Base Ball in Philadelphia

Base Ball in Philadelphia

A History of the Early Game, 1831–1900

John Shiffert

McFarland & Company, Inc., Publishers
Jefferson, North Carolina, and London

LIBRARY OF CONGRESS CATALOGUING-IN-PUBLICATION DATA

Shiffert, John, 1952–
Base ball in Philadelphia : a history of the early game, 1831–1900 / John Shiffert.
p.   cm.

Includes bibliographical references and index.

ISBN-13: 978-0-7864-2795-6
ISBN-10: 0-7864-2795-7
(softcover : 50# alkaline paper) ∞

1. Baseball—Pennsylvania—Philadelphia—History—20th century.
2. Philadelphia Athletics (Baseball team)—History.
I. Title.   II. Title: Baseball in Philadelphia.
GV863.P372S55   2006   796.3570974811—dc22   2006029569

British Library cataloguing data are available

©2006 John Shiffert. All rights reserved

No part of this book may be reproduced or transmitted in any form or by any means, electronic or mechanical, including photocopying or recording, or by any information storage and retrieval system, without permission in writing from the publisher.

On the cover: A replica of a "lemon peel" ball,
such as one used by the Olympic Club *(photograph by Leigh Duncan);*
(left) a photograph of catcher Jack Clements *(courtesy John Thorn);*
(right) a baseball card of Jim Fogarty

Manufactured in the United States of America

McFarland & Company, Inc., Publishers
Box 611, Jefferson, North Carolina 28640
www.mcfarlandpub.com

For my high school history teacher and baseball coach,
Harry Gratwick, for his efforts in both fields.
Thanks, Mr. Gratwick.

Acknowledgments

First, to my father, John Shiffert, for introducing me to baseball and to baseball history, by getting me a copy of *Big-Time Baseball* for Christmas when I was eight years old, and for all his support, encouragement and advice over the years. As the holder of an M.A. in English from the University of Pennsylvania, and an M.B. (Master of Baseball) from the College of Philadelphia Fandom, there is no one better qualified on all counts to acknowledge. By extension, his father, the catcher for one of the Philadelphia club teams of the early twentieth century, the Mermaid A.A., Ralph Milo Shiffert, also deserves mention, since he introduced my father to baseball.

While at least 20 other individuals have directly contributed to this book, two in particular stand out. The first is eminent baseball historian John Thorn, who some 30 years ago, in *A Century of Baseball Lore*, modified and added to an earlier book of historical baseball anecdotes. That book? *Big-Time Baseball*. Thorn more recently generously shared documents and expertise on a number of subjects, including Octavius Catto, the Philadelphia Pythians and baseball's first color line; baseball's origins; and biographical information on many of the now-obscure early heroes of Philadelphia baseball. He also supplied many pictures of these same heroes. His name will appear often in this work, and a great debt is owed him.

Then there's Matthew J. Coyne. He served as my on-site Philadelphia photographer and researcher for this book, helping to pin down the exact site and orientation of the famed Camac Woods grounds, first home of the first Philadelphia Athletics. Matt's brother Andrew Coyne contributed a photo of the Centennial grounds plus innumerable comments and observations.

Several other historians also contributed greatly to this project. Chief among them is David Quentin Voigt, author of the only baseball history series comparable in scope to the late Harold Seymour's work. Not only was Voigt's *American Baseball* (and other writings and presentations) an invaluable source on the early years of baseball, but he personally answered many questions about the early Philadelphia Athletics and the coming of professionalism to the game. Thomas Altherr, David Block and Jerrold Casway were likewise generous with information about early baseball.

My high school history teacher and baseball coach, Harry Gratwick, provided me with my first insight into the allure of history, as well as the highlight of my high school years. One afternoon in 1970, Mr. Gratwick put me in right field for the last inning of the division-clinching game at Friends Central. A lousy baseball player, I had a Moonlight Graham career in high school. He also brought publication of Block's recent landmark work on the origins of baseball to my attention. The great teachers keep on teaching.

Andrew Waskie, Christopher Threston and my friend Dan Rolph of the Historical Society of Pennsylvania contributed information on Octavius Catto, the Philadelphia Pythian club, and the drawing of the color line.

Anyone wishing to write about really early baseball must consult the first book ever written on American sports, Charles Peverelly's long out-of-print *The Book of American Pastimes*. Tom Larwin of the Ted Williams Chapter of SABR was kind enough to share a copy of the Williams Chapter's CD version of *American Pastimes* with me—a magnanimous gesture that really made the first four chapters of this book possible. Also from the ranks of SABR, Frank Vaccaro and Brock Helander contributed their research and insights on Philadelphia baseball from 1877 to 1882.

An information source that is one open to everyone with Internet access is Baseball-Reference.com, the brainchild of Sean Forman, who merits a medal of some kind for his work in this area. David Smith and the Retrosheet website (*www.retrosheet.org*), was also a great help.

I'd also like to thank my friends George Schoener and Jim McSweeney, as well as the Philadelphia Athletics Historical Society's Bob Warrington and Ernie Montella. Thanks also to Bill Deane. When I first began work on this book more than 20 years ago, Bill was the senior research associate at the Hall of Fame and was the first person to lend a hand.

In addition to John Thorn and Matt Coyne's work, Leigh Wills, Louie Maistros and baseball card dealer Larry Fritsch provided photographs. I'm grateful to all for their generosity.

I sincerely hope I haven't forgotten anyone else who contributed to this volume over the 20-plus years it has been in the making. If I have, please forgive the oversight. And thanks.

Table of Contents

Acknowledgments vii
Preface 1
Introduction—Baseball and Philadelphia 3
A Guide to Statistics 7

Part I—The Clubs and the Teams and the City 11

1. The Olympic Days 13
2. The Game Spreads and Philadelphia Grows 21
3. Baseball During the Civil War—Philadelphia Joins the NABBP 31
4. The First Name in Philadelphia Baseball—Athletic 41
5. The Drawing of the Color Line 55
6. The Coming of the Pros 62
7. The National Association Years 71
8. The Centennial City and the First Year of the National League 87
9. The Beer and Whiskey League Comes to Philadelphia 97
10. A Pennant for the Athletics 105
11. The Worcester Ruby Legs and the New Philadelphia Philadelphias 113
12. The Athletics' Riches to Rags Story 129
13. Other Teams, Other Leagues 141
14. War and Peace and War 152
15. The 1890s Phillies—It Was Always Something 161

Part II—A Biographical Dictionary 179

Chapter Notes 269
Bibliography 277
Index 281

Preface

Our perceptions of history are constantly changing. The ways and means by which we can access history are also changing. If someone had told me, when I first began this book in the mid–1980s, that historical documents and reliable statistics would be accessible through my computer, I might have laughed. But the Internet, and with it the proliferation of databases useful to the baseball researcher, has been essential to the writing of this book. Nineteenth-century baseball is an enormous and partly uncharted subject area, and limiting the scope to Philadelphia—one of the biggest of early baseball scenes—reduces the research burden only a little. Without electronic access to newspapers and journal articles, and without the on-line presence of the Nineteenth Century Committee of SABR, this project might not have been completed. Certainly it would not have been completed as quickly.

However, the Internet isn't all that's new since I set out on this project, which was initially to be a history of the American League Philadelphia Athletics. At that time, circa 1984, the only sources of detailed information on early baseball were microfilmed newspapers of varying legibility and archival collections such as the one at the National Baseball Library in Cooperstown, New York. Although I made several trips from my home in Philadelphia to Cooperstown over an eight-year period, and received much assistance there from the library's Bill Deane, it was decidedly slow going, and I eventually put the project aside. There was too little free time to dig out the needed information.

Fortunately for my efforts, and those of a legion of other baseball historians, the accumulated and disseminated knowledge of early baseball was greatly increasing during the 1990s, thanks to books by David Nemec, Marshall Wright, William Ryczek, Dean Sullivan, John Thorn, and many, many others. Thus, when I returned to this still largely unfinished project in 2004, I found a wealth of information on early baseball in Philadelphia, albeit scattered about in some 100 sources, including Harold Seymour's and David Voigt's seminal histories from the 1960s, newly affordable in softcover; the newspaper database ProQuest and lending library of the Society for American Baseball Research (SABR); the records available through websites such as Baseball Reference, Baseball Almanac, and Retrosheet; and any new books and articles by Nemec, Ryczek, and other nineteenth-century historians. And there was more, like the McFarland editions of Francis Richter's and Ernie Lanigan's early baseball histories, Nebraska University Press's reprint of Sol White's 1907 book on early black baseball, and the work of SABR's Nineteenth Century Committee, notably its two volumes of biographies, *Nineteenth Century Stars* and *Baseball's First Stars*.

It should be noted though that baseball history is not limited to baseball sources. Any pastime as deeply ingrained in American history as baseball is also a part of a broader societal fabric—a phenomenon represented by the relationships between Philadelphia's and the game's development, and the story of Octavius Catto, the Philadelphia Pythians, and the drawing of baseball's first color line. This story largely came, not from baseball sources, but from the Pythians' collected archives at the Historical Society of Pennsylvania and from much broader histories of the city and the remarkable Professor Catto.

Even more valuable in this work was the direct personal assistance afforded me by some of this era's notable baseball historians and members of SABR. In the former category, John Thorn and David Voigt proved very generous with their time and expertise. In the latter, Tom Larwin of SABR's Ted Williams (San Diego) Chapter provided a key component of basic source material for baseball before 1867—a CD copy of Charles Peverelly's *Book of American Pastimes*. And, even as my book was going to the publisher, SABR members Brock Helander and Frank Vaccaro were providing missing pieces from the "dark ages" of Philadelphia baseball, from 1877 to 1882. It is my hope that the bibliography of this book may prove of some value to future historians and researchers—I have made it as comprehensive as possible.

Something else had changed by the time I started writing again—the focus of the book. With David Jordan having published his excellent study of Connie Mack's Athletics (*The Athletics of Philadelphia*) in 1999, I found my original idea outdated. I then pondered a history of just the first Athletics' dynasty (1901–1914), before turning to the broader subject of the early years of baseball in Philadelphia. While I had been intrigued enough by the first account of the "original" Athletics that I read (in Fred Lieb's *Connie Mack: Grand Old Man of Baseball*) to include a chapter on that team in the original book, I now found that there was enough information, on-line and in hard copy, to make that fabled team a key component of a new book, one that would start with the game's origins in the City of Brotherly Love and carry the game through to the start of the twentieth century. There was now so much information available—not just on the original Athletics but on the NABBP, the National Association, the early National League, the American Association Athletics and the early Phillies—that the challenge was now to write a comprehensive history without overwhelming the reader with the seemingly endless facts, anecdotes, and historical documents at my disposal. Originally planned as an 80,000-word book, the first draft came in at 180,000 words.

Having spent the better part of two years searching through a vast amount of information on nineteenth century baseball, and culling out the information that pertained to Philadelphia, this book has morphed several times, finally becoming a two-part project. The first part is a detailed history of the teams that came and went across the Philadelphia baseball (or town ball, in the earliest days) scene. Part II consists of a biographical dictionary of Philadelphia's great baseball figures of the nineteenth century. To leave either part out would have left the reader with an incomplete picture of a key time, and a key place, in the development of the National Pastime.

Introduction—
Baseball and Philadelphia

This is the story of baseball in Philadelphia, and baseball and Philadelphia, from the 1831 founding of the first organization in the United States devoted to playing a bat-and-ball game, to the end of the nineteenth century. Philadelphia, Philadelphia organizations, Philadelphia players and Philadelphia administrators all played a vital role in the development of the National Pastime. As historian David Quentin Voigt has said, "Things were happening in Philadelphia."

Before that, things were happening across the Atlantic Ocean, where it has been established by author David Block that the game got its start. In *Baseball Before We Knew It*, Block argues persuasively that baseball evolved from European Longball and other medieval bat and ball games, through Tut Ball, and maybe Stool Ball, into English base-ball, the game that ultimately became baseball.

Block has supported his theory with research into a myriad of other bat and ball games, including three or four passing references to "base-ball" that appear in English literature in the eighteenth century—well-known, though previously puzzling mentions in *The Little Pretty Pocket Book* in 1744 and in the novels *Battleridge* and *Northanger Abbey*. These references puzzled historians because like its predecessor games, English base-ball was a children's game—a fact that might explain why so few allusions to base-ball have been uncovered. As Block writes, "Like many aspects of social and cultural history, especially those involving the diversions of children, (English) baseball was not deemed of any great significance and was not worth writing about."

In America, before 1833, as research by John Thorn and Thomas Altherr has made clear, this was no kids' game. Thus, when two groups of young men banded together to form the first true organized ball club, the Olympic Town Ball Club of Philadelphia, they moved the game in the direction of organized sport. The second such landmark in the game's development came in 1845, when a committee of the Knickerbocker club of New York drew up the 20 rules for what is now considered the game of baseball. After that, the game developed slowly until the late 1850s, when more and more clubs formed in New York, leading to the establishment in 1857 of the National Association of Base Ball Players (NABBP). With the coming of professionalism to baseball, starting in the early 1860s, it was inevitable that a professional organization be formed. That happened in 1871, with the formation of the National Association of Professional Base Ball Players. After problems with scheduling, contract jumping, and gambling doomed the short-lived NA, which had been a co-operative, William Hulbert organized the National League, wresting control from the players and placing it in the hands of the business-minded owners. From that point, baseball entered a whirlwind of development that wouldn't subside until the peace treaty between the National and American Leagues in 1903. Throughout this period Philadelphia was a vitally important baseball scene, and Philadelphian players, owners, and teams were at the center of many of the biggest stories:

1833—Philadelphia Olympic club forms the first true ball-playing club
1865—Al Reach becomes the first baseball player to change cities for a salary, jumping from Brooklyn to Philadelphia (Athletics 1)
1867—The NABBP draws baseball's first color line, despite efforts by Philadelphia Athletics (1) vice president Hicks Hayhurst and Philadelphia civil rights pioneer Octavius Catto to admit the Philadelphia Pythian club to the state and national associations
1871—The first professional league—the National Association—is formed with the Philadelphia Athletics (1) as the first champion
1874—Boston Red Stockings and Philadelphia Athletics (1) make first overseas baseball tour, to Great Britain
1876—The National League is formed, with the Philadelphia Athletics (1) as members
1876—Philadelphia Athletics (1) and New York Mutuals kicked out of National League for the old National Association shortcoming of not completing their schedules
1882—American Association formed by Philadelphian Horace Phillips and O.P. Caylor, with the "new" Philadelphia Athletics (3) as members
1890—The Players League War, led by New York's John M. Ward and (among others) Philadelphia Phillie lieutenants Charlie Buffington, George Wood and Jim Fogarty
1891—The National League and the American Association go to war over the status of former Philadelphia Athletics (3) Harry Stovey and Lou Bierbauer
1891—The American Association folds when the Wagner Brothers, Philadelphia Athletic (4) owners, sell out to the National League
1901—The American League is formed; the Philadelphia Phillies sue the Philadelphia Athletics (6) over the status of superstar Napoleon Lajoie.

The first name in Philadelphia baseball in the nineteenth century was "Athletic." Although no less than six organizations would bear this name between 1860 and 1901, including a series of independent professional teams in the late 1870s and early 1880s and a minor league team in the 1890s, there should be no doubt that the best in baseball in Philadelphia in the nineteenth century usually meant Athletic baseball.

From shortly after the founding of the original Athletic club, the name Athletic would stand astride the Philadelphia baseball world, in the fashion of William Penn looking down from the top of City Hall, for almost a century. While early Philadelphia baseball would have a major role in the game nationally during the nineteenth century, its players, executives, sportswriters and teams would lay the groundwork for baseball in the first half of the twentieth century, when Philadelphia was one of a few cities with two major league franchises. In fact, Philadelphia had been known as "the best baseball city in the world" in the latter part of the nineteenth century, at least according to the definitive non-sporting history of the city, *Philadelphia: A 300 Year History*. This was a not-surprising assessment given first the Athletics' popularity and then the Phillies' attendance records during the 1890s—they had finished either first or second in the National League in attendance every year from 1890 to 1900, with the exception of 1897 and 1898. In the new century, Connie Mack's teams would inherit this tradition of strong local support.

What had happened to the Phillies? How is it that a baseball team that owned Philadelphia in 1900 fell so hard that by 1902, in just their second year, the American League Athletics were outdrawing the Phillies almost four to one? The Phillies were vulnerable as the century turned, thanks partly to the "monopolistic morass," as Harold Seymour called it, that was the National League as the old century closed, but moreso to bad management at Philadelphia Ball Park.

Connie Mack's manifest abilities as a manager and a general manger, a little extra cash, and Phillies principal owner John Rogers' penny-pinching and dishonesty added up to the Phillies falling just short of a pennant in 1901, the year they needed to make a big impression against the first-year interlopers from the American League. After that failure, and after having been devastated by a second year of American League raids, the Phillies were easy prey for Mack's 1902 AL pennant winners, who would ride high for the first 14 years of the American League. Mack put together the AL's first dynasty, finishing first in 1902, 1905, 1910, 1911, 1913 and 1914 and finishing out of the first division only in 1908. Finally, when the Federal League war caused Mack to break up his great team, the Phillies were there to pick up the mantle of excellence, behind Grover Cleveland Alexander and Gavvy Cravath. But a few years after one of Rogers' equally inept successors, William Baker, traded Alexander, Mack was back with an even better team that excelled through 1932.

And then the roof fell in on both franchises, thanks to a lack of money and business acumen. The great Philadelphia baseball men of the nineteenth century—the Al Reaches and Bill Shettslines—had passed from the scene. On the Phillies' part, a string of bad and underfinanced owners—Baker, Gerry Nugent and William Cox—led to 30 years of mostly bad baseball. For the Athletics, once the franchise's bankroll, baseball pioneer and inventor Ben Shibe, died in 1922, the Mack family was on its own. Although Connie was savvy enough to build one more great team, the financial pressures of the Depression on a family that had no other income, plus the owner's advancing age, led to the eventual collapse of the last Philadelphia Athletics team. As the Phillies and Athletics struggled, Philadelphia slipped from the top tier of baseball cities. The Athletics left in 1955 for Kansas City, and Philadelphia became a one-team town. With the Phillies franchise struggling at the gate and in the standings, Philadelphia bore little resemblance to the vibrant and influential baseball city it had been in the nineteenth century. And while the situation has improved, along with the Phillies' fortunes, in recent decades, Philadelphia's connection to the glory days of the Olympics and Athletics seems lost. Early rivals Washington, Boston, and especially New York have all received more attention in the published articles and books on the early game. This book is meant to address that imbalance and contribute, even if modestly, to our understanding of baseball's great rise during the last half of the nineteenth century.

A Guide to Statistics

The source for the post–1870 statistics in this book is Sean Forman's *www.baseball-reference.com*. The pre–1870 stats come from Marshall Wright's book, *The National Association of Base Ball Players, 1857 to 1870*. For those not familiar with the more sophisticated stats, here are some simple explanations of those used in this book.

Adjusted ERA

An earned run average (ERA) around 3.00 was considered the mark of an average pitcher—in the 1960s. In 1908 though, such a mark might have gotten you sent to the Cedar Rapids Canaries. On the other hand, a 3.00 ERA in 2005 would have put you among the league leaders. Thus, while ERA may well be as important a single statistic as there is in assessing a pitcher's competence, it must be put in historical perspective to have real historical meaning. That's where Adjusted ERA (or ERA+ or ERA*) comes in.

Adjusted ERA for a single season is derived by comparing a pitcher's raw ERA against that of his league, and with modification for Park Factors (in other words, whether his home park favored hitters or pitchers, and by how much), producing a percentage that expresses just how good a pitcher was in any one year in terms of keeping earned runs off the board. In the simpler terms of Baseball-Reference.com's Forman, it's the ratio of the league's ERA (adjusted to the pitcher's ballpark) to that of the pitcher.

Taking these same measurements over the course of a pitcher's career gives a career ERA+.

An Adjusted ERA of 100 is exactly the league average. An Adjusted ERA of 110 is 10 percent better than the league average. An Adjusted ERA of 150 or so means you're an ace (although relievers will now commonly have ERA+ over 200). An Adjusted ERA of below 80 means you'd better learn a new pitch, or you're headed back to the minors.

It should be noted that ERA+ in the nineteenth century is probably not as accurate an assessment of a pitcher's competency as it is in the twenty-first century. With a dozen or more errors being made during the course of a game, a pitcher's ultimate effectiveness could vary widely depending on how good (or bad) his fielders were, and on how strict the scoring (as to what was an error) was.

Adjusted OPS

Just like a raw ERA can be misleading, so too can a raw OPS (on base plus slugging—see below). For instance, an OPS of .800 would have been great in 1908, and not so great in 1930. Adjusted OPS (or OPS+ or OPS*) is derived in the same fashion as Adjusted ERA, and produces the same percentage number as Adjusted ERA. As Forman has noted on his Baseball-Reference.com website, OPS+ is essentially OPS normalized to the league. Think of it as a rate above the league average expressed as a percentage. So, an Adjusted OPS of 100 is average, an Adjusted OPS of 150 is Ed Delahanty, and a 50 Adjusted OPS is Doc Bushong.

Batting/On Base/Slugging

A shorthand way to show the "big three" averages for a hitter. If a player's batting average is .333, his on base percentage (OBP) is .400, and his slugging percentage (SLG) is .500, these three stats can be expressed in one line as .333/.400/.500.

The Black Ink Test

Doesn't it make sense that a great hitter in the nineteenth century would dominate the various yearly offensive statistics, just like the great hitters did in 1908, 1930 or 1968? The best way to measure that is through a Bill James invention, the Black Ink Test, a means of assigning a varying number points to a player's credit by means of his leading the league in doubles, triples, home runs, slugging percentage, batting average, runs scored, steals, etc. (When you lead a league in something for a season, the encyclopedias list that stat in bold, or black ink.) The beauty of this measure is that it provides an automatic period adjustment—you get just as much credit for leading your league in hits in 1880 as you do for doing so in 1980.

Isolated Discipline

A means of gauging how willing a batter is to take a walk. By subtracting a hitter's batting average from his on base percentage, isolated discipline gives a better measure than just on base percentage of a hitter's relative ability to get on base by means other than a base hit. An isolated discipline (ID) of over .100 since the 1890s has been traditionally excellent, while an ID below .040 is Rocco Baldelli.

Isolated Power

The slugging percentage version of ID. Subtract a player's batting average from his slugging percentage, and you have a pretty good idea how much power he has. Relative values have varied greatly over the years, running very low in the Deadball eras and very high in the present era.

OPS

If you're looking for a single, simple, easy to obtain statistic that measures offensive performance, it's OPS, also known as on base plus slugging. All you do is add a batter's on base percentage to his slugging percentage, and you've got his OPS. In the current era, you want to have an OPS of at least .800. An OPS of around 1.100 will qualify you to lead the league. On the other side of the coin, an OPS of .600 is the Ordonez Line, named after Rey Ordonez and his career OPS—a figure below which all hitters should be banished to the bench. OPS, while the most popular single method of gauging a hitter's productivity, is *not* perfect, since it does not take into account a player's contributions (or lack thereof) in stolen bases.

Park Factor

Park factor (PF) is a value used to indicate where any particular ballpark in any particular year favors either hitters or pitchers. PF is a number—above 100 is a park good for hitters and below 100 is a park good for pitchers.

Park factor is calculated separately for batters and pitchers. The computation of PF is admittedly daunting. Baseball-Reference.com uses a three-year average park factor for players and teams unless they change home parks. Then a two-year average is used, unless the park existed for only one year. Then a one-year mark is used.

Pythagorean Winning Percentage

Pythagorean winning percentage is an estimate of a team's winning percentage given their runs scored and runs allowed. Developed by Bill James, it can tell you when teams were a bit lucky or unlucky. It is calculated by

$$\frac{(\text{Runs Scored})^{1.83}}{(\text{Runs Scored})^{1.83} + (\text{Runs Allowed})^{1.83}}$$

Range Factor

Combined with the classic fielding percentage stat, the best way of measuring the often immeasurable—fielding skill. Range factor basically measures the average of how many balls a fielder got to in the course of a game—how many plays he made on average every game.

Runs Created

Another James creation, this is a relatively simple means of measuring offensive productivity by calculating how many of the game's basic currency—runs—a player generates, typically for a single season. There are several versions of the runs created formula, but they are based on three factors, "A" "B" and "C" with all the formulas being generated by (A times B) divided by C. In the simplest formula, A is hits plus walks. B is total bases. C is at bats plus walks.

Part I

The Clubs and the Teams and the City

CHAPTER 1

The Olympic Days

Before 1840, young men in Philadelphia were playing bat-and-ball games. More significantly, they were *organizing* to play bat-and-ball games. Most of these games appear to have been versions of rounders or town ball or English base-ball—like so many Philadelphians of that era, imported from England. However, unlike Philly's many Irish, Welsh and English immigrants, rounders and town ball came from the same roots—in this case, English base-ball. Prior to 1800, English base-ball, having migrated to America, begat town ball, bass-ball, baste ball, goal ball and various other-named pastimes, finally leading to base ball, to use the nineteenth century spelling.[1] By whatever name, these varied bat-and-ball sports eventually became widely popular in William Penn's city, but not without some initial growing pains. Nonetheless, as baseball historian David Quentin Voigt has said, "[If] you want to learn the history of nineteenth century baseball, you had better visit Philadelphia. Philadelphia was in the thick of things, it was innovative. Things were happening in Philadelphia that were significant to the growth of the game."[2]

Originally played by young boys as literally a "pass-time," these games came to also be played by the young at heart, in addition to the young. Played as early as the 1820s by what would now be called "Yuppies," young urban professionals who had the spare time, and interest, to revisit the games of their recent youth. As these bat-and-ball games grew in popularity, it became only natural that the proponents of these games would follow the day's most common societal trend, and gather together to form clubs that would further organize this recreation into contests.

Some sources say Athletic was the first Philadelphia base ball club, some say it was Olympic. While Athletic would become the first name in Philadelphia baseball, the Olympic club has the claim as the city's, and the nation's, mother club. There is hard evidence that the Olympic Town Ball Club of Philadelphia had roots that date back to 1831—although it was initially to play town ball, a popular local game in the City of Brotherly Love in the years leading up to the Civil War. This was the foremost innovation spoken of by Voigt, what he refers to as "a group of Philadelphia gentlemen, who were concerned about getting the proper sort of players into the ranks," and thus organized the Olympic Club.[3]

Around this same time, the growth of the sport in Philadelphia was mirrored by the growth of what *New York Daily News* reporter Charles Peverelly, in his 1866 *The Book of American Pastimes*, stated

> has now become beyond question the leading feature of the out-door sports of the United States.... It is a game which is peculiarly suited to the American temperament and disposition; the nine innings are played in the brief space of two and one half hours, or less. From the

moment the first striker takes his position, and poises his bat, it has an excitement and vim about it ... in short, the pastime suits the people, and the people suit the pastime.[4]

The Philadelphia ball-playing pioneers started gathering to play their game at some point during the 1820s. However, they couldn't do so within the city limits of Philadelphia. As Philly baseball fans of the 1920s and '30s and '40s and '50s will recall, the Sunday "Blue Laws" in Philadelphia were still quite strict some 100 years later. In the 1820s, these puritanical decrees weren't just limited to Sundays. To avoid breaking the laws in Philadelphia, early town ball players had to go across the Delaware River to the village of Camden, New Jersey, to play their game, be it on Sunday or any other day of the week. This practice continued into the 1830s when, on the Fourth of July, 1831, a date sometimes given as the founding date for the Olympic Club, the Olympic Club took the Market Street Ferry across to Camden to celebrate the holiday with a game. Although crossing the Delaware at this time was something of a nuisance, there would prove to be one benefit to these trips across the Delaware—by 1833 the Philadelphia Olympics had met up with a similarly-minded, though nameless, group of young ball-playing men, also from Philadelphia, and had united into a single, larger club, now called the Olympic Ball Club of Philadelphia.[5] To show how serious they were, the Olympic Ball Club had a large clubhouse with "Olympic" emblazoned above the door, along with the date "1833." A photo of said clubhouse, located at what is now Broad and Wallace Streets in Philadelphia, featured 30-some Olympics scattered across the front porch.

Peverelly is an excellent source for specifics on the birth of club-based bat-and-ball sports in Philadelphia, and the closest thing to a knowledgeable and contemporary source on the events of the 1830s. However, Peverelly himself wasn't in Philadelphia in 1831 or 1833. But, like every other reporter, he had his sources. Long-time Philadelphia sportswriter Horace Fogel, who also wrote about the Olympic Club in a series of articles in the *Philadelphia Daily Evening Telegraph* in 1908 that were recently brought to light by John Thorn, also wasn't present when the Olympic Club started playing. But, like Peverelly, Fogel had his sources—the same source as Peverelly. In a two-part series in the March 25 and March 26 *Telegraph*, Fogel provides an early counterpoint to the then-just-released Mills Commission's creation of the Doubleday Myth, stating that "we had a baseball club right here in Philadelphia as early as 1833. That organization was known as the 'Olympic Ball Club of Philadelphia.' Evidently this was the first baseball club ever organized; if there had been any others it is unlikely that the Spalding commission would have overlooked more than this one." The source Fogel quotes came from Daniel G. Daley of 305 North 38th Street in West Philadelphia, who had, on February 5, 1908, sent Fogel a copy of a booklet printed in 1866 (note the year) by Philadelphia printer H.B. Ashmead. This booklet contained the constitution and bylaws of "The Olympic Ball Club of Philadelphia, Instituted 1833," as well as a list of officers, a membership roll of the club, the playing rules and an early history of the club. It is the history of the Olympic Club, appearing in the pamphlet's preface, that Fogel quotes extensively from in his two March *Telegraph* articles. Although Peverelly does not give his source in *American Pastimes*, the words he uses to describe the history of the Olympic Club in *American Pastimes* are, in most cases, exactly the same as those used by Fogel some 42 years later. In other words, Peverelly's source of information on Olympic was a copy of the contemporary (for Peverelly) pamphlet that fell into Fogel's hands in 1908.

Peverelly and Fogel both report that the Olympic Club was formed in 1833 by the union of two different ball-playing associations—the term used by both men for the clubs. According to Fogel, one of these groups had been playing on a simple open field off of Market Street in Camden since the spring of 1831. Most likely, this was the group that the original Philadelphia Olympic Club joined with, and that took on the Olympic name. Fogel specifically states, when speaking of the "Fourth of July" club, that this was the case:

The birthplace of base ball? No. The clubhouse of the first ball club? Yes. The Olympic Club house at Broad and Wallace Street (photograph courtesy John Thorn).

> The other association that first assumed the name of the Olympic Ball Club was originally formed for the purpose of playing Town Ball on the Fourth of July. They met occasionally at other times by appointment, but had no regular days or established grounds for some years.[6]

It would appear that two different groups of young Philadelphians, one named Olympic and originally playing on July 4, 1831, and the other a nameless group that started to play in the spring of 1831, or possibly years earlier, both began playing town ball in Camden in 1831. Francis Richter, writing his own history of baseball in 1914, concurs, while giving the summer of 1833 date for the regular organization of Olympic as a town ball club. He also notes that the game had been played in Philadelphia and Camden for some years prior to 1833.[7] Further testimony as to the actual founding of Olympic comes from *The Baseball Chronology*, which states that the club celebrated its fiftieth anniversary on March 31, 1883, which would indicate, in agreement with the 1866 pamphlet, that Olympic considered its origin to date to the start of the 1833 season.[8] A final word on the subject came from the *New York Clipper*, the foremost baseball media outlet of the 1870s and 1880s. In reporting on the death of Olympic Club president Hicks Hayhurst in 1882, the *Clipper* called Olympic, "the oldest ball-playing organization in the country."[9] A notable statement, especially coming from a New York media source.

Initially small numbers of players limited Olympic to at first playing "two-old-cat." Then, the original members invited some of their younger friends to play, with the goal of making enough (a minimum of five players to a side, says Peverelly) to play town ball. "(They) told some of their younger friends of the pleasure and advantage they found in resuming their boyish sports," is how Peverelly (and Fogel) describes the invitation.[10] Soon, 15 or 20 players were taking the ferry over to Camden on Saturdays—the white collar work week at that time allowed for some time off on Saturday—to play town ball. Fogel, who was very pro–Philadelphian, adds that these town ball games "soon changed to Base Ball with nine and sometimes eleven men to a side." Fogel even more boldly states in his March 26, 1908, story that "baseball had its origin in Philadelphia." Going on the evidence from the 1866 pamphlet, Fogel admits that the original Olympic rules, like the rules for town ball, did not provide for a specific number of players and that, due to various controversies that arose during the playing of the weekly games, the rules were actually altered from week to week, "so that it took not a few years until in the opinion of the baseball pioneers the code was finally perfected." Fogel places this landmark on December 13, 1865, at the ninth annual meeting of the National Association of Base Ball Players (NABBP), the first organized league. At that point, says Fogel, "the appended code ... was considered ideal and perfect in all respects."[11] This is a bit of a stretch, implying that the rules approved in 1865 by the NABBP, which were highly detailed, were a direct outgrowth of the Olympic rules from the 1830s. However, according to Thorn, there is some evidence that the Olympic Club was also playing a game more like baseball, a game played on a diamond-shaped field.[12] No doubt that Olympic had rules that were congruent with what the NABBP decided on in 1865, but it's clear from many other sources that the NABBP rules were an outgrowth of the New York Game of the 1840s.

In reality, it's almost impossible to say exactly what game the Olympics were playing, especially due to the variances in terminology at this time. Early baseball expert David Block states, "prior to 1845, baseball in the United States lacked any standardization in rules or semantics. Neighboring communities could be playing identical versions of the game, and yet one might call it 'base ball' and the other 'town ball.' In my view there is no clear evidence prior to the advent of the New York game that varieties of baseball could be reliably distinguished by name, and thus whether the term 'base ball' or 'town ball' was used was a matter of local vernacular."

In regards to this point on terminology, Block notes that later accounts universally agree that the game the Olympics were playing was locally known as town ball, and that considerable evidence exists that town ball was the principal term used for early baseball in the Philadelphia area. Block, in *Baseball Before We Knew It*, also refers to an article from Richter's *Sporting Life* on December 31, 1885, that describes the Olympics' game as consisting of five sticks planted in a 30-foot diameter circle, wherein the runners were put out by soaking. That may not sound like the baseball we know today, but it was

Horace Fogel, during his managerial days in New York. Primarily a sportswriter, in 1908 he claimed the Olympic Club was the first baseball club in America (photograph courtesy John Thorn).

probably not dissimilar to the game the way it was played in most communities in the 1830s.[13]

According to Fogel, two or three members of the Fourth of July Club (the original Olympic Club) eventually began playing regularly in Camden with the nameless group and persuaded all of the original Olympic members to go to Camden on Wednesdays to play on the grounds used by the other club on Saturdays. As a result, an inter-club match — the first of its kind anywhere in America — was arranged sometime in 1833 before the union of the two clubs.[14] Both Peverelly and Fogel understate the importance of this match, following the claim of the 1866 pamphlet that this was merely the first inter-club match among Pennsylvania clubs. Since, according to *American Pastimes*, there weren't any other ball clubs, either formal or informal, anywhere else until at least 1842,[15] this anonymous contest would have to stand as the first ball game between two separate, organized club teams anywhere in the United States.

Although no results of this match were available, even in 1866, this game did serve to better introduce the two clubs to each other, and led directly to the union of the two groups, with the original Olympic Club inviting the other club to play on Wednesdays, and the other club inviting their counterparts to play on Saturdays. As befitted the still-informal nature of the organizations at this time, they did not always meet at regular times or even have their own regular grounds at this time. For that matter, they made their own bats and balls — most likely some form of the "lemon peel" cover baseball, as well.

Both Peverelly and Fogel make note of the bravery of the individuals involved. As Peverelly explains, "So great was the prejudice of the public against the game at that time, that the players were frequently reproved and censured by their friends for degrading themselves by indulging in such a childish amusement, and this prejudice prevailed to a great extent for many years." Peverelly claims the proof of this statement is in the fact that so few other clubs were formed in what he refers to as a "long period" after the founding of the Olympic Club.[16] Indeed, the seminal national organization for baseball, the National Association of Base Ball Players (NABBP), didn't record any games against Philadelphia teams until 1860, and didn't have any Philadelphia members until 1861.[17] On his part, Peverelly does not list the formal organization of any other Philadelphia ball clubs until the founding of the Minerva Club on June 10, 1857. However, that time line really doesn't vary that much from the pattern in New York, where the first hard evidence of an organized ball club was the Knickerbocker Club in 1845 — some 14 years after the Olympic Club formation — and where no other permanent clubs were formed until 1851. Prior to the New York Gotham Club's formal organization sometime in late 1850, the only *lasting* organized bat-and-ball clubs for which we have hard evidence are Olympic in Philadelphia and Knickerbocker in New York. Although New York would have more organized clubs from the early 1850s on — if indeed

A replica of a "lemon peel" ball, such as the Olympic Club made for their own use (photograph by Leigh G. Wills).

Olympic stood alone in Philadelphia until 1857—Philadelphia had established primacy of the first club.

Even the founding of the Minerva Club was still some 26 years in the future when the Olympic Club laid claim to being the first ball club in America, a claim supported by Harold Seymour in *Baseball: The Early Years*. In a passing mention while discussing the Knickerbocker club, Seymour states parenthetically that the Olympic Town Ball Club of Philadelphia was formed about 1833, although he also says he knows little about Olympic, except that it was not a baseball club.[18] Peverelly also says that the Olympic Club was very loosely organized at first, and Fogel states that the original nameless organization had no constitution, bylaws or elected members, although the original Olympic Club did have a written constitution before the union. However, that document, although signed by a few of the other club's members, was largely unknown to them and fell into disuse. This situation would change by 1837.

Following the 1833 fusion, the Olympic Club continued to grow, first adding a third association that had been playing nearby in Camden, and then a fourth group, this time Philadelphians who were largely graduates of the city's already-notable Central High School. This group of Central grads had played town ball for one year in Camden before joining with the Olympic Club. Both of these additions took place, says Fogel, prior to the Olympic Club finally procuring grounds in Philadelphia at Camac Woods at 17th Street and Columbia Avenue—the future site of much significant baseball. This momentous occasion didn't take place until 1857—after 26 years of ballplaying in Camden![19]

According to Peverelly, the Olympic Club did not adopt the NABBP's game—baseball, as it had evolved from the Knickerbockers' original rules—and drop their "time-honored play" in May of 1860, to "press on in the race of progress."[20] Seymour and Richter also concur with this assessment, both stating that Olympic did not take up baseball until 1860.[21] It was a transition that was not without some controversy. Peverelly reports that most of the older members of the Olympic Club, who had been playing their version of the game for almost 30 years, chose an "honorable retirement" rather than play the new game. However, you can't stop progress, and, starting with a July 24, 1860, game against St. George's Cricket Club, most likely at Camac Woods, since it was also the St. George's club's grounds, won by Olympic 25–17, an October 4 win over Athletic 19–18 (Peverelly places this game in 1862), and an October game against Hamilton, won by Olympic 18–16, Philly's mother club took to baseball.[22]

Although Peverelly does not comment on the identity of the Hamilton club, we know that they were another early Philadelphia club, formed in May 1860. According to David Block, the June 16, 1860, *Spirit of the Times* ran the following notice—"Dear Spirit: The Hamilton Base Ball Club was organized in West Philadelphia on the 10th of last month. It has now nearly fifty members. The officers are: C.M. Eakin, President; P.J. Potter, Vice-President; Hugh C. Hanson, Secretary and Treasurer; Ground Committee, Messrs. C.M. Eakin, B.A. Knight, J.C. Williams, C. Ridgway, Dr. McLeod. The playing days are Wednesdays and Saturdays, on the grounds of Prof. Saunders. Very respectfully, Hugh C. Hanson, Sec."

Olympic's baseball hegemony over Philadelphia would last only through the 1861 season, when they went 3–0 in games against Athletic and the Adriatic Club of Newark. By 1864, they were just another baseball club. However, thanks to Fogel and the 1866 pamphlet, we have the entire roster of Olympic from 1833 to 1866. A total of 47 Olympics are listed for the first year (1833), though apparently no new members were added until 1841. It also appears as if the third and fourth (the Central High grads) organizations to join

Olympic, events which Fogel identifies as taking place some years before the club left its Camden playing grounds, did so in 1842, when 10 new members joined, and 1847, when the club added no less than 15 members.

The club's makeup was very typical of the game's early years, and very blue blood, according to Fogel (and Voigt). "This roster furnishes an interesting study in that it reads like a page from the Blue Book of Philadelphia. That the best people of Philadelphia were members of the Olympic Club is made plain from a glance at the names in the appended roster." The rosters Fogel takes out of the 1866 book are sprinkled with good Philadelphian names like Wharton, Emlen, Coxe, Vandusen, Ashmead, Dixon and the like. Of more significance for its baseball pedigree, Olympic's early rosters also bore the names of two of the city's best future professionals; Wes Fisler joined up in 1861 and the future "Count" of the Athletic Club, John Phillips Jenkins Sensenderfer, joined in 1865.

It should be obvious to everyone but Fogel that, even absent Peverelly's comments, the Olympic Ball Club was not playing baseball. Fogel's championing Olympic's game as the precursor of baseball, other than representing a form of parochialism, may have stemmed from the 1866 pamphlet which showed a diamond-based field—a drawing that Fogel had reproduced in the *Telegraph* in 1908.[23] However, that diagram was only taken from the 1866 publication; it didn't necessarily represent the field they used prior to 1860. Nonetheless, the Olympics' organization at such an early date speaks of bat-and-ball games' popularity among a hard core in Philadelphia. According to Dean Sullivan in *Early Innings*, the Olympics were also the first town ball club to draft (1837) and publish (1838) a constitution.

This intriguing document, "instituted" on December 7, 1837, in addition to laying out rules for membership, including a series of fines for various infractions (e.g., 6½ cents for absence from a club roll call, 12½ cents for appearing on club days out of uniform, or with said uniform unclean), also makes a provision for record keeping for their games. Article VI, Section 2—"It shall be his [the club "Recorder"] duty to record in a book, to be provided for the purpose at the expense of the Club, an accurate account of all the games played on Club days, date of the same, names of the players, the number of points made by each [a town ball term], and the grounds used on each occasion." How important was the recorder? Well, Article VI of the constitution provides for an entire series of fines, just for him, for such egregious transgressions as being absent on club days and not keeping the record book in proper order.[24] Thus was born a function that would prove vital to the game for at least the next 170 years or so.

Actually, the document produced by printer John C. Clark in 1838 owes more to *Robert's Rules of Order* than *Beadle's Dime Base-Ball Player*. However, it is possible to glean some information about how the Olympic games transpired, including the fact that the members were required to wear a uniform, "similar in all respects to the pattern uniform owned by the Club." (Article IX, Section 3) As Peverelly reports, said uniform consisted of dark blue pants, a white shirt trimmed with scarlet, and a white cap with blue trim.

Article XIV details the second Thursday of each month as days set apart for practice, or "Club Days," so-named because all the Olympic's games were what we would now call intramural games. Article VIII also sets up provisions for rainouts, "should the weather prove unfavourable on the regular Club day." When the Olympic members gathered on those occasions, two captains were selected and arrangements were made to "play the game which may be agreed upon," a clear indication that the 29 club members listed in the constitution were playing more than one type of bat-and-ball game. Unfortunately, the constitution does not lay out the rules of the various games they were playing.

Article XV then states that the captains would alternate in choosing their players, just like every kid would in playground baseball 130 or so years later, and that the captains would, in effect, act as umpires. If there came a point wherein the captains could not agree, they didn't go to the principal or a teacher to settle the dispute, they turned to the aforementioned recorder—who was also president of the club's board of directors—to adjudicate the dispute. In fact, the constitution states that the recorder, in those cases, "shall be umpire."

This Olympic constitution also includes a preamble that sheds some light on how the members felt about their somewhat controversial—at least at that time and place—sport.

"Field Sports having from time immemorial been the favourite recreation of all classes of men, not merely for the amusement they afford, the bracing and healthy vigour they impart to the human frame, and the hilarity and good feeling they promote; but for their manly and athletic character, and the generous and friendly emulation they encourage and uphold."[25]

Who were these pioneering Olympic individuals? The 1837 constitution, published some six plus years after the two founding groups began playing, and four years after they joined up together, gives a list of 29 members active at that time. It is interesting that the same last name appears twice in five instances—Robb, Desilver, Thomas, Bowlby and Ellmaker account for 10 of the 29 members—leading one to believe that ball playing was a family affair, even back in the 1830s. The 1866 document that Fogel worked from lists no fewer than 47 members in 1833, the true pioneers of ball playing in Philadelphia.

William Whitman	Joseph Thomas	Charles Thomas	Joseph Saxton
Edward Law	Samuel Carpenter	Nicholas Newlin	George Wharton
Edward Hathaway	Charles Desilver	Thomas Robb	Joseph Mort
Lewis Cooper	Robert McCullagh	Peter Ellmaker	Thomas Clark
George Emlen	Joseph Hillborn	Robert Lindsay	Joseph Lewis
John Diehl	George Watson	James Edwards	James Garrigues
Samuel Branson	Edward Guskill	Edward John Fox	Marcellus Coxe
Joseph Reeves	Wm. Hart Carr	George Herse	William Dunlap
Charles Gilpin	Edward Bowlby, Jr.	Samuel Hufty	George Schober
Isaac Jones	John Brenner	John James	Charles Dunn
Samuel Robb	Samuel Bowlby	Frederick Ellmaker	Kirk Wells[26]
Robert Desilver	William Blanchard	Thomas Firth	

The true pioneers, the original heroes, of ball playing as a club in Philadelphia—or anywhere else in America. Gentlemen, take a bow.

♦ CHAPTER 2 ♦

The Game Spreads and Philadelphia Grows

When was what we would now recognize as baseball first played in Philadelphia? Although claims have been put forth for many clubs, there is no clear answer. Olympic's head start notwithstanding, there have been several reports that, when a club that would be called Athletic was founded on April 7, 1860 (some accounts, including one by noted sportswriter Fred Lieb, say this was in 1859[1]), that they were Philly's first baseball club. Charles Peverelly's work, as well as Seymour's, Sullivan's, Richter's, and Fogel's articles, dispute that claim as to the primacy of a club of ballplayers in metropolitan Philadelphia. Still, the issue of the identity of the first *baseball* club in the city is cloudy. However, the weight of the evidence makes it clear that the first *year* that baseball was played in Philadelphia was 1860. Peverelly lists the Keystone Club (November 30, 1859), as well as the Minerva Club (June 10, 1857), as being formed prior to the April 7, 1860, formation date of Athletic. David Voigt credits the Penn Tiger club as adopting the New York game (i.e., the game played and adopted the year before by the NABBP) in 1858.[2] Peverelly does note that Minerva was "one of the oldest Philadelphia clubs." Al Reach, who was just as contemporary as Peverelly, is quoted in the May 19, 1907, *Philadelphia North American* that Minerva was one of the earliest baseball clubs formed in the Quaker City.

Just because a club was organized at a certain date doesn't mean they were playing baseball right from the start. Peverelly does say that Minerva won every game they played from 1857 to 1864 against other clubs, except for two losses to Athletic, with whom they later shared the old St. George club cricket grounds, known as Camac Woods and located between 15th Street and 17th Street and Montgomery Avenue and Columbia Avenue. As additional evidence of Minerva's strength in the years prior to the Civil War, Peverelly notes that, when he was writing in 1866, all of the club's original members and founders were still active. The most prominent of those founders was Theodore E. Wiedersheim, who was first elected club president on April 24, 1858, and who held that office through the time of the publication of *American Pastimes*.[3] Richter, in his history of baseball, identifies Wiedersheim as the organizer of the club, and, as such, includes him among his list of "Leaders in Base Ball" for Philadelphia. Peverelly, who seldom goes into detail on individuals outside of New York, specifically commented on Wiedersheim's efficiency, popularity and worth in leading the Minervas.

Although Peverelly mentions only Olympic, Minerva, Keystone, Athletic and Equity among Philadelphia's pre–Civil War clubs, other clubs for which there is evidence include Mercantile, Pennsylvania, Penn Tiger, Swiftfoot and Winona. If we are to believe Philadelphian Richter, the latter club actually has the honor of being Philadelphia's first baseball club.

> The Winona Club introduced Base Ball, the New York game, in Philadelphia on May 18, 1860, when two nines were formed from the members of the club, and were captained, respectively, by Messrs. Bomeisler and Boyce. The first regular match game was played by teams of the Winona and Equity Clubs on June 11, 1860, the former winning by 39 to 21.[4]

This statement leads to several conclusions. First, that Winona was formed prior to May 18, 1860. Second, that they made some sort of public showing or announcement of an intramural game of baseball, and, as a result, the event at that time was seen as significant. Third, that they were confident, and skilled, enough to shortly thereafter take on Equity (this would be one of only two losses for Equity in 1860) in what appears to be a legitimate claim as the first baseball game played in Philadelphia between opposing clubs. Fourth, that Winona indeed has a strong claim on being Philadelphia's first baseball club.

Winona also had the distinction in 1860 of having at least two notable players as members of the club, although neither would stay long, because Winona as a club did not stay on the scene very long. The younger of the pair, 16-year-old Tom Pratt, served as the club's pitcher, starting a distinguished career in the box that would take him to fame as the star of the undefeated (for two straight years) champion Brooklyn Atlantic club. The older (32 or 33) was established Philadelphia town ball star Hicks Hayhurst, who would later make his name as a center fielder and administrator with the Philadelphia Athletic club.

Among the other early clubs, Mercantile certainly had a loyal following, to the point where the song *Home Run Quick Step* was "respectfully dedicated to the members of the Mercantile Base Ball Club" by John Zebley, Jr., in 1860. In the days before recordings, printed sheet music, complete with elaborately-printed lithograph covers, was both the way that popular music was distributed, and a popular way of celebrating the accomplishments of favorite baseball clubs. Mercantile played at 18th and Master Streets in North Philadelphia, a part of the city that would see many a baseball game played over the next 110 years. In Mercantile's case, they were playing baseball (not town ball) in the then-open fields near the site of Girard College.[5] However, no results or dates of these games are currently available. Most likely, prior to the Civil War, Mercantile's contests (and possibly Penn Tigers') were what would now be called intramural (or intraclub) games, and thus were of no interest to Peverelly, and also didn't cross Richter's radar screen.

Philadelphia's more prominent baseball clubs of the immediate pre–Civil War era, in addition to Olympic, Minerva and Athletic, were Keystone and Equity, the latter club being formed in 1860 just two weeks after Athletic. Although Samuel L. Barnes would be Keystone's organizer and first president, the club's most enduring officer was Francis A. Frazer, elected secretary and treasurer in 1859 and then continuing to serve the club's then–82 members in the former office through 1867. Keystone, who played at 11th and Wharton Streets in white and blue uniforms, is listed as playing a three-game schedule in 1860, defeating a team called Continental 26–11 on the Fourth of July, but losing to the Equity Club 43–20. In September, they lost 48–20 to an outfit by the name of Pennsylvania.[6] Although possibly an informal club—Peverelly doesn't say anything about them—Pennsylvania was, according to Voigt, a rare blue collar team.[7]

While three games may not seem like much, Keystone's opening Independence Day contest may have had great significance, possibly marking the first-ever win by an organized

The cover for the Home Run Quick Step sheet music, dedicated to the Mercantile Club (Library of Congress photograph).

Philadelphia baseball team over an organized baseball team from the city that invented the game. There exists no other evidence of a Philadelphia Continental club, but there was an NABBP member, albeit a fairly anonymous one, by that name in Brooklyn in 1860. According to Henry Chadwick in the 1860 edition of *Beadle's Dime Base-Ball Player*, the Continental club had been founded in the Williamsburgh section of Brooklyn as far back as October 1855.

Despite Keystone's and Olympic's early triumphs, the big name in Philadelphia baseball would soon be Athletic. Dating from April 1860, it is currently the oldest baseball name in near-continual existence. The most likely account of the club's founding comes from Al Reach, who told the same story to the newspapers on at least two different occasions. Although Reach did not join Athletic until 1865, he was a contemporary to the events of 1860, and reported that he heard this account from the original club treasurer, John J. Heisler, a Philadelphia coal merchant by trade, who *was* there. According to Reach's account, which was also basically repeated by Wes Fisler some years later (though with an 1859 date), the original Athletic club was even more musical than Mercantile, getting its start from the members of a prototypical yuppie association, a famous Philadelphia singing organization headquartered at Sixth and Spring Garden streets, the Handel and Haydn.

> The club really got its start in the Handel and Haydn Society, which held its meetings in its hall of Spring Garden Street. All the singers were interested in the game, so that baseball in Philadelphia really had high-class amateur musicians as its sponsors. The meeting to form the club was held in the society's rooms. Mr. Heisler, who was a liberal contributor to the expenses, presided. There was very much discussion over the name to be selected and Mr. Heisler made a short speech in which he said that something suggestive of action, of sport, should be chosen. One man suggested one name and we ran the whole range from Intrepid to Excelsior, when someone called out, "Why not call the club Athletic?" The suggestion was received with a roar of approval and that is how Philadelphia's pennant winners got their name.[8]

Reach would slightly revise this tale in telling it to the *Philadelphia North American* on May 19, 1907, stating at that time that Heisler's speech about choosing a name included the phrase, "It must be an aggressive name, something snappy and bright and athletic." According to Reach in this version, several members picked up on the last word of Heisler's discourse, and liking the sound of it, ran with it. The *North American* also repeated this version of the story in an article on April 2, 1911.

William Emot was elected the Athletics' first president, though Colonel Thomas Fitzgerald would become the club's first significant leader. Not mentioned in any of these accounts of the club's founding is the man usually given credit for starting Athletic, U.S. marshal James N. Kerns. An oversight? Highly unlikely. It would appear that Kerns, who was the club president in 1871 when Athletic joined the National Association (in fact, he was named the first president of the NA) was not part of the club leadership until at least after Peverelly wrote *American Pastimes* in late 1866. Later writers, having the information that Kerns was the leader of Athletic in 1871, and not knowing about the Handel and Haydn Society, assumed he had also founded the club some 11 or 12 years before. However, the testimony of Reach and Fisler clearly refutes that scenario. In reality Fitzgerald, who was sort of a Ben Shibe when the real Ben Shibe was still in the harness-making business, became the club's most notable leader soon after its founding, being elected president three times in all.

Fitzgerald may also have had an even more seminal role in the development of baseball in Philadelphia, at least according to his son, Harrington, who claimed that his father had been a member of the Olympic Town Ball Club and thus, given his membership in Olympic and his key role in the formation, funding and early years of Athletic, he was deserving of the title of father of baseball in Philadelphia. While the elder Fitzgerald did bankroll the early Athletic club, as noted by Reach,[9] the 1833 to 1866 membership rolls of Olympic, reproduced by Horace Fogel in his March 1908 series in the *Philadelphia Daily Evening Telegraph*, do not list a Fitzgerald anywhere therein. Another claim, also by Harrington Fitzgerald, that his father contributed significantly to the Athletic club's famous 1874 trip to England with the Boston Red Stockings, also seems unlikely, unless he did so through his position as publisher of the *Philadelphia Item* newspaper. Thomas Fitzgerald had, eight years before the trip to England, become president of the Equity club.[10] Nevertheless, Reach also considered Fitzgerald, who was also a leading player in his younger days, the "Father of Philadelphia Baseball."[11]

Even at this early date, Athletic members were attired in white trimmed with blue, complete with the big "A" on the uniform chest[12] — the same uniform scheme that Connie Mack cleverly chose in 1901. The only main sartorial difference between the original Athletics and their counterparts 40 years later was that the first team had blue pants with white trim, instead of the reverse.

In its first season, Athletic won its first game against Pennsylvania 27–19 on September 22, 1860, and then subsequently lost to Olympic 19–18 on October 4, in a game at the Camac Woods grounds that the two clubs uneasily shared. It was this latter game that Richter incorrectly states was Athletic's initial baseball game.[13] It's also a game that Peverelly places in 1862. The next Athletic game after the Olympic contest was a loss to Hamilton 51–37 on October 6. This was most likely against the same recently-formed outfit that Olympic defeated at some point in October 1860 — both games coming some three months after Keystone defeated Continental. Although apparently not a major Philadelphia club, and never a member of the NABBP, as were a Brooklyn and a Jersey City club by the same name, the Philly Hamilton did keep playing at least until 1865, when they reappeared back on Athletic's schedule. Following the 1860 Hamilton game, Athletic closed its first season by losing to Equity 29–17.[14]

The best team in Philadelphia in 1860 was probably Equity, organized by Lawrence K. Mann on April 21, 1860. The 1860 season, according to Peverelly, was the "first active ball season in Philadelphia," a statement we can assume means that 1860 was the first season that multiple Philadelphia teams were playing what Peverelly considered base ball— the game as developed by the Knickerbockers and the NABBP. In fact, Equity did claim to be the "Pioneer Base Ball Club of Pennsylvania," and they also claimed to be the first Philadelphia club to play the NABBP game. They were also, according to Peverelly, a member of "the National Baseball Convention" in 1860.

The Winona-Equity opener on June 11 was some three months before Athletic's September 22, 1860, opener, a month before Olympic's 1860 opener, and a week before Keystone's 1860 opener. So, absent more evidence of particularly Minerva's and Keystone's activities prior to 1860, it seems fairer to say that Winona *and* Equity are the best candidates for the honor of being the first Philadelphia club to play baseball on an interclub basis.

Equity followed the June 11 Winona game on June 26 with a contest held at Equity's home grounds — a very oddly-shaped piece of land that would later become known successively as Columbia Park, Centennial Park and Recreation Park. However, in June 1860, it was just another field where baseball was played, in this case, the lot bounded by Ridge and Columbia Avenues, and 24th and 25th Streets. Since Ridge Avenue, along with Germantown Avenue and a few others, was one of the rare thoroughfares that did not follow Philadelphia's famous grid pattern—they follow old Indian trails instead—the lot that was used by Equity was so irregular that the only good explanation for its use as an unenclosed field where baseball games were played was that it was located next to a trolley terminal, allowing the players, and later the fans as well, to ride the then-horse-drawn cars out from Center City to the game. However, this was a redeeming enough feature that the field was used before the Civil War as the home field for Equity, Winona, Swiftfoot and Pennsylvania.[15]

It was against Pennsylvania that Equity played its June 26 game, a wild affair with Equity pulling out a 65–52 win in what Peverelly says was the first game (read: first game under NABBP rules) played in the Commonwealth of Pennsylvania.[16] Even though this wasn't true, Equity's statement about being the first NABBP club in the state is probably true, since Winona was not an NABBP member in 1860.

Just to keep the clubs straight, let's list the roster of all Philadelphia baseball clubs that seem to have been active in 1860 (Penn Tiger doesn't seem to have lasted until 1860), along with the best guess at the dates of their founding, and the best guess as to the date of their first "real baseball" game:

Founding/First Game

Olympic—July 4, 1831 / July 24, 1860
Minerva—June 10, 1857 / ?
Keystone—November 30, 1859 / July 4, 1860
Mercantile—prior to 1860 / intramural games only?
Athletic—April 7, 1860 / September 22, 1860
Equity—April 21, 1860 / June 11, 1860
Winona—prior to May 18, 1860 / June 11, 1860
Hamilton—May 10, 1860 / October 1860
Pennsylvania—Voigt says they were formed early / June 26, 1860

The Philadelphia clubs that were organized made the 1860 season of "'our National Game' one long to be remembered."—especially for Equity. After losing to Winona and conquering Pennsylvania, Equity played two straight games at Ridge and Columbia against Winona, an outfit that Peverelly mentions in passing as being "long since extinct" by the time *American Pastimes* came out in 1866. In these two games, Equity tamed Winona, 59–39 and 58–21 (July 19). Winona did pick up another victory during the year against an unknown opponent, winning behind pitcher Pratt.[17]

After their Winona games, Equity moved on to a rematch with Pennsylvania, this time a 49–23 win. The longer-established Keystones next left Ridge and Columbia on September 15 on the short end of a 42–20 score. Peverelly gives two different scores (43–20 and 42–20) and two different dates, September 15 and September 19, for this game. Equity's five-game winning streak finally came to an end on October 23, 1860, when they lost in their only really low-scoring game of the year, to Hamilton, which was coming off their October 6 win over Athletic. At least, it seems safe to assume that Equity was edged 15–11 by the same Hamilton Club as had also recently played Athletic and Olympic.

Equity's 1860 season finally concluded with what must have been a chilly affair on November 12, defeating Athletic 29–17 to conclude the first season with a 6-2 record.[18]

2. The Game Spreads and Philadelphia Grows 27

While the still-informal nature of the game in Philadelphia precludes the naming of a true champion for 1860, it seems as if Equity had the strongest club, averaging almost 42 runs per game and whipping both Keystone and Athletic—although they did not play Olympic, leaving at least some doubts as to the true top gun in town. In an era when the team with the most wins tended to be viewed as the champion of whatever group they were included in, the final Philadelphia standings for 1860 would be as follows:

Equity	6-2	Hamilton	1-1	Athletic	1-3
Olympic	3-0	Keystone	1-2	Pennsylvania	1-3
Winona	2-2				

A few questions remain unanswered. Who were the Benedict and United clubs Peverelly mentions in passing? And what did Minerva do in 1860? Peverelly doesn't say, except for his statement that their only losses between 1857 and 1864 were to Athletic. Oddly, although he gives a listing of Athletic games from 1860 through 1866, there are no scores for any Athletic games with Minerva in 1860, or any other year up to 1864. In fact, there are no Minerva scores against any other Philadelphia club listed in *American Pastimes*, or against any other club in any other published source, prior to the 1865 season.

For either a lack of information (Minerva and Swiftfoot), or a lack of contests (Olympic), it seems as if Equity should be retroactively awarded the whip pennant, symbolic of a championship in this era, for Philadelphia for 1860. And, maybe it was with this in mind that Peverelly listed the entire hard-hitting Equity starting nine ("first nine" was the term used at that time) for 1860, the only instance where he did that for any Philadelphia team.

P—R.F. Stevens	2B—Frank Knight	RF—C. Fackler
C—W.H. Litzenburg	3B—J.B. Daniels	CF—Weston Fisler
1B—B.F. Shantz	SS—Harry Shantz	LF—B. Loughery

Although it is fun to speculate that perhaps the Shantz' were the first members of future Philadelphia Athletic star Bobby Shantz' family to take up the National Pastime, the most significant players on the 1860 Equity team were center fielder Fisler and pitcher Stevens, both of whom also played in what was essentially a Philadelphia–New York All-Star baseball game on July 24, 1860. Played at the Camac Woods grounds in Philadelphia between a "picked nine" from Philadelphia's Athletic, Olympic, Benedict, Winona, Equity and United clubs[19] and 1860 NABBP unofficial champion Brooklyn Excelsior (they finished 18-2-1 on the year), this historic contest resulted in a 15–4 Brooklyn win[20]—a result that should have brought no shame to the Picked Nine, since the Excelsior pitcher was baseball's first superstar, Jim Creighton.[21] And, since Stevens held Excelsior to 15 runs—they averaged 27 for the year—Philadelphia's first meeting with New York was certainly not a disgrace.

Of more note to Philadelphia fans than the exploits of the 19-year-old Creighton were the exploits of 19-year-old (or possibly 17-year-old) Camden native Weston Dickson Fisler, playing his first baseball season in what would become a notable career in professional baseball (mostly with the Athletics). As such, Fisler was the first great ballplayer—probably better than the older town ball star, Hicks Hayhurst, and a little older than the coming star, Dick McBride—from the Philadelphia area.

In conclusion, although it cannot be said with absolute certainty which organization actually began regularly playing what is now known as baseball first in Philadelphia, or even what the best team of 1860 really was, there's no doubt that, from 1860 on, numerous clubs besides the soon-to-be-famous Athletic were on the Philadelphia baseball scene.

* * *

While it may often seem that New York has been the be all and end all of baseball since 1845, Philadelphia was ideally suited for the game, at least after the prejudice spoken of by Peverelly dissipated, for various demographic and sociological reasons. Starting in 1830, Philadelphia underwent a tremendous period of growth, becoming, by 1860, what Sam Bass Warner, Jr., in *The Private City*, called "something new to the world and new to America—a modern big city." Indeed, the city more than tripled in population, from 161,000 to 565,000 in the years between 1830 and 1860, and more than doubled (from 258,000) in the years between 1840 and 1860, thanks in part to the 1854 decision to extend the city limits to cover all of Philadelphia County, a move that consolidated 28 municipalities with Philadelphia and created boundaries that haven't changed in the past 150 years. Even if the city hadn't consolidated itself with the county, Philadelphia was a "big" city at this time, a significant factor in the potential for the growth of baseball, for the simple reason that the more people there were in any one area, the more people there were who might be available to play baseball. In addition, the city's prosperity, and increasing middle class, also provided more potential "Yuppies," the social class that first played what had been kids' games as adults.

The explosive growth of the city also filled out the city's famous grid pattern of streets that had originally been laid out by William Penn in 1682. By 1860, the grid pattern extended unbroken for six square miles—a testimony to both the success of the city, and the layout of its streets—a pattern that was so popular that it had been copied by Manhattan in 1811, and would be copied throughout the American West for years to come. One of the side effects of that growth on the grid pattern was what Bass characterizes as "the thorough destruction of the informal neighborhood street life which had characterized the small-scale community of the eighteenth-century town." How did Philadelphia and Philadelphians react to that social upheaval? Just like people in cities throughout the land reacted in the mid–nineteenth century (only even more so)—they went out a formed, or joined, a club. As Bass puts it, this was the era of "the urban parish church, the lodge, the benefit association, the social and athletic club, the political club, the fire company, and the gang." In all, Bass estimates there were 1500 organized clubs of various types in Philly in 1861.[22] Enough of these were sporting clubs that, just through sheer numbers, it was inevitable that the level of play would excel and improve to the point where better competition and its fellow traveler, profit motive, would most certainly follow along with the development of the best teams and players. The proof of that would come in the rosters of future Philadelphia teams, rosters that featured a number of home-grown stars—Wes Fisler, Hicks Hayhurst, Dick McBride, Long Levi Meyerle, Harry Stovey, and Jack Clements—just to name some of the best of the nineteenth century.

Interestingly, given the popularity of the singularly American game of baseball, the city was at this time a significant melting pot, without the many and diverse ethnic neighborhoods that would come in the latter part of the century and which, to this day, still characterize Philadelphia. That phenomenon was actually just starting around 1860, when what Bass has characterized as "the full development of the segregated metropolis" was just beginning with a few small enclaves—a downtown (which existed only east of 7th Street, although it was already clustered north and south around Market Street), some manufacturing clusters (that aspect of the city would explode in the latter half of the nineteenth century) and just a few ethnic enclaves. And, indeed, "the people did suit the pastime" since the city was, at this point in its history, largely a British Isles melting pot. Not a small consideration in the growth of baseball, since the bat-and-ball games it was derived from were all essentially British in origin.[23]

Two parts of the city where there weren't many ethnic enclaves, mainly because there was very little there at all, were West Philadelphia and what at that time physically comprised the northwest part of the city, although its designation at that time was Lower North Philadelphia and it is currently known as North Philadelphia. It was in these two areas—most notably the latter—that baseball was first played professionally. Why? A lot of space was needed to play a game that at the time depended on speedy outfielders and not fences to track down balls. Also, what was not needed at first for the more social games of baseball was easy access to the public.

In the midst of this period of baseball and urban growth some baseball clubs played at 32nd and Hamilton Streets in West Philadelphia. Their subsequent relocation from the west side of the Schuylkill River to the east side was a significant one. While the move from what is now known as Philadelphia's University City to North Philadelphia may not seem like a historic event, in reality, the use of grounds at 17th Street and Columbia

Now an inner city intersection, the corner of 17th and Columbia Streets was famous in the 1860s as the Camac Woods grounds, home of the Athletics. The corner shown would have been in deep right field (photograph by Matthew J. Coyne).

Avenue—on what was very largely still undeveloped land, as opposed to the somewhat more built up University of Pennsylvania neighborhood—would pave the way for more than 100 years of Philadelphia baseball. The move also made sense in another logistic fashion—the Market Street Bridge was still the only permanent bridge across the Schuylkill River. Moving to North Philadelphia gave baseball much easier access to the average citizen, most of whom still lived on the east side of the Schuylkill.

Once established in North Philly, amateur, semi-pro and professional teams would continue to play their games within a fairly small section of Philadelphia—a rough square about two miles long and two miles wide—until the Phillies abandoned Connie Mack Stadium and its now crumbling and dangerous neighborhood after the 1970 season. Going back some 110 years though, what is now called North Philly was so unpopulated that only three wards—the 21st, 22nd and 23rd—comprised a huge area that took in pretty much everything north of Montgomery Avenue and west of Kensington Avenue. However, the time was soon coming, thanks in part to the rapid spread of the railroads throughout the city, that the populace would be able to get to the fringes of the city in a relatively short time. Although horse-drawn cars had been operating in the city since 1858, they were more or less limited in service to the old downtown area, well east of Broad Street and far from the West and North Philly locations where baseball was played.[24] The key transportation development in the city, for both baseball and the city as a whole, was the advent of steam railroads in the 1830s and 1840s. This new form of public transportation saw new stations flung all over the hinterlands of the city's landscape because there was a lot of cheap land available out in the direction of Germantown, located northwest of Center City, and other outlying sections of the city.[25] In other words, to get to the growing suburbs north and west of Center City, the railroads (and, eventually, the streetcar lines) first had to go through the Lower North Philadelphia area where baseball would soon become a leading "industry." Philadelphia was growing, and so was baseball.

◆ CHAPTER 3 ◆

Baseball During the Civil War— Philadelphia Joins the NABBP

Despite the long history of Olympic, the previous establishment of Athletic, Keystone, Minerva and Equity, and the games of the 1860 season, the NABBP did not have any Philadelphia members until Olympic, Athletic, Equity and Winona showed up in the 1861 list, along with a couple of fairly anonymous clubs, Benedict and United. This information comes from the definitive source on the NABBP, Marshall Wright's *The National Association of Base Ball Players, 1857–1870*. And it is an important distinction, since, although the main requirement for membership was somewhat vague—that being clubs who attended the national convention or clubs that belonged to a state association—the most important consideration was that the NABBP admitted clubs that played only baseball, not town ball, rounders, or any other bat-and-ball game. So, even though the evidence in Peverelly's 1866 book indicates that several Philly clubs were playing baseball by 1860, it is also true that, thanks to Wright's research, it can be said with a certainty that Olympic, Athletic, Equity, Winona, Benedict and United were playing baseball in 1861. However, only Athletic, Keystone and Olympic seem to have played regularly throughout the Civil War, unquestionably due to a lack of manpower caused by the war—a situation roughly analogous to the situation faced by the minor leagues during World War II.

The available results of the Philadelphia season of 1861 are limited to scores from Olympic, Athletic, and non–NABBP members Keystone and Mercantile. Where was Equity, the unofficial 1860 champions of Philadelphia? A victim of the Civil War, since most of the club's members apparently didn't have the wherewithal to pay someone to take their place in the army—a common practice of the upper and middle class at that time. While the club was in the midst of preparing for the 1861 season, it disbanded until after the end of the war in 1865.[1] Among the teams that did play in 1861, and that Peverelly provides records for, Olympic had the best record, 3-0, followed by Athletic (2-2), Keystone (1-0) and Mercantile (0-1). Two of Olympic's wins came at the expense of Athletic and its 17-year-old pitcher, Tom Pratt, 25–20 and 34–18, but the mother club's biggest victory was also the highlight of the 1861 Philadelphia season and represented another win for the city over a New York area team. On October 5, Athletic had met the Adriatic club of Newark, dropping an 18–17 thriller. A week later, on October 12, Olympic avenged Philadelphia's honor with a solid 25–17 win over the same Newark club.

Although Athletic couldn't take the measure of Olympic in 1861, their 41–13 win over Mercantile on June 19, 1861, was notable in that it saw the first appearance in blue and white of a rather elderly (age 33 or 34) centerfielder who had been a town ball star for years prior to the coming of baseball to Philadelphia. He was Elias "Hicks" Hayhurst,[2] and he would go on to play one of the most significant roles in Philadelphia baseball history prior to his death late in 1882. June 1861 also marked the Athletic debut of a phenom less than half Hayhurst's age. James Dickson "Dick" McBride was a Philadelphia native (as was Hayhurst) and, together with Hayhurst, he would eventually carry Athletic to dynastic status in Philadelphia baseball, and nationally as well.

* * *

According to Wright's information, none of the Philadelphia clubs belonged to the NABBP in 1862. This was almost certainly a war-related development. Wright reports that the December 1861 NABBP convention drew only 34 clubs, just half of the number that attended in 1860, and none of those clubs were from farther away than the wilds of New Jersey. As a result, no Philly clubs would have been NABBP members for 1862. But, even the Civil War couldn't stop the growing baseball rivalry between Philadelphia and Greater New York. In 1862, the association's two top clubs, the champion Eckfords of Brooklyn and the Mutuals of New York, both played series against Philadelphia opposition.[3] While those were important milestones, 1862 was also important to Philadelphia baseball as the season when Athletic first could make its claim as the first name in Philadelphia baseball.

Due to missing box scores, and possibly lessened interest due to the war, which was not going well for the Union at this time, surviving records for the 1862 season are scanty.[4] Between Peverelly's and Wright's works we have scores for four Athletic games — namely two wins and two losses — from 1862. Not that impressive a record, except that one of those wins marked the first time a Philadelphia team had beaten one of the top New York clubs. That momentous occasion was August 28, 1862, and came just one day after the New York Mutual club nipped Olympic 10–7 (Peverelly has the August 27, 1862, Mutual-Olympic game taking place on the same date in 1863) in a low-scoring game the type of which typically brought praise from the cognoscenti like Henry Chadwick. Generally, the lower-scoring the game, the better the fielding and, at this time in the game's development, fielding was clearly the sport's more difficult and valued skill — moreso than either batting or pitching — the former being present in excess and the latter still under severe restrictions in the rule book. The August 28 game saw a little more hitting, as Athletic scored 17 off of Mutual pitcher S. Burns while holding the New Yorkers to 10. Although Athletic subsequently lost a higher-scoring game, 25–32, to the champion 14–2 Eckford club in October, their Mutual win and an 18–19, 19–10 split with Olympic (1–3 in games Peverelly provides scores for) would seem to give evidence that the Philadelphia crown was indeed getting ready to pass into Athletic's hands. So too did the Athletic roster, which boasted two teenage pitchers who would go on to great things in baseball — 17-year-old Dick McBride and 18-year-old Tom Pratt. The two youngsters split the Athletic pitching duties in '62 and, although Pratt would jump to the Brooklyn Atlantic club during 1863, both of these young former cricketeers would have notable success in the box in the future.

Meanwhile, New York was still able to establish its superiority, as Eckford concluded its 1862 season with four straight wins over Philadelphia teams, defeating a picked nine 39–8, Olympic 39–13, Athletic (the 32–25 game) and Keystone 26–2 from October 21 to October 24. Of most note on the NABBP champion Eckford roster in 1862 was the first baseman, Al Reach (he also played some third, short and the outfield), who soon would be starting among the most significant careers in nineteenth century Philadelphia baseball—a career that would last well into the twentieth century.[5]

* * *

The 1863 season marked a giant step for Athletic and Philadelphia baseball. Athletic and Keystone both made it to the December 1862 NABBP convention and, for the first time, a Philadelphia team was a major player in the NABBP. Posting a 7-5 record that gave them both the fourth most wins in NABBP, Athletic showed that Philadelphia baseball had arrived on the national scene.

Athletic's 1863 campaign began with a March 22 game against Nassau of Princeton, a 29–18 win. They then took almost three months off before heading on a historic tour of Greater New York's top baseball clubs. Playing six games in six days in mid–June, Athletic went 2-4 against best the NABBP had to offer:

June 15—defeated Excelsior of Brooklyn 18–17 in 10 innings
June 16—lost to Mutual of New York 17–11
June 17—lost to Eckford of Brooklyn 10–5
June 18—lost to Atlantic of Brooklyn 21–13 (this was a Pratt-McBride pitching matchup)
June 19—defeated Star of Brooklyn 37–17
June 20—lost to Eureka of Newark 8–6

Although Athletic lost four of the six games, none of the defeats were blow-outs, so it must have been clear to the New Yorkers that the Philadelphia team wasn't a bunch of muffins—the term at the time for less skilled players. Further, these were some of Greater New York's top teams. While complete records for Eureka aren't available, the other five clubs Athletic played on tour were a combined 38–16 in 1863. Eckford went 10-0, the first time an NABBP club had gone undefeated on a season in that many games.

The Athletics' tour was big news in both the Philadelphia and New York baseball worlds, and set a pattern for the future, says Wright: "Although they won only two of the six, all parties thoroughly enjoyed the competition. In the years to come, excursions between Philadelphia and New York became a staple of the schedule for most leading clubs."[6]

After the tour, Athletic took another two and a half months off before finishing the season with five wins in six games against more local competition. The lone loss was a 29–13 rematch with Nassau, while Athletic took one more trip, to Altoona to play the Mountain club in the forerunner of many future contests against clubs from central and western Pennsylvania. This one ended up in what would be a fairly typical score for these games, 73–22 Athletic. Why did these small town club teams play the mighty Athletics, since they were getting their brains beat out? Peverelly has an answer of sorts to this: "The Athletics have done more to advance the popularity of the game, by visits to towns and villages where base ball was previously unknown, than almost any other Club in the United States."[7]

A supporting statement as to the Athletic club's motives came from Reach, in the May 19, 1907, *Philadelphia North American*. Reach claimed that the club, while wanting to win games, was also imbued with a higher purpose of showing Philadelphians baseball and traveling around the country spreading interest in the game. In fact, Reach uses the 73–22 waxing of the Altoona club as a "for instance" of Athletic's efforts to spread the word about baseball.

Thus, in 1863 did the Athletic Club of Philadelphia definitively start off on a road that would make it the first name in Philadelphia baseball, partly by spreading the game far and wide beyond Philadelphia. If Equity could be said to have been the best team in Philadelphia in 1860, and Olympic the best in 1861, by 1863 Athletic had pretty surely taken over. It was a road that that would lead to two, or maybe three, unofficial national championships, as well as the first title in the first truly organized baseball league, and a spot in the first permanent sports league in America, establishing a legacy that lasts to the present.

First, though, a word on the nature of championships in the NABBP. In an organization without formal scheduling or any standings, it's pretty hard to determine a true champion. The NABBP didn't even bother with the concept of a champion until sportswriter Henry Chadwick thought it up in 1859, when he declared Atlantic the best in the country. By the next season, the NABBP did have a method of determining a champion in place—even if it doesn't make much sense to modern baseball fans. First, the previous year's defending champion was in the driver's seat, even before the next season opened. Basically, the only way to unseat a defending champion was to take a home-and-home series from them. Or, if the challenger split the home-and-home series (which could be contested over a period of months) with the reigning champs, they'd then play a third, tie-breaking match at a neutral site.[8] Since the NABBP was a very loose confederation of clubs, there was no way to force a champion to actually schedule any other team in a home-and-home, although such series were, in reality, pretty common within limited geographic areas. This odd means of determining a champion would, by the NABBP's reckoning, cost Athletic the championships of 1867 and 1868, and arguably in 1866 as well.

Back to 1863. Who were the Athletics of 1863? Their biggest name was 18-year-old shortstop-pitcher McBride, although their other pitcher at the start of the year, the now–19-year-old Pratt, wasn't bad, either. In fact, Pratt was good enough that Atlantic recruited him away from Athletic in mid-season, most likely with the promise of some form of payment. Although this cost Athletic the services of a fine pitcher, it also was a kind of backhanded compliment and a statement about the caliber of Philadelphia players—especially since McBride would go on to become a better pitcher than Pratt. This maneuver most likely gave the directors of the Athletic club the idea of using the same inducement—money—as a means of building up the club.[9]

A shortstop and a pitcher in 1863, McBride would go on to pitch for Athletic through the 1875 season, winning a certified 149 games from 1871 to 1875 in the National Association, and an estimated 175 games from 1860 to 1870, making him the city's, and baseball's, biggest winner at the time he retired in 1876.

Offensively, the 1863 Athletics were led by catcher Dan Kleinfelder, whose runs average and over was 3,0. At this time, players' offensive averages were expressed as how many runs they scored per game, with the remainder expressed as a single figure, and not a decimal. So, to say that Kleinfelder's runs were 3, 0 is another way of saying he scored an average of exactly three runs a game. As far as totals go, he scored 33 runs in the 11 games he played. And, here's one explanation of why batting skill wasn't so highly valued—almost any muffin could score at least two runs a game. Kleinfelder at 3, 0 was in a five-way tie for third in runs average and over in the NABBP in '63.

* * *

The 1864 season brought pretty much more of the same. Only Athletic and Keystone were NABBP members, although Olympic and Mercantile were still on the scene, along

The one and only James Dickson McBride in his 1874 Athletic uniform. Note the impressive Dundreary whiskers on baseball's first 300 game winner (courtesy John Thorn).

with, presumably, the mysterious Minerva. In nine games against NABBP members, spread out between a June 9 win over Camden (21–10) and a chilly 23–15 win over Keystone on November 24, Athletic went 8-1, finishing tied for third in the NABBP in wins. Only a serious 43–16 pounding by Atlantic and Tom Pratt marred Athletic's record for the year. In fact, Atlantic marred a lot of teams' records in 1864, going 20-0-1 in the first of two successive undefeated seasons for the Brooklyn team and its young ace. In between their first and last games, Athletic's season was highlighted by a 29–12 win over Resolute of Brooklyn, a close win over Keystone (13–8) and an absolute slaughter of Mercantile 68–25. Averaging just over 32 runs per game, Athletic was led once again by Kleinfelder, whose runs average and over was up to 3,7 while he handled both catching and pitching chores—splitting the latter duty with McBride and substitute outfielder-change pitcher Hayhurst.

The other Philadelphia NABBP club, Keystone, had less success, going 1-6 in NABBP action, and giving up 30 runs a game while scoring just less than 15. Their only win was over Camden 17–16, and that was counterbalanced by two losses (44–20 and 19–12) to the New Jersey team. In addition, Atlantic really roughed up Keystone 65–10. Olympic had a little more success as a non–NABBP member, going 2-4 with wins over Resolute (24–23) and Camden (28–23). Olympic also had the misfortune to run afoul of Atlantic 58–11.[10] Thus, as the Civil War entered its final year, Brooklyn fans could indeed point to the superiority of their team over the Philadelphia clubs. However, thanks to Athletic and a new development that would change the game forever, the gap was narrowing. The 1865 season—which was played basically after the war ended—would provide all the proof anyone would need.

* * *

The year 1865 also brought more to Philadelphia, namely, the end of the Civil War. While this was no small occurrence in American history in general, it was especially meaningful in the City of Brotherly Love, since Philadelphia was, in reality, a border city in the unbrotherly War Between the States. Even though the majority of the battles may have been fought in the South, the war's most famous encounter took place about 110 miles west of Philadelphia on Pennsylvania soil in Gettysburg, and the Mason-Dixon Line was and is practically in the city's southern suburbs. Further, the nearest large city to Philadelphia—Baltimore—was hardly a hotbed of Union fervor. A slave-holding city in a slave-holding state. Yankee troops, including some from Philadelphia who weren't even in uniform, were assaulted while marching through Baltimore to Washington in 1861, and Frederick, Maryland's Barbara Frietche, a Union sympathizer, didn't become the subject of a heroic poem by accident.

As happened throughout the North, the firing on Fort Sumter brought out the patriot in Philadelphians, the same Philadelphians who had been stoning abolitionists as part of the Not in My Back Yard (NIMBY) syndrome just a few years before. And, while Philadelphia's initial military quota from the federal War Department was just six regiments, able-bodied men were nonetheless drilling everywhere. While re-enlistments make it impossible to state an accurate number for the white Philadelphians who served in the war, 90,000 would be a good guess.[11] Chances are, more than a few of them were also baseball players, including the members of Equity. Still, even as a city of war, Philadelphia and Philadelphians would have time for baseball.

As awful a disaster as the Civil War was, the conflict's long-term effects on Philadelphia as a whole were surprisingly minimal. Probably the biggest effect was sociological, as the race question was clearly and forcefully raised in a fashion that could not be ignored. And that fashion was first and foremost in the area of public transportation in 1864. Prior to this time, the issue was not segregating black Philadelphians to the back of the bus, it was a matter of them not even being allowed on the "bus" on at least on 11 of the city's 19 streetcar lines. Although black men were serving in the Union armies, both they and their families were not even allowed to board many of the horse cars in Philadelphia. This egregious example of racism first started attracting attention in 1861, and started coming to a head in early 1864, when a group of young black leaders of the Social, Cultural and Statistical Association of Colored People of Philadelphia organized a mass meeting of blacks on March 3 to protest for open streetcars. This meeting, led by the remarkable schoolteacher-activist-baseball player Octavius Valentine Catto, eventually led to more streetcar lines opening their vehicles to "all well-behaved persons." In reality though, total desegregation wouldn't come about until an act of the Pennsylvania legislature in 1867.[12]

While it's true that the developments surrounding the war brought more African Americans to Philadelphia, and those numbers helped contribute to the establishment of black baseball teams like Catto's renowned Pythians, the integration of the streetcar system was a much more significant event. Integration opened up the opportunity for all to travel wherever they wanted within the city—no small thing to the vast majority of the population who did not have their own means of transportation.

In other areas of development and progress, many ambitious plans from the years just prior to the war—like the development of Fairmount Park and America's first zoo—were sidetracked by the war. However, in economic development, wherein prosperity supported baseball's development from a pastime to a profession, as a whole the war really didn't do too much good or bad. Possibly the biggest effect was the failure of the Port of Philadelphia to establish a direct connection with Europe, thus allowing New York to achieve greater pre-eminence in this particular market. In general, wartime activity was too transient to contribute to growth, and economic conditions on the other hand weren't bad enough to create a municipal lassitude deep enough to affect the coming post-war boom that carried on and led up to the city's crowning moment of the latter part of the nineteenth century—the Centennial Exhibition.[13]

The Civil War's effect on Philadelphia baseball was more than just a manpower issue; there is also a socio-economic aspect to the discussion. Prior to the Civil War, baseball was pretty clearly a game of the upper and middle classes. People like Thomas Fitzgerald, John Heisler and Wes Fisler were not only the individuals who drew up the rules of the game, but also the individuals who banded together in the first place to form the first club teams and were, as such, the first players. Why was that? Because baseball was a pastime at first, a game, something that was done literally to pass time. And what class of people had the time to pass—the free time? The middle or upper class. The members of a singing society. The game of the 1850s was one of the hoi polloi, and, maybe it would have stayed that way, at least until the common adoption of the five-day work week, if it hadn't been for the Civil War. A lot of upper and middle class types were able to buy their way out of the army, and, in general, wars are fought in the trenches by and large by the poor. As a result, those individuals who were playing baseball behind the lines were often members of the working class, who were actually being introduced to the game. Did the Civil War serve as a great leveler in terms of bringing the masses to baseball in Philadelphia and elsewhere? It's not an unreasonable assumption.

The evidence indicates that baseball at its highest level, i.e., as played by the teams that belonged to the NABBP, did suffer from the manpower shortage. That much is clear from Wright's, Seymour's and Peverelly's works. Equity was far from the only club that we know had to disband for the duration, Swiftfoot apparently being another Philly victim of the war, and maybe Winona as well. It's also possible that the reason for the lack of results for Minerva during the war was related to a war-slowdown. The number of clubs in the NABBP may have not grown during the war, but it at least maintained pretty close to the status quo during the war years. And, as the war was winding down, at the December 1864 convention, the number shot up to 93, and then skyrocketed in subsequent years, thanks in part to southern teams joining, to the point where the NABBP became so big that it could not administer itself.

In Philadelphia, it is clear that baseball carried on, even in the face of the war and the socio-economic effects of the conflict. Athletic, Keystone, Olympic and Mercantile (and maybe Minerva) played on, although the latter two didn't belong to the NABBP. And, across the Delaware River, Camden continued to field a club team. Meanwhile, a far bigger wartime-related effect on Philadelphia took place off the baseball playing fields, in politics, wherein the Republican Party first rose on its way to taking what would become an iron grip on the city, a hegemony that would last almost 90 years. This political development during the war—which followed the national rise of the Republican Party under Abraham Lincoln—was part of the culmination of about 10 years worth of significant change in the city, beginning with what was literally the biggest development in Philadelphia's history—consolidation.

As Philadelphia and its outlying districts grew in the period from 1845 to 1854, the city itself, which at that time ran only from the Delaware River to the Schuylkill River and from Vine Street on the north to South Street on the south, became harder and harder to administer. While the population within the city boundaries was growing, the populace was also spilling outside the boundaries, and growing at an even faster rate, so much that the police, fire and other services couldn't keep up with what became a patchwork quilt of 13 townships, six boroughs and nine districts. Although this situation was a headache for everyone, law enforcement suffered the most. Various legislative stopgaps, none of which worked, were passed in the years leading up to 1854, leading some outside-the-box thinkers to propose consolidating the small Center City, the area defined by the two rivers, Vine and South Streets, with the outlying districts, forming a veritable super city. Although those suggestions largely fell on deaf legislative years prior to 1854, it was an idea that made too much sense not to happen—even in the face of Harrisburg's traditional antipathy towards the state's largest city. Primarily, Philadelphia needed to expand its tax base to provide all the services needed for a growing urban industrial center. And, although providing support for baseball clubs was hardly the motive that spurred Philadelphia lawyer Eli Kirk Price to champion the consolidation movement, it certainly didn't hurt the growth of those clubs.

By the early 1850s, the center of the region's population wasn't even within the city proper, since 206,885 people lived between the two rivers north of Vine Street, and only 188,802 lived between the two rivers south (i.e., within the city boundaries) of Vine Street. All of the city's newspapers got on the consolidation bandwagon, and helped elect Price to the state Senate, a move that, if it didn't guarantee that consolidation would finally happen, unquestionably smoothed the road to consolidation. On January 3, 1854, Price presented an eloquent and highly-detailed address to the Legislature, including a mass of statistics that featured an estimate that a new charter for a consolidated city would eliminate

A view of mid–nineteenth century Philadelphia, looking west towards the Schuylkill River (Library of Congress photograph).

168 tax collectors, saving the state $100,000 a year. By January 31, the bill had passed both houses, and Governor William Bigler was rousted out of bed just before midnight on February 2 to sign it. In appreciation, Philadelphia named a street after the governor, a street within a long fly ball of the future sites of Veterans Stadium and Citizens Bank Park. A street at the far southern end of what was now, at 129 square miles, the largest city geographically in the country, the second-largest (behind New York) in population, with 565,529 inhabitants in 1860, and the fourth largest in population in the Western world, behind only London, Paris and New York.

Although there were still some 1,500 farms and 10,000 cattle in those 129 square miles,[14] and although Philadelphia was now, in effect, a series of towns connected by railways, the stretching of Philadelphia's boundaries, to where they still remain 150 years later, created a new paradigm for the region. The city would now grow inward, bringing even more people together to all parts of the city, and filling up those empty spaces—though not so fast that there weren't still places to play baseball. Although there were still plenty of wide-open spaces throughout the city, it was around this time that baseball, at least at its highest club level, became almost solely concentrated in a remarkably small area of the city. According to Philadelphia historian and author Bruce Kuklick, prior to the building of Shibe Park in 1909, no less than nine major ball parks were located within a 10-block radius of the North City section of Philadelphia—all established between the years of 1860 and 1901. In addition to the Camac Woods grounds at 17th and Columbia, these most prominently included Jefferson Park (25th and Jefferson), Recreation Park (Columbia, Ridge, 24th and 25th), Oakdale Park (11th and Cumberland), Forepaugh Park (Broad and Dauphin), Columbia Park (29th and Columbia) and the Huntingdon Street Grounds (later Baker Bowl, at Broad and Lehigh, or 15th and Huntingdon). Why was this? Kuklick notes that all nine parks were located between the Pennsylvania and Reading railroad lines, and near the main North City residential areas, without being in the main zones of development. They were also all close to the old diagonal highways, notably Ridge Avenue, which also gave easy access across the standard grid pattern of streets.[15] In other words, ideal locations for spectator sports.

In a baseball sense, the economic success of the city's consolidation, the need to get the still-growing population (a factor in itself that would foster more and better baseball clubs) from place to place within the city, plus the better city services, would soon prove to be a boon to baseball club teams that were undergoing their own radical change. They would soon be professionals, and, just like Philadelphia's boundaries, there would be no turning back, and nothing would ever be the same again.

◆ CHAPTER 4 ◆

The First Name in Philadelphia Baseball— Athletic

It is generally conceded that Jim Creighton was the first individual to be paid a regular salary for the sole purpose of playing baseball. At least, it is known that Creighton was paid before he died in 1862, and that he changed teams a couple of times prior to that, jumping from Niagara of Brooklyn to Star of Brooklyn in mid-season 1859, and then jumping again to Excelsior for the 1860 season.[1] The general consensus is that this 1860 move marked Creighton's transition to the professional ranks, and marks the actual start of professionalism in baseball.[2] This club jumping pattern, which became much more common in another half dozen years or so, was atypical of the genteel club game of the 1850s, when pure amateurism ruled. It is in fact, more typical of the growing professionalism of the latter part of the 1860s, suggesting that Creighton was being to paid, contra to NABBP regulations, to "revolve" from team to team.

Not long after Creighton became a professional, specifically, following the 1864 season, a young Englishman named Alfred James Reach jumped from Eckford to the city of Philadelphia, also no doubt attracted by the lure of filthy lucre, to play baseball for a living, and to play it for Athletic. This despite the fact that it was still against NABBP rules to pay players. While Athletic may not have been the first club team to go under the table to pay players, the club's willingness to do so was a dramatic moment, a major step in the development of the game in the Quaker City. It was also, according to Frank Richter, the first time a team persuaded a player to change cities for a salary. "[Reach] was the first player that there is any record of, to change his address for a stipulated sum," is how he phrased the transaction, also stating that Athletic's offer came in June 1864, in the middle of the previous season.[3]

Reach's reach from Brooklyn to Philadelphia was one of the initial reasons why Athletic was the first, the best, name in baseball in Philadelphia. Claims from New York, Brooklyn and Cincinnati notwithstanding, Philadelphia also had a claim on the first name in baseball in the years after the Civil War—mainly due to the successes of the Athletic Club. Although some sources have the Athletic club playing in the University City section of Philadelphia prior to 1865, that was likely a temporary assignment. Their real home was at the old St. George Cricket Club grounds, known as Camac Woods, with home plate at 17th Street and Columbia Avenue. Most sources say the park was at 15th and Columbia; however, this is not exactly accurate. On-site twenty-first century research by Matthew

J. Coyne has proven that the diamond was actually along 17th Street. Of course, remembering that at first there were no fences, and that part of the early game's charm was in the wide open spaces in the outfield, the Athletic's grounds ran along Columbia Avenue all the way from 17th, two blocks east to 15th. Coyne's observations[4] are backed up by the testimony of Al Reach in the May 19, 1907, *Philadelphia North American*, wherein it is stated that the Camac Woods grounds covered two blocks east and west (16th Street didn't exist between Columbia and Montgomery, the next block to the north) and a block north and south, although it was spoken of as being at 17th and Columbia.

These early, semi-professional Athletics, who evolved into the all-professional Athletics of the avowedly-professional National Association and then into the National League Athletics in 1876, could be said to have won three mythical national titles just after the Civil War, while running up a record of 298-40 between 1860 and 1870. Maybe that's why their white caps carried a blue star. How did they win those mythical, or is it unofficial, national titles? Although the NABBP's arcane, "win-a-home-and-home series with the defending champ" method of deciding a titlist withheld such official NABBP recognition from Athletic, the Philadelphia team did, according to Marshall Wright's research, have the most wins in 1867 and 1868 (tied with Atlantic in the latter year), and another method at this time of deciding a champion was indeed to crown whosoever won the most games in a year (that was the system used by the National Association). Athletic also had the best won-loss percentage, a concept whose time had not yet come, in the NABBP in 1866, a lofty .920.

Of significance to the club's rising prominence in 1865, Athletic played in an intercity tournament in Washington before 6000 fans, including President Andrew Johnson, the first chief executive to see an inter-city game. Also in the tournament were the Washington Nationals (Athletic slaughtered them 87–12) and the Brooklyn Atlantic club,[5] who, by this time, had become the Athletic's biggest rival. Atlantic claimed the national championship for the 1861, 1864, 1865 and 1866 seasons, and even went to the extent of having one of the first baseball cards printed up to commemorate their 1864 season—they had gone undefeated that year. Boldly labeled "Champions of America," this card was a mounted team picture that was presented to opposing teams at the beginning of games during the 1865 season—an early form of gamesmanship.[6]

Whether that ploy worked or not, Atlantic did go undefeated again in 1865, going 18-0 and besting Athletic's outstanding 15-3 NABBP mark, largely due to the fact that one of the 1865 Athletic's three losses was a hotly-contested 21–15 affair on October 30 at 17th and Columbia against Atlantic that drew a huge crowd of as many as (depending on which account you read) 28,000. That was about four times the capacity of the future tenant out beyond the grounds' outfield, Temple University's McGonigle Hall, and they watched from within and without the grounds, climbing trees, peering out of nearby buildings, and even watching from rooftops[7]—a practice that would become far more common 36 years later at Columbia Park and 45 years later at Shibe Park. A week later, on November 6, Atlantic sealed the "official" 1865 whip pennant with another close win over Athletic, this time by a 27–24 score in Brooklyn as the second part of the home-and-home series. Actually, there is some disagreement as to which game of the home-and-home series was in Philly and which was in Brooklyn. The Philly-first version seems the most likely from the weight of the evidence, notably Peverelly giving the details of Athletic's trip to Brooklyn for the November 6 game—they left on November 5 and stayed at Merchant's Hotel.[8]

Prior to the two Atlantic games, Athletic's first NABBP loss of 1865 was an August

10 28–13 defeat by the New York Active club. Some sources say this contest was not played at 17th and Columbia, but rather at 25th and Jefferson Streets—where Athletic would permanently relocate in 1871. Not true, as both geographic evidence and Coyne's research suggest otherwise. According to well-documented protests by the aggrieved Athletic club, this defeat was caused by a lost ball. Seems as if the original ball in use during the contest went over the fence and onto the adjacent grounds of the Wagner Free Institute of Science, and the Wagnerians claimed possession was nine-tenths of the law—and kept the ball.[9] The still-standing Wagner Free Institute of Science building had just been completed that same year at what is now 1700 West Montgomery Avenue, just west across 17th Street from where home plate was at 17th and Montgomery. It would have taken a really long home run to have bounced any kind of ball to 17th and Montgomery from 25th and Jefferson—well over a mile away. Second, as Coyne points out, if the diamond had been based at 15th and Columbia, the ball would still have had to travel more than two full city blocks to get to the Wagner Institute.[10] Thus, the only answer to the actual location and orientation of this famous and historic Philadelphia baseball site is that home plate was located on the southeast corner of the 17th and Montgomery intersection, directly across 17th Street from the Wagner Institute (on the southwest corner) and facing southeast. And, this supposition is supported both by the illustration with the May 19, 1907, *North American* story, showing the playing field with the distinctive Wagner Institute building in the background beyond the first base line, and Reach's remembrance that home plate was so close to the Wagner Institute that many foul balls went into Mr. Wagner's yard. "What he did with them, I don't know," said Reach. Most probably afraid that these baseball ruffians

The Wagner Free Institute of Science, as seen from where the first base line would have been on the Camac Woods grounds. A foul ball landing on the Wagner property from across 17th Street once cost Athletic a game (photograph by Matthew J. Coyne).

might break a window in his new building, or possibly because, as Reach speculated, he didn't like having a noisy ball field so close to his place of study, William Wagner kept the original ball from the Active game (plus many other balls, if Reach is to be believed), and the substitute ball was apparently not to the Athletics' liking, thus causing the loss. This whole tale may sound sort of strange except that, at this time, different makes of baseball differed widely in elasticity, from "dead balls" to "bounding rocks." The substitute sphere must have favored the Actives' style of play, hence Athletic blamed the loss on the lost ball.

Thirteen of Athletic's NABBP 15 wins in 1865 came against competition from outside Philadelphia, since Keystone was the only other Philadelphia club in the NABBP that year. Athletic defeated Keystone in the season opener on June 8 (21–12) and in the season finale on November 11, a 49–5 punishing. Along the way, Athletic's season was also highlighted by defeating Union of Morrisania (31–21 and 26–13) and Excelsior 45–11.

Athletic played a lot more games than just those 18 under the NABBP banner. Counting just those games between NABBP members, Wright comes up with the 15-3 mark. However, Peverelly lists all the games played by Athletic in 1865, and comes up with an overall record of 32-4. By this time, Athletic was sufficiently important that Peverelly gives some details of the various trips taken by the Philadelphia team during the course of the May to December season. In addition to the trip to Washington, he particularly takes note of a five-games-in-five-days trip to New York that "did much to establish their reputation." Athletic took 'em all:

| Eureka | 12–9 | Union | 31–21 | Gotham | 28–20 |
| Eagle | 24–14 | Resolute | 39–14 | | |

To paraphrase Peverelly, if there could be said to be one distinctive moment where a mantle of greatness was passed from New York to a Philadelphia baseball team, this was it.

Peverelly also chronicles Athletic's two trips to western Pennsylvania, games that conclusively proved the difference between a team that would pay an Al Reach to play, and all amateur squads in the hinterlands. Athletic's Pittsburgh tour saw victories for the Philadelphia team by scores like 88–13, 53–6 and 41–8. The results of the second trip, to Williamsport, was a three-team doubleheader on October 20, 1865, with Athletic blasting two non–NABBP teams, Williamsport 101–8 and Danville 162–11. Although basketball-sized scores were not entirely uncommon in that era, 263 runs in two games on the same day has been claimed as a record, although 162 runs in a game involving a high-level team was not a record. According to Francis Richter, that mark was an almost incomprehensible 209, in a win by the Niagaras of Buffalo over the Columbias (who scored 10) in 1869.[11]

The Williamsport and Danville games weren't the only ones in 1865 that Athletic broke into triple figures. They also wiped out National of Jersey City 114–2 and Diamond State of Wilmington 104–7. However, Athletic didn't just run up the score against the little guys, they also led the NABBP in total runs scored, with 604 in 18 games (33.6 per game).

How did they do it? Well, although Al Reach may have scored 34 runs on October 20, he did not lead the Athletic offense that averaged over 49 runs per game for the entire 1865 campaign. Dick McBride, who also played short when he wasn't pitching, and third baseman–outfielder Mike Smith both had runs scored of 4,0 in NABBP games, while Reach's figure was 3,12. As a point of comparison, Mitchell of the Star club led the NABBP in runs average and over, with 5,1. McBride and Smith also had the lowest hands lost (outs made) on the 1865 Athletics at 2,1.

Although Reach may have been paid to come to Philly, the star of the team was McBride. Besides the fact that, over the years, he was both the pitcher and one of the best hitters, his use in 1865 is particularly significant. It was around this time that the shortstop position first took on some of the significance it is now generally accorded—the most important defensive position. When McBride wasn't pitching in 1865, he was playing shortstop, a pattern of usage similar to many high school teams in the present era. The best athlete, the best player, typically pitches and plays shortstop. While it might not be entirely accurate to equate the Athletic game of 1865 to a high school game 140 years later, it's not such a far-fetched analogy—teams playing in both eras generally had somewhat limited player resources, and their game was an as-yet unpolished game.

The 1865 Athletic club was truly the first great baseball team in Philadelphia history. Almost as if to commemorate this high point in Philly sports, the Athletic club, en masse, posed for a group portrait on the front porch of their clubhouse. This picture, originally out of the collection of the late Barry Halper, and first published in the spring 1984 edition of SABR's *The National Pastime*, is a classic. Although mis-identified in 1984 as being the 1860 Athletic club, this shot is the 1865 group, since there on the front row, as large as life and holding a bat about the same size, is Al Reach, who didn't join the team until 1865. Two places to his right is the 20-year-old Dick McBride, looking a lot younger than that without his later trademark Dundreary whiskers. Scattered among the rest of the Athletic club in the photo are the rest of the 1865 first nine, as pictured in other sources. The front row also includes the Gaskill brothers (Charles and E.A.) and a utilityman named Luengene. Along the second row are hard-hitting catcher Dan Kleinfelder, equally hard-hitting third baseman Mike Smith and the impressively Dundrearied Nate Berkenstock. And, modestly in the back, in a spiffy tan vest, is the redoubtable Hicks Hayhurst. Assessing the careers of the men so-illustrated, it is by no means an outrageous statement to say that no less than three deserving Hall of Famers—Reach, McBride and Hayhurst—are pictured. Although the Athletic dynasty would also depend on other fine players in the coming years, notably the versatile and smooth-fielding, good-hitting Wes Fisler and the flamboyant, power-hitting outfielder "Count" Sensenderfer, Reach and McBride on the field and Hayhurst, first in center, and then as one of the first baseball executives, would be the heart of this great team.

Philadelphia's other NABBP entry in 1865—Keystone—didn't have any Hall of Fame caliber players, and didn't fair particularly well, going 4-8 in NABBP games, although they did have the satisfaction of defeating Resolute of Brooklyn twice, upsetting Eckford 18–16 (Eckford finished 8-6 overall) and Empire, and, they did end up with a better record than the venerable Knickerbockers, who were 1-4-1. In all games, Keystone finished 10-10, including a win over Olympic 30–24. Keystone's best hitter was Elias Cope, who pitched, played the outfield, and shortstop—there's another pitcher-shortstop—and scored 3,1 runs. Ned Cuthbert was also a Keystone, and averaged just 1,11 hands lost while playing the outfield and second base.

Although Wright reports on only the two Philly NABBP clubs in 1865, baseball in metropolitan Philadelphia had clearly rebounded after the Civil War, as evidenced by Peverelly's reporting. For instance, Minerva was in action in inter-club games for this season, going 4-6-2 but, more importantly, winning what appears to be some sort of popularity contest at the fair for the Soldiers and Sailors Home, held at the Academy of Music.

The 1865 Keystone club, featuring Ned Cuthbert (far left on second row), Fergy Malone (middle of second row) and Elias Cope (far right on bottom row) (courtesy John Thorn).

According to Peverelly, all the Philadelphia clubs were entered in this competition, with Minerva winning the most votes, 607, to the Young America Cricket Club's (cricket was still popular in Philadelphia) 585 and Athletic's 550.[12] Minerva may not have been able to defeat Athletic on the field—in fact, they lost twice to the Athletic juniors—but they were apparently first in the hearts of Philadelphians. Or, at least, those that attended the fair.

Among the other metropolitan Philadelphia teams in evidence during the 1865 season were Saterlee, Olympic, West Philadelphia, Hamilton (the Philadelphia team—the Brooklyn Hamilton Club last appears in NABBP records during the 1864 season), Ontario, Columbia, Everett, First National and Liberty plus teams from Camden, N.J., Wilmington, Del., and Burlington, N.J. And, returning to the fray after a five-year hiatus caused by the Civil War was Equity. In the spring of 1865, as the war was winding down, Equity was being re-organized. The means of this re-organization was the still-common practice of club teams being formed by pre-existing interest groups or professional groups. In the spring of 1865, a group of employees of the twin titans of the Philadelphia transportation industry, the Pennsylvania and Reading railroads, formed a joint exercise and ballplaying club. This new club was approached by the re-forming Equity group with a proposal to join Equity "en masse." Thus, the two groups were consolidated, with an equal distribution of officers. The "new" Equity then secured grounds, not in North Philadelphia, but, going against the trend, in West Philadelphia, first adjacent to the Saunders Institute, and then at 41st and Lancaster, just down the street from the future playing fields of Drexel University. Harry Shantz, one of the stalwarts of the first Equity club, was still on the scene as the captain of the new Equity club. Colonel Thomas Fitzgerald, one of the original founders of the Athletic club and the publisher of the *Philadelphia City Item*, was the president of Equity. Although the club didn't play any outside games in 1865,[13] they were back in action in 1866, and would be NABBP members in good standing (though not major players) through the 1868 season.[14]

* * *

By the 1866 season, the year when Richter in his history says professionalism "began to pervade the ranks," Athletic began to stand head and shoulders above its fellow Philadelphia clubs, both in terms of the quality of its opposition and the quality of its play, and in terms of the number of top-level games it played. There was also a difference in the Athletic club's means of obtaining players, for this was the team that was already moving towards full-fledged professionalism. Having persuaded Al Reach to come south from Brooklyn for the 1865 season, Athletic now went after a prodigal son, Brooklyn Atlantic ace Tom Pratt, who had just gone 32-0 over the course of the 1864 and 1865 seasons. Pratt did indeed start the 1866 season with Athletic, but now he couldn't beat Dick McBride out as the club's pitcher. After playing a couple of games at third, he returned to Brooklyn in September to pitch for Atlantic and help that club defend its tenuous whip pennant.[15]

Athletic was even better than during the war years, and even more popular among Philadelphia fans. In fact, the club counted no fewer than 371 members at this time, and it's doubtful many of them were singers. On the field in 1866, Athletic lost only to Atlantic and the Unions of Morrisania in what would be the first of the Philadelphia team's mythical national championship seasons. Wright gives them credit for a 23-2 season, while Peverelly, writing just after the 1866 season concluded, records a remarkable 39-2 year, listing 16 more wins, many against badly outmatched Philadelphia clubs. Although Athletic was clearly the cream of the crop in Philadelphia by this time, the size of that crop was also significant—they played 14 different Philadelphia-area teams. Among Athletic's Philadelphia-area victims were Quickstep (99–6), Chester (80–12), Hamilton (50–5 and 63–10), West Philadelphia (44–19 and 67–11), Alert (67–25—Lip Pike hit six home runs in this game, including five in a row—and 100–5), Philadelphia (68–10 and 58–15), Germantown (79–14), Columbia (65–6 and 63–25), Camden (49–11 and 33–4), Olympic

(57–16), Frankford (55–5), Mount Holly (71–32), Keystone (40–16 and 27–23) and Batchelor (50–9 and 36–15—they would later be better known as a rowing club).[16] The average score of these games against local competition was 56–13. And that doesn't include the May 9, 1866, season opener in New Castle, Delaware, against Lenapi. Athletic won that one 131–9 and hit a record 19 home runs.[17] That record lasted only until August, when they hit 29 home runs in the 100–5 win over Alert.[18] In the NABBP games that Wright records, Athletic scored an association-leading 1287 runs, while giving up just 350. That's a not-much-closer average score of 51–14. As a point of reference, during the Red Stockings' fabled 57-0 1869 season, the Cincinnati team outscored its opposition—admittedly a better overall level of opposition than Athletic faced in 1866—by an average score of 42–10.

It should be noted that 1866 was, as Wright points out, an expansion year for the NABBP. Following the end of the Civil War, membership in the association more than tripled at its December 1865 meeting, meaning a lot of what were then called "country clubs" were admitted to membership, and would subsequently become what are now called "cannon fodder" for Athletic, et al. As would happen in 1961 and 1993, expansion brought scoring records, and, it also brought a general expansion of the sport to Philadelphia. Additional NABBP teams in the City of Brotherly Love in 1866 in addition to Keystone (5-5-1) and Olympic (3-4) included Equity, Minerva and Swiftfoot (although they didn't play any games), along with Mt. Airy.

Athletic was undefeated going into its October 1866 series with Atlantic and Tom Pratt. Included in the Philadelphia team's record was a 33–20 win over Union, a team that would finish 25-3 in NABBP games, in June. Although by October Atlantic had already lost to New York–area teams Irvington and Eureka, they had won their second encounters against both teams, and had not yet played the tie-breaker. Hence, the official defending champs were still holding the whip pennant. Athletic fans were undoubtedly recalling the two close losses to Atlantic in 1865 as Athletic prepared to contest the Brooklyn club in a home-and-home series that would most likely decide the official NABBP title—a series that some say was also the first official inter-city championship series. Although that claim is hard to substantiate, there's no denying the excitement generated by the Athletic-Atlantic series, or by just Athletic. The team was so popular by this time that David Voigt notes they were charging 10 cents admission to their intrasquad games![19]

The first game, on October 1, 1866, was one of the notable landmarks of the sport in the city of Philadelphia. Handbills proclaimed it "The Great Game for the Championship of the United States." A total of 8,000 tickets were sold prior to game time, a number that was impressive for this era, considering that Philadelphia had less than 600,000 residents and little public transportation to North Philadelphia at this time. Trouble was, somewhere between 22,000 and 32,000 additional fans showed up on game day. Businesses closed, bosses and their clerks bet on the game—similar to a modern day World Series game. Certainly, if 40,000 souls were present that day, they represented the largest crowd ever to see an (attempted) baseball game in Philadelphia or anywhere else up to that time. Richter admits to a crowd of 30,000 as being the largest to that time.[20] Whatever the actual total, the massive throng led to a bonanza for the ancestors of Philly's present day scalpers who were getting an outrageous $5 per for good spots *outside the park* by game time.

It was a madhouse. A squadron of special police couldn't control the crowd, which included a fair number of Brooklyn fans who had journeyed south for the game. With the police highly outnumbered, the crowd took up positions wherever they well pleased, both inside and outside the park. This was actually quite easy to do, since, like every other ball field in the city, the grounds at 17th and Columbia were not fenced in, at least not in the sense that ball fields would be 15 or so years later. Outside of a picket fence around the entire grounds, there were no fences at Camac Woods at this time. Just to make things more chaotic, flocks of gamblers walked through the huge crowd, waving wads of greenbacks and taking bets from everyone and anyone. As a result, there were so many spectators on the field that they actually encroached on the infield itself. Overflow crowds would commonly stand around in the outfield during baseball's early years, but this was a bit much. The field was literally unplayable due to the crowd, and the game had to be called—possibly because Atlantic refused to play unless the field was cleared—after one (some sources say two) innings.[21]

Illustrating how difficult it is to get a story straight after some 140 years, the Spring 1984 issue of SABR's *The National Pastime*, which also proclaims this game as widely regarded as the most important played up to that time, includes a reproduction of an Athletic-Atlantic scorecard, reputed to be from this truncated game—a scorecard showing an 18–9 Athletic win. How was that possible? Did they actually complete the game, maybe at some remote location? No. The scorecard in question has Tom Berry playing third base for Athletic, and he didn't join the team until 1867. This is actually the scorecard from Athletic's 18–9 win over Atlantic on August 31, 1868.

So much for Game One. Game Two was not only played, but was a lot saner as well—a 27–17 Atlantic win in Brooklyn two weeks later. The two teams then returned to Philadelphia—certainly with some trepidation—for the next game on October 22, although a story in the *Philadelphia North American* on April 2, 1911, claims that the third game was first played on October 21, and resulted in a 33–33, seven-inning tie that was called by darkness. This might account for Francis Richter's statement that the October 22 game was actually a replay, and not a regularly-scheduled contest.[22] Whatever did or did not happen on the 21st—Marshall Wright does not list an October 21 game in his records—the two teams were at it again at Camac Woods on October 22. This time, the Athletic offense, led by Al Reach and Wes Fisler, who scored six and five runs each without making an out between them, asserted itself. Scoring 22 runs in the last three innings of a contest cut short to seven innings by rain and darkness, the home team prevailed 31–12 in front of 20,000. According to Dick McBride, this win assured the Athletic club's reputation.[23]

The only way the Athletics were able to keep the fans manageable this time—Richter puts the crowd at only an unlikely 8,000—was to hire special police and build a true fence around the field. This was the first time that a Philadelphia park had been so enclosed. Oddly enough, in light of the experience of the first game, Athletics' officials built a fenced in area big enough to hold only 3,000 people. This time the fans paid a dollar apiece, four times the price of admission for the October 1 game, to get in—most likely leaving 17,000 unpaid spectators outside the fence.

Unfortunately for Athletic, given the fact that the home-and-home series was now tied at a game each, a dispute over gate receipts kept a deciding game from being played.[24] This was no small matter for the theoretically amateur Athletics and Atlantics—$3000 was a lot of money and the individual Athletics and Atlantics were each pocketing $200 after the gate receipts were divided,[25] this in addition to Al Reach, Lip Pike, Patsy Dockney, Dick McBride, Tom Pratt and maybe a couple of other top players, who were also getting around $20 a week in salary. This dispute kept Athletic from getting a shot at the "official" NABBP crown, although the Philadelphia newspapers (notably the *North American* in 1907 and 1911) would later claim the October 23 game was for the "Championship of America."

Since Atlantic never played Union at all in 1866, the diadem thus remained in Brooklyn after they waxed Eureka 38–13 in the tie-breaker of their series and edged Irvington 12–6 in 10 innings in their third game with the New Jersey squad. Undeterred by the fact that Union and Athletic both had better records, and that they hadn't even played Union, Atlantic claimed the title, despite the fact that the three powerhouses' NABBP records looked like this:

Athletic	23-2	Union 25-3	Atlantic	17-3

So, not for the last time would Athletic fail to be officially crowned by the NABBP, despite having the best record in the nation. They also had the best offense in the NABBP— maybe, the best of all-time. No less than seven Athletics—Dick McBride (160), Dan Kleinfelder (141), Al Reach (134), Isaac Wilkins (125), Patsy Dockney (118), Lip Pike (100) and Charles Gaskill (100) scored in triple digits during the 25-game NABBP season. McBride, playing third and short when he wasn't pitching, not only led the NABBP in total runs scored, and runs average and over (6,10), he set association records in both categories. But then, Kleinfelder and Reach also broke the old total runs scored record, and Pike (6,4) and change pitcher-outfielder-third baseman-business manager Hicks Hayhurst, although pushing 40, joined McBride in breaking the old runs average and over standard (with 6,4). Wes Fisler, over the succeeding years the team's third-best player after McBride and Reach, had a runs average and over of 5,5—and he had bad year, since he was last among the regulars.[26]

Although 1866 being an expansion year had something to do with Athletic's scoring outburst and overall success, there was another factor to the Philadelphia team's dominance, and, it got them in dutch with the then still ostensibly amateur NABBP—paying salaries to their stars. Athletic was publicly accused, by no less a figure than Harry Wright, of paying $20 a week in salary to McBride, Pike and Dockney—the first time that paying players was made a public issue. Of course, a couple of years later, Harry Wright himself would be a paid professional in Cincinnati, but this was still 1866. Oddly, Reach, the team's first imported star and its longest-standing professional, was not included in the NABBP's indictment. That failing could be explained if the rules were such that the association could bring actions against transgressors only in the year the felony took place. Or, it may have even been a deliberate oversight by Wright, a long-time friend of Reach's. Whatever the reason, when neither the plaintiff nor the defendants appeared for the hearing before the NABBP's Judiciary Committee, the matter was tabled and never re-opened,[27] maybe because the rest of the Athletics were getting money through the division of gate receipts[28]—a practice that several teams had been following for some time, and a less controversial one at this point than paying salaries.

Pike and Dockney, like Reach before them, had clearly been paid by Athletic to jump from their New York–based teams. Considering McBride had been their star long before even Reach showed up, and that he was still the best player on the team, it would have been pretty weak not to have paid him as well. As for the other two, Pike had broken in with Atlantic in July 1865 as a sub at the age of 20. Someone in the Athletic organization must have seen his potential, and he ended up in Athletic white and blue in 1866—certainly a sweet acquisition from their biggest rival. A left-handed infielder like Reach, Pike would spend only the 1866 season in Philadelphia, revolving to Mutual in 1867 and, eventually, back to Atlantic in 1869. He would ultimately appear for 11 different top-level teams in a playing career that would last off-and-on all the way until 1887.

Dockney was, in 1866, a better-established pro than Pike, having broken in with Gotham in 1864, and serving as their regular catcher in both '64 and '65 before becoming Athletic's catcher in '66. He, too, lasted just one year in Philadelphia, also ending up with Mutual by 1868. He also played for Buckeye of Cincinnati that year. While it may not necessarily be to Athletic's credit as an amateur organization, the practice of revolving from city to city for money, clearly a more significant move for a player than just changing clubs within a city, since it involved re-locating the player and his family, can be said to have been initiated in Philadelphia. Maybe not a high point in the history of amateur sports, but certainly a seminal moment in the development of baseball as a professional sport, both in Philadelphia and nationwide. In general, Philadelphia was making waves elsewhere in the NABBP. As Harold Seymour stated, Philadelphia had five times as many clubs as New York City by the late 1860s, although the 10th annual convention of the NABBP in December 1866 shows membership in that group consisting of 73 clubs from New York State and 48 from Pennsylvania. By the 11th convention, held on December 11, 1867, the NABBP was meeting, in the person of 70 clubs and eight state associations, at the Chestnut Street Theatre in Philadelphia.[29]

* * *

The 1867 baseball season mirrored a tremendous upsurge of the sport's popularity in Philadelphia, far beyond anything Peverelly could have imagined writing on the eve of the new season. No less than 50 Philly teams were NABBP members, and even though Athletic dominated the field once again, they were hardly alone in providing the City of Brotherly Love with excellent baseball. Although only Keystone (a 19–14 loss) and Quaker City (a 16–10 loss) were able to give Athletic even a close game among Philadelphia teams, they certainly were able to hold their own against other competitors. Newcomer Quaker City, and their new pitcher, former Athletic-Atlantic Tom Pratt, finished 28-9, the third highest number of wins in the NABBP. Keystone was 21-6-1 and tied for the fifth highest number of wins. In addition, Geary, led by hometown hero Levi Meyerle, finished 19-6 and tied for seventh in wins. Another new club, Typographical, which probably had something to do with a printing organization as well as typographical errors, had a winning record, as did Artic.

At the start of the season, you have to think that Athletic's fans were expecting another triumphant campaign, considering that their favorites were coming off such a successful 1866 season, and also considering Athletic had shown a willingness to go out and get the best talent. However, Athletic had also opened Pandora's Box as far as the practice of bringing in talent from out of town. If players could be paid to come to Philly, they could also be paid to return to New York, as was the case with Lip Pike in 1867. But, even the loss of a Lip Pike didn't slow down the Athletic machine in 1867; they just brought in Ned Cuthbert from Keystone and John Radcliff from Camden—both of whom would become well-known as revolvers—and marched on to victory.

And what a march it was. Although suffering two exceedingly close losses to Mutual (21–23 and 17–18), and a third to their old nemesis, Atlantic (28–16), Athletic ran the table the rest of the way, going 44-3, and winning 15 more games than any other NABBP club, including a 26 game winning streak to start the season. Although the Washington Nationals' tour through the Midwest is generally considered the big story of the 1867 season, in a large part because no Eastern team had ever "gone west" on tour before, National was decidedly the second-best club to Athletic, despite running up scores like 106–26 and

113–26 against Western of Indianapolis and Union of St. Louis. First of all, National lost on the tour to the upstart Rockford Forest City club, and 16-year-old pitcher Al Spalding, 29–23, and more significantly, they closed the season in November by getting blistered 35–12 by Athletic. Since Athletic also defeated Mutual (who finished the year 23-6-1) 18–16 and Atlantic 28–8, there should be no doubt that, in fact, the best team in baseball in 1867 was playing its home games at 17th and Columbia. Still, Union of Morrisania (21–8 overall) was the official NABBP champion of 1867, by virtue of beating 1866 champion Atlantic (who finished 19-5-1 in '67) twice—although that was well after Athletic had warmed the Morrisania 23–10 and 36–32.

Long before closing the season in November with wins over National, Olympic of Washington and Bristol, Athletic had begun its triumphant 1867 season in April and May by warming up against local teams before heading to New England and easily sweeping games in Portland, Boston and Hartford. Playing locally again, along with a few games against Union, Mutual (a rare, close 18–16 win) and Eckford, Athletic ran its winning streak to August 28 before the first loss to Mutual. After three more wins, they shockingly lost back-to-back games on September 16 and September 18 to Atlantic and Mutual. Thus chastened, they won out, taking their last 15 games. Once again, Athletic was an offensive juggernaut, scoring 2198 runs and averaging just under 47 per game while giving up just 14 runs per game. This time, Al Reach set an NABBP record for runs scored, with 270, just edging out Dick McBride (265) and the marvelously-named John Phillips Jenkins "Count" Sensenderfer (263), playing his first season as a regular in the Athletic outfield. The regular nine that posted a .936 winning percentage, an NABBP record for that many games, until Athletic broke it the next year, were:

1B—Dan Kleinfelder	3B—West Fisler	OF—Ned Cuthbert
2B—Al Reach	OF—Count Sensenderfer	C—John Radcliff
SS—Isaac Wilkins	OF—Tom Berry	P—Dick McBride[30]

As noted, Athletic didn't seem to miss revolvers Pike or Dockney in the least, moving the ubiquitous Fisler over to third, which is where Pike had played mostly in 1866, and bringing in Radcliff to catch.

Quaker City's first year in the NABBP was also successful, although they didn't play as tough a schedule as Athletic. As previously noted, they did manage to hold Athletic to a more-than-respectable 16–10 score in their second match after getting their doors blown off 57–8 in the first encounter. Among non–Philadelphia opponents, Quaker City's only notable foes were Union, Irvington and Atlantic. Although they lost 20–10 to Union and 24–21 to Atlantic, Quaker City did have a big win (17–14) over the New Jersey boys, which may not sound like a big deal, but this was a team that featured two future Cincinnati Red Stockings, Andy Leonard and Charlie Sweasy, as well as famed early junkballer Rynie Wolters. Quaker City was led by outfielder-pitcher-second baseman John Chapman, whose runs average and over was 5,3. Chapman was a long-established player, having been playing for Greater New York teams since 1860, and having played for Atlantic in 1866, leading one to speculate that he was paid by Quaker City to leave Brooklyn for the Quaker City in 1867. Other notable names on this team included Fergy Malone, who had started his career with Athletic in 1864, and pitcher Pratt. The pattern should be clear. As Athletic brought in paid players from either other local teams or out-of-town clubs, their former players were moving on to help boost other Philadelphia teams. Hence, through the mechanism of paying stars to play for Athletic, the first name in Philadelphia baseball was also helping spread the wealth among other local teams.

Whereas a newcomer was the second best team in Philly in 1867, one of the old guard, Keystone, also had a pretty good year, a landmark year, or at least a landmark week. Playing their ninth year of baseball, Keystone went 21-6-1 with six and eight game winning streaks. Although Keystone picked up a nice win over Mutual (28–20) on August 30 in their first '67 game outside of Philly, the highlight of their season was unquestionably a trip to Brooklyn in October. On three consecutive days, October 2, 3 and 4, Keystone played Excelsior, Atlantic and Eckford—three teams with six NABBP titles between them—and beat all three. The scores were, in order, 20–15, 21–18 and 31–13—all indicative of the somewhat lower-scoring, scientific type of game Keystone played when they were playing at their best, as opposed to Athletic's high-scoring, blow-their-doors off style of play. Although Athletic had previously established that one Philadelphia team could compete and beat the New York teams, these three days in October 1867 sent an even stronger message to NYC—Philly was *not* a one-team town, and the top New York teams couldn't take any of the top Philadelphia teams for granted.

The team that held its opponents to just less than 20 runs per game over the course of the season while scoring just more than 30 was a fairly anonymous group—no big names like McBride or Fisler or Reach. Elias Cope was still around, playing outfield, shortstop and pitching. Billy Dick, who was in the middle of a solid NABBP career mostly with Keystone, although he also played with Olympic of Washington and Union of Lansingburgh, was the leading hitter at second base, with a runs average and over of 3,12. And, former Athletic Mike Smith got in seven games in his last NABBP season.

Looking at the year as a whole, Keystone could be said to have had two separate seasons. Up through about Labor Day, Keystone played a lot of pretty high-scoring games and went 11–5. This stretch of the season was not without its high points, including the six game winning streak, two wins over Quaker City, and the Mutual win. However, starting with a September 14 game with Pastime of Baltimore (a 39–9 win), Keystone gave up an average of just under 11½ runs per game the rest of the way, and didn't lose a game on the field—a forfeit loss to Quaker City and a 12–12 tie with Atlantic were the only blemishes on their record after September 10. For this era, that was tremendous defense, the caliber of the '66 Athletics or the '69 Red Stockings.

In addition to Athletic, Quaker City and Keystone playing a national schedule, there was also a spirited competition among Philadelphia teams that had never before played the larger stage. Foremost among these teams was Geary. Although their 19-6 record gave them the seventh-highest number of wins in the NABBP, all were earned in intra–Philadelphia competition against the likes of the Chestnut Street Theatre, Amateur, South Penn, Philadelphia, Excelsior of Philadelphia, Excelsior of Coatesville, Commonwealth, S.J. Randall, Artic and Harry Clay. The main reason to notice Geary was their pitcher, the hulking, 6-1, 180 pound Philadelphia native Long Levi Meyerle. Playing in his first NABBP season at the age of either 22 or 18 (his year of birth has been given as both 1845 and 1849), Meyerle was pitching for Geary on the still-common sandlot theory that the best player pitches. Meyerle wasn't really a pitcher, or even much of a fielder, but he sure could hit. He led Geary with a solid runs average and over of 4,10—and he was just getting started. After another year pitching for Geary, he would end up where a lot of the best Philadelphia players ended up—Athletic—and there he would build a legend that included the highest single season betting average ever recorded in a professional baseball league.

The 1867 season was a watershed year for baseball in Philadelphia. The city's teams had, in effect, divided themselves up into three categories—national-class teams, local-class teams, and a few clubs that played pretty evenly in both worlds. The top national-class teams—Athletic, Quaker City and Keystone—proved they could compete with anyone. The top local-class teams—Geary and Brandywine (of West Chester, Pennsylvania) ran up imposing records against local competition. Brandywine's success was in part due to a player named Sheppard, who was third in the NABBP in runs average and over with a whopping 7,7. Other teams like Commonwealth, Typographical and Artic all had success as well. And even West Philadelphia, at 5-12, could boast of victories over Eckford and Keystone. In fact, West Philadelphia played a pretty tough schedule; along with games against the big three national powers and Brandywine, they also played, in addition to Eckford, two games with Mutual and two games with Atlantic. To keep up with that imposing schedule, West Philly had three noteworthy players. The revolving Ned Cuthbert was now on the west side of the Schuylkill River, along with an up-and-coming young pitcher named Cherokee Fisher, and a youngster who would become a long-time local star (he also played some for Geary in '67), George Bechtel.

Here are the records of Philly's top NABBP teams for 1867:

Athletic	44-3	Commonwealth	11-11-2	Bachelor	2-8
Quaker City	28-9	Typographical	9-6	Union	2-8
Keystone	21-6-1	Artic	8-6	Alvin	0-5
Geary	19-6	West Philadelphia	5-12	Harry Clay	0-7
Brandywine	12-3	Camden	2-5		

And this doesn't even acknowledge the other 35 or so NABBP members from the Philadelphia area—including Equity, Minerva and Olympic—that there are no published records for. Things had changed a lot since 1860, and they would change a lot more by the time the 1871 season would start even though the biggest potential change—integration—would die aborning.

◆ CHAPTER 5 ◆

The Drawing of the Color Line

Perhaps the greatest potential change that baseball could have made on nineteenth century America never took place. Just two years after the end of the Civil War, Philadelphia, and America, was a racially polarized society. Although the struggle to integrate the horse cars was one that Octavius Catto would eventually win, the struggle for some form of equal recognition in baseball would prove to be a far harder battle, one that would ultimately not be won until long after he was dead.

One of the clubs that did not officially join the NABBP, or even officially attend the December 1867 NABBP meeting in Philadelphia, although as a local club, they had quite logically applied for membership while the meeting was in town, was one of the city's best, Pythian. This club had another, unfortunate, distinction—one that would mirror the desegregation struggles of both Philadelphia and other large Northern cities in this era—they were the first African American club ever banned from joining an association of baseball clubs or teams, because 1867 also marked the first drawing of a color line in baseball. And, unlike the unwritten rule along these lines that governed organized baseball from the last years of the nineteenth century until 1945, this was a written injunction, at least written into the rules of the NABBP. However, let us not judge either the NABBP or the Pennsylvania State Convention of Base Ball Players, the state organization that Pythian tried to join first, too harshly, even though Pythian was for all practical purposes banned from both groups. As John Thorn has observed, we should not think of those whose drew the color line, including, on the NABBP's behalf, prominent New York Knickerbocker James Whyte Davis, "as being 'racist' or even racialist." Thorn points out that many researchers and scholars, when talking about nineteenth century color lines, "miss the point of the nation's pervasively derogatory attitude towards African-Americans." Even Abraham Lincoln was guilty of this attitude, he adds.[1] While Lincoln was opposed to and offended by slavery, he did not consider the white and black races equal. During one of his 1858 debates with Stephen Douglas he said, "I am not, nor have ever been in favor of bringing about in any way the social and political equality of the white and black races ... there must be the position of superior and inferior, and I as much as any other man am in favor of having the superior position assigned to the white race."[2] Perhaps with this statement in mind, famed abolitionist Frederick Douglass once called Lincoln, "preeminently the white man's president, entirely devoted to the welfare of white men."[3] It is not surprising that the pervasive racial attitudes were strong enough to not only keep Pythian out of "organized" baseball, but to also cost Pythian founder Octavius Catto his life some four years later.

It is easy to focus on what Thorn refers to as "bad guys" in the color line dramas — NABBP Nominating Committee acting chair Davis in 1867, and Cap Anson in the better-known incidents of the 1880s and '90s. And while their actions may ultimately do them no credit, it is also incorrect to give them credit for solely drawing the color line. To do so is to give the rooster credit for making the sun come up. The Davises and the Ansons were just in the right place at the right time to have their expressions of a common societal attitude become the focal point of their respective controversies.

There is also another reason to suspend a blanket judgment of at least the Pennsylvania Association. The Pythian club was *invited* to join the Pennsylvania group. Invited as worthy competitors by several notable Philadelphia ballplayers, the most significant of whom was Athletic's Hicks Hayhurst, a friend of Catto's and an umpire at Philadelphia black baseball games. The evidence of this invitation comes from three sources: baseball author (*The Integration of Baseball in Philadelphia*) and historian Christopher Threston, Catto biographer Andrew Waskie of Temple University, and a remarkable entry in the Philadelphia Pythian papers, now in the collection of The Historical Society of Pennsylvania. This latter source, in the form of a hand-written report from the Pythian representative to the October 1867 Pennsylvania State Convention was first unearthed by the late black baseball expert and historian Jerry Malloy in 1997, and then brought to light recently by Thorn. "Report of a Delegate of the Pythian to the Pennsylvania State Convention" is dated October 18, 1867, and tells of the events of October 16, 1867, at the Court House in Harrisburg, Pennsylvania, wherein Pythian attempted to join the Pennsylvania association. Malloy believed that the delegate was Raymond Burr, a member of Pythian's 1868 second nine, although he had also played with the first nine in 1867.

The Pythian delegate (hereinafter identified as Burr for purposes of clarity) met the night before the convention with Hicks Hayhurst, at the time the vice president of the Athletic club, and another representative of Athletic named Ellis, as well as with some other, unnamed delegates. The next day, at the actual meeting, Hayhurst introduced Burr to the Pennsylvania Convention president, Judge Rose, who was also a prominent member of the NABBP. Hayhurst was then appointed to a committee on credentials — the committee that would decide what clubs would join the Pennsylvania association. While this committee was making its report, the rest of the delegates "clustered together in small groups to discuss what action ought to be taken on the admittance of the Pythian delegate."

According to Burr, Hayhurst, Pennsylvania State Convention secretary Domer and President Rose were in favor of Pythian's admittance, "still, the majority of the delegates were opposed to it." Hayhurst, et al., then suggested that Pythian withdraw its application, so to as avoid being blackballed (Burr actually used the term "blackballed" in his report). Pythian refused to do so, and, when the Credential Committee made its report, they "reported favorably in all the credentials presented to them." However, according to Burr, his club's credentials, despite the presence of Hayhurst on the committee, were deliberately left out of the committee's report — thus nicely sidestepping the issue entirely. Although Rogers of Philadelphia's Batchelor club and Hayhurst continued to advocate Pythian's acceptance — the committee was discharged and an attempt by Rogers to have Pythian's credentials voted on separately was tabled. Finally, just before the convention adjourned, Burr did indeed withdraw the club's application. Nonetheless, he went out of his way to close his report by commenting on "the kind attention which these gentlemen showed him and their expression of friendship for our club." That friendship notwithstanding, while the Pennsylvania Convention did not actually de jure draw the color line, they sure drew it de facto.[4]

Two months later, in December 1867 at the Chestnut Street Theater in Philadelphia, the drama was repeated at the NABBP annual meeting. Although the outcome this time was quite clear, there are several questions raised by the report of the NABBP Nominating Committee, which was chaired by Davis and included Dr. William H. Bell, a player from New York's Eclectic club, and later a member of New York's Social club, William E. Simm (or Sinn) and, according to Thorn, Walter T. Avery. Davis et al. "responded to the petition for membership by the Pythians of Philadelphia by rejecting any club composed of persons of color, or any portion of them." Although the NABBP committee didn't mention what color they were discriminating against, it's a pretty good guess it was black, and not purple or magenta. And, that was indeed the end result of the committee report, to ban African Americans from the NABBP. However, when you look at the entire committee report, as reproduced by Dean Sullivan in *Early Innings* from the December 19, 1867, *Ball Players' Chronicle*, it raises as many questions as it answers. Here is the entire text of the sixth section of the report of the 1867 NABBP Nominating Committee:

> Your committee would beg to add, that it has been quite impossible for them to ascertain the condition, character, and standing of all the clubs, in different parts of the country, as required by the Constitution, and can only assume that the applications made are based upon good faith. It is not presumed by your committee that any club who have applied are composed of persons of color, or any portion of them; and the recommendations of your committee in this report are based upon this view, and they unanimously report against the admission of any club which may be composed of one or more colored persons.[5]

The previous five sections of the Nominating Committee report deal exclusively with the status of various clubs, and groups of clubs, that were applying to the NABBP. In none of these is there a word about persons of color. Then we come to the sixth, and closing section. The first sentence seems to be pretty harmless; there *were* standards that member clubs had to adhere to, and the NABBP was getting so big and widespread that it was impossible to ascertain if all the applicants met their gentlemanly standards. It's the second sentence (which the first sentence sets up) that is either deliberately disingenuous, or is just an outright lie. It is well-established that Pythian had applied to both the Pennsylvania Convention and the NABBP for membership in 1867. Membership in the Pennsylvania group would have, by the rules the NABBP also established at the 1867 meeting, also made Pythian NABBP members. It is inconceivable that Davis' committee didn't know about the Pennsylvania application two months before, if for no other reason than Pennsylvania Association president Judge Rose was a prominent enough member of the NABBP to have been seated on the dais at the previous NABBP meeting in late 1866. And, it is certain that Davis, et al., had to have known that a black club was applying for NABBP membership, even if they didn't follow Philadelphia baseball and its clubs at all. This meeting was in Philadelphia, and Pythian, as a Philadelphia club, clearly must have had a representative at the Chestnut Street Theater along with their application. After all, they'd sent Raymond Burr all the way to Harrisburg for the Pennsylvania meeting, and Threston says that Octavius Catto himself was trying to get Pythian into the NABBP,[6] partly for economic reasons so they could play white teams for bigger gates, though financial concerns were hardly Catto's main reason for starting a baseball team—he was out to end Jim Crow. It is equally inconceivable that no one at the NABBP convention had heard of Octavius Catto.

"It is not presumed by your committee that any club who have applied are composed of persons of color?" Was the Nominating Committee trying to make it seem like they were not specifically discriminating against Pythian? Were they trying to soften the blow of the color line, even though the drawing of such a line certainly would have been societally-popular at the time? Were they afraid of the potential popular clout of Octavius Catto, who was the preeminent Civil Rights leader of this time? Were they just so arrogant given the support of the mores of white society that they just didn't care what they said? Or did they just lie, for whatever reason?

Another question is raised by a seemingly innocuous reference in the fifth section of the Nominating Committee report, which states that the applications of two clubs were too informal to be noticed by the committee. One of the clubs mentioned is specifically identified as Excelsior of Philadelphia. Now, Excelsior was a very common name among baseball clubs at this time. Marshall Wright lists no fewer than 23 Excelsiors, including the famous Brooklyn outfit, in *The National Association of Base Ball Players*. However, one club he may not have listed was another black Philadelphia club. Pythian was not the only black baseball club in Philadelphia at this time. The second best African American team

One of the great men of nineteenth century Philadelphia: civil rights leader, educator, baseball player-pioneer-promoter Octavius Valentine Catto (courtesy Dr. Andrew Waskie).

in Philly probably belonged to Excelsior. Did the black Excelsior club also apply to the NABBP in December 1867? And were they turned down on a technicality? It's hard to say. Or was there another explanation? Wright shows an Excelsior club of Philadelphia on the NABBP membership rolls for the 1867 season—so they had joined the NABBP at the annual convention in New York after the end of the 1866 season. This was the team that Geary defeated 60–19 during the summer of 1867. The 1870 NABBP season also had a Philadelphia Excelsior team that was whipped 80–4 and 32–2 by Athletic. Could this 1867 team that played Geary have been the black Philadelphia Excelsior? Could the NABBP have found out during the 1867 season that they'd "accidentally" admitted a black club at their 1866 meeting in New York, when there may not have been an Excelsior representative present, and then moved to bar Excelsior after the fact at the December 1867 meeting? Is the first sentence of section six of the report an apology or an explanation to the general membership for letting Excelsior "pass" for the 1867 season? Or were there two different Excelsior teams in Philly, a white team and a black team?[7] One thing is for certain: the NABBP team that Athletic beat so badly in 1870 could hardly have been the black Excelsior team because of the 1867 color line. Intriguing possibilities, and, at the moment, unanswered questions.

An equally intriguing question is, why? Why draw the color line, and why draw it now? Was it strictly because of the Pythian application? Had the issue of "colored" clubs never come up before, even though they had been around in New York since at least 1859?[8] Had they just discovered Excelsior in their midst? Was it just codifying something the NABBP, and society as a whole, approved of? Was it just putting into writing an unwritten law, such as baseball had from the 1890s until 1945? Whatever was really meant by the report of the NABBP Nominating Committee, it is worth noting that, in introducing the report of the Nominating Committee, the minutes of the meeting go out of the way to declare that, "the feature of it [the Nominating Committee report] being the recommendation to exclude colored clubs from representation in the Association, the object being to keep out of the Convention the discussion of any subject having a political bearing, as this undoubtedly had."[9] A reference to the just-finished Civil War, which certainly was of "political bearing?" Maybe. A wish to just avoid political issues, and not a statement of segregation? Possibly, although Robert Peterson, in *Only the Ball Was White*, rejects this possibility, saying that the drawing of the first color line was a matter of simple prejudice, mainly due to the still highly-social nature of baseball games. Was this a reference to Octavius Catto, who certainly was a political figure? Maybe more likely. Unquestionably this was a political subject—the nation's hottest political subject of the late 1860s and early 1870s.[10]

The NABBP also proclaimed in its December 1867 minutes, with a good deal more candor, that, "if colored clubs were admitted there would be in all probability some division of feeling, whereas, by excluding them no injury could result to anyone."[11] Threston says that those individuals who controlled or owned NABBP clubs, and the NABBP itself, "were afraid that crowds would stay away from the games if black players were used."[12] The economic motive? Possibly. Finally, a societally-significant assessment on the subject of the effect of potential admittance of African American clubs to the NABBP comes from Waskie, who asks, "My, how that might have altered society?"[13] As it was, this ruling against Pythian by whatever contorted logic was the drawing of the first official color line in baseball history.

That black baseball clubs should have come about at this time in Philadelphia (or anywhere else) should not come as a shock. As no less a figure than W.E.B. DuBois noted at length in *The Philadelphia Negro: A Social Study*, African Americans were already socially isolated by segregation. On top of that, they faced the same pressures that drove whites into forming clubs and associations. Combine these two sociological factors, and it should come as no surprise that African Americans formed their own schools, banks, literary societies, newspapers and other such institutions at this time. Another noted black baseball historian, Jules Tygiel, writing in the fourth edition of *Total Baseball*, states that there is scattered evidence of blacks playing baseball prior to the Civil War, but that the first recorded black clubs do seem to have been formed in Northern cities just after the war.[14] Sullivan, in *Early Innings*, pre-supposes that blacks and whites played with and against each other in the 1860s. Given the climate of segregation it seems as if these occurrences were few and far between, although the summer 1867 Geary-Excelsior game may be an exception.

* * *

Undeterred by the NABBP's snub, Pythian carried on, with all the trappings of their almost-peers in the NABBP—preprinted scorecards, silk banners worn on the players' sleeves on game day (gray silk with black print in their case), a total of no less than four complete nines, etc. One source says the club was founded by former cricketeers James

Francis and Francis Wood in 1867, two years after the Excelsior club was formed as Philadelphia's first African American baseball club.[15] More common is an 1866 founding date by Catto, who thereafter played second base, shortstop, batted second and captained and managed and promoted the team. The hard-hitting Pythians, according to their archival records at The Historical Society of Pennsylvania, won eight of nine games against other black teams in 1867, including a road trip to Washington in August where they rolled over Alert 52–25 in just five innings, and then came back two days later to defeat Mutual 50–43. As would also be the case 40 to 70 years later, black teams at this time were often given the same names as famous lily-white teams. Although Pythian usually had to play in South Philly or over in Camden,[16] they also were able to take part in another practice that would be well-known 70 years later—borrowing the white teams' grounds to play—notably when Pythian defeated Harrisburg's Monrovia club 59–27 at the original Columbia Park (bordered by 24th and 25th Streets and Columbia and Ridge) on October 22, 1867—ironically, the same week as the Pennsylvania Convention. As much a group of pioneers as the original Olympics of 1831 and 1833, the main Pythian lineup in 1867 included, in addition to Catto:

> pitcher John Cannon (who also batted leadoff)
> shortstop James Sparrow
> outfielder-catcher John Graham
> first baseman Jefferson Cavens
> outfielder-catcher Spencer Hanly
> third basemen Joshua Adkins and Frank Jones
> outfielder Francis Jones[17]

Of course, since white teams wouldn't play Pythian, they needed other African American clubs to compete against. Excelsior and Orion were the most notable of these other organizations that were formed in Philadelphia around this same time. In October 1867, Excelsior traveled to the capital of the NABBP, Brooklyn, to face the Monitor and Unique clubs of that city, the latter game being billed as the "championship of colored clubs." Although this claim seems rather iffy, since Pythian had already walloped Excelsior 35–16, the game attracted a large crowd of *both* black and white spectators, and was preceded by Excelsior marching around the field behind a fife and drum corps. They then whipped their hosts 37–24[18] winning another of those mythical titles for Philadelphia—and maybe in the process alerting the NABBP that they had previously admitted a "colored" club into their tight fraternity for the 1867 season. Although there are still pieces missing to this puzzle, those that we have fit in intriguing fashion.

Despite Excelsior's success, Pythian appears to have been the superior club. Catto and his teammates also won a "World's Colored Championship" game, this one against the Unique club of Chicago, and Threston quotes fellow black baseball historian Neil Lanctot to the effect that Pythian's success led to Philadelphia briefly becoming known as the capital of black baseball.[19]

In later years, the NABBP ban notwithstanding, Pythian would indeed play some games against white teams, including a September 16, 1869, game against NABBP member City Item. Pythian beat their fellow Philadelphians 27–17 in that contest, a notable accomplishment since City Item went 5-3 against its regular NABBP competition that year. This contest has also been clamed, by Tygiel, to not only be the first-ever win for an all-black team over an all-white team, but also, the first game *ever* between an all-black team and an all-white team.[20] David Voigt has also said that Pythian played an 1869 game with the ultimate in old-line Philly clubs, the "snobbish" Olympic—a contest that ended up in an Olympic victory.[21] These contests aside, Wright says that Pythian, and any other African American clubs, were never allowed to join the NABBP, being treated more as curiosities than anything else.[22] This statement would seem to support the theory that the NABBP was banning "colored" clubs more out of a wish to avoid controversy than anything else—not that their motives made much difference in the development of baseball, in Philadelphia or anywhere else. As Waskie has indicated—a loss to society, in both Philadelphia and ultimately the nation.

Another loss to Philadelphia came some two years after Pythian's historic win over City Item. Philadelphia's Renaissance Man, as Waskie refers to him, was walking home after exercising his newly-won right to vote—a right that he was instrumental in obtaining through his work to help pass the 15th Amendment, guaranteeing voting rights for black males. Election Day was October 10, 1871, and Octavius Catto was shot twice in the back, dying at the age of 32.[23] And while the 15th Amendment was certainly his most significant mark on American history, it is also true that the baseball team he used as another means to battle Jim Crow, the Pythians, lived on at least in spirit. Threston says that the original Pythian club soon disbanded after Catto's violent death, leading to the end of Philly's reign as the capital of black baseball.[24] Still, when the first African American professional baseball league, the National Colored Baseball League, began play in May 1887, one of the eight teams was the Philadelphia Pythians,[25] most probably named in tribute to Octavius Catto and his fellow pioneers.

♦ CHAPTER 6 ♦

The Coming of the Pros

Although it is a matter of the most common record that the Cincinnati Red Stockings of 1869 were the first professional baseball team, that truism is actually a matter of interpretation. Harry Wright's most famous team may well have been the first club recruited from the start of the season as all-professionals. And, they were the first openly announced all-professional team. Or, as David Voigt has said, they may have been the first all-salaried team. In reality, what the Red Stockings were was the first paid team that had been recruited from all over the country, with only first baseman Charlie Gould a native of Cincinnati. But, it is possible that one of the first baseball teams to put nine professional players on the field at the same time was Athletic—and that was in 1868.

In support of this hypothesis, Voigt has pointed to evidence in numerous sources, notably the Henry Chadwick scrapbooks, and the *New York Clipper*, that what he (Voigt) refers to as "creeping commercialism" in baseball was well advanced by the start of the 1868 campaign. Indeed, Voigt points out a quote from the Chadwick scrapbooks to the effect that by 1868 baseball was a business, and that the same Chadwick scrapbooks contain several of the great sportswriter's articles, written before the start of the 1868 season, on the prevalence of professional trends in baseball.[1] As Voigt also says in his landmark work, *American Baseball*, "With high-priced stars raising the costs of competition among 'amateur' clubs, many were obliged to seek new ways of meeting costs of travel, maintenance, and equipment. Now, the ethic of victory first touched off a talent hunt among clubs, which soon relegated the gentlemen members to the side lines."[2]

Voigt's primary source on creeping commercialism is Chadwick's scrapbooks. Speaking some 40 years after the publication of *American Baseball*, Voigt reiterated his contention, derived from Chadwick and the *New York Clipper*, that in 1868 baseball was a business. Certainly Athletic was, by this time, one of the more business-like operations, with a history of paying players dating back to Reach's joining the team in 1865. Although no definitive proof exists, Voigt has also recently said he would support the possibility that Athletic paid its entire starting nine in one fashion or another in 1868.[3]

The 1868 Athletic club played like pros, going a stunning 47–3 with 25- and 20-game winning streaks against top competition in the northeast and Midwest. Looking at the Athletic first nine, it's not a stretch to believe that they were all professionals. Here are the regulars for the season that ran from May 1, 1868 (a 61–8 win over Commonwealth), to October 31, 1868 (a 25–17 upset loss to Nassau):

1B—Wes Fisler	3B—Tom Berry	OF—Harry Schafer
2B—Al Reach	OF—Count Sensenderfer	C—John Radcliff
SS—Isaac Wilkins	OF—Ned Cuthbert	P—Dick McBride[4]

All but Schafer, the team's new recruit from Philadelphia's Artic club, and it's pretty easy to guess why he changed teams, played in at least 40 of Athletic's 50 games. Reach and McBride were clearly professionals at this point. It's also pretty easy to believe that established revolvers like Cuthbert and Radcliff were being paid. Shortstop Wilkins had been on the team since 1863, and had already been honored as the top hitter at his position. Think it might have taken some money to keep him in blue and white? The Count, after breaking in with Olympic in 1865, had jumped to Athletic in 1866 and was now in his third season with the team. He'd been the top hitter at his position the year before, and he'd probably already been paid in 1866 to leave Olympic. Tom Berry joined Athletic in 1867. There shouldn't be much doubt of his status, since his former club, Keystone, charged him with "leaving them for no reason to join the Athletics in violation of the amenities of honor and confidence."[5] That leaves only Wes Fisler, the team's third best player behind McBride and Reach. According to his own testimony, given to a *Philadelphia Press Sunday Magazine* reporter in 1918 or 1919, some 50 years after the fact, he played for Athletic without getting paid for three years after joining the team for the 1866 season. This seems a little hard to believe, especially since Fisler claimed that the other players on the team told him he was being foolish to play for free, implying that everyone else was getting paid. Now, as to when Fisler went in to ask for a salary, a request that was quickly granted, maybe it was three years, maybe it was two years after joining Athletic—after more than 50 years, his memory may or may not have been accurate.

For all intents and purposes, the 1868 Athletics were a professional baseball team, one that the *New York Clipper* acknowledged as being number one in 1868—Athletic received a gold medal from the nation's foremost sporting paper signifying the best record in the land for 1868—even if the NABBP didn't.

For the 1868 season, Mutual ended up as the official NABBP titlists, because they had taken two straight from Atlantic, who had, in turn, previously taken two from the 1867 defending champs, Union of Morrisiana. It didn't matter that Athletic had beaten Atlantic twice, including the 18–9 game appearing in the scorecard in *The National Pastime* (the other game was 37–13), because Atlantic didn't hold the pennant at that time, Union did. Let's do a chronology of the key games of 1868 between Athletic, Atlantic, Union and Mutual, to try and straighten this out. Union still held the 1867 pennant going into September 1868:

8/31	Athletic 18, Atlantic 9
9/7	Athletic 37, Atlantic 13
9/10	Atlantic 31, Union 7
9/21	Athletic 51, Mutual 24
10/5	Atlantic 24, Union 8—the pennant passes from Union to Atlantic
10/12	Mutual 25, Atlantic 22
10/14	Mutual 25, Athletic 15
10/26	Mutual 28, Atlantic 17—the pennant passes from Atlantic to Mutual

Athletic didn't play Union at all in 1868 and played Mutual only twice, splitting the games. If the Philadelphia team had won a third contest, played after the October 26 Mutual-Atlantic game, the whip pennant would have officially been Athletic's. As it was, the fact that the top five NABBP teams' final records looked like this officially meant nothing:

Athletic	47-3	Union	37-6	Mutual	31-10
Atlantic	47-7	Cincinnati	36-7		

As for the official whip pennant, one reason it wasn't decided until so late in the season is that Athletic, Atlantic and Union all toured extensively earlier in the season, Athletic starting off with a 39–5 June 1 win over Olympic of Pittsburgh and not returning to Philadelphia for a month. Sitting on an 8-0 record when they left town, Athletic proceeded to win 17 more in a row before the nineteenth century equivalent of jet lag caught up with them in Rochester on June 29. Having played 17 games in the previous 27 days in an era when train travel was painfully slow, leaving almost no time to rest, and having gone as far west as St. Louis, Athletic and Dick McBride's arm must have been dragging when they faced Excelsior of Rochester. After only giving up as many as 21 runs in a game once all year, McBride was touched for 26 by Excelsior in a 26–20 loss. "The Athletic club should not have extended its tour into the present week ... the result has been seen today ... when they have met defeat at the hands of a second rate club," wrote the correspondent for the *Philadelphia Post*. Yes, baseball was big enough in Philadelphia that the newspapers were sending reporters on the road to cover Athletic games.

Taking a month off after the tour to rest, Athletic came back with a vengeance, winning another 20 straight, including games over Olympic of Washington (35–27), both the Atlantic wins, Union of Lansingburgh (36–28), Eckford (26–20), Mutual and the Red Stockings (15–12)—all top teams. The first Atlantic win, 18–9 on August 31, was another fence-breaker, in that the crowds at Camac Woods (15,000 this time, according to the April 2, 1911, *Philadelphia North American*) once again broke down the fences in the rush to see the game.

The October 14 loss to Mutual finally broke this string, but, the season was almost over anyway, with just two wins over the Olympic club of Philadelphia, and the last-game-of-the-season loss to Nassau remaining. Although Athletic was still winning with heavy hitting—they led the NABBP with 1980 runs scored (just short of 40 a game)—McBride's pitching was also worth noting as he held opponents to single digits in scoring 15 times during the year, as Athletic gave up an average of just 14.74 runs per game.

Individually, it was another big year for the Athletic players. Catcher Radcliff led the NABBP in runs scored with 240, and Wes Fisler, his reputation as a defensive star notwithstanding, was third in the association with 231. Al Reach led the team in runs average and over with 5,6—a mark that tied him for second in the NABBP. The 1868 season also marked the introduction of some new statistics—thanks to Henry Chadwick,[6] notably hits and total bases. Although not every club kept up with the new stats, Fisler was the first player to lead the NABBP in total bases per game, with 6,21. Putting that in modern terms, he averaged the equivalent of better than three doubles a game for 47 games. He was also second in total bases, with 304. Another measure of the excellence of the individual Athletic players came from the *New York Clipper*. While awarding the Athletic club the gold medal as the top team of 1868, the *Clipper* also awarded five Athletic players each a gold badge for having the best "batting average" at their position—meaning runs average and over, not batting average as we now know it. Dick McBride was the top hitting pitcher, ditto catcher Radcliff, first baseman Fisler, second baseman Reach and center fielder Sensenderfer.

From Wright's 1868 results, it seems obvious that the rest of the Philadelphia NABBP clubs were significantly slower than Athletic in adjusting to the advent of the professional game. None of the other Philadelphia NABBP members played more than 22 games—even long-time member Keystone was a dreary 5-10-1 after going 21-6-1 in 1867—and none won more than half of their games. Athletic was now a colossus astride Philadelphia baseball. The oldest club of all, Olympic, had the second best record, breaking even in 22 games despite being outscored 571–554. The Olympic roster was largely undistinguished, except for breaking in a young (17) shortstop that would play in just five games in his NABBP debut. Although he only scored 10 runs in those games, Philadelphia native Chick Fulmer would go on to a long and significant career in baseball, and making a name for himself as one of the best fielding shortstop-second basemen of his era.

Among the other clubs, Geary went 7–6 with Levi Meyerle on the mound, leading the team in scoring (4,1) and pitching to the Allison brothers, Art and Doug. The latter Allison, and Meyerle, would find themselves on opposite sides as full-fledged pros in 1869, Long Levi with Athletic and Allison with the Red Stockings. In fact, Doug Allison revolved to Cincinnati during the 1868 season, and played more games, 27 to 10, with the Red Stockings that year than he did with Geary. Other Philadelphia NABBP members in '68 included Harry Clay (4-3), Commonwealth (4-6), Chestnut Street Theater (2-3), Malvern (2-5) and Batchelor (1-4).

The handwriting was on the wall, the day of the pure amateur club as a dominant force in the top level of baseball had passed. From now on, the pros would play the best brand of ball.

* * *

The big story of the 1869 season was the "eclectic" Cincinnati Red Stockings, a paid team with players drawn from all over the east and midwest. Chadwick, at the beginning of the baseball season of 1869, said that several commercialized teams stood ready to take the field, not just the Red Stockings. Chadwick at the time singled out the Unions of Lansingburg, The Troy Haymakers, Athletic, and the Baltimore, Maryland, club as being the most notable in this regard in 1869.[7]

Over the years, the Red Stockings have taken on a mythic quality. The facts are as follows. Given the game's New York origins, many of the Red Stockings were from the New York area. The nation's second hotbed of baseball, Philadelphia, had just a single representative on the Cincinnati nine, Doug Allison, who had already jumped from Geary the year before. Nonetheless, this is not a story without an additional Philadelphia sub-plot— in this case, how the Red Stockings club assembled its 1869 team. Club president Aaron Champion started out his recruiting campaign by appointing club members George Ellard and Alfred Gosham as a committee of two. And, they came up with the simple idea of buying the nine winners of the *Clipper's* 1868 gold awards. At one point, the committee claimed it had signed five of the nine 1868 medalists. Although Voigt, in reporting on this action, doesn't identify which five the Red Stockings signed, it's a pretty good guess they were mostly members of Athletic. In fact, if Ellard and Gosham had been able to pull off this raid, Athletic would have lost a goodly portion of its first nine to Cincinnati. And, without any kind of reserve clause, there was nothing stopping Ellard and Gosham from doing just that, except a larger infusion of cash from the players' 1868 teams.

That's exactly what happened. Either Ellard or Gosham spilled the beans on their plans to a reporter a little too early, the story hit the newspapers, and there was a mad scramble for other teams to re-sign some of the best players in the land. As a result, not one Philadelphia player ended up in Cincinnati. Was it loyalty to Athletic? That's where almost all of the better Philadelphia players were by this time. Or was it a matter of money? One of those who actually did sign with the Stockings, and then jumped back to Athletic for more money was John Radcliff.[8] It was not the first or last time he would revolve—he didn't even spend the entire 1869 season with Athletic. So maybe the Athletic player's motives were mixed at best.

Whatever their motives, the Athletic players had another fine season in 1869. Maybe not up to the standards of the previous three years, but not bad. They finished third in their professional games with a 15-7 record, and 45-8 overall, also the third best overall mark. Although the Red Stockings may have missed out on Dick McBride, Al Reach, Wes Fisler, et al., Harry Wright still had enough connections, after Ellard and Gosham failed, to put together a team that won all 19 of its games against professional opponents, and 57 straight in all. The final standings for the first official professional baseball season were as follows:

Cincinnati	19-0	Olympic (DC)	9-12
Atlantic	15-6-1	Maryland	7-12
Athletic	15-7	National (DC)	4-12
Eckford	15-8	Keystone	3-17
Union (Troy)	12-8-1	Forest City (OH)	1-6
Mutual	11-15	Irvington (NJ)	0-8[9]

Even though Athletic didn't lose any players to the Red Stockings, there was some turnover in the lineup:

1B—Wes Fisler	OF—Ned Cuthbert
2B—Al Reach	OF—Levi Meyerle
SS—Tom Berry	C—John McMullin
3B—Jim Foran	P—Dick McBride
OF—Count Sensenderfer	

McBride, in addition to doing the pitching, also served as the playing manager. As for the rest of the team, Wilkins was moved out of the shortstop position after being a regular since 1863, Berry moved to short, and rookie Foran was brought in to play third. In the outfield, Levi Meyerle had arrived from Geary to wear the white and blue, replacing Harry Schaefer. Finally, with Radcliff jumping back and forth between Athletic and Keystone (he played in 30 games for Athletic, five for Keystone) McMullin was brought in from the Cincinnati Buckeyes to also catch. As might be expected, this team didn't come cheap. Voigt says they were paid between $600 and $1500 apiece[10] in comparison to the Red Stockings' salary range of $600 to $1400.

Although there was no doubt that the undefeated Cincinnati Red Stockings were the champions of 1869, the 1869 Athletics did have a few distinctive moments, including drawing a huge crowd to 17th & Columbia on June 21 to see them take on the touring Red Stockings. As author Darryl Brock notes in his historical novel, *If I Never Get Back*, Philadelphia was indeed baseball crazy in that summer of '69, as 20,000 fans turned out in 100 degree heat for the Athletics–Red Stockings game. Led by George Wright's two triples and a home run, plus some excellent fielding, the Reds prevailed 27–18—Athletic's first loss of the year after 11 wins. According to Brock, the newspaper reports of the game focused more on the Stockings' fielding, especially Philadelphia native Allison, than any other aspect of the contest.[11] This was a common angle in the reporting of mid–nineteenth century baseball since even a simple fly ball, to say nothing of a foul tip to the catcher, could prove to be an adventure. Athletic would later travel to Cincinnati at the end of the season, and lose an even closer game on October 18, 17–12.

Athletic also had the distinction in 1869 of playing a controversial July 5 slug-a-thon before another 15,000 fans in Brooklyn against Atlantic, where the final score stood Atlantic

51, Athletic 48. By some accounts the highest scoring game ever between two all-professional teams, and one that bore out Athletic's long-standing reputation as a hard-hitting team, this contest also added to the Athletic-Atlantic rivalry when the Brooklyn team complained that Athletic had brought a professional ringer to the Capitoline Grounds — none other than John Radcliff. Accused of using a revolver, and with 15,000 in the stands, representing a pretty penny in gate receipts, the Athletic and Atlantic announced just before game time that the contest would be a "social" game, in effect, a "friendly" to use the modern-day soccer term. Or, if you wish, an exhibition game that didn't count towards the season's win total. The crowd was not amused.[12] However, the game is listed in Marshall Wright's accounts of the 1869 season as one of each team's professional contests. Moreover, Radcliff had played for Athletic throughout 1868, and would play just five games for Keystone in 1869. Since this was the middle of the season — Athletic's 15th game — the assumption must be that Radcliff had already jumped Athletic early in the year, and had then returned sometime before the July 5 game, leading to the revolver accusation.

Otherwise, it was a typical Athletic year. In a year that saw a lot of scoring, they scored a ton of runs, hitting triple figures twice and averaging 43.4 per game, actually more than the Red Stockings' 42 per game. However, Dick McBride had an off-year, due to illness,[13] appearing in just 34 games as the team allowed 20.6 runs per game, maybe because Meyerle and McMullin also pitched, or maybe because everyone was running up the score. Al Reach was the hitting star at 9,5 runs average and over — a huge number, but nowhere near that of the Stockings' George Wright, who had an incredible 10,44. To give some example of just how offensive a game this was in '69, it has been calculated that Wright's batting average for the year was .629, with 47 home runs in 57 games.[14]

Keystone had much less success in '69, winning just three of their 20 professional games, including five losses to Athletic, and finishing 12-21-1 overall. A couple of days after the Athletic–Red Stockings game, Keystone lost a sloppy, slugging 45–30 contest to the Red Stockings before another big crowd on the wet 17th and Columbia field. The highlights of their professional season were a couple of wins over Maryland (31-24, 26–11) and one over Olympic of Washington (45-31). Despite their overall losing record in 34 games, Keystone actually outscored their opponents on the year, averaging 32.4 runs per game and giving up just 27.2. What happened was they ran up a lot of big wins against Philadelphia amateur teams — Chestnut Street Theater, Rescue, Expert, City Item — early in the year, in effect padding their scoring totals. City Item (5-4) and Olympic (5-10), the two teams that also played Pythian during the 1869 season, were Philadelphia's most notable amateur teams during the year.

* * *

By the time the 1870 season started, baseball and most of the NABBP still hadn't really adjusted to the Red Stockings' dramatic move in the early spring of 1869. There were a few teams that saw the future as clearly as Harry Wright, and as a continuation of their scrambling after the abortive Ellard-Gosham raids in early 1869, jumped into professionalism with both spikes. Among the Philadelphia teams, only Athletic really managed to ride the tide of professionalism successfully. Although Keystone declared itself pro for 1869, their 3-17 record didn't impress anyone, and the club reverted back to amateur status for the 1870 season.

This time, the Red Stockings were standing with a pat hand — a not illogical move

Left: Another noted revolver, and also maybe the first man to slide into a base, Ned Cuthbert. **Right:** George Bechtel (note misspelling on photograph), revolver and possible hippodromer (both photographs courtesy John Thorn).

after going 57-0 in 1869. In 1870 the raiders were from Chicago—another indication of the game's spreading popularity through the midwest. And, this time, the raiders had more success in Philadelphia. Whereas the Red Stockings had tried to actively buy up what was in effect the 1868 NABBP All-Star team, the new team from Chicago, known as the White Stockings, took a different route. They advertised. Late in 1869, a series of ads appeared in the *New York Clipper*, seeking players for a team in Chicago.[15] And, probably to the surprise of the Athletic directors, Ned Cuthbert and Levi Meyerle both left their hometown to sign with the White Stockings. In addition to having to come up with replacements for two-thirds of their outfield, Athletic also needed a catcher—John McMullin had gone to pitch for the Troy Haymakers. To fill his spot behind the plate Athletic turned to an old friend and well-known revolver, Fergy Malone, who had last worn the white and blue in 1864. Since then, Malone had put together an impressive travelogue, mostly as a catcher, sometimes as an infielder, playing for Keystone, Quaker City and the Olympics of Washington, which is where Athletic recruited him for the 1870 season. With Tom Berry moving from the infield to the outfield to fill one of the holes there, an even older pro than Malone came on board in the person of former Athletic and Atlantic ace Tom Pratt, back from another stay with Atlantic. Actually, he was only 26 years old, and he still couldn't beat out Dick McBride as Athletic's main pitcher, so Pratt played third base in 1870 in what is essentially his last hurrah as a ballplayer. By 1870 he was pretty much a fill-in,[16] mainly because he never was a very good hitter, possibly indicating that Athletic had trouble filling that hole. The other outfield spot went to Philly native George Bechtel, a former Geary and West Philadelphia player who really hadn't established himself yet as a top player, although he would later do so in a career that would last into the National League era.

Although Athletic seems to have had a little more trouble filling its roster spots in 1870, maybe because, unlike the Red and White Stockings, they weren't recruiting nationwide, they still had a pretty good year, again finishing third among the professional teams with a record of 26-11-1. The newspapers published what Marshall Wright refers to as the first-ever standings, showing how the top five of the 15 professional NABBP teams were faring. At season's end, it looked like this:

Cincinnati	27-6-1	Athletic	26-11-1	Atlantic	20-16
Chicago	22-7	Mutual	29-15-3		

None of the other 10 pro teams had a winning record, indicating the gap that separated not just the amateurs from the pros, but the top pros from everyone else. The fact that the top two pro teams were the ones that had recruited nationally was most probably not one that was lost on the directors of Athletic, Mutual, etc.

The difference between the pro and amateur teams was shown even more clearly by the results of the games between the pros and the amateurs. Counting all their games, no fewer than six pro teams played better than .700 ball on the year. Here are their records, as compiled by Wright, including all games, and just those games the pros played against amateurs:

	All Games	*Games vs. Amateurs*
Mutual	68-17-3	39-2
Cincinnati	67-6-1	40-0
Chicago	65-8	43-1
Athletic	65-11-1	39-0
Forest City (IL)	42-13-1	32-0
Atlantic	41-17	21-1

The top six pro teams went 214-4 against amateur opponents, a .982 winning percentage.

The 1870 season was also known for the end of the Red Stockings' winning streak, in the historic 8-7, 11 inning game in Brooklyn against Atlantic. Having finished the 1869 season undefeated, the Stockings returned to Philadelphia in 1870, just one week after Atlantic ended their fabled streak on June 14, and nipped Athletic 27–25 in a June 22 game, one of the last Athletic would play at 17th and Columbia, and where the fans backed up traffic and surrounded the field so completely that the Stockings had to climb the fence in center field to get into the park.[17] The highlight of Athletic's year came in Cincinnati on July 27 when they became the second team to defeat the professional Red Stockings, and the first team to defeat Cincinnati's pros on their home grounds. The score was 11–7 on July 27, 1870.

In keeping with the split in the standings, the stats for the pro teams were also kept in two categories—those run up against just pro teams, and those in all games. In professional play, Wes Fisler even out-hit George Wright, banging out 85 hits for 139 total bases in 36 pro games, for averages (they were now using the decimal system, instead of average and over) of 2.36 and 3.86—the last three figures leading the way for pro games. Fergy Malone, with 86 hits, edged teammate Fisler by one for the most number of safeties in the professional season. Overall, scoring was down in 1870, probably due to the increasing sophistication and skill—to say nothing of the experience gained by playing more games during the year—of the professional players. Athletic averaged just 28.9 runs per game for all games, but gave up just 9.2 runs per game.

The season concluded in November 1870, with the final annual convention of the NABBP. The *New York Clipper* even pronounced the death of the NABBP as the meeting was closing, due to what Marshall Wright terms "the great gulf between the amateurs and the professionals."[18] As a result, when Athletic next took the field, it would be as a part of the first real baseball league—a league of professionals. Baseball was coming to another paradigm shift.

♦ CHAPTER 7 ♦

The National Association Years

During the National Association's run from 1871 to 1875 it was known as "Harry Wright's League." And there was some degree of truth in that. Wright was a major force in forming the NA. Wright's Boston Red Stockings did dominate the standings, winning four out of the five NA pennants, and it was Wright's Red Stockings that, during the NA years, took baseball's first international trip. But, the National Association wasn't all Harry Wright and Boston. Philadelphia baseball, especially the Philadelphia Athletics, played a major role in most of the major baseball events that took place from the March 1871 founding of the National Association to the February 1876 founding—which was, in fact, a virtual coup d'etat—of the National League.

Marshall Wright's account of the final year of the NABBP makes it clear that the old association had both grown too big to be managed, and also was suffering from a terminal split between two factions—the amateurs and the pros. As Voigt put it in *American Baseball*, "The fall meeting of the Association was a fiery affair marked by hot words between the two camps, and it ended with the amateurs staging a walkout."[1] The majority of the NABBP walked out into true obscurity. Although amateur baseball would continue to thrive in the United States, and does so to this day, it would never again really hold center stage, either in Philadelphia, or anywhere else. And, although club teams would continue to flourish in Philadelphia, even existing to the present in organizations like the Penndel League, and although college, high school and eventually Little League baseball would provide a structure for the amateur game, and entertainment for many, the main plot line in the story of Philadelphia baseball, and the highest level of Philadelphia baseball, passed inexorably into the hands of the professionals. In 1871, that meant the Athletic Club. From here on in, the amateur clubs would appear in the public eye only as a footnote.

On the other hand, Athletic's stigma of having professional players certainly went by the books in 1871, in part due to the success and publicity that surrounded the 1869 Cincinnati Red Stockings, but moreso because the Athletics joined the National Association of Professional Base Ball Players. According to Henry Chadwick, writing in the *New York Clipper* and so quoted by Dean Sullivan in *Early Innings*, the genesis for the NA came from Nick Young, at the time the secretary of the Olympic Club of Washington. Young suggested to his fellow secretaries of the other professional clubs that they should get together in March 1871, to arrange the dates for the respective tours their clubs would take. It was the proverbial dark and stormy St. Patrick's Day night when the representatives of 10 professional teams met and quickly moved on to far more than just setting a schedule for the upcoming year. Although J.W. Schofield of the Troy Haymakers first held the gavel, it was Athletic president and U. S. marshal James M. Kerns who was shortly elected chairman, and who fired the first shot in the battle with the soon-to-be-dying NABBP.[2] Kerns began his tenure by sounding something like Jefferson Davis, and stating that the amateurs, who had held their convention the day before in Brooklyn, were hostile to the professionals' agenda, and had thus forced Athletic, et al., to take action. And, indeed, Kerns just wasn't blowing hot air. Dr. L.B. Jones of the still-ostensibly amateur Excelsior Club had just sent the *Clipper* a letter, basically stating that the professionals were ruining the Great American Game—a disingenuous statement if there ever was one, since Excelsior was the team that first paid Jim Creighton!

Following Kerns' remarks, Schofield, Alex Davidson and Harry Wright were directed to form a committee to decide what to do. In what was not exactly a shock, they came back with a recommendation that the clubs present form an association of professionals. And so it was done, with Kerns now being elected president of the National Association, with J.S. Evans of Cleveland vice president, Young secretary and Schofield treasurer.[3] Professional baseball was now truly on its way, and Philadelphia, in the persona of Athletic, would be leading the way.

How important was Athletic to the new association? Well, it may or may not have been in conjunction with Athletic having been jobbed out of several NABBP titles, but Chadwick reported in the March 26 *Clipper* that the first thing done at the March 17 meeting in reference to the rules for determining the championship was the reading of a series of resolutions adopted by the Athletic Club, governing their own actions in conjunction with the championship. These resolutions in essence stated that Athletic would play no exhibition or social matches and the estimate as to what would constitute the championship would be based solely on what we would now call won-loss percentage, although at the time it was phrased as the smallest percentage of losses. Athletic was clearly very important to this new organization, even though a proposal from Nick Young, to award the championship to the team with the most wins, ultimately carried the day.[4]

* * *

The Athletic Club was now playing at Jefferson Park (sometimes it was called Athletic Park), located at 25th and Jefferson Streets in North Philadelphia. Their Camac Woods grounds at 17th and Columbia having been sold out from underneath them after the 1870 season, Athletic went a little farther west and built Philadelphia's first permanently enclosed ball ground on the site of their former secondary field. Jefferson Park seated about 5,000 with very short fences down the lines and a 500-foot Grand Canyon of Pennsylvania in center field. Proving that there is nothing new under the baseball sun, the park included a swimming pool beyond the right field fence—only about 130 years before the Arizona Diamondbacks first came up with the same ballpark gimmick. As Philadelphia's first true baseball venue, Jefferson Park would get a lot of use over the years, being used by five different pro teams from 1871 to 1891.[5]

By the end of the first year of the NA, Philadelphia held even more importance in baseball, and had the distinction of winning the first organized league pennant in baseball history.[6] Their record? A somewhat murky 22–7, just ahead of the Chicago White Stockings (20–9) and the preseason favorite Boston Red Stockings (22–10). Actually, just as disputes on who won the whip pennant had plagued the NABBP, disputes over the league champion would flare up in two of the National Association's first three years, though for different reasons and as a part of a larger problem, the issue of the eligibility of revolvers.

In fairness to the competition, it should be noted that Mrs. O'Leary's cow kicking over that lantern and starting the Chicago fire proved to be something of a handicap to the White Stockings, who had to finish their 1871 season on the road. Furthermore, the favored Red Stockings, under the able direction of former Cincinnati Red Stockings boss Harry Wright, did indeed sweep the next four NA pennants. Still, when the dust finally settled after the 1871 season, something that didn't happen until early November, the champions were the Philadelphia Athletics.

The Athletics of 1871 were a formidable lot, made up almost entirely of native Philadelphians and led by third baseman Long Levi Meyerle, who set an all-time major league baseball batting average record of .492, long-time pitching star Dick McBride (20–5), and Al Reach (.353), the oldest regular at 31 and already the owner of the sporting goods firm that still bears his name. The major changes in the lineup from the 1870 NABBP squad were the addition of Meyerle, who returned home to Philadelphia from Chicago, putting Tom Pratt out of a job at third, and Ned Cuthbert, revolving back to Philly to replace Tom Berry in the outfield. Other than George Bechtel and George Heubel splitting an outfield spot, it was otherwise the same lineup that Athletic had fielded in 1870:

C—Fergy Malone	OF—Ned Cuthbert
1B—Wes Fisler	OF—Count Sensenderfer
2B—Al Reach	OF—George Bechtel and George Heubel
3B—Levi Meyerle	P—Dick McBride
SS—John Radcliff	

Exactly who managed this aggregation has been the subject of some varying interpretation in modern times, since the modern definition of manager really didn't exist at this time. McBride, as captain, led the team on the field. He was, in modern terminology, the manager. Hicks Hayhurst, though commonly referred to at the time as the team's manager, was an administrator, something like a modern day business manager. A more accurate title for Hayhurst would be the team secretary, since he scheduled games, kept count of the receipts and the like. As was the case with the rest of the team's directors, Hayhurst was well-connected in Philadelphia. By now a city councilman with ties to the city's tax collection functions, Hayhurst was the most visible Athletic among the directors, who also included several billiard parlor owners and liquor store owners. They were all also good Republicans, an affiliation that would increasingly help the team's clout as the city became a Republican stronghold after the Civil War.[7]

On the field, there was no doubt who the main man was in 1871. A 6-1, 177 pound DH born 100 years too soon, since he played the field equally poorly at every position but catcher. Meyerle also hit a league-leading four home runs in '71, drove in 40 runs in 26 games, scored 45 runs and had an adjusted OPS of 241. His record .700 slugging percentage would go unsurpassed in major league baseball until Babe Ruth's 1920 campaign, 50 seasons later. Meyerle would later go on to play for three more Philadelphia professional teams, the National Association White Stockings, the '76 National League Athletics and the '84 Union Association Keystones. A .353 hitter in his National Association career, he also hit a combined .329 in the NL and the UA. Long Levi may not have been much of a fielder, but he could hit.

This was basically an all–Philadelphia metropolitan area team—a situation that was already unusual in professional baseball—and it was also a virtual All-Star team, two situations that also say something about the quality of players from Philadelphia. In addition to returnees Meyerle and Cuthbert, and long-time Athletics McBride and Reach, the

5–6 Camden duo of Fisler and Radcliff had been top players since at least 1866, the only difference being that Radcliff was a notorious revolver and suspected hippodromer, and Fisler was a squeaky clean Athletic. The Count, another Philadelphian, had been on board since 1867. And even Irish native Malone, the only non–Philadelphian outside of Englishman–New Yorker Reach among the regulars, had been bouncing back and forth between Philadelphia and Washington for a few years.

The 1871 club opened on May 20 with an 11–8 loss in Boston, Al Spalding getting the win over McBride. Their first win came on June 3, a 15–5 blitz of the Troy Haymakers — a still not-uncommon score for 1871. Although the game's and the players' growing sophistication in terms of both pitching and fielding skills was bringing down the overall scoring, this was still a high offense era; in 28 games the Athletics scored 376 runs and they were only second in the league in scoring, since Boston scored 401 runs.

The third and fifth games of the season, against the Rockford Forest Citys, turned out to be extremely important to the outcome of the season. Rockford first came to Jefferson Park on June 5, and shockingly took an 11–5 lead into the ninth inning. Although the Athletics rallied for five runs, they fell one short, and lost 11–10. Then, 10 days later and still on a tour of the east, the Forest Citys returned to Philadelphia and this time won 10–7. However, as would often the case in the NA, all was not as it seemed. The definitive story of this first professional league, by William Ryczek, is titled *Blackguards and Red Stockings*, not a bad four-word review of the years from 1871 to 1875. Certainly, what would be considered extra-legal events took place, and the first of these involved the Rockford Forest Citys. As Ryczek explains, 25 of Rockford's 27 games in 1871 were tainted, because the Forest Citys were using a player who was clearly ineligible under NA rules. And two of those games were the June victories over Athletic.

Veteran catcher Scott Hastings, the Forest Citys' regular backstop in 1870, on April 16, 1871, was in the New Orleans Lone Stars' lineup for what we would now consider an exhibition game against the Chicago White Stockings, who were making a preseason tour of the south. Hastings' next action was on May 6, in the Forest Citys' NA opener with Cleveland. Now, this may not have been a big deal to the Lone Stars, who weren't in the association, but it was clearly against the NA rules which prohibited a member of any club from playing with another club for 60 days. Despite the fact that other NA teams protested Hastings' use in championship games, and despite the fact that his status was questioned in print during the season, Rockford kept using him, thus setting up forfeits for 25 of their games. The matter of Hastings' eligibility, and the status of 25 of Rockford's games, would eventually come up in November, to be decided by the league's Judiciary Committee.[8]

In the interim, the season continued, even as various versions of the league standings were published, partly due to the potential Rockford forfeit question, and partly due to other issues, such as what constituted an exhibition game (there were no formally set schedules at this time), and the circumstance of teams coming into and going out of the league. Undaunted, the Athletics rolled through the summer, moving into first place in early July with a six-game wining streak and scoring runs by the bushel, including a 49–33 orgy in Troy on June 28, a game most likely played with Troy's favored lively ball. By the start of September, the pennant race was a three-team affair between Philadelphia, Boston and Chicago, with Athletic either in the lead, or tied with Chicago. However Athletic's situation was precarious, since Meyerle, Reach, Malone, Heubel, Sensenderfer and, most importantly of all, McBride, were hobbling. Sensenderfer's knee injury — suffered while stealing second during an exhibition game with Rockford — was the most serious; he was out for the year and would play only another 24 games in the National Association. McBride missed three straight games, forcing Bechtel to the mound for a September 2 win over the New York Mutuals (9–8) and September 4 and September 9 losses to the Mutuals and Boston (wherein he gave up a total of 35 runs). And, although McBride was back for an 11–6 win over Chicago on September 18, the White Stockings tied for the lead on September 29 with a 10–8 win over Boston, while the Athletics sat by—not playing a regular game from September 18 to October 9 (the day after Chicago burned). However, Chicago could never get past a tie for first with Athletic, mainly because, in their October 9 and October 18 games, Philadelphia showed its class, defeating Troy and New York 15–13 and 21–7 respectively. This set up a final game with Chicago. The question was, where were they going to play, with the Windy City now a smoldering pile of ashes.[9]

Even though the various forfeits had not yet been officially determined and other issues, included the status of George Hall of the Washington Olympics and the disbanding of the Fort Wayne Kekiongas, continued to muddy the waters, Ryczek points out that there seemed to be a general consensus in the newspapers at the time that the Athletic–White Stocking game of October 30 would decide the pennant. Most accounts from 1871 seemed to indicate that a Chicago win would give Boston the crown while the Athletics had control of their own destiny. In reality, when looked at after the fact, the October 30 game, technically a Chicago home game though held at the Union Grounds in Brooklyn, was almost a winner-take-all. The Athletics would take the whip pennant outright with a win, and Chicago would have thrown the race into a disputed tie with a win, causing untold chaos in the process.

While the White Stockings were homeless for this climactic game, the Athletics were Reachless—the Scratcher, as he was known, was out. However, they did have McBride, despite accounts over the years that he was injured for this game, and that, as a result, Bechtel took his place in the box against George "The Charmer" Zettlein. Fisler moved over to play second (he was an excellent fielder there, too) and Heubel played first. That still left a hole in the outfield. To the surprise of everyone, and to add even more drama to the day, 40-year-old Nate Berkenstock, a regular on the great Athletics teams of the 1860s, came out of retirement to play right field.

Although the aged Berkenstock made a fine running catch in the outfield to save a run, the star of the game was McBride. In arguably the biggest game of his career, McBride shut down the White Stockings in what would be the Athletics' lowest-scoring game of the year, thanks in part to some fine fielding by shortstop Radcliff. Hits by Fisler and the day's other hero—naturally enough Meyerle, who had three hits for the game—brought in a run in the second. Errors by Zettlein and shortstop Ed Duffy gave Philly another solo run in the third and McBride did the rest, actually taking a 4–0 shutout into the ninth. Although Chicago scored a lone run in the last frame, in just one hour and 35 minutes McBride had pitched what was unquestionably his team to the championship by the score of 4–1.[10] When the various legal issues of forfeits and the like were finally resolved in November, it was decided that the final standings were:

Philadelphia	22-7	Boston	22-10
Chicago	20-9		

Pretty much any way you slice it, the Philadelphia Athletics were ultimately crowned the first true professional baseball champions and were awarded the whip pennant, which they hung in a saloon—drawing a rebuke from Harry Wright in the process.[11] And while

Harry may have been right about the Athletics' lack of respect for the pennant, there can be no denying the significance of the 1871 pennant, and the 1871 season—marking the end of the reign of a great team, the second great baseball dynasty, and most assuredly the finest team Philadelphia would see until Connie Mack was managing his first dynasty from 1901 to 1914. In the baseball seasons leading up to 1871, only Atlantic could match the Athletics for sustained brilliance over a period of years. And while both Atlantic and, briefly, the Cincinnati Red Stockings could make claims as being the best team in baseball, in reality, from 1866 to 1871 that title belonged in Philadelphia. The Athletics of 1866 to 1871 represented the high water mark of baseball in Philadelphia in the nineteenth century. After all that, the remaining four seasons of the National Association would, in many ways, be an anticlimax.

* * *

Three factors—injuries, age and the lack of what would later be called a reserve clause—led to more turnover in 1872 in the first nine than the Athletic club had seen since back in its pre–NABBP days. Sensenderfer's injury limited him to part-time status, and Reach's advancing age—he had played ball regularly since 1858 and would turn 32 (old for this era) early in the 1872 season—also made him a part-time player. These were no small losses, since Reach was an all-time All-Star and the slick-fielding Count had hit .323 and scored 38 runs in 1871. In addition, Radcliff went back to his favorite pastime, revolving, while Bechtel and Heubel also left town.

To re-supply the team, Hayhurst and McBride brought in the third baseman from the 1871 Forest Citys, 20-year-old Adrian Constantine Anson. Former Villanova University player Denny Mack followed Anson from Rockford and took over first, moving the accommodating and versatile Fisler to second to replace Reach. When Chicago folded for lack of a city to call home, Fred Treacey was brought in to replace the Count in center. The final piece was former Troy player Mike McGeary, who would play short and catcher. What about Long Levi? Well, the star of the 1871 season was asked to try right field to make room for what proved to be Athletic's number one acquisition, "Baby" or "The Marshalltown Infant" as Anson was known in those days. This move wasn't entirely successful. Although Anson hit .415 and led the league in on-base percentage (.455), Meyerle, perhaps distracted by trying to play the outfield, fell off to .329, just above the team average of .317.

Although this may have looked like a stronger Athletic team, one that was favored to win another pennant, especially with the White Stockings folding, that would not be the case. Although Philadelphia still posted an excellent 30-14 record, that was good for only second place, seven and a half games behind Boston. After winning their first six games, the Athletics then lost to the Red Stockings and spent the rest of the season trying to catch up to Boston while McBride shuffled players around the field. Of course, with Boston at 18-1 by June 24, no amount of shuffling in the world would have made much difference. Except for Heubel and Bechtel sharing an outfield spot, Philadelphia had gone with pretty much a set lineup in 1871, except when accommodating for injuries. In '72, Malone and McGeary (he would hit .360, second on the team to Anson) split the catching, Mack (he led the NA in walks, with 23) and Malone divided up the time at first, McGeary and Mack split the shortstop duties, and a total of four different players—Treacey, Meyerle, Cuthbert and Reach—played at least 20 games in the outfield. Whether this did any good or not is debatable, since it's pretty hard to outmaneuver a team that finishes 39-8 as Boston did.

The Athletics put up a struggle, though. A 9–1 win by the redoubtable McBride in front of 5,000 fans at Jefferson Park on July 27 gave Boston just its third loss of the year, and pulled Athletic within four and a half games of first. However, Philadelphia never got any closer, and, when the Red Stockings knocked McBride around by a 16–4 score on September 5, the Athletics were seven and a half back and the race was over.[12]

* * *

The loss of the 1872 pennant may have come as a surprise to Philadelphia baseball fans, but the 1873 season would bring even bigger surprises, including the Athletics' first real local challenger since the early 1860s. The '73 season also featured the biggest Philadelphia baseball collapse prior to 1964, and the first, though hardly the last, successful player raids in Philadelphia baseball history. At the middle of the major Philadelphia baseball events was a new team, officially known as the Philadelphia White Stockings, but also familiarly known as the Whites, Philadelphias, or sometimes, the Phillies.[13]

The White Stockings were by far the most imposing of the NA's three new teams for 1873, because, in a series of moves that would be repeated 28 years later, the White Stockings built a excellent team by raiding their Philadelphia brethren. In 1901, the players in question were Nap Lajoie, Chick Fraser and Strawberry Bill Bernhard, and they were going from the Phillies to the Athletics. In 1873, the players were Long Levi Meyerle (he would hit .349 for his new team), Ned Cuthbert (he would score 78 runs in 51 games), Fergy Malone, Denny Mack and Fred Treacey—and they were going *from* the Athletics *to* the Phillies. The White Stockings took five of the Athletics' nine regulars—a catcher, two outfielders and two infielders—and left the first name in Philadelphia baseball temporarily with just four starters, although two were the steadfastly loyal McBride and Fisler. Even though this was perfectly within the rules of the reserve clauseless NA, one can only imagine the hue and cry in Philadelphia—especially at 25th and Jefferson Streets, where the Athletics initially refused to let the raiders play. Finally, for an appropriate rental fee, the Athletics admitted the White Stockings to their grounds, thus setting up the best Philadelphia baseball rivalry to date.[14]

On the Athletics' part, they had bigger problems to deal with. Like, putting together a team. Fortunately for McBride and Hayhurst, the NA had lost several teams between the 1872 and 1873 seasons, throwing a number of established professionals out of work. So, from the Middletown Mansfields came John Clapp and Tim Murnane, while Cherokee Fisher came in from the Lord Baltimores and Ezra Sutton from the Cleveland Forest Citys. Nevertheless, these weren't the old, homegrown Athletics of old, and it showed. The new rivalry took on a decidedly one-sided flavor as the White Stockings took the first eight games between the two teams. Despite the uneven nature of the 1873 Athletics–White Stockings rivalry, the games were a hit with Philadelphia baseball fans, no doubt in part because so many old Athletics were wearing white socks, instead of blue. The outcome of the second game of the series, on May 14, might also have revved up interest, as the two teams battled in an extremely rare 5–4, 13 inning contest. With the still-high scores of this era, extra inning games were quite unusual, and a 13-inning game was almost unheard of. According to Ryczek, the last time two top teams had played that long a game was back in 1865.

The third game between the two, on June 11, drew somewhere around 10,000 people and a $5000 gate to a park that only held 5,000, causing a large number of people to congregate in the outfield, and encroaching on the respective right fielders, George Bechtel (who had returned to Philadelphia with the White Stockings after a year with the New York Mutuals) and Cherokee Fisher. However, the $5000 gate was chickenfeed compared to how much was bet on the game (a 7–5 White Stocking win)—a rumored $100,000! Ten days later, another 5,000 saw another White Stockings' win, this time by a 17–5 score.[15]

Although it must have been small consolation to McBride, Hayhurst, et al., the Athletics weren't the only team to fall prey to the White Stockings' veterans in the first part of the season. Along with the purloined Athletics, manager Malone also had a fine double-play combination in Chick Fulmer and Jimmy Wood (he joined the team in Bob Addy's place in July—a move that would have large consequences), and former Chicago White Stockings pitcher George Zettlein on the mound. The White Stockings opened the season on April 21 with an 11–3 win over Athletic, and then followed that up two days later with an 8–5 win over Al Spalding and the Red Stockings. Having taken the measure of the NA's two best pitchers in three days, the Whites won five in a row to start the season, split their next four games, and then won 10 straight (including a 22–8 win over Boston), to go 17-2. The streak finally ended at Boston in an 11–6 loss on June 17. Even so, the Whites had a three-and-a-half game lead over Boston and Athletic, a lead that only expanded when they ripped off another 10 game winning streak wherein they scored in double figures in every single game. After edging Boston 18–17 on July 10, the White Stockings were 27-3, and held an eight-game lead over both Boston and Philadelphia. Henry Chadwick himself declared the pennant race over, though Harry Wright disagreed, writing to Hicks Hayhurst, "Let us get our and your second wind, then look out Philadelphias."

As was typically the case during the five NA seasons, most of the '73 teams played very few league games during the months of July and August, usually using that time to go on a tour of exhibition games before ramping up for the fall season and the climax to the official pennant race. That's not what happened in 1873, when the White Stockings, possibly starting what would be a tradition for millions of twentieth century Philadelphians, spent almost three weeks "Down the Shore." Following the July 10 win over Boston, the Whites didn't play another game of any kind until July 30, spending the intervening time celebrating their successful first half on vacation in Cape May, New Jersey.[16] Even then, Victorian Cape May was a pretty staid place; however, the White Stockings apparently found a way to live it up. Or, at least, that seems to be the case, since they were seemingly unprepared for the resumption of their profession when they next re-took the field. The team that had won 27 of its first 30 games lost five straight, including two to Boston 23–10 (their first game after vacation) and 11–8 (on August 16). Still, at that point, the Red Stockings and the Athletics trailed by five and a half games, although the Baltimore Canaries had snuck into second, just two and a half back.

At this point though, it seemed as if the Whites got over their case of sunburn. They won seven of their next nine games, including a 9–4 win over Boston on August 18, and 6–5 and 14–7 wins over Athletic. At the conclusion of the latter game, on September 22, they still held a lead, but it was down to three games over the now red-hot Red Stockings. In the 17 games since the July 30 contest with the Whites, Boston had gone 14-2-1. In addition, the Philadelphia team had other problems; while in Chicago to play a neutral site game, Denny Mack was run down by a horse and severely injured (although he would return to the lineup later in the year) and Zettlein was reported to be in ill health, although in these more discrete days, newspaper reports of an individual's "illness" could have either meant they were sick or hung over.

Just as the pennant race was really heating up, the issues of ineligible players, forfeits, and teams dropping out of the league once again came up. This time, the player in question was Addy, who had started the year with the Whites, played one game in Chicago with a group from Rockford, and was now ending the campaign with the Red Stockings. Did Addy's participation on that Rockford nine make him ineligible for Boston's use? It was a question that would be brought up before the league's Judiciary Committee after the season. In addition, the Resolutes and Marylands had both dropped out of the league and two other players, T.J. Donnelly and Doug Allison, had eligibility questions.[17]

What caused the White Stockings to unravel? Ryczek speculates they were throwing games. There's no doubt there was a lot of money around, as indicated by the betting on the early-season Athletics game. Whatever the reason, with the season on the line between September 25 and October 4, the Whites lost six straight, now falling two games behind the Red Stockings, who had gone 4–0 in the same period. Although no proof of White Stockings tanking has ever been established, at the very least the Whites' player use in the closing weeks was odd, as was the behavior of some of their players. Ryczek tells of on-the-field, mid-game contretemps, especially involving the now-former captain-manager Malone and Wood, who was now captain-manager.

On September 29, the Whites lost to Athletic for the first time all year, in what must have been a sweet 7–6 win for the older team. At 34–12, the Whites now led 32–13 Boston by one and a half games. The next day, for the first time all year, Zettlein did not pitch for the Philadelphias. Bechtel, who had been the Athletics' change pitcher in 1871, was sent out to face Baltimore in this key contest. He lost 10–6, and then, the very next day (October 1), he was back pitching against the awful Washington Nationals, losing 14–13 and putting the Whites in a virtual tie with Boston, after the latter team defeated the Brooklyn Atlantics 8–6. The Whites had blown an eight game lead in 18 games. Not as bad as the 1964 Phillies' six-and-a-half game lead in 10 games, but bad enough.

	W	L	Pct.	GB
Boston	33	13	.717	-
Philadelphia	34	14	.708	-

The Nationals game was a weird one. In addition to Bechtel pitching, shortstop Fulmer caught (the only game in '73 he would appear in behind the plate), catcher Malone played short (the only time he played there this year), and Denny Mack, normally the first baseman, played right. With Washington holding a 14–1 lead, Wood switched Malone and Fulmer back to their normal positions, only to see Fulmer kick a ball and a Whites' rally come up one run short, thanks largely to a baserunning error by utilityman Jim Devlin.

The very next day, October 2, the Whites and the Reds met before 4,000 fans at Jefferson Park, with first place on the line. This time, Zettlein was the starting pitcher, and he was staked to a 4–0 lead. Had he been held out of the previous games because of an injury? An illness? A hangover? No one knows. Could Wood have been resting him against two bad teams so he wouldn't have to pitch on four straight days? Unlikely, but possible, since playing league games on four consecutive days was unusual at this time, and it certainly would have been a stress on the pitcher's arm. Even throwing underhand, a couple of hundred pitches over each of four consecutive days would have been tough, especially if it wasn't commonly done and especially if the pitcher threw as hard as Zettlein did. Still, these were the only two games all year that Zettlein didn't start. Whatever was going on, Boston took a 7–5 lead into the fourth, when the Whites, and captain Wood in particular, lost it—their heads, the game, and the season. In the fourth, Wood botched a fly ball and a throw from Fulmer to start the fun, in both cases pitching a fit on the field and allowing a total of three Boston runners to score in the process. Obviously not the coolest head in North Philly this day, Wood in the fifth removed Zettlein and put Fulmer, who had almost no experience pitching, in his place. The Charmer went to first, Devlin to third and the awkward Meyerle took over Fulmer's spot at short. Boston won the game 18–7.[18]

If there were Boo-Birds in Philadelphia in 1873, they would have let Wood, Meyerle, Zettlein, Cuthbert, Malone, Devlin and Treacey know it, though maybe for another reason as well. Although it was supposed to have been kept a secret, the word had been out for more than a month that those seven stalwarts of the Philadelphias had already signed with another team for the 1874 season. Another team of White Stockings, only this one in Chicago. In the first-ever mid-season raid of one team upon another, the newly reformed Chicago White Stockings had pulled a "what goes around, comes around" on the Philadelphia White Stockings, mimicking the Philadelphias' early 1873 raid on the Athletics, and making off with the heart of the Philadelphia team for the next year—and as early as August 1873. Phillies president George Young screamed bloody murder, but, there was nothing either he or the NA could do about the piracy, since there was no rule against it.[19] This, then, may have been another explanation for the Philadelphians' strange and lackluster play late in the 1873 season—they were already looking west towards Chicago and the 1874 season. Or, it may just have been they were distracted by their now-hostile fans. Although the White Stockings were 8–5 at Jefferson Park from the beginning of August to the end of the season, it's still easy to picture the outrage of the fans.

Losing to the Mutuals 5–4 two days after the 18–7 disaster against Boston just drove the nail in the coffin. When the season officially ended on the field with a 12–1 November 1 loss to the Atlantics, the top of the NA standings looked like this:

	W	L	Pct.	GB
Boston	43	16	.729	-
Whites	36	17	.679	4
Baltimore	34	22	.607	7½
Athletics	28	23	.549	11

After starting 27-3, the White Stockings had lost 14 of their last 23 games. They were 2-12 outside of the one stretch where they won seven of nine. The Red Stockings, on the other hand, had gone 24-2 from the August 18 loss to the Whites until two meaningless losses to Athletic in the last two games of the year. The Athletics, after their mid-summer layoff, were never a factor in the race, except as a spoiler, going 11-13 from mid–August on, despite Anson's .398 average and good old Wes Fisler's .344 mark. Following the close of the regular season, the two Philadelphia teams tried to make a little extra money with two November exhibition games, but drew only 500 chilled fans to the final affair. However, overall it had been a good season for Philadelphia baseball. There was clearly room in town for two major league teams, with the newcomer Whites making a net profit of $4000.[20]

Even after the two November exhibitions, the season wasn't over as far as the White Stockings were concerned. After it was all over but the shouting, they did some shouting, trying to convince the NA's Judiciary Committee that the Red Stockings' Addy was an ineligible player for part of the second half of the year. Basically, the Philadelphia team claimed that the July 4 game he took part in in Chicago for Rockford, which didn't have a team in the NA in 1873, was a regular game, thus making him ineligible for the next 60 days. Although the game in question was clearly a pick-up contest, the dispute wasn't resolved in Boston's favor until early 1874.

Shortly thereafter, in a classic case of locking the barn door after the horse escapes, the Judiciary Committee passed a rule that any player signing with another team for the next season before the current season was over could be expelled or would have to forfeit his salary. Like many NA rules, this one turned out to be ignored in practice.[21]

* * *

The Philadelphias now faced a major rebuilding job—even to the point of changing their name. It would seem as if the Chicago ball club had also stolen the "White Stockings" moniker as well, since Philadelphia changed both the color of its socks and its official name, to the Pearls, for the 1874 season. However, the team was still more commonly called the Philadelphias or the Phillies.[22] Playing under that name in 1874 would be just three survivors of the 1873 collapse—Mack, Fulmer and Bechtel. Worse yet for the Philadelphias, the Athletics would also steal from them in 1874. They would steal back the spotlight of Philadelphia baseball, by teaming up with the Boston Red Stockings on the first game's first trip abroad—back to England, the mother country of baseball.

While we now know that baseball originated in England from the game of English base ball,[23] Harry Wright, from whose fertile brain the idea for the trip seems to have sprung, was trying to bring what he considered a new game back to his mother country. Whatever Wright's knowledge, or lack thereof, of the origins of baseball, he first approached the Athletics to propose that both teams journey to England, with Wright's Boston team, during the middle of the 1874 season in the months of July and August, those times being typically reserved for tours and exhibitions. This would be the tour of all tours, and a series of exhibitions the likes of which England had never seen. Or so Wright thought.

Even odder than Wright's seeming lack of knowledge of the role of his home country in his profession was, in fact, the reception the Red Stockings and Athletics received in England. Despite the fact that there almost had to be some people who watched the American baseball games in 1874 who were alive when Jane Austen wrote *Northanger Abbey* with its reference to baseball in 1798, no one seemed to know what to make of this strange game the Colonials were playing. Nowhere in any of the literature about the trip does there appear any reference of someone exclaiming, "This bloody game looks familiar to something I played when I was a nipper." For instance, in *American Baseball*, Voigt quotes the editor of *London Field* magazine as describing baseball as being the cricket of the American continent, considerably altered,[24] with no mention of English base ball. However, Ryczek has found an intriguing reference in the coverage of the Americans' tour. The *New York Clipper* reported after the fact in September 1874 that the British press, in coincidental and incorrect agreement with Chadwick, thought that baseball came from rounders, while also mentioning that the Prince of Wales had played a game of baseball in 1748.[25] Still, the otherwise massive unfamiliarity with the game the Americans were playing would seem to support the theory that English base ball had died out well before 1874.

After a New York meeting with Athletics president James Ferguson, Wright was confident enough of his scheme that he sent Al Spalding to England to make arrangements for the trip with the officials of the Marylebone Cricket Club. However, the negotiations were not all tea and crumpets. As Voigt points out, the Royal St. Andrews club of cricket finally decided to welcome and host the Americans only after Spalding agreed to a joint baseball-cricket tour, beginning in late July 1874 and running through the month of August.

This would come as a surprise to Wright. Although the old cricketeer had expected to play a few games of his old sport in his old country, he initially had no idea that the baseball tour was expected to be a two-sport affair, and that he was supposed to provide top-notch cricket players.[26] Fortunately for Wright, he had two such cricket stars on his own team, his brother George, and himself. He also brought along a ringer, their younger brother Sam, still another of the Wright family cricket stars.[27] It was also Harry's good fortune that the other team he chose happened to also have a first-rate cricket bowler on their squad. That would be Dick McBride who, like George Wright, could seemingly do anything needed with a bat and ball.

The 14 baseball games, wherein the Athletics went 6-8, on the tour weren't attended very well, even though the British press was impressed and curious about the game. Basically, the baseball games drew like a game that was unknown to the natives, thus leading to an overall loss of $2500. The Athletics, with greater travelling expenses, lost $1800 of that total. As for the cricket matches, while it is true that the joint American team went 6-0-1 against the British in cricket games, that was largely due to the fact that their hosts let them use 18 players against the standard 11-man British squad. It was also widely reported that the way the Americans played the British game wasn't, for want of a better word, "cricket." Instead of just trying to block the ball from hitting the wicket, they swung away like early-day Shawon Dunstons, hacking wildly at every pitch they could reach.[28]

The trip to England was ballyhooed as the highlight of the 1874 NA campaign, and it was a lot more interesting than the rest of the 1874 regular season, which saw another Red Stockings pennant, with the 42-23 New York Mutuals as the only close pursuer. The Mutes managed to finish second despite the loss of center fielder Dave Eggler, who journeyed south to Philadelphia as the centerpiece of the Pearls' massive rebuilding effort that consisted entirely of picking up players from New York and Baltimore. Joining Eggler from the Mutuals were catcher Nat Hicks and infielder Jim Holdsworth. Baltimore contributed pitcher Candy Cummings, who was becoming known as another professional revolver, along with an even more notorious revolver, John Radcliff. Also coming from Baltimore were the sinister and talented Bill Craver and outfielder Tom York. In the end, none of them did much good, as the Pearls fell from a close second in 1873 to a distant (17 games out) fourth in 1874, with a record of just 29-29. Adding Craver and Radcliff to the team also didn't do anything for what Ryczek terms was the Philadelphias' reputation for shady play, either. And what of those blackguards in White Stockings from Chicago? They finished behind the Pearls, with a 28-31 record, so there was some justice in the 1874 season.

Meanwhile, although the Athletics had finished a distant fourth in 1873, they chose to basically stand pat, adding just second baseman Joe Battin from an Easton, Pennsylvania, amateur team in place of Cherokee Fisher, who, like Craver, was a former Troy Haymaker who carried a somewhat shady image with him throughout baseballdom. The Athletics' basic mistake in 1874 was one that would be repeated time and again throughout baseball over the next 130 years. They held on too long to their stars. The veterans of the 1860s — notably Reach, Fisler and Sensenderfer — were getting old, and, even when they were replaced, they were replaced by players like Battin. And, even though McBride was still a top pitcher, his batting average fell to .217 in '74. Reach was almost through — he hit just .127 in 14 games. Although Fisler still hit .328, he was able to play only 37 games and score 26 runs. And the Count had been done in by his 1871 knee injury. As a result, the Athletics ended up third, at 33-23, five games ahead of the Pearls and 12 games behind the 52-18 Red Stockings.

* * *

The 1875 season saw baseball news made in The City of Brotherly Love from an unexpected source, one of the game's true Philadelphia pioneers, Elias "Hicks" Hayhurst. Like McBride a long-time Athletic, Hayhurst had, also like McBride, stayed with his old club through thick and thin, becoming one of the city's leading and best-connected figures inside and outside of sports. One proof of his status was the Pythian episode in 1867— only a man of Hayhurst's status would have had the standing to propose admitting a black team to the NABBP, and only a man of Hayhurst's status could have come so close to pulling it off. So, it must have been a shocker in 1875 when Hayhurst announced he was leaving his post as manager of the Athletics to form a new professional baseball team in Philadelphia, a move that would prove to be Hayhurst's only real mistake in all his years in Philadelphia baseball.

Perhaps it was the baseball fervor generated by the rivalry between the Athletics and the Whites-Pearls. Maybe it was the financial success of the newcomer Pearls. Perhaps it was a move designed to ride the wave of excitement and civic pride rising with the coming Centennial. Whatever it was, it was a mistake having three all-professional baseball teams in Philadelphia. Remarkably, it was a mistake that would be repeated twice more in the coming years—once in 1884 and once in 1890—proving that indeed those who do not learn from history are doomed to repeat it.

Logically enough, Hayhurst called his new team the Centennials. To start the ball rolling, he needed a place to play, since the Jefferson Street Grounds were pretty well taken by the Athletics and Pearls. Hayhurst found available the very oddly-shaped piece of ground that he himself had played on back in the early 1860s. Bordered by Ridge and Columbia Avenues and 24th and 25th Streets, this "block" took its odd shape from the meandering path of Ridge Avenue—the old Indian trail that had been turned into a city street, running all the way out past the city line and into Montgomery County and leaving the baseball grounds with a field that was 300' down the left field line, 331' to dead center, 369' to right-center and 247' down the right field line. Apparently the odd dimensions didn't bother Hayhurst or the earlier club teams, nor would it bother the Phillies in 1883, since it had been a baseball field since at least 1860, and maybe earlier than that, thanks to its location next to the streetcar line terminal.

The Centennials leveled and sodded the field, threw up a 10-foot high fence around the property (the first time these particular grounds had been enclosed), built some grandstands and a club house and announced that admission to their new Centennial Grounds would be 25 cents.[29] Hayhurst also announced that some familiar faces would be on the nine—George Bechtel, John Radcliff (despite the fact that he had been suspended for suspicion of throwing a game in 1874), Bill Craver and Fred Treacey. Here was Mistake Number One—these were the only four experienced professionals Hayhurst was able to sign for the Centennials. The rest of the team were local amateurs and semi-pros, and the days were long past when your average local club player could keep up with the professionals.

Mistake Number Two—Craver, as well as Radcliff, didn't exactly have a sterling reputation. And Treacey was one of the 1874 revolvers who signed with the Chicago White Stockings while still under contract with the Philadelphia White Stockings. As a result, Treacey may have well been persona non grata in Philly, or it may have been that he wasn't that big a hit with the fans in the first place because he also wasn't very good—his career average in this high-scoring era was only .244.

Mistake Number Three—trying to add another new team to an already-crowded market, especially one that was still feeling some of the effect of the Panic of 1873.

As everyone knows, it's three strikes and you're out in baseball. The Centennials went 2-12, with Bechtel, the former Athletic change pitcher in the box (in addition, he also led the team in runs scored—12, doubles—5, batting average—.279 and RBIs—7), and were the first 1875 NA team to fold, leaving Bechtel free to return to the Athletics. Well, not exactly for free. There was a price on his head, as well as on Craver's head. In fact, the final act of the Philadelphia Centennials was to establish a precedent for all time in baseball—the first-ever player transaction between two teams.

Before that happened, the Centennials did have at least one highlight, a May 6 11–2 win over the Athletics. However, they were clearly outmatched, scoring only 70 runs and giving up 138 in their 14 games. Several "crowds" of around 100 would also seem to indicate a clear answer to the question as to whether or not Philadelphia could support three teams. Still, there may have been extenuating circumstances to the team's demise following their May 24 5–0 loss to Boston. Ryczek points out that the average attendance for the four Centennial games where such figures are available was just short of a respectable 1,000. They only drew really poorly when one of the other two Philadelphia teams were playing at home on the same day. Now, maybe the directors of the Centennials saw the handwriting on the wall after 12 losses in 14 games, and two terrible turnouts when either the Athletics or Philadelphias were also playing at home. Or maybe, suggests Ryczek, they saw a chance to turn a profit and get out while the getting was good, although that doesn't sound like something Hayhurst would do.

The Athletics were short-handed, thanks to injuries to Dave Eggler and Fisler, and, as a result, they were turning a covetous eye towards former Athletic Bechtel and Craver. And, although it was against the NA rules to sign players while they were under contract to another team, well, that hadn't stopped the Chicago White Stockings in 1873. Of course, no one had yet tried to sign another team's players and then use them during the same season. According to Ryczek, the Centennials stockholders came up with the unique (for 1875) idea of releasing Bechtel and Craver from their contracts—for a price. One of the Athletics' stockholders came up with $1500, and the Athletics became the first team in history to purchase a couple of players from another team—certainly a landmark moment in the development of the competitive game. And, since Bechtel and Craver were the Centennials' two best players, Ryczek and Francis Richter both assert that the dissolution of the Centennials was a direct result of the player transfer.[30] This would also result in Treacey going back to the Philadelphias and two of the Centennials' former amateurs, second baseman Ed Somerville and catcher Tim McGinley, hooking up with the NA's New Haven Elm Citys.

In one of his many philosophical moments, Richter also suggested there was further fallout of this first player transaction, noting, "It was a peculiar fact that the first sale of players brought retribution with it, as Craver turned out to be crooked, and Bechtel took Anson's place so often that the latter became dissatisfied and later seceded to the Chicago club."[31] Given Anson's temperament—the term "prima donna" seems to fit here—it is certainly believable that he went into a snit after being unseated by Bechtel (they both played a lot in the outfield that year), and was thus more willing to participate in the upcoming player movements of 1876.

Meanwhile, the better-established Athletics and Pearls-Phillies-White Stockings carried on in the face of Boston's overwhelming superiority and subsequent 71-8 record. The Athletics had some slight consolation by running up what would normally be a pennant-winning record of 53-20, a .726 winning percentage. In 1875 though, all this got them was second, 15 games behind the rampaging Red Stockings. It's a measure of just how good Boston was to look at the Athletic lineup:

    C—John Clapp   OF—George Hall
    1B—Wes Fisler   OF—Dave Eggler
    2B—Bill Craver   OF—George Bechtel
    3B—Ezra Sutton   P—Dick McBride
    SS—Davy Force

McBride went 44-14 with an Adjusted ERA of 133 and hit .270 (which turned out to be the second-lowest mark on the team). Cap Anson? As Richter noted, he didn't even have a regular job on this powerhouse. He played first for 32 games, was in the outfield for 25, caught for 13 and played third in another five, posting an Adjusted OPS of 139.

Although McBride and Anson may seem like the most important players on the 1875 Athletics, in reality, little Davy Force would have an even bigger effect on baseball, inside and outside of Philadelphia, at least for the next year. The 5-4, 130 pound Force was one of baseball's first great defensive shortstops, as indicated by his .896 fielding percentage (against a league average of .849) and his 4.73 range factor (against a league average of 4.46). He was also a good hitter during his National Association years, posting Adjusted OPS figures of 97, 177, 138, 111 and 136 from 1871 to 1875. Thus, when he signed contracts with the both the Chicago White Stockings (September 18, 1874) and the Athletics (December 5, 1874) for the 1875 season, there was a great hue and cry, especially in Chicago, after Force expressed a desire to play in the City of Brotherly Love. While the Athletics weren't really doing much more than the White Stockings had

The man whose contract jumping helped bring down the National Association, Davy Force (courtesy John Thorn).

done to the Pearls for the 1874 season—that is, contravening association rules by signing a player for the next season before his current contract was up—somehow the White Stockings' William Hulbert didn't see it that way. After a couple of trips through the NA Judiciary Committee, that august group eventually ruled in favor of the Athletics in what could hardly have been a shocking development, since the committee at that time was comprised of Messrs. Van Delft, Bulkley, Hayhurst, Concannon and Spering—the latter three worthies representing, in order, the Philadelphia Centennials, the Philadelphia Pearls and the Philadelphia Athletics![32] The fix was in. Hulbert, and an equally-incensed Harry Wright, would neither forgive nor forget this instance of Philadelphia justice.

Against the backdrop of the Force Case, the 1875 season would be somewhat anticlimactic, particularly in light of what would happen in 1876. Against the Red Stockings' Hall of Fame crew featuring the Wright Brothers, Spalding and Jim O'Rourke, the NA in general, including the Athletics with Davy Force, and the Pearls, didn't have much of a chance. Even Long Levi couldn't keep the Pearls from finishing fifth at 37-31, with almost as many rumors about foul play as they had losses, and a $3000 bill at year's end for the players' back salaries (Athletic was reportedly $5000 in arrears of their players' salaries).[33] Most of the rumors swirled around infielder Mike McGeary, a Philadelphia native who started the season as the Pearls' manager. In August, McGeary accused George Zettlein and Fred Treacey of fixing a game. Those two responded that McGeary was the crooked one. Although all three were acquitted of any charges, McGeary was replaced as manager and the Pearls' reputation took another hit.[34]

The season's one highlight for the Pearls, outside of Meyerle's hitting, took place on July 28 when young Joe Borden, fresh off the amateur Doerr club and pitching under the pseudonym Josephs, took the pitcher's box against the Chicago White Stockings and proceeded to throw a 4–0, no-hit, no-run game, the first no-hitter in Philadelphia professional baseball, as well as the only no-hitter in the NA's five years.[35]

♦ CHAPTER 8 ♦

The Centennial City and the First Year of the National League

The 10 years immediately following the Civil War were significant ones for Philadelphia, and not just on the baseball diamonds of North Philadelphia. The period from 1865 to 1875 marked an era of general good feeling in the city, and not just because the war was over. Even one of the most traumatic episodes in American history, the assassination of Abraham Lincoln, and the subsequent public outpouring of grief, seemed to have a salutary effect on the city, as did the troops returning home. The angst of the loss of the president was soon replaced by a good humor, a feeling of a new beginning and a new approach to all aspects of life in the city.[1]

The city's recovery and thriving wasn't hurt by the fact that the Centennial was coming either. For the 10 years from 1865 to 1875 were marked throughout by the anticipation of the biggest block party in Philadelphia's history—the 100th anniversary of the Declaration of Independence and the founding of the United States. Against such a backdrop, against such general municipal excitement, is it any wonder that the Philadelphia Athletics and baseball were riding a wave of popularity throughout the decade? However, the Athletics were also ultimately facing a twin-edged sword, as the Centennial whose coming generated so much enthusiasm in Philadelphia would also end up being a major cause of the downfall of the first name in Philadelphia baseball.

However, that was still in the future as the 1870s started, and growth was the watchword in Philadelphia. Growth in population (674,000 in 1870, 817,000 by 1876), populated areas, building, industry, commerce, cultural and educational activities and, yes, growth in baseball. By now the heavily populated portion of the city had far outgrown the area between the Delaware and Schuylkill Rivers, following both rivers north and south and crossing over the Schuylkill, thanks in part to four new bridges, into West Philadelphia—where the Centennial would soon be held and where many early clubs had once played in open fields—which were also getting scarcer in North Philadelphia as the city expanded in that direction as well. What Philadelphia was doing was, in reality, taking advantage of its unique geography. Unlike the other major northeastern cities—mainly New York–Manhattan and Boston—Philly was not constricted by an island or the Atlantic Ocean. And while the two rivers may have formed a temporary barrier, they were soon overcome by moving north and west. Unlike New York–Manhattan, which was already growing vertically, Philadelphia and Philadelphians had room to spread out in more single-family dwellings. By 1867, 4500 such homes were being added annually to the housing supply—certainly a much more pleasant prospect for the collective municipal mindset than the already-teeming tenements of New York.[2]

As Philadelphia was growing out during the 1870s, this brought to new prominence the need to get around the city. While the horse-drawn streetcar system was important enough in Catto's day to make its integration a major event in the city, some 10 years later public transportation was becoming a major industry, and a major force in the city—and for baseball, since the ability to get to the games for an increasing number of people depended on being able to ride there in a streetcar—a phenomenon that would last well into the twentieth century.

In Philadelphia in the 1870s, as in every other decade, opportunity abhorred a vacuum. In this case, into the shortage of public transportation stepped Peter A.B. Widener, a butcher who made a small fortune selling mutton to the federal troops during the war, and a large fortune selling seats on the now-integrated streetcars after the war. Along with his partner, Western Pennsylvania oil baron William Elkins, Widener started buying up the individual streetcar lines right and left just before the Centennial, eventually forming what would become the Philadelphia Rapid Transit Company (PRT) and then the Philadelphia Transportation Company (PTC).[3]

As to who was riding Widener's streetcars, there were indeed now blacks aboard, but the majority of the new riders, and new immigrants, were Irish and Germans, who had a little more disposable income to stop by at 25th and Jefferson, since this was the period where Philadelphia industry established itself as a world of skilled and semi-skilled—which is to say better paid than unskilled—laborers. The first great industrial city of America, Philadelphia was a leading urban manufacturing center, but one made up of relatively small firms[4] with a little better paid workers than say, the miners of central Pennsylvania or the steel workers of Pittsburgh. And, in addition to having some extra money, these workers also had some extra time, either for their own recreation, or to watch others at sport.

This trend, which in reality started well before the Civil War, helps explain in part the proliferation of amateur baseball clubs in Philadelphia in the years before the war. It also shows why, in 1867 and 1868, Philadelphia put together the largest park in the country totally within a city's boundaries. Fairmount Park, which would eventually stretch for some 13 miles along both banks of the Schuylkill River and the Wissahickon Creek, was another indication of the city's maturation, and its focus on recreation—something the original Olympics had to journey to Camden to enjoy just 35 years earlier.

So, Philadelphia was growing throughout the decade following the war. Even the Panic of 1873, which was kicked off on September 18 when the New York branch of the Philadelphia banking firm of Jay Cooke and Company failed, couldn't really damage the city or its financial institutions, although it might have had a hand in a dampening of the baseball fervor (and attendance) during the 1874 season. The Jay Cooke flop burst the classic inflationary bubble that had formed after the Civil War, and three more Philadelphia banks, not to mention Jay Cooke's home branch, also went belly up before the end of the winter. Although most Philadelphia banks stayed open, many of the small factories did close, throwing a lot of workers onto the street.[5] As baseball would find out again some 60 years later, these conditions were not good for baseball attendance.

* * *

The Athletics' distinguished history did not serve them very well when the National Association met its untimely—at least from the Athletics' point of view—demise. The way the game was played on the highest professional level had reached a crossroads during the 1875 season, and unquestionably needed to be revised, if not reformed. In other words, it was time for another paradigm shift in baseball. Francis Richter, among many others, thought that's what the establishment of the National League brought about. "The organization marked a new era in Base Ball, inasmuch as the new organization lifted the game out of the slough into which it had fallen, purged it of everything that was dishonest, and made it popular and respected."[6]

However, the means by which this was done turned out to be a classic case of the ends justifying the means, and the end result proved (temporarily) fatal to the "big league" pretensions of Philadelphia baseball. In fact, the immediate ends almost proved fatal to "major league" baseball as well. David Voigt pulls no punches on this one:

> Baseball mythmakers depicted the National League of 1876 as a reforming force for major league baseball. The legend tells how the white knights of the league quickly brought honesty and prosperity to baseball by overcoming the discredited Association. In truth, it did neither.... The moralizing founders undermined the stability of the league by barring membership to New York and Philadelphia, two of the most lucrative cities.[7]

As the 1875 season progressed, it was clear that the essentially weak and disorganized NA was in trouble—in trouble from revolving, hippodroming, a gross competitive imbalance, schedules not being fulfilled and teams dropping out right and left, inflated player salaries and other woes. Enter William A. Hulbert, Albert Spalding and their plan for a new league—a league of baseball clubs, not baseball players, to be called just the National League. However, the Athletics would enter the NL under a double whammy—as a weakened team, bereft of its best player, and facing the worst off-the-field competitive situation imaginable.

The Red Stockings' level of domination of the NA was, quite simply, bad for baseball, demoralizing the other teams, most of which had no chance against Wright's powerhouse. Added to the problems of players jumping from team to team at the merest suggestion of a better deal, drinking, gambling and rowdyism (among players and fans), the National Association was a mess. One of the basic reasons for this on-going fiasco was the lack of a strong central organization, brought about by the fact that the entrance fee for a team was only $10. Into this disorganized rabble stepped William Hulbert, one of the charter stockholders of the second iteration of the Chicago White Stockings, and a man whose business practices and sentiments were in keeping with the great robber barons of America's late nineteenth century. During Chicago's first road trip to Boston in June 1875, Hulbert arranged for a secret meeting with the Red Stockings' Spalding, and offered him a $4000 contract, probably the biggest such contract up until that time, to come to Chicago to manage and pitch for the White Stockings in 1876. Hulbert had obviously planned his strategy well. In tempting Spalding to revolve, he probably knew that Spalding was highly ambitious, in addition to being a pretty good pitcher, and he certainly played on the fact that the pitcher was originally from Rockford, Illinois, just west of Chicago. Hulbert chose his man well. Not only did Spalding tell him he'd come back west, but that he'd bring with him three more of Boston's best players—Cal McVey, Ross Barnes and Deacon White. By the end of June, all four had signed Chicago contracts for 1876, in direct violation of NA rules.[8]

Now, this raid on Beantown, surely the boldest such move since the original Boston

Braves dumped that tea into the harbor, was not going to go unnoticed. Hulbert had thought ahead as to what might happen when word got out that he had signed Boston's "Big Four." He and his White Stockings would be expelled from the National Association. Considering the $10 membership fee, that was hardly a major financial consideration; however, it would leave the White Stockings an independent team, with no real championship pretensions. And, if there was one thing Hulbert wanted to do, in addition to making money, it was to be number one. So, he and Spalding put their heads together again. The NA was due to meet in March 1876, wherein the number one item on the agenda would most likely be the expulsion of the Chicago team. Hulbert figured they would anticipate the NA's actions, and form their own (new) league, and see who would expel whom.[9]

In January 1876, Hulbert met in Louisville with representatives of three other midwestern teams, the NA's St. Louis squad and independent outfits from Cincinnati and Louisville, and convinced them that a better organized new league was needed in the belief that "existing circumstances demand prompt and vigorous action."[10] What Hulbert wanted was to make major league baseball a business, run on business principles for the first time, and he wanted it to be done his way. And, of course, he wanted to keep the Big Four as well. Harold Seymour refers to Hulbert's motives as "a mixture of idealism and materialism."[11] And, unquestionably, Hulbert also wanted a winning team. In fact, Voigt says that Hulbert, following his piracy of the Big Four, was worried about a counterplot from the eastern teams that would put control of the association in Philadelphia (Harry Wright, as it turns out, had a similar issue with the City of Brotherly Love), and worse yet, force him to relinquish the Big Four.[12]

Jump ahead one month, to February 2, 1876. A mighty nor'easter is blasting the Middle Atlantic states. Wind gusts of 70 MPH are blowing everything in Manhattan into either the rivers or the harbor. Inside the Grand Central Hotel, things are hot.[13] William Hulbert is holding individual secret meetings with the representatives of the Philadelphia Athletics, the New York Mutuals, the Hartford Dark Blues, and of all teams, the Boston Red Stockings. Just how Hulbert managed to get Boston to this meeting, scheduled a month before the regular March NA meeting, is another story, involving Harry Wright. At first blush, it would seem at this point in time that Boston would have considered Hulbert in the same fashion as Larry Lucchino now thinks of George Steinbrenner. However, Wright was nobody's fool and he saw the weaknesses of the NA as clearly as anybody. Moreover, Hulbert and Spalding had gone out of their way to personally cultivate Wright to back their scheme, even asking Harry for his ideas about changing the structure of baseball, something Wright essentially knew was necessary. On his part, the Father of Professional Baseball recognized from the start that Hulbert's plan would eliminate the weaker franchises who so blithely dropped in and dropped out of the NA, thus making this new enterprise a more profitable one. No less than 15 clubs were already seeking to join the NA for the 1876 season, and, in that rush of weak sisters, Wright foresaw potential economic disaster.

Still, Harry Wright was a baseball man, and like any successful baseball executive, he probably believed on some level that, even without the Big Four, he could still rebuild his Red Stockings into a championship club—as long as those blackguards in Philadelphia didn't get their way. According to David Voigt, Wright had yet another motive for throwing in with Hulbert and Spalding: the Davy Force case. Both Wright and Hulbert remembered the ruling by the association's Judiciary Committee, headed by NA and Athletics president Chris Spering, that assigned Force to the Athletics instead of the White

Sox for the 1875 season. And, even though Wright wasn't directly involved, he didn't like the outcome. "Embittered over what he perceived as a clumsy attempt by the Athletics to dominate the Association and fearful of further plots, he wanted to crush the Philadelphians."[14]

Of course, what Hulbert would end up doing, pirating the Big Four and then personally forming his own league so he could keep them, was very similar to what his White Stockings had done to the Philadelphia White Stockings in 1873, and what the Athletics had done in the Force case, and what the White Stockings were currently seemingly in the midst of doing with the Athletics' best player.

What Hulbert was proposing was a structure that, for the first time, would create a labor-management arrangement in baseball, with the latter having the upper hand. In Spalding's words, management would be given the upper hand in the conflict between capital and labor in the great tradition of John Stuart Mill. When the eastern owners, none of whom objected to the concept of making money, quickly fell in line, baseball was no longer a hobby (at least not at the top level), it was a business. And, it was better organized.[15]

Still, the move was not without opposition, including some from Philadelphia. Even though the Athletics had been the premier name in Philadelphia baseball for more than a decade, some questions were raised as to why the Athletics, and not the Philadelphias-Pearls were brought into the NL, in light of the new rule that a city could be represented by just one franchise. The answer to that one seems pretty simple. In addition to the Athletics' long-standing status as the top club in Philadelphia, they were one of the two or three most successful teams in baseball, having won three mythical championships in the late 1860s, and the first NA pennant in 1871. You have to think that Hulbert figured out the Athletics would be a little better draw than the Philadelphians. Another factor was the Philadelphians' reputation for hippodroming, something Hulbert badly wanted to stamp out, although he did let the New York Mutuals, who were infamous for crooked play, into the league. Or, it may have been that Hulbert felt he owed the Athletics something for stealing their best player.

Sometimes lost in the fuss over the pirating of the Big Four is the fact that Hulbert had also signed Adrian Anson away from the Athletics. There are two versions of what happened. The first comes from Donald Dewey and Nicholas Acocella in the *Encyclopedia of Major League Baseball Teams*. They claim, "In exchange for gaining exclusive right to the Philadelphia territory, it [the Athletics] had to surrender first baseman Cap Anson to the Chicago franchise headed by NL founder William Hulbert."[16] That sounds like the kind of coup that Hulbert would pull, especially since, with six other teams already in his pocket, he had a fair amount of leverage in deciding who he let into the National League from the City of Brotherly Love.

The other, more common version of Anson's Philadelphia leave-taking is simpler—Hulbert pulled the same stunt on the Athletics that he pulled on the Red Stockings. Like he did with the Big Four, he signed Anson away from his original team during the 1875 season, long before the February 1876 meeting in New York. Francis Richter subscribed to that version, as did Harold Seymour, as does Bill James, as do most present-day historians. In fact, it seems fairly sure that Anson actually tried to buy his own contract back from Hulbert when his fiancée, a Philadelphia girl, objected to his playing in Chicago.[17]

What really happened? The best guess is that Anson, like the Big Four of Boston, did indeed sign with Hulbert in the summer of 1875 for the 1876 season. Then, during the February 2, 1876, meeting, or possibly during a subsequent meeting, Hulbert cut a deal with the Athletics, giving them the rights to the NL's Philadelphia market in exchange for the White Stockings keeping Anson, who would later try to buy back his 1876 contract, to no avail. The key to this puzzle is Voigt's statement that Hulbert was worried about a counterplot from the eastern teams that would force him to relinquish his ill-gotten gains, i.e., Anson and the Big Four of Boston. Thus, to forestall such an occurrence, Hulbert got Harry Wright's buy-in to his grand design, and basically coerced the Athletics into giving up any claim to Anson so they could join the league.

So, the National League was an idea whose time had come, even if it came about the wrong way. However, the timing was awful from the perspective of Philadelphia and the city's first name in baseball. For, this was 1876, the 100th anniversary of the founding of the United States. In a nation, and a city, already imbued with a sense of its own history, nothing less than a great exposition would do to celebrate the centennial of the United States. And, quite naturally, there was only one place to hold such an affair—the founding city of the U.S., the Cradle of Liberty, Philadelphia. And, it was a rousing success, both as an economic exhibition, and for the city's psyche. As Dorothy Gondos Beers noted in *Philadelphia: A 300 Year History*, "Over and above the economic benefits Philadelphia had acquired a sense of accomplishment, a conviction that its citizens could achieve results.... The Centennial was altogether a lesson of self-respect for the city; it showed its present greatness and its potentialities." Even the *Chicago Tribune* noticed that the staid old Philadelphia was gone, and that the city was now as cosmopolitan as Paris and as lively as Chicago.[18]

Now, at first glance this might seem like a promoter's dream come true: millions of people—virtually the whole world—coming to Philadelphia, now the second-largest city in the country, in the year when the Athletics would join a new and more professional league that would establish itself as unquestionably the best baseball organization in existence. But, it didn't work that way, and the Centennial turned out to be not a blessing, but a curse for baseball in the city. It brought a wave of excitement, people, notoriety and yes, money, to Philadelphia. But, none of that would be translated into gate attendance for the Athletics. The problem was that Philadelphia *was* the center of the world during 1876, and as many, including novelist Albert E. Idell, have pointed out, the world was interested in the Centennial. Americans, yes they were interested in baseball, Brazilians, not really. And, the time had not yet come when a tourist, visiting a strange city for the first time, would go out of his way to take in a ballgame. Maybe they would stop by the Philadelphia Zoo, located essentially next door to the Centennial grounds (the zoo set an admissions record in 1876 that would not be topped for 70 years), but they weren't going to hie on over to North Philly to watch the Athletics. For that matter, as Idell also made clear in his novel *Centennial Summer*, Philadelphians were themselves fixated on the 200 plus buildings within the Centennial grounds, so they weren't going out of their way to take in ballgames either.[19] This should not come as all that shocking a development, since Philadelphia's citizens had been hearing about this worldwide celebration of the nation's first 100 years since Professor John L. Campbell of Wabash College in Indiana had written to Mayor Morton McMichael in 1866, suggesting such an event. Now, as to why the Athletics' owners, who had also been hearing about this for 10 years, didn't move to make some steps to promote their team to the crowds....

The world was coming to Philadelphia, a total of 10.2 million strong during the course of the exhibition's six months (May 10 to November 10, starting less than three weeks after the baseball season, and running a month and a half after its conclusion), but this was a mixed blessing at best, since the world outside of the U.S. didn't know baseball from rounders, and was far more interested in U.S. Grant, the emperor of Brazil and all the other dignitaries visiting the Centennial, to say nothing of the exhibits from around the world, including a demonstration of Alexander Graham Bell's new invention, the telephone, the Statue of Liberty's torch, Japanese art exhibits, the Pullman Palace Car and exotic plants from all over the world in Horticultural Hall. In fact, visitors to the Centennial didn't even have to leave the grounds; two huge wooden hotels were built on site, to encourage visitors to stay nearby.

The organizers of the Centennial, in casting around for a spot to build the exposition, had hit on Belmont Plateau, the west side of Fairmount Park, as the location for their exhibits. The Fairmount Park location was just across the Schuylkill River in West Philadelphia, not really all that far (less than five miles) from the Athletics' Jefferson Street grounds.[20] However, it might as well have been on the moon. In 1876 there weren't that many convenient ways across the river, at least not from North Philadelphia. Basically, the new Girard Avenue bridge was about it. And, although the city did build a railroad spur from the Richmond Street Station right onto the exposition grounds, that line didn't go by 25th and Jefferson, and it probably wouldn't have mattered if it did—the patrons of the Centennial were far more interested in the new city that had been built on Belmont Plateau than the Athletics. As big as professional baseball still was in Philadelphia, it couldn't, or didn't, compete with a World's Fair.

Facing competition for attendees from the biggest thing ever to hit Philadelphia, the Athletics didn't have much of a chance to draw many people to North Philly, especially since the team they put on the field wasn't very good in context to its immediate compe-

A period postcard showing the grounds of the Philadelphia Centennial. Competition from the Centennial was one of the causes of the Athletics' financial failure in 1876 (courtesy Andrew Coyne).

tition anyway. While Hulbert may or may not have realized this, he nonetheless found it necessary to include teams from the two largest cities—New York and Philadelphia—in the National League, in theory a wise move to give the new organization both a commanding presence in the more populous east and to successfully cripple the National Association. And, even though the Athletics were one of only three teams (along with the Mutuals and Boston) to participate in all five seasons of the National Association, they were hardly in a favored position when the National League was formed, partly because the league's, and Hulbert's, power base was in the Midwest.

* * *

Let's compare the 1875 Athletics team that finished second in the NA with a sterling 53-20 mark, to the 1876 National League Athletics that finished seventh with a 14-45 record.

1875 (BA/SLG)
C—John Clapp .264/.339
1B—Wes Fisler .276/.347
2B—Bill Craver .319/.469
3B—Ezra Sutton .324/.402
SS—Davy Force .311/.394
OF—George Hall .299/.427
OF—Dave Eggler .302/.393
OF—George Bechtel .280/.343
UT—Adrian Anson .325/.390
UT—John Richmond .200/.216
P—Dick McBride .270/.304—44-14, 1.97 ERA

1876 (BA/SLG)
C—Fergy Malone .229/.250
1B—Ezra Sutton .297/.419
2B—Wes Fisler .288/.360
3B—Levi Meyerle .340/.449
SS—Davy Force .232/.254
OF—George Hall .366/.545
OF—Dave Eggler .299/.322
OF—William Coon .227/.259
P—Lon Knight .250/.312—10-33, 2.62 ERA
P—George Zettlein .211/.242—4-20, 3.88 ERA

At first glance, the big differences are the absence of Anson and McBride. Anson, of course, was in Chicago. McBride, after 16 years, more than 300 wins, and who knows how many pitches, finally had his strong right arm give out. Released by the Athletics even before 1875 was over (he was released in the middle of a game, for that matter), he pitched in just four games for Boston in 1876, including three in a row in June, and was done with major league baseball at the age of 31. In retrospect, although much has been made of Anson's switch from the Athletics to the White Stockings, it was the loss of Dick McBride that was the single biggest blow to Philadelphia on the field in 1876. With McBride still able to throw 538 innings in 1875, the Athletics had finished third in the NA in ERA. With Lon Knight, McBride's change pitcher in '75, and an over-the-hill George Zettlein (his Adjusted ERA was 62) handling the pitching in 1876, the Athletics were seventh in the NL in ERA, and gave up double figures in runs in 22 of their 59 games.

Manager Al Wright, a former sportswriter for the *Philadelphia Sunday Mercury*, couldn't seem to figure out who he wanted to start in the box, basically working one pitcher, then the other, for extended periods. Knight started the first nine games with some success—they were 4-5 at that point—and, after trying Meyerle twice, Wright then started Zettlein in nine of the next 10 games. Then, it was back to Knight for the next five, of which he won three, bringing their record back to 8-15, after which Zettlein was out there for 14 of the next 15, only three of which were wins. By this point, it's not hard to imagine that both pitchers were confused, since the practice at this time was still to pretty much stick with one pitcher. Knight then finished out the season by starting 16 of the last 19 games. However, the relative success he'd had earlier in the year—he was 7-6 at one point— wasn't there, as the Athletics won only three of those 16 games. Perhaps indicative of the problems Zettlein and Knight had, it took double figure scoring by Philadelphia to take nine of their 14 victories.

Although less of a factor, the offense, despite big years from Meyerle, Hall (the National League's first home run champ, with five) and Sutton, couldn't overcome bad years by Malone and Force, and the loss of Anson, and finished fifth in the league in runs scored, after having been second in the last year of the association. The Athletics' fielding didn't help the cause, either. Everywhere but at shortstop—where Force was—they were below the league fielding percentage for that position. The odd thing was, this wasn't that bad a team. Meyerle, Hall, Force and Sutton were excellent players and pretty much still prime time performers. However, Fisler and Malone were both 34, and playing in their last season of major league competition. All in all, it still added up to a bad team in the context of their league. Having culled the weak sisters out of the National Association, the National League, with only eight teams, was unquestionably a stronger circuit than its predecessor in terms of the level of play.

There were a few other highlights during the season, notably hosting the first-ever National League game at Jefferson Park. The Athletics entertained Harry Wright's Boston Red Stockings on April 22, 1876. On a cloudy day in front of a less-than-capacity 3,000 spectators, the Red Stockings scored two runs in the ninth inning on Knight to pull out a 6–5 win for Yeadon, Pennsylvania, native Joe Borden.[21] One person who did not make it out to Jefferson Park that day was President Ulysses S. Grant. Although the president was in Philadelphia on April 22, the practice of the chief executive throwing out the first ball wouldn't start until 1910, and besides, Grant was in town with his wife to get a sneak preview of the Centennial.[22]

Given a bad team and the competition from the Centennial, the Athletics also faced competition from another source. Although left out of the National League, the Philadelphias didn't pack up and go away. They played partway through the 1876 season as an independent professional team, apparently in the same ballpark on Jefferson Street as the Athletics. Then there was an "X" factor in the 1876 season. Ever since the White Stockings blew the 1873 pennant, allegations of throwing games had hung over Philadelphia baseball. Could it be that, during 1876, the Athletics, who were uncharacteristically losing games, were tarnished by proximity to the Philadelphias and their bad rep? Could that have hurt attendance as well?

When it came time for the 1876 season's final road trip, Athletics president George W. Thompson found he didn't have the train fare necessary to send the team west to Chicago and St. Louis. In trying to meet the Athletics' commitments, and following their final home game on September 16, he offered Hulbert's White Stockings and the St. Louis Brown Stockings 80 percent of the gate receipts if they would come east and play in Philadelphia instead. However, Hulbert's memory was remarkably short when it came to the reasons why the Athletics were in a financial bind. Remarkably, Hulbert answered Thompson back by complaining about the loss of five games from his own schedule, as far back as 1874! He also told Thompson he should have explained the situation prior to the White Stockings making their eastern swing, two weeks earlier.[23] The White Stockings and the Browns didn't come, and the Athletics couldn't afford to go. Everybody stayed home, Thompson canceling the eight-game road trip as well as a final three game series with the Mutuals.

That's the story of the final weeks of the 1876 season as it has always been told. However, SABR member Frank Vaccaro tells another story on his website, AllGamesBaseball.com. According to Vaccaro, the NL distributed its 1876 schedule in quarters, with the final stage being released late in August, after the Athletics had already set up a series of potentially lucrative exhibition games—something all the 1876 NL teams did to make money and fill in around the brief league schedule. Although a week without NL games was set up from August 28 to September 3, Vaccaro says there were still conflicts between the Athletics' exhibition schedule and the league schedule when it resumed on September 5, with Chicago and St. Louis visiting Philadelphia. According to Vaccaro, the Athletics would have had to break too many money-making commitments if they had gone west, so they just ignored the league schedule,[24] although that may have been because they needed the money they would garner from the exhibition games.

Whatever the reason for the Athletics' actions, they were expelled from the league at the December 1876 meeting, which shouldn't have been totally unexpected, since one of the rules in Hulbert's new constitution was that teams had to complete their full schedule. However, Voigt says the draconian action, which was taken by Hulbert himself, since he was now National League president, shocked everybody, including Spalding and Wright, no great supporter of the Athletics. Here's what Voigt says about the decision:

> Spalding described a pathetic scene in which a weeping Athletics president begged for another chance. It moved Wright to intervene and to plead that the Athletics had "repented and ... put on clean linen." But Hulbert was pitiless; after presenting charges, he demanded and got a unanimous vote for dismissal.[25]

A dramatic scene—and maybe one backed by an ulterior motive. In the April 1, 1894, *Chicago Daily Tribune* (an article discovered by Vaccaro) a sportswriter from that era, as part of a lengthy conversation with one of the local "cranks" from the 1870s, includes a remarkable statement about Cap Anson and the 1876 season: "Anson put in his first year here, having a contract to go back to Philadelphia, but the Athletics were thrown out and he staid [sic] here and has been here ever since."[26] If there ever was a hidden agenda for expelling the Athletics from the National League, this was it. The National League president who threw out the Athletics and the president of Anson's 1876 team, the Chicago White Stockings, were one and the same—William Hulbert. After 15 seasons of playing at the highest level of baseball, the original Philadelphia Athletics had been summarily dismissed from the national scene—by William Hulbert.

◆ CHAPTER 9 ◆

The Beer and Whiskey League Comes to Philadelphia

After the 1876 season, the Athletics resumed life as one of the hundreds of independent clubs playing ball throughout the nation, initially as part of the loosely-organized League Alliance. Over the next few years, according the historian Jerrold Casway, teams called Athletics drifted in and out of several regional leagues as semi-pro teams,[1] and the name wasn't seen in the best baseball circles until 1882, when the American Association was formed in competition to the National League. Whatever anyone may think of William Hulbert's actions or motives in the formation of the National League, at least it's pretty clear what happened and when in 1876. As befitting an organization also known as the "Beer and Whiskey League" (most of the owners were in spirits-related businesses) and about which Francis Richter would say, "it paltered through 10 years of varying fortunes, always handicapped by incompetence and deceit,"[2] the exact chronology of the formation of the American Association, and Philadelphia's role in same, is open to interpretation, depending on which story you believe.

The most significant action for any Philadelphia team between 1877 and 1882 came during the 1881 season, when a squad known as the Athletics, and owned primarily by theatrical producer Bill Sharsig, made a western tour through Pittsburgh, Columbus, Louisville and Cincinnati—ending up in St. Louis at the invitation of Albert Spink, St. Louis baseball booster and future publisher of *The Sporting News*.[3] This team was managed along its trip by Philadelphian Horace Phillips, also known as "Hustling Horace."

However, these Athletics were not the same team founded by the singing society in 1860. There are two versions of these Athletics' start-up. One comes from Donald Dewey and Nicholas Acocella in the *Encyclopedia of Major League Baseball Teams,* who state that this particular team of Athletics was *started* by Sharsig, after borrowing his mother's life savings. In a similar vein, Casway says that this last embodiment of the Philadelphia A's merely laid claim to the name.[4] On the other hand, David Nemec, in his history of the AA, *The Beer & Whiskey League*, says that Sharsig, along with former player Charlie Mason, *re-organized* the Athletics as a semi-pro club in 1880.[5] The true story? The previous 1880 Athletics team, that included Mason as player, had folded in the summer of 1880. Mason then partnered with Sharsig (the money man) in a September 1880 "pick-up" of the earlier team, the second 1880 Athletics including a few of the previous team's players, including Mason.[6] Phillips joined in as manager some time before the start of the 1881 season, leaving the team before the organization of the AA. Also involved, most likely after the Athletics' application to the AA, was someone Sharsig presumably met in the entertainment industry, Lew Simmons—a minstrel by trade.

One of the significant aspects of the 1881 trip was that none of the cities the Athletics visited was affiliated with the National League, and all were cities with major league pretensions. According to Richter, "This tour aroused Base Ball interest to such a degree that Justus Thorner, of Cincinnati, and H.D. McKnight, of Pittsburgh, set about the task of organizing a new league of national proportions."[7] While there was some truth in Richter's statement, a lot of other things happened, and several other people got involved, before Thorner and McKnight came on the scene. A series of meetings were held in September, October and November 1881, in various locations and with various participants. The first was held in a Philadelphia hotel room in September, between the 28-year-old Phillips and one of the great baseball writers of the nineteenth century—Oliver Hazard Perry (O.P. or Opie) Caylor of the *Cincinnati Commercial*. At the time of this meeting, Phillips had jumped ship from Sharsig's Athletics, since both Harold Seymour and David Nemec identify him at this time as being the manager of the newly-reformed Philadelphias team, run by Al Reach.

One thing that does seem clear is that Hustling Horace was in the middle of things from the beginning. Caylor, who had previously been working with Thorner, ex-president of the National League's Cincinnati franchise, on trying to bring about the return to major leagues of the Queen City, was in Philadelphia because a postcard from Phillips had fallen into his hands. It seems as if, sparked by his tour with the Athletics, Phillips had been emboldened enough to send out postcards to prominent baseball figures in the cities the Athletics had visited, inviting them to a meeting in Philadelphia. However, only Caylor from Cincinnati responded to the invitation. Undaunted, Phillips and Caylor talked most of the night, and they pressed on, planning another meeting,[8] although exactly what happened in regards to that meeting is a little murky. Probably the best known part of this story involves somebody, maybe Phillips, maybe Caylor, sending telegrams (or postcards) to everyone who didn't attend the first meeting, implying that they were the only city that did not send a representative, and inviting them to another meeting. What's uncertain is whether these missives were sent from the under-attended meeting in Philadelphia, or from an under-attended second meeting in Pittsburgh in October. There's also a parallel story that Caylor, finding himself in a Pittsburgh saloon, asked the barkeeper, a baseball fan named Al Pratt, if he had any local connections. Pratt, in turn, is supposed to have introduced Caylor to Denny McKnight.[9]

These were all preliminaries to a November 2, 1881, meeting at the Gibson House in Cincinnati—the Queen City reps and Phillips were the driving forces behind the new league—which stands as the first formal meeting of the American Association. McKnight (representing Pittsburgh) and Thorner were there, as were Caylor and Phillips. However, much to Hustling Horace's dismay, so was a representative from his old team, a player on the 1881 Athletics and now the Athletics' shortstop-manager, Chick Fulmer. Others in attendance included representatives from New York, Brooklyn, St. Louis, Louisville and Boston, although the latter three cities in attendance represented just one team or faction. As a result the first order of business on November 2 was to try and settle the territorial disputes between the Athletics and Philadelphias, and the Metropolitans (New York) and Atlantics (Brooklyn).

In the case of the two Philadelphia candidates, this proved to be easier said than done. First, Fulmer claimed that the Athletics could put up $5000 that very day. Considering it was only six years since the National Association required just a $10 admission fee, this must have impressed the rest of the group. Undeterred, Phillips said the Philadelphias also had plenty of financial backing—which would have been true if Reach, already a wealthy

9. The Beer and Whiskey League Comes to Philadelphia 99

The peripatetic Chick Fulmer sits third from the left in the middle row of this picture of the 1876 Louisville Grays. In 1882, he jumped from the Philadelphia Athletics to the Cincinnati Red Stockings before the first AA season opened (courtesy John Thorn).

man, was the owner. While the two greater New York factions then took center stage to argue their cases, Caylor pulled Phillips aside and suggested that, since Philly was vital to the success of this new American Association, he and Fulmer should consolidate their efforts. Both parties agreed—if only temporarily. The next day, McKnight was formally elected the first president of the American Association, while Fulmer, ostensibly representing a team called the Philadelphia Athletics, was elected to the board of directors. Where was Phillips? Caylor had previously convinced Hustling Horace, apparently as early as the October meeting, that although the two of them were the real founders of the league, they needed to stay in the background as much as possible.[10]

When the meeting ended, the various participants, now representing AA teams in Philadelphia, Pittsburgh, St. Louis, Cincinnati, Louisville and Brooklyn, scattered throughout the east and midwest to start recruiting players, with the popular wisdom holding that the Athletics, as well as the Louisville Eclipse and Chris Von der Ahe's St. Louis Browns had a leg up, since they were already-established semi-pro teams. However, Cincinnati had a secret weapon—O.P. Caylor, and he helped recruit a team that would end up by far the best in the AA in 1882.

The principals re-assembled in Philadelphia for the association's spring meeting on March 13, 1882. Quite a lot had happened in the preceding four months, including Brooklyn having to withdraw for lack of a playing field (Baltimore joined in their place), and the Philadelphia group having once again split into two factions, although Seymour says the Athletics and Philadelphias never really did consolidate. Whether or not the two Philadelphia teams ever formally and truly joined together, pretty much everybody agrees that the Athletics finally got the nod from the association because they had access to playing grounds. Sharsig had had the foresight to keep his rights on the Oakdale Grounds at 11th and Cumberland, where his "re-organized" Athletics had played some in 1880.[11]

Part of the fallout of this pas de deux by the two Philadelphia teams was the exclusion of Horace Phillips from his brainchild. Phillips stuck with Reach's Philadelphias, and had been aced out of a spot in the association when the league went with the Athletics—who were now without the services of Chick Fulmer as well. Correctly believing that Caylor and Cincinnati had their act together better than any of the other five teams, Fulmer, a highly-prized defensive shortstop-second baseman, had left the Athletics and joined up with the Reds.[12] This series of moves also left Al Reach and his Philadelphias out of the association. Reach's partner, Ben Shibe, who at first owned a piece of the Philadelphias, then became a minority partner in the Sharsig-Simmons-Mason Athletics.[13]

Horace Phillips wasn't called Hustling for nothing though. He went back to managing Reach's Philadelphias in the League Alliance until a July 30 contretemps in an exhibition game between St. Louis and Cincinnati led to a call to fire AA umpire Tom Carey. McKnight backed the Browns' lobbying to can Carey and, in his place, called Phillips back from the Philadelphias—to umpire in the association. However, McKnight changed his mind before Phillips could actually start umpiring, deciding he needed help with running the Pittsburgh Alleghenys. Although Pratt was managing the Pittsburgh team, and would do for the entire year, Phillips was hired on in some executive capacity with the team, so that McKnight could better devote himself to his duties of running the association.[14]

First, though, came the start of the 1882 season in the American Association, wherein the Athletics had the Philadelphia major league field entirely to themselves. The field they had, Oakdale Park, was a little—so little that it boosted offensive totals 12 percent during the A's one year there—wooden park located at 11th and Cumberland Streets in North Philadelphia that had been a popular amateur field since just after the Civil War. However, Oakdale was just a stopgap for Sharsig and company. Ultimately a means to obtain the AA franchise, the park was sold off after the 1882 season and the Athletics moved "back" to the Jefferson Street Grounds, former home of two of the three Philadelphia National Association teams as well as the 1876 National League Athletics.[15]

Bereft of Chick Fulmer, their best player from the 1881 season who was also going to be the Athletics' manager as well in 1882, the three Athletics owners' first jobs were to find a second baseman and a manager. The latter slot ended up going to a "big" name veteran ballplayer, 29-year-old Juice Latham. Other than playing in the National Association in 1875, and spending 1877 with the ill-fated Louisville Grays team that threw the National League pennant, Latham had played in the minors, mostly in his hometown of Utica, New York, for the last decade. The "big" part came from the fact that, by the time he got to Philadelphia, the 5-8 Latham was well on his way to 250 pounds. Fulmer's second base spot went to one of the Athletics' five Philadelphia natives, major league rookie John "Cub" Stricker. Although he would hit only .217 in 1882, he had an excellent year in the field, with both his fielding (.904 to .882) and range factors (6.81 to 5.79) well above the association averages. Born John A. Streaker in Philadelphia on February 15, 1860, he had played baseball under the name Stricker in Philadelphia since 1879. As for the "Cub" moniker, he was one of the smallest men to play major league baseball, standing just 5-3 and weighing 138 pounds. That handicap notwithstanding, he would go on to an 11-year, 1196-game major league career through the 1885 season, mostly in Cleveland and Philadelphia. Although he never hit much, his career Adjusted OPS being just 78, he got by on quickness, stealing as many as 86 bases in a year, and retiring with a range factor above the league average (5.97 to 5.79). In all, a dozen players would see action in more than 20 games for the 1882 Athletics, and Stricker would by far have the longest major league career. Not one regular on the 1882 Athletics had played in the National League in 1881. Sharsig, Simmons and Mason put their team together partly from their 1881 semi-pros—Stricker, catcher Jack O'Brien, outfielder Jud Birchall, pitcher Sam Weaver and pitcher Doc Landis—plus whatever spare parts they could find.

And what did that get Philadelphia for 1882? Surprisingly, second place, with a 41-34 record. Although all observers on the baseball scene in 1882 agreed that the association was weaker than the league, looking at the Athletics' roster and their yearly records, it is tempting to conclude that either Latham was a tremendous manager, or the Athletics were real lucky. The Cincinnati Red Stockings had by far the best team, running off to an 11-and-a-half game margin of victory, although the Athletics were in first in early June and kept it close until the end of July, when they were just three games out, before slowly falling back. Even though they were still only four-and-a-half out on August 20, they ended up finishing just ahead of Louisville, Pittsburgh and St. Louis in what became a tighter race for second than there was for first.

On May 2 at Oakdale Park the second major league incarnation of the Philadelphia Athletics took the field against the hastily-assembled Baltimore Orioles. Here's the lineup Latham put in the field that day for what would become a 10–7 Philadelphia win:

RF—Jerry Dorgan	LF—Jud Birchall	3B—Bob Blakiston
SS—Lew Say	P—Sam Weaver	2B—Cub Stricker
1B—Juice Latham	C—Jack O'Brien	CF—Doc Landis[16]

Leadoff man Dorgan, despite supposedly being a player of promise, had just 10 games of previous major league experience, with Worcester in 1880. He would play only 44 of the Athletics' 75 games and hit .282 in '82. Shortstop Say, like Latham, was a National Association player put out of major league work years before by that league's folding. Although he and his younger brother Jimmy were both fine defensive shortstops, neither hit much (Lew .226, Jimmy .207) in splitting the position, and each would play only a couple of years more in the majors. On a team that totaled just five home runs and 21 triples on the year, Germantown native Birchall, who'd been playing in Philly since 1877, was as good a cleanup hitter as Latham had—he finished the year with 12 doubles, and led the squad in runs scored with 65. Still, the best hitter on the team, and its unquestioned MVP was catcher and Philadelphia native Jack O'Brien.

One of the Athletics' semi-pro players from 1881, O'Brien was making his major league debut on May 2, 1882, at the age of 22, although he'd been playing independent ball in Philly since at least 1880. O'Brien would catch 45 of the Athletics' games, switching off mostly with Dorgan, and appear in the outfield in another 18. Finishing the year at .303/.339/.419, he would end up in the top 10 in the AA in nine offensive categories, including fourth in home runs (3), OPS (.758), on base percentage (.339) and batting average as one of only four .300 hitters in the entire league. Although 1882 was his best year—the quality of play in the AA got better very quickly—he would stay on as the Athletics' pretty-much regular catcher until 1886, and then return to the team for his final season in 1890.

Blakiston, the team's only rookie not from Philadelphia—he was a San Franciscan—hit .228 on the year and didn't last long past a part-time job in 1883. He was, however, at least an interesting character. Born Robert Blackstone, he claimed to be a descendent of *the* Blackstone, of English jurisprudence fame.[17] The number nine hole batter, Doc Landis, was another Philadelphian from the 1881 team who had been playing top level ball in Philly as far back as 1877. He was designated the change pitcher for this game and was quickly sent to Baltimore, where he became the Orioles' primary man in the box for his one major league season—a 12-28 record (1-1 with the Athletics). Yet another player without experience in either the NL or the NA, John Mansell, the youngest of three baseball-playing brothers, ended up playing more centerfield for the Athletics than anyone else, however, he was injured part-way through the year and released, ending his major league tenure on July 22.

One player who was not in the Athletics lineup, nor on their roster on May 2, was second baseman-shortstop John "Dasher" Troy—the cause of the first big blow up between the association and the league. Even though he'd played in only 11 games for the Detroit Wolverines in 1881, Hulbert and his cronies in the league considered Troy, and Sam Wise, another Detroit sub who signed with the AA Reds around the same time, its property, and raised the roof when he signed with the Athletics before the 1882 season started. Understand that the Troy and Wise contracts were not property of the Detroit NL team at the time they signed with the association, and, and such, they were not contract jumpers. As a couple of scrubs, they hadn't been reserved by the Wolverines, who, at this time, could invoke the reserve clause on only five players. Hulbert did not want this new venture using National League players. When Troy and Wise subsequently broke their AA contracts and jumped back to the National League, McKnight made the statement that the league saw the association as a dangerous rival, and, by pirating Troy and Wise back again, were trying to break up the AA. Lew Simmons, far from the coolest head in Athletic management, was equally distressed at Detroit's "stealing" of his player. Thus was drawn a battle line that would flare up from time to time throughout the American Association's entire 10-year existence, and which started immediately after l'affair Troy-Wise with the AA 1) allowing blacklisted NL players to apply to the new league, 2) creating its own minor league farm system, and 3) starting legal action to recover players from the NL.[18]

The bulk of the Athletics' pitching in 1882 would be done by Sam Weaver and Bill Sweeney, but Latham gave no fewer than five other players a chance to start in the box. This was somewhat of an unusual use of pitchers in a league where the Reds' top three pitchers started 79 of their 80 games, the Pittsburgh Alleghenys' top three pitchers started 75 of their 79 games, and Tony Mullane by himself started 55 of Louisville's 80 games.

After playing center for the opener, Landis started the next two association games for Philadelphia against Baltimore, and then was sent over to the Orioles. Although Weaver started seven of the next 10 games, Latham also gave starts to Charlie Reynolds (a 9–8 win and a 9–3 loss) and Ed Halbriter (a 12–8 loss), thus accounting for the sum total of those two worthies' major league careers. For the month of June, Latham more or less alternated Weaver with Frank Mountain in the box. Mountain was pretty bad, going 2-6 in his eight starts, with an Adjusted ERA of 76. His last start came on June 20, a week before the Athletics brought in Bill Sweeney to take his place. Mountain had a tough year, bouncing back and forth between the Athletics and the Worcester Ruby Legs of the National League, and going 4-22 overall. Still, it may have been that Latham thought he saw something in Mountain. The young — he turned 22 during the season — pitcher came back with Columbus' AA franchise in 1883 and 1884 and won 49 games.

For the last three months of the season, Latham alternated Sam Weaver and Bill Sweeney in the box. Weaver, though hardly a star, was a known commodity, having pitched for Philadelphia teams throughout the 1870s and '80s. Sweeney, on the other hand, is something of a mystery. Although he pitched in the major leagues for only six years between 1875 and 1886, Weaver managed to pitch for three different Philadelphia teams in three different leagues. Born on July 10, 1855, in Philadelphia, Weaver pitched a six-inning, 17–2 complete game win for the Philadelphia Pearls on October 25, 1875 — the last game of the season, and the Pearls' last game in the majors — striking out 12. That was his only major league experience until he became the Milwaukee Grays' main starter in 1878, going 12-31 despite a 1.95 ERA (Adjusted ERA 135). After pitching for the 1880 and '81 Athletics, he went 26-15 with an Adjusted ERA of 109 in 1882. Although Nemec says Weaver "drifted off" to another team in 1883, in this case the Louisville Eclipse, for whom he went 26-22, the more likely the cause of his drift was Bobby Mathews, the ace Sharsig brought in for 1883 to lead them to fame and fortune. Weaver next showed up in Philadelphia in 1884 with the Union Association Keystones (5-10) before finishing his career with two losses for the 1886 Athletics. Overall, he went 70-80 in his major league career, 32-27 during his four stays in Philadelphia.

Right-handed pitcher William J. Sweeney is one of the mystery men of the game. He first appeared in the Athletics' lineup on June 27, playing in the outfield, and he started his first game in the pitcher's box on June 30, a 7–1 win over the Alleghenys. He would eventually start 20 games for the Athletics, going 9-10 with about a league-average 2.91 ERA, and playing five games in the outfield, batting .159 overall. Where was he playing beforehand? Where did he come from? Where was he born? How did the Athletics find him? How old was he? Did he bat left-handed or right-handed? All unknowns. Nemec has a sketch of him drawn in 1880 in *The Beer & Whiskey League*, and reports that he went back to pitching in the minors for Cleveland of the Western League after an 1884 season wherein he won 40 games for the Baltimore Monumentals of the Union Association, making Sweeney the only pitcher in major league history to win 40 games (40-21, 2.59 ERA with 374 strikeouts in 538 innings) in his last major league season.[19] Since he died in Philadelphia on August 2, 1903, we might postulate that, like many of his 1882 Athletics teammates, he was a native Philadelphian.

Between the rookies, the NA left-overs, the mysterious and unsettled pitching staff, it had actually been a pretty good return to the big leagues for Philadelphia, and although no attendance figures are available for Oakdale Park, it is known that the Athletics made money on the year, as did all the 1882 AA teams.[20] However, that wasn't enough for Sharsig, Simmons and Mason. Carrying the proudest name in Philadelphia sports, they wanted more—a better park, better players, and another title to add to the name Athletic. They would get all three in 1883, thanks in part to the best all-round player the AA would ever see, and a little spitballer that most people thought was over the hill.

♦ CHAPTER 10 ♦

A Pennant for the Athletics

In the 30 years between the original Athletics' 1871 pennant, and the advent of Connie Mack's sixth version of the Athletics in 1901, Philadelphia baseball fans had a lot to cheer about but never so much as during the 1883 season, when the third generation Athletics brought the city its only first place finish within a 31-year (1871 to 1902) span. In addition, 1883 marked the return of the National League to Philadelphia. Although this was an event with more long-term significance than the Athletics' championship, it was not so recognized at the time since not only were the Athletics big winners and the Phillies big losers, but the Athletics were the established team, carrying the more recognizable name. The big baseball story in Philly in '83 was the Athletics.

Although the Athletics had certainly been successful in 1882, there were big changes in store for 1883. This was due to a variety of circumstances—Oakdale Park being sold,[1] players changing teams, and the aggressive posture of the pennant-winning Cincinnati squad—O.P. Caylor wasn't letting any grass grow under his Red Stockings in his attempt to win another title. As they often did in these days of limited reserve clauses, players were jumping to and fro in the winter of 1882-83, especially in light of the Troy-Wise case. With Juice Latham having taken his large self, he was now nicknamed "Jumbo," to Louisville, the Athletics first needed a manager, or, at least, someone to run the team on the field. Exactly who this was is a matter of some dispute. Most of the encyclopedias say that Simmons, the former minstrel, was the Athletics' manager in 1883. However, Simmons' main skills were verbal—singing and debating—and he was hardly a "baseball man." Thus, it is easier to believe other sources, including the Baseball-Reference website, that team captain Lon Knight was the de facto manager of the '83 Athletics.[2] This would not have been an unusual development, since this was still the era when the captain really did most of what is now called managing. For instance, New York Giants "manager" Jim Mutrie, a couple of years after this, would spend games running about the stands in a top hat and tails, exhorting the fans with the Giants' slogan, "We are the People." Maybe that's what Simmons did after the games started; as a former minstrel, he would have made a good early day Phillie Phantic. Simmons' biggest contribution to the 1883 season may have been his attendance at the February 17, 1883, meeting in New York between the association and the league, where a temporary peace was formed, most notably by the association agreeing to honor the league's reserve rule (the AA did not have a reserve rule at this point), which now extended to 11 players per team, and the league grudgingly granting the association "major league" status.[3]

Alonzo Knight was still another Philadelphia native, and a former Athletic in both the National Association and the National League, who left the major leagues along with the original Athletics when they were shown the door by William Hulbert in 1876. He reappeared in Worcester in 1880 as an outfielder, and then spent the 1881 and 1882 seasons as a regular outfielder for the Detroit Wolverines. After he hit only .207 in 1882, Detroit decided not to reserve him, and he was free to come back home to Philadelphia as field captain and right fielder, and to have his best single season in the process, finishing third in the association in doubles (23) and fourth in runs scored (98), as well as making the top 10 in triples (9), RBIs (53) and extra-base hits (33). And that's how the Athletics won the pennant—they could hit, hit for power, and get on base. For the year, the Athletics finished 66-32, and led the league in most of the significant offensive categories, including runs (720, or 7.3 per game), hits, doubles, walks, batting average and on base percentage. They were second in home runs and slugging percentage. So potent was their offense that no less than four of their players were among the top seven in the AA in runs scored.

The three owners and Knight needed a place to put all these hitters. With Oakdale Park, which really wasn't satisfactory anyway, having been sold to a developer who thought the land too valuable for a ballpark, Sharsig went back to the Athletics' roots—Jefferson Park, at 25th and Jefferson—where the original Athletics had moved when their field at Camac Woods had been sold out from under them in 1870. The Athletics celebrated their return to their new-old renovated field on April 7, 1883, by shutting out Yale (whose team included a pitcher named Daniel Jones, who would play a much larger role in the Athletics' season) 12–0. After three more exhibition wins against the Hartsville, Auburn and

The nineteenth century Athletics have not been totally forgotten in Philadelphia. Pictured is part of Athletic Recreation Center in the 1400 block of North 27th Street, the former site of Jefferson Park and the only former major league baseball site in the city of Philadelphia still used for recreational purposes. The entire complex is now known as "Athletic Square" in honor of Harry Stovey, Bobby Matthews, Billy Sharsig, et al. (courtesy Matthew J. Coyne).

Trenton clubs, they came up against the Phillies, in Philly's first City Series.[4] The teams split six games. The Phillies, who had just been hastily thrown together by Al Reach and Bob Ferguson, won the first three, and the Athletics the final three. That may not have boded well for the quality of the AA's play as opposed to that of the league, but it was relatively speaking a good sign for the Athletics. The other three AA teams that played preseason exhibitions against league counterparts—Pittsburgh, Baltimore and New York—went 1-24.[5] So, it may have been with good reason that the Athletics were considered the favorites before the AA started its second season.

What may or may not have seemed reasonable, at least to the players, was a set of 10 rules of conduct that the Athletics' three owners also set in place before the season started. In keeping somewhat with the moralities of the 1880s, Sharsig, Simmons and Mason decreed that their players were, among other things, prohibited from smoking after eating their pre-game meal, and consorting with members of the opposite sex while in uniform. They also imposed an 11:30 p.m. curfew after road games.[6] Whatever the players seemed to think about the rules, it must not have affected their play on the field in a negative fashion, as they won their first four games, lost a 15–7 slugfest at Baltimore, and then proceeded to win 13 of their next 14, so that after the first game of a May 30 doubleheader, they stood 17–2, probably causing the rest of the association to ask, "Who are these guys?"

First and foremost, they were Harry Stovey. The big prize in the Athletics' talent hunt over the winter of 1882–83, Harry Duffield Stow could do everything on a ball field, and do it all better than almost anyone else in baseball at this time. A native Philadelphian with one of the best pedigrees imaginable—he was related to John Stow, one of the 1753 recasters of the Liberty Bell—he changed his last name to Stovey when he first entered professional baseball, so his mother wouldn't know. That debut came late in the 1877 season, as a pitcher with the original Philadelphia Athletics, then playing in the League Alliance. By the 1883 season, he was a 26-year-old, three-year veteran of the National League. And, unlike many of the players who jumped to the AA, he was anything but a scrub or an afterthought. The only explanation as to why the league let him get away was that his 1882 team, the Worcester Ruby Legs, had disbanded and the franchise that took their place, the Phillies, had a right to only the Worcester franchise, and not its players. Thus, Stovey was a free agent, not reserved by any team, and slipped through the cracks to the Athletics. As a Philadelphia native, Stovey was in the unique position of having a choice as to where to come home to after the 1882 season. That he chose the Athletics would have significant consequences for baseball, and not just in Philadelphia, for the next nine years. In fact, Stovey was so good, and so valuable, that David Nemec says that AA officials artificially inflated his batting averages in their official reports just to make the league even more jealous that they'd lost a star of such magnitude.

Stovey didn't need any artificial PR help, and you have to think that the league knew very well what they'd lost. Before he'd ever set foot in Jefferson Park, he'd led the National League in triples, extra-base hits and home runs, all with Worcester in his rookie season of 1880. He'd also finished in the top five in OPS, total bases, slugging percentage, doubles and runs scored in his first three years in the NL, alternating between first base and the outfield. And, he could run, too. "Stovey was also a daring and intelligent baserunner who, at one time, was credited (erroneously) with the single-season record for stolen bases and who is believed by many authorities to have pioneered the use of sliding pads," says Nemec.[7] A better-than-average fielder with a good arm, a legacy of his pitching days, and excellent range, Stovey could truly do it all on a diamond.

However, even Harry Stovey couldn't win a pennant by himself. He had a little help. In this case, little meant 5-5, 140 pound right-handed pitcher Bobby Mathews. The two pitchers who had handled the chores in the box for the Athletics in the second half of the 1882 season, Sam Weaver and Bill Sweeney, were both elsewhere and the only other 1882 Athletics' hurler to throw more than 17 innings, Frank Mountain, was long gone. Hence, captain Knight needed an entire new pitching staff. Although they ultimately had five pitchers play significant roles during the year, there shouldn't be much doubt that Mathews, despite his small size, was expected to carry the load. The National Association's ERA champion in 1874, he had also led the NA in strikeouts twice, while throwing what was probably the first spitball in history. In fact, he was throwing the pitch back in the NABBP days, and baffling hitters with it. By 1883 he was 31 years old, had won 191 games since his NA debut with Fort Wayne in 1871, and was coming off something of a comeback season with the National League's Boston Red Caps, wherein he went 19-15 with a league average ERA of 2.87. After winning only 20 major league games since 1877 — mostly due to bad teams, unstable teams and a couple of trips out of the major leagues — he had spent 1882 splitting the Boston mound duties with Jim Whitney. Boston apparently decided to reserve only one pitcher for 1883, and kept Whitney. Mathews was, as the 1883 season opened, essentially a good, though somewhat elderly for the time, major league pitcher. And that was a fairly rare commodity in the AA's second season. On his part, Mathews would open the Athletics' 1883 season on May 1 with a 4–0 shutout of Pittsburgh, the only shutout Philadelphia would have all year. Mathews would go 30-13 with an Adjusted ERA of 141 (actual ERA 2.46) as the bellwether of the team's pitching staff. The rest of the Athletics' hurlers included another veteran, 30-year-old George Bradley, and another refugee from the defunct Worcester team, Fred Corey. Nineteen-year-old Jersey Bakely was also around, mostly at the start of the year, and former Yalie Daniel Jones, now known as Jumping Jack Jones, would appear late in the year, though in a significant cameo role as Mathews wore down.

George Washington "Grin" Bradley, like Mathews, was a veteran of the National Association and the early days of the National League. From his performance in the NL's inaugural season, the Reading, Pennsylvania, native still holds the major league record (in a tie with Grover Cleveland Alexander) for shutouts in a season, with 16. However, his first two years in the box, when he went 78-45 for St. Louis, were by far his best. Except for 1880 with Providence (13–8) he hadn't had a winning season since 1876, and had pitched just 18 games for the Cleveland Blues in 1882. He was seemingly just another pitcher who had thrown his arm out by pitching almost 2000 innings in his first four seasons, which is probably why he was available to the Athletics for $500 from the NL Cleveland Spiders in mid–June. Although he'd pitch only 214 innings in 1883—not a lot at this time—he would go 16-7 with a 110 Adjusted ERA as Mathews' (who pitched 44 games and 381 innings) main back-up. When Bradley wasn't pitching, he was otherwise earning his keep as the team's most regular third baseman.

Corey had done all of his previous major league pitching in New England, with Providence and Worcester. Actually, pitching was his second job; he played 237 games at third and pitched in 93 games during his seven-year career, when he also wasn't playing outfield (83 games) or short (38 games). He also played 11 games at second, seven at first and caught once for good measure. Although there was a lot less specialization in baseball in this era, there weren't many people who appeared at all the positions. Since he really hadn't been a very good pitcher for Providence and Worcester (16-39), it's logical to wonder why the

Athletics wanted him in the first place, especially since he was coming off a 1-13 year in the box, a season where he'd actually played short more than he'd pitched. In the end, Sharsig and Knight wanted him as a spare infielder who could also pitch in a pinch. In fact, he ended up splitting the third base position with Bradley. Corey ended up playing 34 games at third, and pitching in only 18. But, he did have his first-ever winning season in the box, going 10-7 with a 102 Adjusted ERA.

However, the Athletics initially faced starting the season with just a utility player (Corey) backing up their little ace, since Bradley didn't join up with the team from Cleveland until June 12. Casting about for help, they came across Edward "Jersey" Bakely from across the Delaware River. A native of Blackwood, New Jersey, Bakely had just turned 19 a month before his major league debut, a 5–3 win against the Metropolitans that boosted the Athletics' record to 6-1. He would end up starting seven of the Athletics' first 22 games (Corey pitched only twice in that span), going 5-2. After his June 2 start against Columbus, and an 8–6 loss, he wasn't heard from again until August 6, when he started one last time and was bombed by Baltimore 14–9. Unlike many prodigies, he would have a fairly long, though not terribly successful, career, pitching off-and-on in the majors until he was 27 in 1891, going 76-125 overall. And, he would re-appear in Philadelphia in 1884.

So, captain Knight started the year with a pitching staff of Mathews, backed up by a teenager and a third baseman. As great as Mathews was—he started the season 13-2—he wasn't doing it all by himself. In the context of the AA's second season, he had a pretty good lineup behind him, although this may be the only time in major league history that a pitcher-third baseman and a third baseman-pitcher platooned at the hot corner.

The 1883 Athletics:

C—Jack O'Brien	3B—George Bradley	OF—Jud Birchall
1B—Harry Stovey	Frank Corey	OF—Lon Knight
2B—Cub Stricker	SS—Mike Moynahan	OF—Bob Blakiston

Blakiston, who was moved off of third base by the Corey-Bradley combo, didn't play all that much, only getting 167 at-bats on the year, nowhere near as many as Bradley (312) and Corey (298). Two other players, Ed Rowen and Bill Crowley, also saw a fair amount of action, Rowen as O'Brien's backup, while Crowley, O'Brien and Blakiston basically split the third outfield position. Even though the Athletics had finished second in 1882, Sharsig had made wholesale changes for 1883—only his three 1881 regulars, O'Brien, Stricker and Birchall, were back at their same positions.

The 1882 Athletics:

C—Jack O' Brien	3B—Bob Blakiston	OF—John Mansell
1B—Juice Latham	SS—Lou Say	OF—Jerry Dorgan
2B—Cub Stricker	OF—Jud Birchall	

In addition to having a superstar at first, and Knight having his best season in the outfield, the other spot where the 1883 team improved the most was the double play combination. Stricker began to show the skills that would keep him in the majors for 11 years, raising his average to .273. Moynahan was a revelation, and a huge upgrade from the Say brothers. An infielder-outfielder for three National League teams in 1880 and 1881, Moynahan was the AA's top shortstop in 1883, hitting .310/.360/.412 and finishing in the top 10 in the association in 14 different batting categories, including second in walks (31), third in on base percentage (.360) and fourth in RBIs (67). Out of the majors in '82, he came to the Athletics from the Philadelphias—the independent team, not the new National

League franchise. Just the fact that he was able to play was remarkable, because he'd broken a finger on his throwing hand so badly in May 1882 that part of the digit had to be amputated.[8] He also fell fast, playing just 13 major league games in 1884 and not even being able to keep a job in the minors by year's end.

Although no team by this point in the game's sophistication could maintain a 17-2 start, the Athletics were able to build up a five-and-a-half game lead on the defending champion Cincinnati Red Stockings by early June. However, Mathews cooled off from his hot start, and Bradley wasn't much help as he started only three games between June 12 and July 10. After the Athletics lost three straight in Cincinnati to Will White, the 22-11 Browns momentarily took over first place on June 20, a half game ahead of 21-11 Philadelphia and Louisville, and a game ahead of 20-11 Cincinnati. Although the Metropolitans would come on strong later in the year, the standings on June 20 pretty much reflected the AA's season

Five foot, three inch Cub Stricker, second baseman for the Athletics' 1883 pennant winners (Library of Congress photograph).

as a whole: Columbus, Pittsburgh and Baltimore were terrible, eventually going a collective 91-200, and the other five teams were pretty good.

A couple of wins from Corey, and Mathews getting back on track, soon helped the Athletics back into first. In fact, after an 11–1 loss to the Reds on June 20, they proceeded to win six straight—four by Mathews, two by Corey, although they also scored seven runs or more in five of those wins. By the end of July, Philadelphia, St. Louis and Cincinnati were pulling away, thanks in part to a 22–7 run that took the Athletics through to August 4. At that point, they were back in first by two games over the equally-hot St. Louis Browns, while the Reds were once again five-and-a-half back and the Colonels trailed by seven. On August 21, Caylor's Red Stockings came to Jefferson Park and took three out of four, putting the Browns (52-24) back in first by a game over the 50-24 Athletics, but only bringing Cincy within five-and-a-half again. The Reds never really made another move, possibly because they were pitching Will White, admittedly a great pitcher (he'd end up leading the association in wins with 43 and ERA with 2.09), almost every day, and the Athletics had come up with a secret weapon. Although Bradley was now taking a regular turn in the box, little Bobby Mathews' arm was hanging—he went 16 days, from September 1 to September 17, without pitching at all, which would have put Knight in a tremendous bind, if it wasn't for the addition of Jumping Jack Jones.

Daniel Albion Jones was a 22-year-old pitcher out of Yale who originally signed with one of the Athletics' two favorite League feeder teams—the Detroit Wolverines—for the 1883 season. Jones went 6-5 with an 89 Adjusted ERA in 12 games for Detroit, who apparently decided they didn't need him. Philadelphia most certainly did, and he took the box for the first time on September 4, beating Tony Mullane and the Browns 11–1. He beat them 5–4 again the next day, and then won two from Columbus in the next series—all this during the period when Mathews wasn't pitching. Jones' timely arrival in Philadelphia boosted the Athletics' lead to three games, the largest it had been since mid–June. It also didn't hurt that Bradley won three straight decisions during his time as well. In fact, the Athletics won seven in a row while Mathews was out, with Bradley and Jones getting all the wins. While it is true that Mathews was their ace for most of the year, the Athletics were carried down the stretch by Grin Bradley and Jumping Jack Jones.

When Mathews came back on September 18, his hitters won two sloppy games for him, 13–12 over Cincinnati and 13–11 over the only other pennant contender left, St. Louis. This second game gave Philadelphia—who had been playing on the road since September 9—a three-and-a-half game lead with six games to go. Although Jones lost the second game of the series 9–6 the next day, the lead was back up to three-and-a-half, with just four games to go, on September 23 when Bradley cruised to a key 9–2 win. With their magic number at one, the Athletics went to Louisville to play the respectable Eclipse, while the Browns took on the awful Alleghenys. Philadelphia, with Bradley and Mathews pitching, then lost their first two games, while St. Louis won both, cutting the lead back to a game-and-a-half with the Athletics having two games to go, and the Browns one.[9] The Athletics still needed one more win, and it was time for Jumping Jack Jones again.

The day was Friday, September 28, 1883. The Browns had the day off, and the Athletics continued their series in Louisville. Back in Philadelphia, thousands stood outside the telegraph offices, waiting for the results and bringing traffic in the streets to a standstill.[10] And while Jones wasn't great, he was good enough to run his Athletics' record to 5-2 (with an Adjusted ERA of 132) with a dramatic 7–6 win over Guy Hecker in 10 innings. Fittingly enough, the pennant-winning run was scored by Harry Stovey, who walked, went to second on a wild pitch, to third on a single by captain Knight and scored on a single by Moynahan.[11] For the first time since 1871 the Philadelphia Athletics were champions.

Two day later, the Athletics lost their last game, and the Browns won theirs, making it close—Athletics 66–32, Browns 65–33. A series of post-season exhibition losses to the Phillies, Providence and Buffalo quickly scotched the talk of a post-season series between the Athletics and the league champion Boston Beaneaters. Indeed, after the Athletics, who may have been worn out by the pennant chase, lost five out of nine exhibition games to the 17-81 Phillies,[12] the *Inquirer* reported that the scheduled "World Series" with the Beaneaters was called off[13]—probably the better for the reputation of Philadelphia baseball.

How important was Stovey to the Athletics' win? Individually, the only players who could have competed with him for the MVP Award would have been the Pittsburgh Alleghenys' Ed Swartwood (a league-leading .356 batting average), Will White and New York Metropolitans' ace Tim Keefe (41-27, 361 strikeouts). Stovey led the circuit in a 98 game season in runs (110), doubles (31), home runs (a major league record-setting 14), total bases (213), extra-base hits (51) and slugging percentage (.506). Although stolen bases weren't kept at that time, he probably was near the top there as well. He was also eighth in batting average (.302), sixth in on base percentage (.346) and fourth in hits (128).

A huge mob met the Athletics' train at the Broad Street Station when they returned home from Louisville, with Jones, Moynahan and Stovey being the heroes of the day. Presaging what would become a twentieth century Philadelphia tradition, more than a half million people lined Broad Street on October 12 for a victory parade.[14] Nemec reproduces a period-typical cartoon of the 1883 champs, marching home behind Sharsig, Mason and Simmons, the players mostly on crutches or with their arms in slings, and the owners carrying bags of cash. While Stovey would go on to a fabulous career, this was the one moment in the sun for Jones and Moynahan. Jones, who had already earned a dental degree at Yale, decided to take his baseball earnings and set up a dental practice. He never played baseball again,[15] going out in a blaze of glory on September 28, 1883.

Overall, the Athletics were eminently successful in 1883, despite the first year competition from the National League Phillies. This was a logical development, since the already-established Athletics, bearing a famous name, were on their way to a pennant in a tight race, and the first year Phillies were finishing last with a terrible 17-81 mark. In fact, over their first two years, the AA Athletics made an estimated profit variously quoted as being between $200,000 and $300,000—an unheard of sum for that time.[16] As for the Phillies, 1883 wouldn't be quite so successful, even though their very appearance in the National League was, looking at the long term, an event of major significance to both major league baseball and Philadelphia.

♦ CHAPTER 11 ♦

The Worcester Ruby Legs and the New Philadelphia Philadelphias

Even prior to the 1883 kickoff for a "new" team of Phillies, Philadelphia had had its baseball troubles—revolving, hippodroming, failed teams, bad teams, blown pennants, being left out of leagues, being booted out of leagues—Philadelphia had seen it all prior to 1883. Still, Philadelphia was also right in the middle of practically every major baseball happening in the period from 1866 to 1883, either for good or for bad. The founding of the new Philadelphia Philadelphias came as part of what would be the first significant expansion by the National League.

While the Athletics brought Philadelphia back in to the national spotlight in the American Association in 1882, and into an even bigger spotlight in 1883 with the AA pennant, there were those who thought that what the city really needed was a National League team. Fortunately for Philadelphia, this latter group included Abraham G. Mills and Arthur Soden, and their support would lead to the establishment of the second team of Philadelphia Phillies.

The creation of the National League Phillies has commonly been misconstrued as a franchise shift, with the National League moving the Worcester Ruby Legs (or Brown Stockings) franchise from a small market to a big market. While it is true that the National League coveted the Philadelphia market which was proving so lucrative to the American Association, it wasn't a franchise shift. The National League needed to muscle out some of its smaller franchise cities, and, more importantly, it needed the power and prestige of New York and Philadelphia to survive against the American Association. Philadelphia, on its part, was still on a roll after the Centennial, and was able to show it had the ability to support two major league teams.

It started when William Hulbert dropped dead of a heart attack on April 10, 1882,[1] an event that didn't draw too many tears in Philly, and didn't really hurt the National League very much. In spite of Hulbert's posturing and blustering after his highly suspicious expulsion of the Athletics after the 1876 season, the NL was struggling, and one reason was because Philadelphia and New York weren't fielding NL teams. As American Association president Denny McKnight was prone to point out during the 1882 season, the six cities in the AA actually had a larger population base, by somewhere between a half million and a million (depending on what source you read), than the eight cities in the NL.[2] Even in 1882, it was a little hard to sell a league as "major" when half of its teams were in Troy, Worcester, Providence and Buffalo.

Hulbert's death initially brought Boston Red Stockings owner Soden into control of the league. As David Nemec notes in *The Beer & Whiskey League*, the practical-minded Soden wasn't about to leave the nation's two largest cities to the rival American Association.[3] Mills then took over as NL president after Soden served briefly as interim president—just long enough to get the ball rolling on expansion into New York and Philadelphia. Although A.G. had been the "prosecuting attorney" in the case of the expulsion of the Athletics and the Mutuals in 1876,[4] he also shared Soden's view that the National League was floundering while playing musical franchises from 1876 to 1882 and trying to fight off the advances of the aggressive Denny McKnight and his compatriots in the AA. When the association announced it was awarding a franchise to John Day's New York Metropolitans for the 1883 season, Mills figured out something had to be done to help preserve his league. He needed, the National League needed, New York and Philadelphia.

It took a little behind-the-scenes maneuvering to make it happen, though. First, Troy and Worcester had to be persuaded to give up their teams after a September 1882 meeting in Philadelphia that, in effect, expelled them.[5] The next step was to find an owner for virtually nothing, since all that was being transferred to Philadelphia was the right to a franchise, not the team or its players—not that anyone might have wanted most of the players that went just 18-66. Mills needed the best he could find to take on the AA Athletics, and he found an old Athletic, as Al Reach re-entered the national baseball scene. Actually, Reach had never left baseball, he had just stopped playing. In fact, well before he had stopped playing after the 1878 season, Reach was a big name in baseball, on the supply side. While he was still a regular player with the old Athletics, Reach had gone into the sporting goods business, at first on his own in retail, and then with native Philadelphian, manufacturer and inventor Ben Shibe as a manufacturer. By the time Mills, who had known Reach when they were both players before the war,[6] contacted him about owning the Philadelphia franchise, the Scratcher was already a captain of industry in his adopted hometown.

Moreover, he was still an active player, from a management perspective, in Philadelphia baseball, having revived the Philadelphias, most likely just prior to the 1882 season.[7] This move was done in conjunction with partner Shibe, who himself had sponsored his own semi-pro team from 1877 to 1881—a platform that Reach may have used in the re-creation of the Philadelphias and ultimately, the NL Phillies. Thus, while Reach would be one of the partners of record for the new Phillies, Ben Shibe also had a hand in at least the initial development of the National League club.

However, Shibe was not an owner of the National League Phillies. When the franchise was formally incorporated in November 1882, with Reach heading a group of Philadelphia investors, Shibe wasn't part of the deal. Perhaps he was too busy running the manufacturing end of their growing sporting goods business. Reach's main partner in the Phillies was lawyer John I. Rogers. A native Philadelphian, born on May 27, 1844, Rogers was active in local politics and held a law degree from the University of Pennsylvania. At one time a state legislator and judge advocate of the Pennsylvania National Guard, giving him the rank of colonel, Rogers, like Reach, was at first a minority partner in the Phillies. However, Reach was initially named president and Rogers club secretary—positions from which they gained majority control of the franchise by the end of the 1880s.

From the very beginning, there was an obvious disconnect between Reach and Rogers.[8] Reach was more interested in the game itself, and in its ability to promote the sale of sporting goods. Rogers, on the other hand, was looking for direct profit from his investment,[9] and would let little or nothing stand in his way, a fact that would come out more than once in the future, in part because Rogers also tended to be arrogant and overbearing.[10]

* * *

When the Phillies were first constituted as a National League team, Rogers left the running of the team up to Reach. One of the first jobs Reach faced was making the little park at Ridge and Columbia something akin to a major league facility. Although Reach's Philadelphias had been playing there for a year, and he had already made some improvements over what was left of the NA Centennial Park from 1875, he now added a small upper deck behind home plate, put an awning over the press box, painted the seats red and the walls white.[11]

This was really just window-dressing compared to the real job at hand—finding a major league team to show up at Recreation Park on May 1, 1883, for the Phillies' first game. This outfit has typically been characterized as a bunch of minor leaguers, pick-up players, local sandlotters, semi-pros and cast-offs—a not unreasonable assumption, since the first-year Phillies would go 17-81, setting the franchise record for the worst single season record in their very first year. However, that's not exactly true. Although four players from the 1882 Philadelphias stuck around, of the team's 11 regular players who batted more than 140 times, only four had never before played in the major leagues (and only one of those was a regular in the field), and only two were from Philadelphia. What was true is that the team's two main pitchers, John Coleman and Art Hagan, were both 20-year-old

The first home of the National League Phillies, Recreation Park, with the 1884 team. Fourth from the left is 20-year-old rookie Charlie Ferguson. The gent in the dark suit and bowler, back by the grandstand, may well be Harry Wright. Note the players' benches on the right side by the grandstand, and the tops of the Philadelphia row houses, visible between the first and second decks (courtesy John Thorn).

rookies. Still, despite the fact that Reach did not have the title to any of Worcester's players, this was not a team of unknowns.

The best known of the original Phillies, and indeed the first Phillie player, was Bob "Death to Flying Things" Ferguson. In his first personnel move as president, Reach had selected an old adversary as manager.[12] Although they'd never played on the same team, Reach and Ferguson had played against each other starting back in 1865. Typically described by adjectives such as tyrannical, short-tempered, authoritative and tactless, Ferguson had also managed just about every team he had played on since 1869, when he led the Brooklyn Atlantics to their historic, streak-breaking win over the Cincinnati Red Stockings by becoming the first acknowledged switch-hitter in the bottom of the 11th inning.[13] In addition to his rather over-bearing personality, Ferguson was also fearless—imagine the nerve it must have taken to hit left-handed for the first time under those circumstances—competitive, intelligent, one of the best fielders in his day (hence the "Death to Flying Things" nickname), financially astute, and a leader—he had been president of the National Association from 1872 to 1875.[14] This the was the man Reach selected, not only to run the Phillies, but also to play second base, run the team's business office, and recruit the rest of the players as well. Ferguson, by now 38 years old and also known as "Old Fergy," was nothing if not versatile.

The team he put together may not have been unknowns, but, they weren't very good either. And Ferguson lasted only 17 games (a 4-13 record) as manager, before being replaced by third baseman-outfielder Blondie Purcell. Depending on who you read, this precipitous action was either initiated by Reach (due to a lack of success on the field), Ferguson himself (he was tired of losing) or by the rest of the players, who were tired of Ferguson. Old Fergy did stay on to man second base and the business office for the rest of the year, with more success in the latter than the former. The clearly over-the-hill as a player Ferguson hit just .258 and led NL second basemen in errors with 88. Fortunately for Reach, Rogers and their fellow stockholders, financial acumen doesn't fade in your late 30s. Despite the Phillies' awful record, Ferguson was still sharp enough with the pen that the team actually made money, although a special dispensation from the league that allowed them to sell tickets for 25 cents a head, to better compete with the popular Athletics, certainly helped as well.[15]

As to the rest of the team that Ferguson put together, part of the problem was that all of the defunct Ruby Legs players with any real skills had already been snapped up by other teams before Ferguson could start recruiting.[16] The one exception to this situation appears to be the big one that got away—Harry Stovey. By far Worcester's best player, Stovey could have thrown his lot with either the Athletics or the Phillies, says Nemec.[17] For whatever reason—maybe he saw what the rest of the Phillies team was going to be like—he chose the Athletics and the AA.

For the players who did make up the first Phillies team, the regular lineup looked like this:

Position—Name (Previous ML experience)
C—Emil Gross (three years/NL)
1B—Sid Farrar (rookie)
2B—Bob Ferguson (since 1865)
3B—Blondie Purcell (three years/NL)
SS—Bill McClellan (2 years/ NL)
OF—Jack Manning (since 1873)

Position—Name (Previous ML experience)
OF—Bill Harbridge (since 1875)
OF—Fred Lewis (27 games in 1881 with Boston NL)
C/OF—Frank Ringo (rookie)
3B—Fred Warner (since 1875)
P—John Coleman (rookie)
P—Art Hagan (rookie)

This was the team that finished last in the National League in runs scored, batting average, slugging percentage, on base average, hits allowed and runs allowed—a consistent, across the board performance. Indicative of the changing nature of the game, when Ferguson and Reach went out recruiting, they no longer relied on local players. Only Harbridge and Warner were from Philadelphia, and both of them had major league experience dating back to the National Association. In fact, Warner had played for both the Athletics and Centennials in 1875. Manning, Lewis and McClellan had all played for the 1882 Phillies, as had sub pitcher and outfielder Jack Neagle.

Catcher Emil Gross was by far the team's offensive star. Having formerly caught for the National League Providence Grays from 1879 to 1881, he was a three-year major league veteran who had posted Adjusted OPS figures of 115 or above in all three years. At the age of 25 he led the Phillies with a .307/.342/.489 year and an Adjusted OPS of 158. However, 1884 was his last year in the majors, and even then he could catch on with only Cincinnati and Pittsburgh in the quasi-major Union Association. Possibly his .789 fielding percentage with the 1883 Phillies had something to do with his major league career ending at the age of 26, despite a career Adjusted OPS of 146. In addition to managers Ferguson and Purcell, the other notable name in the first Phillies lineup was that of the first baseman—Sid Farrar. However, Sid would be far better known for an off-the-field accomplishment than he would be for batting ninth most of the time for the Phillies. Sid had a daughter named Geraldine, who would become one of America's first music and film stars as one of the great opera singers and entertainment personalities of her time. As for Sid, he had an Adjusted OPS of 77 in his rookie year of 1883. Nevertheless, he did last another seven years in Philadelphia baseball, all but the last (1890 in the Players League) with the Phillies.

Purcell was sort of an odd choice to take over the managerial reins from Ferguson. He had just turned 29, had never captained a team before and, in fact, had less top level experience than Manning, Harbridge or Warner—or Reach. One wonders if the Scratcher was tempted to come out of the executive suite and try and straighten things out himself. Purcell got stuck with the job and, in between playing third, the outfield and pitching 11 games (2-6 with a 70 Adjusted ERA), he led the Phillies to a 13-68 record the rest of the way. He never managed again but he did play another seven years, largely with the Athletics.

Pitcher John Coleman has become something of a minor cult figure among the cognoscenti of nineteenth century baseball, mainly because he set two all-time records that, barring an unforeseen major change in the game, will never be approached. Coleman started 61 of the Phillies' 99 games (he also relieved four times), threw 538 innings, and was the losing pitcher 48 times. Only four other pitchers have ever managed to lose 40 times in a year, with Will White's 42 in 1880 being the closest to Coleman's landmark (12-48, 63 Adjusted ERA) season. In addition, his 772 hits allowed also stands alone as a record, far above Bobby Matthews' 693 in 1876. Undeterred by this rude welcome to the national game, Coleman soldiered on for another seven years, alternating between Philadelphia and

Pittsburgh, although he wisely devoted most of his time to the outfield, where he had played 31 games while not pitching for the 1883 Phillies. An average hitter in the outfield—his career Adjusted OPS was exactly 100—his career mark as a pitcher was 23-72 with an Adjusted ERA of 67.

Coleman and the Phillies inaugurated Recreation Park as a major league field on April 2, 1883. Having spent spring training at the little Ridge and Columbia field, the Phillies were ready to take on one of the city's many semipro clubs, Ashland of Manayunk, in their first exhibition game. Coleman sent Ashland back to the mill town on the Schuylkill River without a hit.[18] The Phillies also warmed up for their first regular season by splitting six exhibition games with the Athletics.[19] However, neither the Athletics nor Ashland were quite the caliber of the first real competition the Phillies would face when they opened their first National League season at Recreation Park on May 1. The opposition that day was provided by the Providence Grays and Charlie Radbourne. Although the Phillies staked Coleman to a 3–0 lead after seven innings, the Grays scored four in the eighth to win 4–3 and give Radbourne the first of his 48 wins and Coleman the first of his 48 losses.

All things considered, the opening game was one of the highlights of a season that included eight straight losses to start (including a 24–6 slaughter at the hands of Radbourne and Providence in the third game), a 29–4 loss to Boston, a 28–0 loss to Radbourne and Providence (in the midst of a 14-game losing streak) and a 1–0 no-hit loss to one-armed Hugh Daily and the Cleveland Blues. The Phillies didn't win a game until a 12–1 victory at Chicago in their ninth contest. Even then, poor Coleman didn't get the win. The starter on that historic occasion was Neagle, who spelled Coleman every fourth game or so until mid–June, when he jumped to the American Association, taking a 1-7 record with him. Things got so bad that Reach, showing a promotional spirit along with his entrepreneurial spirit, offered two free streetcar tickets (worth 12 cents) to every fan who bought a 50 cent admission ticket. (Recreation Park was next to a horse car barn.) Only when that ploy failed did Reach successfully petition the National League to allow him to drop the cost of a ticket to 25 cents. To pick up a few extra dollars to help Ferguson keep the bottom line in shape, Reach also rented out Recreation Park for bicycle racing and college football games.

Still, the 1883 season did end on a positive note for the Phillies. After splitting the six exhibition games with the Athletics in the spring, and then being outdrawn by the AA team at the gate during the regular season,[20] the outlook didn't look good as they picked up the city series with the Athletics just two days after the conquering heroes returned home from winning the AA pennant. When the A's waltzed to an 11–2 win in the first game on October 3, the betting crowd was wagering that the Phillies wouldn't win a single game of the fall series.[21] Surprise—Reach's team ended up winning five of the nine games[22] to salvage at least some local pride.

* * *

While Reach may or may not have been tempted to shake things up during the 1883 season, he wasted no time in doing so after the Phillies' first campaign finally ended after the Athletics series—rife with rumors that the team would fold.[23] However, the rumormongers underestimated the determination of Al Reach, a man who had never failed at anything he set out to accomplish. Still, Reach had a problem, namely a team that had come very close to setting a record for the worst record to date in the National League. Having previously turned unsuccessfully to a former competitor from New York who was one of the best-known names in baseball, Reach now decided to call in the big gun. Another former New Yorker whose baseball pedigree went back even further than Ferguson's, even further than Reach himself. To literally try and save the Phillies franchise, Reach turned to the biggest name in professional baseball, a man who, like Reach himself, had never failed at anything he had attempted in sports. Reach asked the Father of Professional Baseball, Harry Wright, to come to Philadelphia to take over managing the Phillies. It was a move that would save the franchise, though it would prove to be a relationship that was not without irony.

First, Harry Wright was, in 1884, the biggest winner among baseball managers. And yet, even though he did save Reach's franchise, the Phillies finished as high as second only once in his tenure. Did that make his stay in Philly ultimately a failure? That would be a harsh judgement, since he not only took an awful team to contention in two years, but he also ran up the best managerial record in Phillies history.

Wright had quite a history with Philadelphia, dating back to 1869, when he took his Cincinnati Red Stockings into Philadelphia to play the Athletics and Keystones as part of the Stockings' historic, unbeaten tour. Although Wright escaped the baseball-crazy City of Brotherly Love unscathed then, he had many an additional run-in with Philadelphia teams in the years afterwards, not the least of which was the Force case. He also didn't much seem to like the Pearls, nee White Stockings, nor was he impressed at their run at unseating his Boston Red Stockings in 1873. In fact he wrote a letter during the White Stockings' Cape May vacation to Athletics boss Hicks Hayhurst, suggesting as much.[24] This wasn't Wright's only famous correspondence with Hayhurst. He had also exchanged some fairly pointed comments with Hayhurst in 1871, after the Athletics had taken the first NA pennant, on the subject of the Athletics in effect dissing said pennant by hanging it in a saloon.[25]

So, Wright had a history with Philadelphia, and it wasn't a particularly good one. Still, when Reach came calling, Wright said yes, for what would basically be his last stop in baseball. Why did he do it? You have to think the answer is that Harry Wright was, above all else, a competitor, a man who, like Al Reach, loved a challenge. He had never failed at anything he'd ever tried in baseball, since his playing days with Knickerbocker, and here was an old compatriot offering him a challenge. How could he refuse? Fortunately for baseball in Philadelphia, he didn't.

The hiring of Harry Wright was just the first step in making the Phillies a real major league team. There was still the little matter of getting better players. However, one showed up right away, thanks to an offer from Reach that lured him away from the independent Richmond, Virginia, club. He was 21-year-old Charlottesville, Virginia, native Charles Ferguson,[26] and he was all ballplayer, from his handlebar mustache to his talented right arm and fast feet. In 1884, by far his worst year, he accounted for more than 40 percent of the team's total innings pitched, 417 out of 981, while going 21-25. He also played five games in the outfield, hitting .246/.311/.305 overall, which may not sound like much, but his Adjusted OPS was 99—almost exactly the league average. And he would get far better in the coming years.

Ferguson represented just the most notable of the roster changes that would lift the Phillies to a 39-73 sixth place finish in 1884. An even younger player, 20-year-old outfielder Jim Fogarty came east from San Francisco, initially to play for the Phillies' reserve team. However, that reserve team never materialized and Wright, discovering that the young Californian could play the outfield as well as a young Harry Wright, stuck him in the starting lineup in right field against Detroit on May 1, Opening Day. Although he never really became any more than an average hitter, his fielding kept him in the Phillies' lineup until he jumped to the Players League in 1890.[27]

Fully half of the Phillies' regulars were new in 1884, with only Purcell, Farrar, McClellan and Manning surviving the start of the Wright Era. Only Manning really posed much of an offensive threat in '84, posting a 134 Adjusted OPS on the strength of .271/.334/.394 numbers, as the team finished sixth in runs scored with 549. However, that was better than the pitchers accomplished. They finished dead last in runs allowed (824) and ERA (3.93). John Coleman (5-15) was still around, although his 61 Adjusted ERA still wasn't exactly a plus. The team's best pitcher was actually 19-year-old Bill Vinton, who went 10-10 despite an excellent 2.23 ERA.

Although Reach and Wright had turned fully half the team over, and although they had improved by 15 games over 1883's disaster, the Phillies really weren't very strong in any aspect of the game in 1884, leading one to conclude that their sixth place finish was a tribute to Wright as much as anything. If that was the case, it was only fair that, under the terms of his contract with Reach, Harry took home 25 percent of the team's $6,082.79 profit.[28] And the Phillies, especially their pitching, would improve dramatically over the next few years.

* * *

It only took until 1885 to show real improvement. The team jumped over .500 to 56–54 and finished third as Ferguson won 26 games and started to really show why Richmond was so unhappy to lose him. Among his 26 wins was the Phillies' first regular season no-hitter, a 1–0 gem over the defending National League champion Providence Grays on August 29 at Recreation Park. In addition to going 26-20 as a pitcher in 405 innings, Ferguson also became the team's best hitter, posting a 144 Adjusted OPS largely on the strength of a .306 average and 23 walks in 235 at-bats (a .368 on base average) that included 16 games in the outfield when he wasn't pitching.

Ferguson also had some help in the pitcher's box. Another 22-year-old, Ed Daily, had been purchased from the Harrisburg club in the off-season. Together, he and Ferguson essentially alternated in the box during the 1885 season, picking up all but four of the team's 56 wins between them. In addition to his 26-24 record, Daily threw more innings than Ferguson, 440 in all, and almost exactly matched him in ERA—Daily was 2.21 (126 Adjusted), Ferguson, 2.22 (125 Adjusted). Together, they helped the Phillies finish third in runs allowed (511)—a good thing, because they were only fifth in runs scored (513). The offense was not helped much by the main new addition to the lineup, a local youngster who had caught nine games for the Phillies in 1884 as a 19-year-old after his Philadelphia Keystone team in the Union Association had folded. He hit only .191 with a .498 OPS in 1885, but the perspicacious Wright must have seen something he liked, despite the fact that the young Philadelphian threw left-handed. Jack Clements would stay with the Phillies even after Harry Wright left the team, becoming one of the great catchers of the nineteenth century and the first catcher to appear in 1000 major league games.

* * *

Not one to rest on his laurels, Wright brought in some new faces for 1886, and was rewarded with a 71–43 fourth place finish that would prove to be the team's best won-loss record until 1976. One of these new faces finally represented one of the Worcester Ruby

Legs showing up in a Phillies uniform, although it happened because his previous team, the Providence Grays, folded and, in effect, made him an early version of a free agent. Although Arthur Irwin didn't hit much at short, he was a fine fielder, and a certain upgrade from Charlie Bastian, who had hit .167 with no power (14 extra-base hits) and a terrible strikeout-walk ratio of 82–35 in an era when nobody struck out very much—in fact he led the NL in Ks in 1885.

Wright also brought in three notable players from the Detroit Wolverines: catcher Deacon McGuire, outfielder George Wood and pitcher Dan Casey.[29] Although McGuire, 22, hit just .198 while spelling Clements (who hit .205), he was in the third year of a playing career that would take him all the way to 1912. Casey also had his claim to fame, in that he later in life claimed to be "Casey at the Bat" of Ernest Thayer's famous poem—a claim that must have been a little hard to take from a career .162 hitter. Wood was just a good outfielder who had led the NL in home runs in 1882, and would finish second in triples (15) in 1886. Still, the Phillies were just fifth in the league in runs scored with 621.

Although Casey may not have been much with the bat, he teamed with Ferguson and Daily to make for the best pitching in the National League. All three hurlers, Casey (24-18) the lefty and Ferguson (30-9) and Daily (16-9) the righties, were 23 years old, and together they helped the Phillies to lead the NL in ERA (2.45) and runs allowed (498). Ferguson (1.98) was second in the league in ERA while Casey (2.41) was sixth. Daily, although he wasn't particularly good out of the pitcher's box, played 56 games in the outfield and pitched in 27, hitting .227/.244/.327. Then there was Ferguson. After this season, he probably could have run for mayor of Philadelphia. Although his hitting fell off to a .253 average, he still showed good plate discipline (a .346 on base percentage) and his Adjusted OPS was still over 100 (102). And he'd get better in 1887.

The tables had been turned in the City of Brotherly Love. For the first time since the early 1860s, the Athletics were no longer the first name in Philadelphia baseball. The Phillies had taken over the Athletics' city, a move that also proved that timing is everything, because, as would happen in the late 1880s and the late 1940s, the Phillies' ascendancy would mean the end for two different teams of Athletics.

* * *

After five years in the league, the 1887 Phillies were ready for prime time. For the first time, they were outdrawing the Athletics at the gate[30] by a simple means—the Phillies now had a better team. While the Athletics were falling below .500 after their 1883 pennant, the Phillies were now winning, thanks to Harry Wright. In one of the ironies of Philadelphia baseball, Harry Wright, who had wished to bring about the downfall of the Athletics in his late National Association years, was now actually doing so—from a base in Philadelphia.

The first and biggest news in Philadelphia baseball in 1887 was the opening of the first truly modern ballpark in America, bounded by Broad, 15th, Lehigh and Huntingdon streets. The first park with something other than a wooden superstructure, the Philadelphia Baseball Park, also known as the Huntingdon Street Grounds, was built a little north and east of old Recreation Park, though still within the basic confines of the North Philadelphia area that had been home to Philadelphia baseball since the Civil War era. The reason for the move was simple. Recreation Park, on its best days, could really hold only about 6,500 people, which included 1,500 in the grandstand, 2,000 in the outfield bleachers and the rest standing. The oddly-shaped plot of land the park stood on, besides producing its unique dimensions, was simply too small for the type of operation envisioned by the ambitious Reach, Rogers and Wright.

Thus was built, on the site of an old dump with Cohosksink Creek running through it (it took 120,000 wagon loads of dirt to bring the field level), and at a cost of $101,000, the finest stadium in America, and a virtual castle, at least from the outside. The brainchild of the multi-talented Reach, it was built of wood and brick, and initially seating 12,500, partly in brick exterior pavilions (another first). The Huntingdon Street Grounds was a wooden showplace with a brick exterior (not the cantilever steel and brick structure—that came in 1894) that included three main turrets, the largest of which towered 165 feet over the main entrance at 15th Street and Huntingdon Avenue—an impressive facility that could have been called The House that Ferguson Built.

The home of the Phillies for 51½ years, the Huntingdon Street Grounds would later be called Baker Bowl, after future Phillies pinchpenny owner William Baker. Throughout its existence, it would also be known for its strange dimensions. In 1886 Reach still had a wide choice of property available in North Philadelphia. For instance, he could have tried to purchase a bigger lot just six blocks to the west (i.e., six blocks closer to the old Recreation Park) at 21st Street and Lehigh. That land was still available more than 20 years later (partly because it was next to the Smallpox Hospital), when Reach's partner, Ben Shibe, decided to move his Athletics there. The plot of land he chose in 1887, bordered by Broad Street on the east, 15th Street on the west, Huntingdon Street on the south and Lehigh Avenue on the north, was extremely rectangular, for the simple reason that Broad and 15th Streets were a lot closer together than Huntingdon and Lehigh. Reach, possibly because he was a left-handed hitter in his playing days, but mostly so the late afternoon sun wouldn't shine in the batters' eyes, laid out the park with home plate at the 15th and Huntingdon corner, producing a very deep left field towards the faraway Lehigh Avenue, and a very shallow right field fronting on the adjacent Broad Street.

Initially, this produced a playing field that was somewhere between 400 feet and 500 feet (depending on what source you believe) from home to the left field wall, 408 feet to center field (there was no seating in the outfield at first) and a little over 300 feet down the right field line. With further building in later years, notably the rebuilding following a major fire in 1894, these dimensions would become even more extreme, as right field shrunk to 272 feet and left 341 feet. The lot was also rather small, at least by later standards, which led to the stands sitting right on top of the field. In other words, from Day One (a Park Factor of 106 in 1887), it was a hitters' park.

It also was a bicyclist's park. To make a few extra dollars, maybe to pay for those three brick turrets, a quarter-mile track was constructed around the outskirts of the playing field, to take advantage of the 1880s craze for long-distance bicycle racing. The track was 15 feet wide with appropriately banked turns, making for some interesting adventures for opposing outfielders who weren't used to running up an incline to catch a fly ball.

The hitters who benefited from Philadelphia Park did so right away. Although the Phillies' 1887 lineup wasn't significantly different than the 1886 crew, they now scored 901 runs, second in the league, and came on strong in the season's second half to eventually battle the Detroit Wolverines for supremacy of the National League mainly because, even with the short right field, the Phillies' pitchers also still managed to lead the league in runs allowed, with 702. And, even though they fell three and a half games short in second place, with a record (75-48) slightly worse than 1886's fourth place, this was a season to remember.

The 1887 Phillies at the Huntingdon Street Grounds. The first row seated includes Mike Piazza look-alike Sid Farrar (far left), Harry Wright (center), Jack Clements (to the right of Harry) and Charlie Buffington (far right). The back row features Art Irwin (far left), Dan Casey (next to Irwin), Joe Mulvey (third from right), Jim Fogarty (without a team sweater) and Charlie Ferguson (far right) (courtesy John Thorn).

It started on April 30, with the grand opening of the Philadelphia Ball Park, an opening that indicated the changing status of baseball, not only in Philadelphia, but also nationally. Whereas the game was originally a very Yuppie affair, the game and its public perception changed over the years. As professionalism also brought with it gamblers, contract jumping and the like, the game went from a genteel sport to a rather gamey business, in both reality and in the eyes of the public and the media. And this judgment applied to both the players and the fans. However, the opening of Philadelphia Ball Park was a major moment in the history of sports in Philadelphia. For the first time, a new athletic facility was opened with grand fanfare and celebration. In the past, a Jefferson Park or a Recreation Park was inaugurated by just playing the first game. However, for the new home of the Phillies, the city rolled out the red carpet. Mayor Edwin Fitler was there, along with Beck's Military Band, most of the other prominent city officials, and a good collection of socialites.

Also present were some 20,000 fans, including 3,000 there by invitation of Reach, Rogers and the Phillies. Some of them may well have been fans of the current Athletics. That's because, in an unprecedented show of Brotherly Love, the Athletics had moved their April 30 game against Brooklyn at Jefferson Park up several hours. Now, it may have been that the Athletics were realistic enough to recognize that, if they played at the same time as the Philadelphia Park opening, virtually no one would show up at Jefferson Park. However, there does seem to have been some genuine cooperation between the two teams.

The opposition for the opener was the New York Giants. Since the park held only 12,500, that meant that approximately 7,500 people were standing in various places around the park, a large number of them behind ropes in the outfield. Since neither the outfield nor the foul territory was very big anyway, this situation helped lead to a high-scoring game, won 19–10 (in only eight innings) by the Phillies behind Charlie Ferguson, over future Hall of Famer Tim Keefe. Just to get Philadelphia Park off on the right foot, the first nine Phillies batters, starting with leadoff hitter Ed Andrews, hit safely and scored in the first inning.[31]

The 1887 pennant race turned out to be one of the early National League's great finishes. In addition to the eventual champion Wolverines, who led for most of the year before having to hold off a furious finish by the Phillies, the defending champion Chicago White Stockings were in the mix, despite having sold their superstar King Kelly to Boston. The Giants were also a contender, and the Beaneaters, bolstered by Kelly, were respectable most of the year.

For the Phillies, although Andrews had his best season at the plate (he hit .325), Wood was the first hitter to take advantage of the cozy dimensions (he hit a career-high 14 home runs, including the park's first, and finished fourth in the league). Clements also made a big jump to .280, and Ferguson was the team's best hitter, but the key to the Phillies' 1887 success was the pitching staff, which managed to excel despite the chummy surroundings. In fact, if the Phillies of the 1890s had pitching as good as the 1887 team, there would have been pennants flying at 15th and Huntingdon long before 1915. Daily was a flop and was sold to Washington in June, but a better replacement was at hand in the person of Charlie Buffington, who had been brought in from Boston and who had won as many as 47 games as recently as 1884. Even with Buffington (21-17) and Ferguson (22-10, and third in the NL with a 3.00 ERA) around, the staff's unquestioned ace was Casey, who went 28-13 and led the league in ERA (2.86) and shutouts (4). It was an uncommonly strong three-man staff despite the fact that Wright seems to have been in the process of turning Ferguson into an early version of Babe Ruth. Ferguson pitched in 37 games (less than either Casey or Buffington), played second in 27 games, the outfield in six and third base in five. All the moving around didn't seem to hurt him any more than it would the Babe in 1919, as Charlie led the team in RBIs with 85, still had a fine strikeout-walk ratio (19-34) and showed increasing power, raising his slugging percentage to .470 on the strength of 14 doubles, six triples and three home runs. If Ferguson had batted enough, he would have been fifth in the league in batting average (.337) and third in on base percentage (.417). In fact, if he could have maintained his RBI rate over a full season of at-bats, he would have set a major league record. Just how much of this improvement was due to Philadelphia Park—he was a switch-hitter, so he could take advantage of the short right field against right-handed pitchers—and how much was due to the natural maturation of the talented, now 24-year-old Ferguson is hard to say. In either case, he was now a star of the first magnitude.

Despite the excellence of the 1887 team, they were just nosed out of the pennant by Detroit, not the first or last time a Philadelphia team would come up just short. They started slowly and still stood at just .500 (38-38) after losing to the Wolverines 9–6 on August 3.

At that point they were in fifth place, nine and a half games back. And then they got hot after Wright made a key change. In an attempt to get Ferguson's bat in the lineup more, he started the Virginian in the pitchers' box only three times between July 20 and September 15. With Ferguson playing mostly second base, the Phillies went 21-7 from August 3 to September 10, jumping to third place, though still seven and a half games behind the Wolverines.

And then they got really hot. After losing three straight at Chicago, the Phillies ran off a 16-game wining streak—the last 16 games of the season—with one 5–5 tie with New York on the next-to-last day. Never has major league baseball seen such a finishing kick. Wright decided to restore Ferguson to the regular rotation for the final push, and he won all seven of his starts between September 16 and the final game on October 8.[32] On those days when he didn't pitch, Ferguson was on second, where his hot bat helped the other pitchers. Alas, it was just a little too late. The Wolverines won often enough that the Phillies ran out of time. The three-and-a-half game margin on the final day was as close as they got to Detroit. However, if the season had gone another 10 days or two weeks....

* * *

But, it didn't, and, even worse, there would never be another season of any kind for Charlie Ferguson. After the close call in 1887, optimism had to be running high around Philadelphia Park in the spring of 1888. A large part of this optimism was based on the statement, made at the beginning of spring training by Harry Wright, that Ferguson would play second base whenever he wasn't pitching. According to Harry, he was the best second baseman in the league.[33] But, on April 13, the club announced that Ferguson was ill. It was typhoid fever and although reports over the next two weeks seemed to be optimistic as to his eventual recovery, he died on April 29 at the age of 25,[34] and the Phillies, who would never become noted for their good luck over the next 118 years or so, had suffered their biggest loss—a brilliant pitcher, hitter, fielder and runner—right from almost the very start.

Still, the 1888 season had to go on, and Reach and Wright had to find, on short notice, a pitcher *and* a second baseman to take Ferguson's place. In another irony, the keystone performer they were forced to buy in July 1888, in a pricey ($1900) purchase from Wheeling in the Tri-State League—forced because holdover second baseman Charlie Bastain couldn't hit or field—would become both one of the team's great stars, and another super talent who would die in mid-career: Ed Delahanty. For a pitcher, they turned to a native of nearby Camden, signing a tough little 21-year-old who was rightly at the time called "Kid" Gleason. However, while Delahanty would go on to the Hall of Fame (as an outfielder), and Gleason would go on to a 22-year career (mostly as a second baseman), neither was of much help in 1888. Gleason went 7-16 with a 104 Adjusted ERA, and Delahanty hit .228/.261/.293. In general, the team struggled terribly on offense, and slumped to a 69-61 third place finish. Among the 10 regular hitters, only Wood had an Adjusted OPS as high as exactly 100, and the team finished sixth in runs (535), on base average (.269) and slugging percentage (.290).

Although Gleason was merely an average pitcher in 1888, and Casey flopped (14-18, 93) after his big year, Buffington was brilliant (28-17, 154) and Ben Sanders, a newcomer brought in from Canton, was equally as good (19-10, 155). As a team, the Phillies were second in ERA (2.38) and runs allowed (509), despite Philadelphia Park still playing to a 105 as a hitters' park. Imagine how good their pitching might have been with Charlie

Ferguson getting 30 to 40 starts in place of either Casey or Gleason. While it is usually true that no single player is so great that his loss will by definition cripple a team, you have to wonder about the case of Charlie Ferguson. The Phillies wouldn't have made up the 14 and a half games they were in arrears of the league-leading Giants, but, you have to think they would have been in the race, since they had lost both their best pitcher *and* the "best second baseman in the league."

Perhaps it was the frustration of losing such a talent as Charlie Ferguson. Maybe it was the slump to a 69-61 season. Whatever the cause, the 1888 season seems to have been a starting point for the establishment of what is now a long-standing reputation of Philadelphia fans as being a tough audience. According to author Robert Smith, it was during the 1888 season that umpire Phil Powers was forced to pull out a revolver to stop Phillies fans from disputing one of his calls. Smith also says that Powers' pistol-packing ways were not unusual. At this time, umpires generally were packing heat when they came to Philly.[35]

* * *

If 1888 was a shock at Broad and Huntingdon, then 1889 was just plain dreary. The Phillies fell to fourth place and a 63-64 record with a team that had neither a good offense (fifth in runs scored) nor good pitching (fourth in runs allowed). And yet, looked at in hindsight, there were a couple of positive signs. One was something everyone who followed baseball realized. The Phillies had taken advantage of the dissolution of the Detroit Wolverines to buy the former champions' best player. Although Detroit had won the 1887 pennant by outlasting the Phillies, the team went belly-up after the 1888 season and its best players were sold off throughout baseball. Reach and Wright, in another of their inspired moments in the player acquisition game, turned up with Big Sam Thompson[36] to play right field and become the second in a long line of left-handed sluggers to take advantage of the close proximity of Broad Street to home plate at Philadelphia Park. In addition to being the only Phillie over 100 in Adjusted OPS (125) in 1889, Thompson led the National League with 20 home runs, and finished third in doubles (36), fourth in total bases (262) and fifth in RBIs (111) and slugging (.492). And he was just getting started.

So was the other cause for optimism, the young second baseman who had failed to do much in 1888 to help the fans forget Charlie Ferguson. Even though he was hampered by injuries in 1889, Ed Delahanty, now splitting his playing time between the outfield and second base, raised his average to .293. The other youngster Reach and Wright had brought in in 1888 to try and replace Ferguson, pitcher Kid Gleason, continued to struggle, going 9-15 with a terrible 5.58 ERA. With Dan Casey continuing his regressing with a 6-10 mark and a decent (115 Adjusted) 3.77 ERA in just 153 innings, the pitching staff was bailed out by Buffington (28-16, 134) and Sanders (19-18, 122).

* * *

If Philadelphia baseball fans thought 1888 was traumatic, and 1889 dull, well, they hadn't seen anything like the 1890 season and the Brotherhood of Professional Ball Players in effect leading the biggest strike in sports history—forming its own league in competition to both the National League and the American Association. Unlike the 1884 Union Association war, which really didn't affect the Phillies at all, the Players League war of 1890 had a major effect on everyone in baseball, since a large number of the best and best-known players jumped their contracts with great gusto, ultimately leading to three major leagues functioning at the same time (including three Philadelphia teams), and practically bleeding each other dry. In 1890 on the field, success often meant making do with whatever players you could hold on to.

In Philadelphia, at least at 15th and Huntingdon, financial success and on-the-field success were pretty well assured by Reach and sporting goods partner Ben Shibe's foresight. With the Brotherhood strike looming in late 1889, Reach and Shibe took out their own form of strike insurance—they sold all of their retail sporting goods outlets to the voracious A.G. Spalding for $100,000.[37] Thus financially fortified, Reach was better able to keep the team together than most of his National League compatriots (who lost something like 80 percent of their players). Still, there were significant losses. From the beginning, they were fated to lose Wood, Buffington and Fogarty, since they were three of the leaders of the Brotherhood. However, they didn't like the idea of also losing Thompson, Delahanty, Clements, back-up catcher Pop Schriver and infielders Joe Mulvey and Al Myers. So, Reach pried open his checkbook, and induced the aforementioned six players to jump back to the Phillies from the Players League, making them scabs of a sort. However, the Brotherhood raised the ante again, and Delahanty defected once again to his hometown team in Cleveland, while Mulvey went to the PL Philadelphia Quakers to play for Buffington. Even more dramatic, Reach's co-owner, John Rogers, an attorney by trade, went to court to unsuccessfully try and keep shortstop Bill Hallman from jumping to the Quakers.[38] Rogers' efforts would prove to be both quixotic and a little puzzling, since Hallman had hit .253/.313/.346 for the worst Adjusted OPS (78) on the team in 1889.

When the dust settled, the Phillies had also lost first baseman Farrar, Hallman, third baseman Mulvey, and pitchers Ben Sanders and Dan Casey (who ended up with Syracuse in the American Association) in addition to Fogarty, Wood and Buffington. If the truth be told, outside of the three Brotherhood ringleaders, only the loss of Sanders was really significant. With both of 1889's top pitchers gone, Wright turned to little (5-7, 160) Kid Gleason, who responded with a still-standing team record 38 wins in an exhausting 506 innings, 54 complete games, and a 138 Adjusted ERA. A rookie from nearby Milford, New Jersey, Tom Vickery, served as the number two man, going 24-22 with a 106 Adjusted ERA. However, that wasn't enough to keep the team from finishing sixth in runs allowed (707) as Philadelphia Park continued to favor the hitters (103 Park Factor).

Those hitters, to a certain extent presaging what would happen for most of the rest of the Gay Nineties in Philadelphia, had a good year, scoring 823 runs, good for third in the league and helping the Phillies to a 78-54 record and a third place finish, nine and a half games behind Brooklyn. If one were to single out a single player most responsible for the offensive upsurge, it wasn't Thompson, who had sort of an off-year (.313/.371/.443), nor was it Clements, although he had upped his numbers to .315/.392/.472. No, the star of the show was purchased from the failing Kansas City team of the American Association (most of the Brotherhood members were from the National League) to play left field and leadoff for the 1890 Phillies. He was Sliding Billy Hamilton, an excellent replacement for the departed Fogarty who, like Fogarty, was extremely fast, drew a lot of walks, and was a good fielder. Unlike Fogarty though, Hamilton could hit, .325 in 1890 with a .430 on base percentage and a league-leading 102 steals under the different scoring rules of the 1890s. Only Clements, who as a catcher played in only 97 games, had a higher Adjusted OPS than Hamilton's 139. And, Sliding Billy was just getting started as well. Together with Thompson and Delahanty (after his one-year hiatus in the PL), he would form one of the great outfields in major league history in the coming years. An all–Hall of Fame outfield.

The slings and arrows of the 1890 season didn't end with Reach, Rogers and Wright trying to hold their team together. The Phillies started strong but, in late May with the team in first place, they were hit with one of the most bizarre problems of all—manager Harry Wright went blind.[39] It has been suggested, perhaps somewhat facetiously, that Wright's problem came from poring over too many box scores. While it's true that Harry kept his own highly detailed box scores, and was a devoted enough studier of them and of statistics in general[40] to qualify for posthumous membership in the Society for American Baseball Research, that claim seems a bit far-fetched. A more likely explanation might have been a sinus problem of the type that almost cost George Sisler his sight in 1923. Whatever the cause, Wright was forced to the sidelines with Clements (who was only 25), Reach himself, and finally shortstop Bob Allen (he was only 22, making him the youngest manager in major league history) taking over as interim managers until Wright's vision cleared up in late July and he returned to the bench. Although the Phillies still clung to first place over the Bridegrooms as late as August 1, they were ultimately no match for the Brooklyn team, which was then in the midst of a nine-game winning streak, to be followed later in the month by another nine-game streak,[41] that put the pennant race out of the Phillies' reach—a frustrating circumstance for the Phillies that would be repeated throughout the coming decade.

♦ CHAPTER 12 ♦

The Athletics' Riches to Rags Story

The Athletics were riding on top of the world—the Philadelphia sporting world, that is—following the 1883 season. They were the American Association champions, they had made something like a quarter of a million dollars over their first two seasons, they had the best player in the AA (Harry Stovey) and an ace pitcher (Bobby Mathews) and even though they had lost five of nine games to the Phillies in the postseason exhibition series, life was still good for Billy Sharsig, Lew Simmons and Charlie Mason. And yet, in less than seven years, the franchise would be disbanded and taken over by the American Association, and 30-some years of baseball excellence in Philadelphia under the name Athletic would come to a crashing end. What happened?

As is usually the case in tales of woe such as this, there is no simple answer. Rather, a combination of factors brought down the Athletics—a change in ownership and bad management, greatly increased competitive pressure from the Phillies, greatly increased marquee presence from the Phillies, the basic weaknesses of the American Association, the Players League War, instability in a pitching staff that couldn't match up to the heavy hitters that manned the field, and finally, after the 1890 season, another change in ownership to a pair of quick buck artists—they all played a role in the fall of the Athletics.

The first change in the executive suite came after the four so-so seasons that followed the 1883 pennant. After finishing seventh, fourth, sixth and fifth and never getting closer to the top of the league than 14 games, falling profits caused Sharsig, Simmons and Mason to bring in an outsider to run the operation for the 1888 season. He was H.C. Pennypacker, who would prove to be one of the first in a long line of bad executives in Philadelphia baseball. There are actually two versions of this transaction. One is that the original owners hired Pennypacker as club president.[1] The second scenario is that Simmons and Mason outright sold their portions of the club to Pennypacker and his partner, William Whittaker, while Sharsig stayed on as manager and part-owner. Probably the most accurate statement comes from Francis Richter, who was there at the time. Richter states that the 1888 season was the year "the Athletic Club was purchased by Messrs. Whittaker, Pennypacker and Sharsig."[2] The fact is that Pennypacker was running the club in 1888, and would be the de facto owner, along with Whittaker, when the club went belly-up in 1890.[3]

Pennypacker's most obvious move as Athletics president in 1888 was to defy a new AA rule that raised the price of admissions from 25 cents to 50 cents. Philadelphia fans, thrifty sorts by nature who liked the traditional 25 cent ducats of the AA, were rebelling against the price increase, and staying away in droves. Pennypacker, recognizing this, unilaterally lowered the Athletics' ticket price back to 25 cents in July 1888—to be soon followed by the rest of the AA.[4] However, that maneuver, while helping the bottom line in 1888, ultimately didn't stop the Athletics' slide.

One of the other reasons the Athletics were experiencing a slide at the gate was the Phillies. Although Philadelphia as a whole was big enough to support two professional baseball teams, there may be some question whether the same neighborhood—North Philadelphia—was big enough to adequately support two teams at this time. Especially when one team was on the rise and the other team seemed to be more interested in fighting front office battles. AA historian David Nemec puts the Athletics' problem succinctly: "Long notorious for their front office squabbling, the A's had become the most ineptly run club in the Association, barring only Louisville, after the original group of ownership had sold out."[5] This perception was especially damaging to the Athletics since the front men for the Phillies, Al Reach and Harry Wright, were the two most distinguished gentlemen in professional baseball.

The key period of competition between the two teams was the period from 1884 to 1887. In 1883, the Athletics had established themselves as the top dog in town. However, the Athletics fell back to seventh in 1884 while the Phillies moved up to sixth. Even though the Athletics at 61-46 had a better record than the Phillies' 39-73, the two teams were moving in opposite directions. By 1885, the roles were completely reversed, as the two teams passed like high speed elevators going opposite directions—the Phillies toward the penthouse and the Athletics towards the cellar. Just two years after taking the AA title, the Athletics were under .500 (in fourth place) at 55-57. And, just two years after going 17-81, the Phillies were over .500 at 56-54, and in third place. The situation only got worse for the Athletics in 1886. They fell to sixth with a 63-72 mark while the Phillies posted what would be their best record for 90 years, 71-43. Philadelphia may love baseball, but Philadelphia fans love a winner, as the final version of the Athletics found out from 1949 to 1954, and the present-day Phillies have found out in trying to compete for the autumnal entertainment dollar with the Philadelphia Eagles football team.

The Athletics' competitive state vs. the Phillies' really hit rock bottom in 1887. The Phillies moved into the showplace of baseball in Philadelphia Park, a move occasioned by the team's success at the gate and the hottest superstar in town, Charlie Ferguson. Even the city's established star, Philadelphian Harry Stovey, had been eclipsed by the new star in town.

While the Athletics were fighting what looked to be a losing battle against the Phillies, the American Association itself wasn't much help to them. Long derided as the "Beer and Whiskey League," such an image would not generally go over well in a city that to this day still has "State Stores" selling liquor, and would still have Blue Laws prohibiting Sunday baseball for another 50 years. However, those surface issues were minor, compared to the basic flaws of the AA. It was Francis Richter, a supporter of the association who was also a part of its rise and fall, who said it the best. "After a splendid start it paltered through 10 years of varying fortunes, always handicapped by incompetence and deceit."[6] Such an organization was more likely to raise its ticket prices across the board to the detriment of individual teams (as the AA did in 1888) than it was to lower ticket prices in a city to help one of its teams compete against the other league (as the National League did for the Phillies in 1883). As a result, the Athletics got very little assistance from their league in their battle with the interlopers, a situation that was only exacerbated by the 1890 Players League war. Even though the Brotherhood initially made a bid to keep the association neutral in its war with the National League, the AA was severely rocked by the war, and nowhere was it rocked harder than in Philadelphia. Harold Seymour, in *Baseball: The Early Years*, explains the relationship between the three leagues:

> The struggle for players between the rival leagues hit the American Association hard. In a shrewd bid for Association neutrality, Ward promised at the outset that its players would remain untouched. In fact, he went to a special Association meeting December 4 to explore the possibility of amalgamating the Players' League and the Association. The rumor was that the two circuits would combine their teams in certain cities to form a single ten-club league.... For a while, the National League was very much worried that the "unnatural alliance" between the Association and the Players' League might materialize.... But, fortunately for the National League, nothing came of all this. The result was that the Association was soundly buffeted by the other two parties to the baseball triangle. The Players' League raided it, and the war strategy of the National League weakened it.[7]

When all was said and done, the association lost 30 players to the Players League, nowhere near what the NL lost, but enough to further unbalance an unstable organization. And, the same was true in spades for the Athletics. Already suffering from bad management, they accounted for one-sixth of the association's losses—Henry Larkin, Lou Bierbauer, Lave Cross, Gus Weyhing and the biggest prize of all, the AA's best player, Harry Stovey.

One reason the Athletics were in such bad shape at the start of the Players League war was the state of their pitching. From 1884 to 1889, the Athletics typically fielded a team of hard-hitters and less-accomplished pitchers. During those six seasons, only twice did their ranking in runs allowed in the AA even match their ranking in runs scored.

	Runs Scored	*Runs Allowed*
1884	3rd	9th
1885	1st	8th
1886	6th	8th
1887	5th	5th
1888	1st	3rd
1889	4th	4th

* * *

Coming off their 1883 title, where the Athletics were first in runs scored and fourth in runs allowed, complacency was not a problem. Sharsig turned over a large part of the team. Only Stovey, Cub Stricker, captain-manager Lon Knight and Jud Birchall returned for 1884 among the regulars. However, the offense didn't suffer that much, because one of the new players brought in was Henry Larkin. A 24-year-old rookie from nearby Reading, Pennsylvania, Larkin could *hit*. If it wasn't for the presence of Stovey on the team, he would have been the Athletics' big gun until he too jumped to the Players League in 1890. Unlike Stovey, he was slow afoot and not a good fielder. Still, a career Adjusted OPS of 141 is nothing to sneeze at, and he was already the Athletics' second-best hitter as a rookie going .276/.324/.423 in 85 games. With the addition of Larkin, the '84 Athletics, in addition to finishing third in runs, led the AA in batting average (.276) and slugging percentage (.379), and were second in on base percentage.

As for the pitching, that was the reason the 12-team AA's six-team pennant race in 1884 wasn't a seven-team race. The Athletics undoubtedly derived scant consolation from their 61-46 mark, since it landed them in the second division, 14½ games behind the New

York Metropolitans. Although Bobby Mathews again won 30 games (30-18), he did not have anywhere near the year he had in 1883, since it was only the Athletics' hard hitting that got him to 30 victories. His Adjusted ERA was just 101. The other major factor in the pitching slide was the loss of George Bradley, the number two pitcher in 1883, in a nasty salary dispute. Bradley jumped to the Union Association as part of the UA war of 1884, a conflict that also saw Sharsig lift pitcher Bollicky Billy Taylor from the UA St. Louis Maroons, and the UA Chicago Browns make off with Athletics rookie hurler Al Atkinson, both of these latter moves happening in mid-season.[8] The Athletics got the better of the exchange, since Taylor went 18-12 with a team-best 133 Adjusted ERA for Philadelphia, while Atkinson's 1884 service in Philly produced just an 11-11 mark and an 80 Adjusted ERA, although he did throw a 10-1 no-hitter against Pittsburgh on May 24.[9]

* * *

The imbalance between Philly's offense and defense just got worse in 1885, as the Athletics managed to finish under .500 despite leading the AA in runs scored (764), hits (1099), doubles (169), home runs (30), batting average (.265), on base percentage (.303) and slugging percentage (.365). The main abusers of opposing pitchers were once again Stovey and Larkin, with the latter finishing second in the AA in runs, on base percentage and RBIs, and third in batting average, slugging average and total bases. Even though Stovey finished behind Larkin in Adjusted OPS (174 to 163), he had no cause to be ashamed, since he led the AA in home runs (13) and runs scored (130) and was third in hits (153) and on base percentage (.371). In all, a typical Stovey year. Starting in 1883, when he set the single-season home run record (14), 1887 was the only season Stovey didn't lead the AA in at least one major offensive category.

Stovey and Larkin had some additional help in 1885 in the person of a refugee from the National League Phillies who had first caught on at the Jefferson Street Grounds late in the 1884 season. Since John Coleman's pitching talents were no longer desired at Recreation Park, the still just 21-year-old walked down the street to 25th and Jefferson and offered his services to the Athletics. Although he was a little better pitcher in the AA (6-7 in 19 games over four seasons), Sharsig and company probably appreciated him more for his hitting in 1885—a 133 Adjusted OPS in 96 games and top-10 finishes in the AA in batting average (.299), on base percentage (.345), slugging percentage (.415), OPS (.760), RBIs (70), and Adjusted OPS.

The pitching was basically a case of Bobby Mathews' last big year, plus whatever non-entities were around when the little spitballer wasn't available. Tom Lovett would be a star in 1890 (30-11 for Brooklyn in the NL), but he was 7-8 with a 93 Adjusted ERA in 1885. Seventeen-year-old Ed Knouff (7-6, 94) was a local teenager recruited in July to try and get somebody out when Mathews wasn't pitching. A good story, but unfortunately he never was much good, going 20-20 for his career. Undaunted by Knouff's less-than-rousing success, the Athletics would bring in an even younger Pennsylvanian to pitch a couple of years later. Finally, Ed Cushman (3-7, 98) was similarly forgettable (62-80 for his career) and even Coleman got eight turns in the box, going 2-2 with a league-average ERA at 3.43. That left the 33-year-old Mathews, who went 30-17 with a 142 Adjusted ERA in 422 innings—more than 40 percent of the team's total pitching for the year—the last heroic effort of a career that stretched back to the NABBP days and his hometown of Baltimore.

The Athletics' most significant action in conjunction with the 1885 season took place off the field—the first real signs of unrest among Sharsig, Simmons and Mason. In December

1884, Simmons announced that he was taking over as field manager in 1885 because the team had lost $20,000 in 1884, and blamed Harry Stovey, of all people, for the team's slump in the season just past. Since Stovey's 186 Adjusted OPS in 1884 was the highest of his glittering career, this claim made as much sense as the former minstrel thinking he could run a baseball team on the field. The determination of exactly who was running the Athletics on the field at any one time has been somewhat of a mystery; different sources will list any one of the three owners, plus different players, for various times in the years up until 1888, when Sharsig took over as the "manager." Although elsewhere in Philadelphia Harry Wright was still functioning as the Phillies' manager in what had been for a number of years the traditional fashion — a combination field manager, general manager and travelling secretary rolled up into one — it was at about this time that major league teams were starting to split up the all-encompassing duties of the position of on-the-field leader. Starting in professional baseball with Wright's role with the 1869 Cincinnati Red Stockings, the team captain generally served as the chief strategist during games, made overall strategic policy, including player moves, and made arrangements for the team to get from place to place. Although the Athletics' overall management may have been royally confused, the team did have a very specific policy that split the functions of club secretary and on-the-field manager into two different jobs. Harold Seymour explains that, "Clubs began putting the business details into the hands of a separate man, called the manager, whose job really corresponded to that of a modern club secretary. This left the captain free to concentrate on directing the team on the field." Seymour also gives the Athletics' owners' policy on the subject:

> The Captain shall have absolute control in directing, placing and playing the men during games and practices, without interference from anyone, the manager being as much under his control in these instances as any other men.[10]

Under this policy, the uniformed individual known as the captain (Lon Knight in 1883) was serving as the de facto manager, using the terminology of the twenty-first century. Meanwhile, the individual known as the manager in the 1880s was in reality not running the team during the games. This seems to have been the situation with the Phillies as late as 1896 when Billy Nash was brought in to manage the team on the field, while Bill Shettsline handled "strategic policy." This was also the arrangement the Athletics had as far back as 1869 or 1870, with captain Dick McBride running the team on the field and manager Hicks Hayhurst handling the more executive duties.

Simmons, in addition to his patently absurd claim about Stovey's performance in 1884, also cited an incident in 1884 wherein he stated that Stovey was too drunk to play, a common-enough claim in the 1880s, but not in conjunction with an upstanding citizen like Stovey. Both Sharsig and Mason jumped to their star's support, praising Stovey and bewailing Simmons' statements. Stovey also wrote a long and eloquent letter to Richter at the *Sporting Life*, defending himself. The end result was that Stovey was appointed manager-captain for 1885 and Simmons was moved to the bottom of the management totem pole.[11]

* * *

Then came 1886, and just about everyone but Stovey (155) and Larkin (162) had off-years. With the St. Louis Browns of Chris Von der Ahe reaching their pinnacle and defeating the Chicago White Stockings in the World's Series, the Athletics were left in the dust, finishing a poor sixth with their worst won-loss percentage (.467) to date. Possibly this is what set Lew Simmons off again. After a 5–4 loss at Jefferson Park to the last-place Baltimore Orioles on June 18, Simmons stormed into the Athletics' clubhouse to berate the team in general—he threatened to suspend the lot—and shortstop Joe Quest, whose error had cost them the game, in particular. This despite the fact that, going into the game, the Athletics were 22-19, good for fourth place and just three games out of first. Team policy aside, Simmons apparently at this point did take over the team on the field for a while. Fortunately for the Athletics, Sharsig was able regain control in time to keep them in sixth place; they had been headed for the cellar with Simmons actually handling the on-the-field manging.[12]

Even with 14 top–10 finishes in various statistical categories between them, Stovey and Larkin couldn't carry the offense to better than sixth in runs scored. And, with Mathews' strong right arm finally faltering at the age of 34, the pitching was in even worse disarray, finishing last in runs allowed. Little Bobby was able to throw only 198 innings, going 13-9 with an Adjusted ERA of 89. Al Atkinson, returning to the fold, was just as mediocre, going 25-17 in 397 innings with an identical 89 Adjusted ERA. The rest of the staff, Bill Hart (9-13, 110), Ted Kennedy (5-15, 77) and Cyclone Miller (10-8, 118), were also collectively average.

The only really interesting news for 1886 was the arrival of two young rookies who would both make their mark in the baseball world, though for somewhat different reasons. Lou Bierbauer was a 20-year-old second baseman from Erie, Pennsylvania. Although Bierbauer would never be much of a hitter (his career Adjusted OPS was 83) he was an excellent fielder at second, perhaps trailing only Hall of Famer Bid McPhee in the quality of his work among nineteenth century keystone men. His career fielding percentage was .935 (the league average was .922) and his range factor was 6.07

Lou Bierbauer in his second year with the Athletics (1887). He would become a cause celebre in 1891 (Library of Congress photograph).

to the league's 5.74. The Athletics' failure to reserve him after he jumped to the Players League would set off the second NL-AA war, leading to both the AA's eventually downfall and a new nickname for the NL's Pittsburgh franchise.

The other newcomer was a skinny, 23-year-old catcher from Massachusetts, Wilbert Robinson, whom Sharsig found playing in the New England League with Haverhill.[13] Although Robbie was later known as a devoted family man, he had a slightly different reputation in Philadelphia. Seems as if he was in charge of the Athletics' Ladies Auxiliary during his stay in the City of Brotherly Love. And, according to sportswriter and Philadelphia native Fred Lieb, some of the Auxiliary members themselves had slightly tarnished reputations — they were known as the "Big Bosom 'A' gals."[14] Whatever his off-the-field chores may have entailed, Robinson would play four and a half seasons with the Athletics, never posting an Adjusted OPS over 83, before moving on to Baltimore, Brooklyn and greater glory in the Hall of Fame as sort of a Lifetime Achievement member.

* * *

By 1887, it's possible that those few Philly fans that could drag themselves away from the Phillies' new Philadelphia Ball Park might have had trouble recognizing the Athletics. By now a totally average team being completely outshone by the hard-charging second place Phillies of Harry Wright and Charlie Ferguson, about the only aspects of the Athletics that would seem familiar were Harry Stovey and Henry Larkin. At the age of 35, Bobby Mathews made his last appearance in a major league uniform at season's end on October 10, starting the last game of a dreary season at Jefferson Park against the Brooklyn Trolley Dodgers, just his seventh appearance in 1887 (3-4, 64). Although Mathews had beaten the same Brooklyn team 10–3 just three days before for the last of his 300+ professional victories, he was unable to repeat the magic on the 10th, losing 7–5, and finishing the Athletics' season at 64-69 in fifth place. The new ace in town was 20-year-old Gus Weyhing, who was just starting what would be a distinguished career in Philadelphia baseball with a 26-28 record and a 101 Adjusted ERA. Weyhing and another 20-year-old rookie, Ed Seward (25-25, 104), were the workhorses of the 1887 staff, pitching 466 and 471 innings respectively.

Bill Sharsig must have had a fascination with young pitchers. Either that, or Mathews' looming retirement caused the Athletics to go to extreme lengths in the search for pitching help. The Athletics' other claim to fame in the pitchers' box in 1887 was Fred Chapman, who started a game against Cleveland on July 22, 1887. The 5-8, 165 pound Chapman, from Little Cooley, Pennsylvania, lasted all five innings of the game, giving up eight hits, two walks and four earned runs while striking out four in his only major league appearance. Although he was trailing 6–2 when he left the game, he escaped without a loss when the Athletics won the game on a forfeit. Not a great performance, but not terrible either, since Chapman was still four months short of his 15th birthday — the youngest person to ever appear in a major league baseball game — more than a year younger than the Cincinnati Reds' Joe Nuxhall was in 1944. In fact, Chapman is still the youngest person to ever play as a major league professional athlete in the United States — some 60 days younger than DC United's 14-year-old wunderkind, Freddy Adu, was in his debut.

Aside from the Chapman sideshow, the other new name of significance in the 1887 lineup was 21-year-old third baseman Denny Lyons. Although he'd played four games with Providence in the National League in 1884, and 32 games with the Athletics in 1885, he was virtually a rookie, and one that hadn't really impressed anyone, hitting .201 with no power. However, he would total 209 hits in 1887, good for a .367/.421/.523 line (161 Adjusted OPS) and finishing in the top five in five different statistical categories — batting, slugging, on base, total bases and hits. Just for good measure, he also set an all-time record for putouts by a third baseman (255) and put up a consecutive game hitting streak that would not be topped until Joe DiMaggio's 56-game streak. Admittedly, this latter feat is somewhat subject to interpretation. The 1887 season was the year that walks counted as hits in both the NL and the AA. During the course of a 52-game streak in 1887, Lyons had base hits in 50 of the 52 games, while drawing a walk in the other two games wherein he did not hit safely. So, under 1887 rules, he had a 52-game hitting streak.[15]

* * *

Philadelphia's baseball fortunes made a dramatic shift in 1888, first with the death of Charlie Ferguson and the Phillies' resultant malaise, and second with a revival by the Athletics. The offense bounced back to once again lead the AA in runs scored (827), hits (1209), doubles (183), triples (89), batting (.250) and slugging (.344). Even the pitching, led by Weyhing and Seward rebounded, and finished third in runs allowed (594) as the Athletics returned to the pennant race for the first time since 1883.

Offensively, the most important addition was a gift from the pennant-winning AA powerhouse St. Louis Browns. Von der Ahe had grown tired of outfielder Curt Welch's dissolute (the nineteenth century sportswriters' code for "he drank too much") ways, and sold him to Philadelphia for $3000. Although Von der Ahe would also send shortstop Bill Gleason to Philadelphia in a trade for three spare parts — catcher Jocko Milligan (although he was an excellent hitter, Robinson had taken his job), outfielder Fred Mann and infielder Chippy McGarr — Welch was the big prize that Sharsig garnered from the first of Von der Ahe's Finley–esque fire sales. A superb defensive outfielder, Welch would have his best offensive season in 1888, with an Adjusted OPS of 129 and finishing in the top 10 in the AA in on base

Another AA star who has never gotten his due — Denny Lyons (card from Larry Fritsch, Stevens Point, WI, photograph by Leigh G. Wills).

percentage (.355), runs (125), hits (155), doubles (22) and stolen bases (95). Generally, Welch was another Jim Fogarty—a fast, good fielding outfielder who really couldn't hit very well. As usual, Stovey, Larkin and Lyons had big years, although Stovey's only league-leading total was 20 triples. However, his all-around offensive excellence gave him an Adjusted OPS of 164, second in the AA to Cincinnati's John Reilly.

What was out of the usual, at least since 1883, was the pitching. The two young hurlers, Weyhing and Seward, not only dominated, they practically did all the pitching, combining to throw 923 of the team's 1208 total innings. For good measure, they each also tossed a no-hitter, Seward on July 26 against Cincinnati (12-2) and Weyhing five days later, a 4–0 shutout of Kansas City.[16] Mike Mattimore (15-10, 221 IP) in his only decent year, was the only other pitcher with more than 31 innings. The 21-year-old Seward threw an exhausting 519 innings, the third most in major league baseball in 1888, starting 57 games, and completing 57 games. After throwing 470 innings in 1887 to go with his 519 in 1888, Seward would pitch a total of 490 innings in the rest of his career. However, in 1888, he was great, going 35-19 with a 149 Adjusted ERA. Compared to those numbers, Weyhing seemed like a slacker, going 28-18 in 404 innings with a 133 Adjusted ERA.

Largely as a result of Seward's and Weyhing's heroics, although Welch helped, too, the Athletics were once again hot stuff in Philly, going 81-52 and finishing third. They were part of a four-team pennant race through July, keeping up with their benefactors, the Browns, the Brooklyn Bridegrooms and the Cincinnati Reds. Although Seward lost a tough 2–1 decision to the Reds in front of an overflow 12,000 fans at Jefferson Park on July 28,[17] knocking the Athletics five and a half games back in fourth place, the team then won seven straight. Coming in to a two-game series on August 7 against the Browns the Athletics were in second, just three games out. However they could only split with the Browns at home, Weyhing losing the first game 5–4, and then immediately traveled to St. Louis, where they lost two and tied one. By August 30, the Athletics, despite another seven-game winning streak, were still in second, but now they were six and a half games behind St. Louis. A 3–2 Seward loss to the Browns and pitcher Silver King on September 1 knocked them seven and a half back and, despite the fact that they then ran off their third seven game winning streak at a key point in the season, the Athletics never could get any closer than four games after that. They reached that final high point following an 8–3 Seward win over Baltimore in the first half of a September 12 doubleheader. From that point on, they went just 13-15 to finish third,[18] 10 games back of St. Louis and three and a half behind the Bridegrooms.

* * *

Although the Athletics would also finish third in 1889 (75-58), they had already reached their peak on September 12, 1888. The AA race in 1889 was strictly a two team affair pitting the Browns against another recipient of Von der Ahe's generosity, the Brooklyn Bridegrooms. Featuring both of the Browns' old aces in Parisian Bob Caruthers and Dave "Scissors" Foutz, the 'Grooms would not be left at the altar in '89, finishing two games up on St. Louis and 16 games ahead of Philadelphia. As a result, the best news for the Athletics was that the team had made a $30,000 profit on the 1888 pennant race.[19] The worst news was that the Brotherhood war was brewing, and, $30,000 in the black to the contrary, Pennypacker would manage to run the team into the ground before the end of the 1890 season.

The Athletics were an average fourth in runs scored and runs allowed in 1889, although they actually scored almost 100 more runs than they gave up (880-787). As usual, Stovey, Lyons and Larkin created a ton of runs—in fact, they were first (114), fifth (100) and sixth (91) in the AA in runs created. For good measure, Stovey also led the AA in home runs (19), RBIs (119), slugging (.525), runs (152), total bases (292) and extra base hits (70)—all in just 137 games.

Seward, clearly wearied by the monstrous load he had carried in 1888 and 1889, could pitch "only" 320 innings, going 21-15 with just a 95 Adjusted ERA. Weyhing took over as the ace, throwing 449 innings and going 30-21 with a 128 Adjusted ERA. Twenty-one-year-old curveballer Sadie McMahon, a year younger than Seward and Weyhing, escaped from Wilmington, Delaware, to spell the two iron men with 242 innings and a 14-12, 107 mark on his way to becoming the Athletics' ace in 1890. While "escaped" may not be exactly the right word, it's not far wrong—in 1888 McMahon had narrowly escaped a prison sentence for manslaughter in his hometown. He had been accused of killing a peanut vendor at the Wilmington Forepaugh Circus. And while McMahon was found innocent of that crime, he would soon be a witness to another manslaughter, in Philadelphia, in 1890.

* * *

Having lost five key players, including the AA's best (Stovey), the second part of their one-two punch (Larkin), and their ace (Weyhing) to the Players League, the Athletics were forced to do a major reconstruction project for the 1890 season. Sharsig, still around as manager, apparently because he still had a piece of the team, brought in rookie Dennis Fitzgerald to play short. However, he hurt his ankle in the second game, and gave way to another rookie, 19-year-old Philadelphian Ben Conroy. Jack O'Brien was brought back from exile—after five years with the Athletics, he had been sent to Brooklyn after the 1886 season for having too many shouting matches with Simmons—to play first base. The Shaffer brothers, 38-year-old Orator, who had been in the minors for four years, and 23-year-old Taylor, who hadn't played in the majors since the Union Association, came aboard to fill the holes at second and in the outfield. Sharsig still had Welch and long-time Philadelphia favorite Blondie Purcell to man the rest of his outfield, and he still had Denny Lyons from the team's previous big three. Also, Wilbert Robinson was still around to catch.

C—Wilbert Robinson	3B—Denny Lyons	OF—Curt Welch
1B—Jack O'Brien	SS—Ben Conroy	OF—Orator Shafer
2B—Taylor Shafer	OF—Blondie Purcell	

This was the patchwork team Sharsig fielded, largely behind Sadie McMahon. Ed Seward was still around, but the suspicion was the PL didn't want him because he had thrown his arm out. Seward was able to pitch 154 innings in 21 games, going 6-12 with an Adjusted ERA of 81. If Sharsig is to be given credit for making chicken salad out of chicken feathers with the players he put on the field, then he must also be given the blame for overworking Ed Seward. The almost totally anonymous Ed Green (all that's known about him is that he was 40 years old in 1890 and had never pitched previously in the majors) and Duke Esper, just starting his nine-year career, also worked more than 100 innings for Sharsig in 1890. McMahon, at age 22, threw 410 innings and went 29-18 with a 115 Adjusted ERA.

Behind Lyons' outstanding hitting (a 194 Adjusted OPS—he would lead the AA in on base, slugging and OPS in 1890) and McMahon's pitching, Sharsig actually had this ragtag crew playing good baseball. O'Brien and Welch had pretty good years, and the AA had been weakened by the Players League raids, but there was no easy explanation as to how Sharsig had them in the lead for a good part of the early season, and how they were still in first place as late as July 17 with a record of 43-27. All this despite the fact that Lyons was injured off and on, and both Taylor Shafer and Conroy were proving they could not hit major league pitching. In addition, Sharsig's pitching was so bad behind McMahon that he even tried Grasshopper Jim Whitney, who had been a great pitcher in the early 1880s, but who would be dead of tuberculosis by May 1891, for six games.[20]

Following a 15–9 win over Columbus on July 17, a six-game losing streak knocked the Athletics out of first, and by the end of the month, they were third, five games back. And, the worst was most certainly yet to come, because, although the Athletics had been leading the AA pennant race for most of the first part of the year, they were suffering at the gate in competition with the Phillies and the Players League Quakers. As was the case in all the markets where the PL was going head to head with the two established leagues, Philadelphia baseball was suffering. And, in this case, it was the Athletics who were suffering the most, being financially handicapped by the overly-generous salaries Pennypacker and Whittaker were paying themselves.[21] Combine that financial drain with the attendance drop-off, which undoubtedly became more severe as the Athletics, having played over their heads all season long, started to lose, and there was a formula for disaster.

If that were the case, then the association was a party to the crime. While Nemec is correct in that the Athletics were very poorly run, he is also correct in that the AA, to its own detriment, did little to solve the situation until it was too late. As one of his eight reasons why the association ultimately succumbed to the National League, Nemec noted that the AA had ignored "the deteriorating situation in Philadelphia until the Athletics' franchise had become almost unsalvageable ... someone ... should have noticed that things were coming apart and sounded the alarm."[22]

The Athletics went 5-14 in August, dropping to sixth place with a record of 51-50 by the end of the month. They had gone 8-23 since leading the league on July 17. And the worst was still to come. As the Athletics continued to lose, going 3-7 for the first 16 days of September, the red ink mounted and the players threatened to strike over a little matter of not being paid.[23] On September 17, with the Athletics now $17,000 in the hole, Pennypacker and Whittaker pulled the plug, releasing almost all the players, and disbanding the Philadelphia Athletics.[24] Finally, in a classic case of too little, too late, the American Association stepped in to help out Philadelphia. Having already had the Brooklyn Gladiators fold earlier in the year, the AA apparently decided it couldn't afford to lose another team, taking over the franchise and sending the Athletics on an extended road trip under the direction of the great survivor, Billy Sharsig.

The team they sent was a bunch of amateurs, semi-pros and other professional nonentities. Despite reports that all the previous 1980 Athletics had been released, there was at least one who stayed to the bitter end, 40-year-old pitcher Ed Green. The winning pitcher in the Athletics' 6–0 triumph over Baltimore at Jefferson Park on September 14, Green would start five more times after September 17, losing all five of those starts. An understandable result, since the Athletics lost 22 straight games to close out the season, finishing 54-78 in seventh place, ahead of only the now-defunct Gladiators. What of Ed Green? In his only major league season the Philadelphia native was 7-15 in 25 games and 191 innings with that one shutout of Baltimore—the last win for this version of the Athletics—and a 5.80 ERA (66 Adjusted). Not great, but this was an era when you almost never saw a player in his 40s. Green was the second-oldest player in the league (Orator Shaffer was third oldest), and by two years the oldest pitcher. And, he did better than his two main pitching compatriots on the 22-game death march. Charlie Stecher went 0-10 with a 10.32 ERA and Ed O'Neil (who had pitched two games for the AA Toledo Maumees earlier in the year) was 0-6 with a 9.69 ERA. All things considered, Green deserved a medal of some kind, especially in light of the team he ended up pitching with. The 1890 Athletics, being in the position of amateurs facing pros 22 times, lost 16 of those games by giving up 10 runs or more (with a high of 22).[25]

The other individual deserving of praise in this disaster was Sharsig. He was sent on the road trip by the AA with $245 to pay his cast of non-entities on a per diem basis— they weren't even signed to regular contracts. That got him as far as Louisville, where the Athletics were killed in five games by the now-first-place Cyclones. However, the gate receipts for the five games allowed Sharsig to keep them going, and to pay his players in cash after each game. Finally returning home to Philadelphia after 17 road games (and 17 losses), the Athletics lost five more to Rochester and Syracuse (all but one loss coming by double digits) to end the season on October 12—after which Jefferson Park was sold in a sheriff's sale to help meet the team's debts. Only Johnny Ray, the groundskeeper, and Billy Sharsig were there at the end to represent the first name in Philadelphia baseball.[26]

♦ CHAPTER 13 ♦

Other Teams, Other Leagues

Philadelphia had been a great baseball town since before there was baseball. Never was there a shortage of individuals willing to play—and watch—the amalgamation of bat-and-ball games originally imported from Western Europe that included town ball and cricket. Starting around 1860, and accelerating following the Civil War, baseball became the dominant sport in the city. As a result of the war's role in bringing the faster, more comprehensible sport directly into the mainstream of Philadelphia society, the number of baseball clubs in the city grew exponentially after the war. Athletic and Keystone may have been the only openly professional clubs by the watershed year of 1869, but they weren't the only top clubs, anymore than they had been some five years before. Dozens and dozens of Philadelphia teams joined the NABBP in its latter years.

The names of these largely amateur clubs may be footnotes in Philadelphia baseball history, but, at the time they were very important to Philadelphia baseball fans and baseball history, spreading the game and its popularity to the point where there was a fan base that could support two, or briefly, three, professional teams almost continuously for 85 years, as well as a huge number of amateur and semi-pro teams. The highlights of Philly baseball outside of the National Association, National League and American Association tell a tale of some excellent players who passed through, or came up through, the independent ranks before moving on to greater fame and glory. Not only did these independent teams often serve a development function for players, but also for the three best-known leagues of the nineteenth century.

By 1868, Philadelphia was represented in the NABBP by 44 clubs and there must have been a goodly number of non–NABBP clubs, since the roster of NABBP-member teams from the city changed dramatically from season to season in these years. Although the 1868 list had Athletic, Olympic, Keystone, Equity, Minerva and Geary, a score of new names had appeared, many of which would drop out of the NABBP by 1869—Alpha, Amateur, Armstrong, Athenian, Belmont, Cold Spring, Contest, Dirigo, First Ward, Harry Clay, Korndaffer, Marion, Masonic, Mutual, Pacific, Penn Treaty, Ralston, Reno, Rittenhouse, S.J. Randall, Spartacus, Trix, W.H. Patterson and more.

In 1869, Philadelphia was represented in the NABBP by just 17 amateur clubs, as well as the professional Athletic and Keystone. At least one of these 17 names was still an old familiar one, dating back 40 years or so. Olympic went 5-10 in 1869, scoring 305 runs and allowing 345. The remainder of Philadelphia's 1869 teams still contained familiar names like Geary, City Item and Chestnut Street Theater, but there were also many newer ones, sometimes representing Philadelphia's many neighborhoods, like Roxborough and Wissahickon (from Germantown). In 1870, the number of Philadelphia amateur clubs in the

NABBP was back up to 21. This group included the now-amateur Keystone club (they went 2-12, having scaled back their baseball ambitions greatly), Olympic, West Philadelphia, Cohocksink, Mount Vernon, and two Pastime clubs. In the majority, these teams seem to have represented North Philadelphia, where most of the major playing grounds were anyway, and the northwest Philadelphia neighborhoods like Germantown, Roxborough and Manayunk.[1]

The Athletics in 1871 played just 29 games within the National Association; they must have had a lot of local opposition during the season since they didn't have the financial resources to spend six months touring the country between NA games. NA teams also used the better amateur teams as a form of minor leagues, signing the amateurs' better players to fill holes. One such team, mentioned by William Ryczek in *Blackguards and Red Stockings*, was the Easton, Pennsylvania, club that defeated the Athletics, White Stockings and Brooklyn Atlantics in 1874, thanks in part to having George Bradley, who would throw 16 shutouts for the 1876 National League St. Louis Browns, as their pitcher. Most of the 1879 Easton team became the 1880 Athletics and other Easton alumni of note included Chick Fulmer, Denny Mack, Jim Devlin, Joe Battin, Bill Parks, John Abadie and Tom Miller.[2]

* * *

The biggest development in Philadelphia-area baseball outside of this arena took place between 1866 and 1875. In 1872, the University of Pennsylvania had sold its campus in the heavily-developed area of 9th and Chestnut Streets, and had moved to the relatively wide-open spaces of West Philadelphia, to the 3400 block of Walnut Street, where the university bought part of Alexander Hamilton's eighteenth century Woodlands estate at a cost of $8000 an acre.[3] Although 34th and Walnut was no longer a woodlands in the early 1870s, there apparently were enough wide open spaces—neighboring Drexel University wouldn't be founded until 1893—that the Penn Quakers decided to take up baseball as a sport.

Penn's first team, playing during the 1875 season, featured future dentist and catcher Albert "Doc" Bushong, who also found the time to play in one game for the Brooklyn Atlantic club in the NA that year, collegiate eligibility rules being a little different then than now. Bushong would go on to play five games for the Athletics in 1876, and 13 years in all in the major leagues, thus becoming the first of 53 former University of Pennsylvania players to be so employed. As would later be the case with other Philadelphia colleges, Penn would become part of the feeder system for the major leagues, in addition to being a home for the best in amateur baseball. In the absence of the minor league farm systems that developed in the twentieth century, no less than 21 former Penn Quakers from the years between 1875 and 1900 played major league baseball, with Phillies centerfielder Roy Thomas and defensive standout Bushong having the best and longest careers.

Meanwhile, just west of the city, in a region that grew up around the mighty Pennsylvania Railroad's Main Line, another college, Villanova University, was taking up baseball. The Wildcats started even earlier than the Penn Quakers, playing their first game on May 2, 1866, against the Philadelphia Central Club and winning 74–9. An almost equally-lopsided result came from Villanova's first intercollegiate game, a 66–21 thrashing of Haverford College.

The catcher and president of that first Villanova B.B.C. (Base Ball Club), as the Main Line team was known, was an Easton native, Dennis McGee. Playing under the name Denny Mack, he later became Villanova's first major leaguer,[4] playing for seven different teams, including the original Athletics and the Philadelphia Pearls, in three different leagues. Although he never hit very much (.228/.273/.271), Mack played in 373 games from 1871 to 1883, primarily at first base and shortstop. Although 48 former Villanova Wildcats would go on to play major league baseball, only two, Mack and late 1890s Phillies pitcher Red Donahue, would play in the nineteenth century.

* * *

With only the Athletics being taken into the National League for 1876, the Pearls were left to an independent existence, the same fate that would befall the Athletics the next year. Both Athletics and Philadelphias would continue to be familiar names, though hardly the only names, in the thriving Quaker City baseball scene in the years from 1876 to 1882. The Pearls soldiered on part-way through the 1876 season until disbanding, with most of the team joining a professional club in Harrisburg. The 1876 Philadelphias featured at least four very decent players, notably a big name in the pitcher's box, George Zettlein. The Charmer started the season with his old (he had played with the Pearls in 1873 and 1875) team, despite allegations made at the end of the previous year regarding his throwing games. After going 3–2 with the Pearls-Phillies, he was picked up by the National League Athletics, for whom he went 4-20 for the balance of the 1876 season. Shortstop Candy Nelson was in the middle of a very lengthy career in 1876 while leftfielder Orator Shaffer, a native Philadelphian who had played 10 games for Hartford and the Mutuals in the National Association in 1874 and 19 games for the NA Philadelphias in 1875, was early in a career that would last all the way to the Players League war in 1890.[5] A fourth player who had played professionally previously in Philadelphia was former Centennial, and future AA Athletic executive, Charlie Mason.

Villanova University's first major leaguer, Denny Mack (courtesy John Thorn).

When the Athletics left the NL after the 1876 season, they took the same route as the Pearls-Phillies—they became an independent team, and one that employed more than a couple of good players over the next few years. Both the level of baseball activity and the interest in baseball in Philadelphia did not wane in the period from 1877 to 1882, despite occasional potshots from out-of-town newspapers, claiming that the Philadelphias' reputation for hippodroming had caused the professional game to go to the dogs in Philly.[6] A more correct interpretation would be that Philadelphia didn't really need the National League from 1877 to 1882. At this early point in its development, the National League was barely more than a baseball-playing organization with pretensions of grandeur as there was plenty of good baseball being played outside of the league. As Harold Seymour noted in *Baseball: The Early Years*, "For several years after their Athletics were cast out by the National League, Philadelphia fans followed several clubs who played under the names 'Philadelphias' and 'Athletics.'"[7] Thanks to research by SABR members Brock Helander and Frank Vaccaro, the lineage of these teams has recently become clearer.

The best of these teams was probably the 1877 version of the Athletics. At the very least, it was a team local fans could relate to. Still playing at 25th and Jefferson, with Al Reach initially set to be the captain (field manager); none other than Hicks Hayhurst returned to his old job as (business) manager while 1876 field manager Al Wright served as secretary. Fergy Malone actually started the season as field manager.[8] On the field, Reach (139 hits in 94 games) and Wes Fisler (129 hits in 96 games) were playing their last competitive seasons, but Levi Meyerle still had enough left in his bat to be picked up by the Cincinnati Red Stockings mid-way through the 1877 campaign, and to hit .327 in National League competition. Chick Fulmer also made an appearance for a couple of months. Even Count Sensenderfer, whose bad knee seems to have healed, was on the roster after several years as an executive with the Athletics. Sam Weaver was a solid pitcher, as was a youngster who was just breaking in—Harry Stovey. Beating Chicago 6–5 on September 4, 1877, in his first action, he also scored 28 runs and 24 games, and soon moved to first base and the outfield.[9]

These Philadelphia favorites were not the only recognizable names on the 1877 Athletics. Dave Eggler, the Athletics' center fielder in 1875 and 1876, stayed around for the first part of 1877 before he was picked up by Hulbert's Chicago White Stockings, despite the fact that he was hitting just .194 for Philadelphia. John Montgomery Ward, recently kicked out of Penn State University for fighting, saw his first professional action in 1877 as a 17-year-old curveball pitcher for the Athletics. If George Bradley, fresh off his 45-win, 16-shutout 1876 season with the St. Louis Browns, hadn't reneged on his 1877 contract with the Athletics,[10] they would have employed a more notable crew of pitchers than any of the league teams. The 1877 Athletics had a virtual all-star team (minus a catcher) under contract at one time or another, and that's not counting Cap Anson, who signed with the '77 Athletics but went back to Chicago when the White Stockings' owner, William Hulbert, banished the Athletics to the League Alliance.[11]

1b—Wes Fisler	3b—Levi Meyerle	OF—Harry Stovey
2b—Al Reach	OF—John Montgomery Ward	P—George Bradley
SS—Chick Fulmer	OF—Dave Eggler	

Briefly joining the Athletics in the loosely-organized League Alliance in 1877 were the Philadelphias. Initially under the management of former Athletic-Philadelphia outfielder-pitcher John McMullin, they added Malone as their manager when he was pushed out of the Athletics in early May. Also on this team, at least until early June, were George Bechtel, Horace Phillips (who would later manage the team), Jud Birchall and J.M. Ward. According to Vaccaro, in June McMullin took six of his players and formed another short-lived Philadelphias team that broke up on July 28.[12]

A dissenting opinion on the best Philadelphia team of this interregnum comes from the late Philadelphia baseball historian Ed "Dutchy" Doyle. Speaking at a symposium on Philadelphia's Baseball History at the Historical Society of Pennsylvania on February 24, 1990, Doyle stated that probably the best baseball team in the area in the period from 1877 to 1881 was the Shibe Ball Club, sponsored by future American League Athletics owner Ben Shibe.[13] Exactly how good the Shibe Club was is hard to say; they may have been just a local club that would later seem more important because of their sponsor. They did have at least one first-rate ballplayer, Philadelphia native Tom "Oyster" Burns, who began his rise to an 11-year career as a major league outfielder in 1880 with Shibe.[14] Doyle also claimed in 1990 that Shibe "got rid" of this team when the American Association came to town in 1882,[15] however, it is also possible that he merged this semi-pro outfit into or with the independent Reach Philadelphias.

Despite their sterling 1877 lineup, the Athletics underwent a re-organization for the 1878 season. On March 30, 1878, the team was re-organized under the management of 1876 manager Al Wright who was planning to have Reach, Fisler, Meyerle, Mason and Count Sensenderfer on the nine,[16] which played this year at Oakdale Park. However, it seems as if Fisler and Reach retired, and Meyerle played for Springfield in the International Association in '78.[17]

As for the Philadelphias, they apparently took a year hiatus when Fergy Malone left town for Baltimore.[18] Still, new teams continued to make the scene, notably the Philadelphia Defiance Club, which, after playing a partial season in 1877, played in the National Base Ball Association (not to be confused with the old, now defunct National Association) in 1878 and '79.[19] In fact, Defiance, with Doc Landis on the squad, may have been the city's strongest club in '79, defeating both the Philadelphias—managed by William Warr and featuring youngsters Cub Stricker and Pop Corkhill—and the Athletics for the "Pennsylvania championship."[20] According to Vaccaro's information, this team of Philadelphias was another Fergy Malone production (in fact, they were known as Malone's Philadelphias), playing at Oakdale Park, and they joined the National Association in June.[21]

The second Athletics reorganization took place in 1880. This "new" Athletic team, now playing in the National Association of Base Ball Clubs, featured Jack O'Brien, Charlie Mason, Doc Landis and future AA star Tip O'Neill and played its games at Oakdale Park, which they shared with the still-amateur Olympics. Formed largely from the 1879 Easton team, this squad of Athletics foundered when the National Association failed in the summer of 1880.[22] However, the pieces of this failure are what Bill Sharsig re-organized even before the 1880 season ended, becoming the AA Athletics. Corroboration for this seminal development, and the separate status of the various Athletic organizations, is found in the June 6, 1884, *New York Times*, wherein it is reported that Sharsig had been sued by what claimed to be the "original" Athletic baseball club (whoever that might have been) over the use of the name Athletic. The injunction wasn't granted, and it was noted that Sharsig had been using the name for four years, or since 1880.[23]

Sharsig's team, referred to in the September 1, 1880, *Brooklyn Eagle* as "the new nine," was a different crew than the first 1880 team, with just O'Brien and Mason remaining among the top players, and being joined by a new captain—Chick Fulmer—and other Philly favorites like Sam Weaver and Jud Birchall. Sharsig arranged for this Athletic team to play through September and October at both Oakdale Park and what would later be called Recreation Park.[24]

Meanwhile, Hustling Horace Phillips was supposed to be back in town in March 1880, completing the organization of another team of Philadelphias and featuring old-timers Fisler, Meyerle and Eggler. However, Phillips ended up managing in Baltimore and Rochester in 1880, and it appears as if the 1880 Philadelphias never came together.[25] Then, according to Helander, the Philadelphias lasted for about a month in 1881 with Billy Barnie as manager. Only Sharsig's Athletics, playing in the Eastern League and then taking their tour through Pittsburgh, Columbus, Louisville, Cincinnati and St. Louis, seem to have represented Philadelphia throughout 1881 with a team now managed by Phillips and including at one time or another Fulmer, Birchall, Stricker, Weaver, O'Brien, Landis, Mason and future AA star Arlie Latham.[26]

The Philadelphias returned with an entirely new team in 1882 under Al Reach, a move that may have built upon the Shibe Ball Club. Reach, who established the team and became treasurer, also obtained the title to the oddly-shaped grounds at Ridge and Columbia, aka Recreation Park, where the Philadelphias and the Athletics had both played some previously.[27] Playing in a two-team League Alliance with the New York Metropolitans they featured four players good enough to play in the National League in 1883 (Lewis, Manning, McClellan and Neagle), plus 1883 Athletic shortstop Mike Moynahan, and future stars Latham and Charlie Buffington (before he joined the NL's Boston Red Caps).[28]

When the Philadelphias were left out of the AA in favor of the Athletics, Reach went ahead with his plans for the 1882 season. Reach cleared his little plot at Ridge and Columbia, re-sodded the grounds, built a three-section wooden grandstand, and, on April 8, 1882, Recreation Park opened for the independent Phillies,[29] who would go on to play a lengthy schedule of 140 games, and included at various times Doc Bushong (he caught five games), Cannonball Morris (another catcher, although he'd make his name later as a pitcher), Bald Bill Barnie (1b), and Frank Fennelly (he played a little third along with Latham). They were now managed by the Athletics' 1881 manager, Hustling Horace Phillips, at least until the AA called him back midway through the 1882 season, and Barnie took over the captaincy-managerial reins.[30]

With Helander and Vaccaro having done much to straighten the tangled web of Philadelphia baseball from 1876 to 1882, here is a chronology of what appear to be the four top organizations in that period:

1876—Athletics (National League); Philadelphias (independent, folded mid-season)
1877—Athletics (from NL to League Alliance); Philadelphias (League Alliance, folded mid-season); Defiance (independent, partial season); Shibe (independent)
1878—"Re-organized" Athletics (independent); Defiance (National Association); Shibe (independent)
1879—Athletics (independent); "New" Malone's Philadelphias (National Association); Defiance (National Association, won Pennsylvania championship then disbanded in late August); Shibe (independent)
1880—"New and re-organized" Athletics (National Association, folded mid-season); Sharsig's Athletics (formed in September); Shibe (independent)
1881—Sharsig's Athletics (Eastern League); Philadelphias (lasted for one month); Shibe (independent)
1882—Sharsig's Athletics (from EL to American Association), Reach's Philadelphias (may have merged with Shibe, League Alliance, left out of AA).

* * *

Another development in Philadelphia baseball around this time was the re-establishment of the city as one of the top centers for black baseball. After the original Pythian club disbanded in the wake of the death of Octavius Catto, two top flight African American semi-pro teams, Orion and Mutual, were formed, helping pave the way for what historian Christopher Threston says was the formation of the first black professional team, the Keystone Athletics, in May 1885. That outfit lasted only two months in Philadelphia before relocating to Long Island and merging with the Manhattan club of Washington, D.C., and the Philadelphia Orion club to form the Cuban Giants, the first black touring professional baseball team.[31]

A slightly different version of this transition comes from Robert Peterson's *Only the Ball Was White*. Peterson reports that although black baseball pioneer and historian Sol White did give credit to the Long Island Cuban Giants for being the first team of professional African Americans in 1885, earlier reports in Francis Richter's *Sporting Life* (1884) and the *Cincinnati Enquirer* (1882) give evidence that either the Philadelphia Orion club or the Philadelphia Mutual club were professionals. Peterson also says that the Orions and the Mutuals were still playing as professional teams in the late 1880s.[32]

* * *

One can imagine that it was the 1882 success of the independent Phillies more than the failure of the 1875 National Association Centennials that carried the most weight in 1884 when the Athletics and the Phillies were joined by a third Philadelphia team purporting to hold major league status, and also carrying a fine old Philadelphia baseball name— the Keystones of the Union Association. The league's key organizational meeting was held in Philadelphia on December 18, 1883, at the Bingham House, and brought together the Keystones, the Chicago Browns, the semi-pro Washington Nationals, the Baltimore Monumentals and UA organizer Henry Lucas' St. Louis Maroons. Teams from Boston and Cincinnati (headed by Justus Thorner, who had just been squeezed out of the AA Cincy team) soon joined, finally followed by the Altoona Mountain Citys. Although this squad was apparently not the same Altoona Mountain club that the original Athletics had drubbed so unmercifully back in 1863, they were at least the heirs to that tradition. The most obscure city to ever hold a major league franchise lost that franchise after going 6-19 and disbanding on May 29.[33]

In a similar fashion, the Keystones were not the same team that was founded in 1859 in Philadelphia; they just borrowed a famous Philadelphia baseball name. They also borrowed a couple of other famous Philadelphia players' names—Tom Pratt and Fergy Malone. Trouble was, they were both over 40 at this point, and even though the 42-year-old Malone did play one game for the Keystones (he caught and went one for four), neither was of much help, either on the field or as a draw against the Phillies and the Athletics. Pratt, who had done quite well out of baseball with his Pratt Brothers company (a paint dealership),[34] is typically listed as one of the two main financial backers of the team, along with a young man (he was just 20 at the time) who would go on to become one of the notable people in Philadelphia baseball, William "Billy" Shettsline. Although Shettsline's having the money to back the team seems unlikely, the Keystones did get off the ground, with the 44-year-old Pratt, whose Philadelphia baseball career stretched back to at least 1860, taking over as manager after Malone went 11-30 in the same role. He posted a somewhat better 10-16 mark, but it wasn't good enough to keep the team from folding in early August, $10,000 in debt.[35] It's also possible that another factor in the Keystones' lack of success was Pratt's choice of a playing field. Bucking what was already a 25-year-long tradition in Philadelphia of teams playing in North Philly, Keystone Park was located in South Philadelphia, on the east side of Broad Street, at the intersection of Broad and Moore. Pratt apparently didn't have enough time to secure a real grounds—Keystone Park was actually the former home of the city's Forepaugh Circus.[36]

On the field, Harry Wright himself probably couldn't have done much with this bunch of Keystones. For while it was theoretically possible to scare up a representative team on short notice, the fact is that the team Pratt scared up was closer to reprehensible. Only left fielder Buster Hoover, who hit .364/.390/.495 to finish second in the UA in batting average and third in on-base and slugging, was really representative of being a good player, although the team's 19-year-old rookie catcher-outfielder was both a crowd-pleaser and hit a decent .282 with three home runs in 41 games. The opportunistic Wright, now running the Phillies, picked up both Hoover and the young catcher when the Keystones folded, but, Harry batted only .500 in this respect. Hoover played just 64 more major league games, and never hit over .217 again. Now the catcher, undaunted by the fact that he threw left-handed, became one of the great backstops of the nineteenth century, and the first man to catch 1,000 major league games—Philadelphian Jack Clements.

As for the rest of the team, pitcher Jersey Bakely, who led the UA in losses with 30, would hang around for four more years. Shortstop Henry Esterday played three more years, but never hit over .190, and third baseman Jerry McCormick had played 93 games with Baltimore of the AA the year before. They had the longest major league careers, outside of Clements. Pratt even resorted to bringing his old teammate, 38-year-old Levi Meyerle, out of retirement to play three games at first and right field. He had a double in 11 at-bats, and made four errors. No wonder Lucas had to bring in the Wilmington Quicksteps to take the Keystones' place. Still, despite this fiasco, it would be only another six years before ambitious souls would once again try to establish a third major league team in Philadelphia.

* * *

The Players Brotherhood and the 1890 Players League, spearheaded by John Montgomery Ward, right from the start must have considered Philadelphia a vital cog in their venture, despite the previous failures to establish a third major league team in the city. Only in Brooklyn (which was still a separate city from New York) and Philadelphia were three teams going head to head to head, leading one to assume that, by placing a third team in Philadelphia to take on the by-now well-established Phillies and Athletics, Ward, et al., must have felt it was both important to have a presence in the Quaker City, and that such a venture would succeed. As it turned out, Ward was only partly correct in his assumptions. The Philadelphia Quakers did outdraw the Athletics at the gate, although the Quakers in turn were outdrawn by the Phillies, who led the National League in attendance (148,000) and were the only NL team to outdraw their Players League counterpart.[37] On the other hand, David Voigt, in *American Baseball*, says that the Players' Philadelphia franchise was shaky, and the most vulnerable spot among the new league's eight teams.[38] While the Quakers did give the Players League a presence in what was unquestionably an important baseball city, Ward made the mistake of turning to the wrong source of money to bolster the franchise. When original primary investor J.M. Vanderslice ran into monetary troubles in July the Quakers were rescued by the team's minority stockholders, brothers and meat wholesalers George and J. Earl Wagner,[39] who turned out to be very good at dealing in meat—both the livestock and baseball varieties.

Vanderslice and the team's player representative, George Wood, built a team with a very heavily Phillie look—a not surprising development since Wood had been the Phillies' left fielder in 1889.

	1889 Phillies	*1890 Quakers*
C	Jack Clements	Jocko Milligan
1B	Sid Farrar	Sid Farrar
2B	Al Myers	John Pickett
3B	Joe Mulvey	Joe Mulvey

	1889 Phillies	*1890 Quakers*
SS	Bill Hallman	Billy Shindle
OF	Jim Fogarty	Jim Fogarty
OF	Sam Thompson	Mike Griffin
OF	George Wood	George Wood
UT	Ed Delahanty	Bill Hallman
UT	Pop Schriver	Lave Cross
P	Charlie Buffington	Charlie Buffington
P	Ben Sanders	Ben Sanders
P	Kid Gleason	Phil Knell
P	Dan Casey	Bill Husted

The Phillies, thanks to the continuing presence of Harry Wright and the loyalty he engendered, and the money Al Reach had squirreled away after selling his retail operation to Al Spalding, actually suffered the fewest losses among National League teams. However, all of the Phillies deserters stayed in town in what was still the biggest intra-city raid since the White Stockings made off with most of the Athletics' regulars in 1873. As a result, Philadelphia fans were undoubtedly saying, "Gee, these guys look familiar," when they went to Forepaugh Park (also known as Brotherhood Park), now located at the corner of Broad and Dauphin Streets, to see the 1890 Quakers. In a throwback to the 1884 UA Keystones, the Quakers were using the new home of the Forepaugh Circus, although the circus by this time had moved to North Philly, closer to the foci of the city's traditional baseball activity. In this case, a lot closer, since all three Philadelphia major league teams were now playing in separate parks just four blocks apart.[40]

On April 30, 1890, no less than 17,182 fans jammed the little (only 420 feet to dead center—a relatively short distance in these days of big outfields) wooden park to see the former Phillies, now Quakers, take on the Boston Reds in the home opener, a 9–6 home team loss to a home town pitcher, Philly native Matt Kilroy.[41] The Quakers had split their previous six road games, pretty much giving an indication of how the rest of the year would go on the field. Under the management of Phillies deserters Fogarty (7-9 in the first 16 games) and then Buffington, the Quakers played pretty close to .500 ball throughout the year, finishing at 68-63, good for fifth place, 14 games behind the Reds.

Although undistinguished on the field, the Quakers' real significance was behind the scenes, where, in March 1890, Philadelphia lawyers for the first time came onto the baseball stage with a vengeance. In a move that would precede the raids of Connie Mack and the Phillies' reaction some 11 years later, Phillies' co-owner and lawyer John Rogers sued the Quakers with the goal of retaining contract-jumper Bill Hallman. Remarkably enough, Philadelphia Common Pleas Court judge M. Russell Thayer ruled in the Quakers' favor, on the grounds that Hallman's Phillies contract, or at least that portion of it that contained the reserve clause, lacked mutuality, in that it bound the player to the club for as long as the club desired, but the club could release itself from any obligation to the player with just 10 days notice.[42] The remarkable part wasn't Judge Thayer's ruling, it was the fact that it had so few repercussions throughout baseball. You would think that, after the judge released Hallman from any obligation to the Phillies—in other words, he was free to play for the Quakers in 1890—that every time a player wanted to jump his contract, the name of M. Russell Thayer would have been invoked, to the point where the reserve clause would have been revoked.

Actually, the Hallman case was far from unique. Suits instituted by National League clubs to overturn the contract jumping of Buck Ewing, George Gore, Hardie Richardson,

Tim Keefe and Ward himself all had the same result as the Hallman case.[43] Why then did the reserve clause exist into the twentieth century? Apparently because the clause itself, or at least the enforcing of the clause within a league, was not illegal. After all, players jumped contracts by the dozens during the American League–National League War of 1901–1903, without anyone actually successfully suing, with the exception of the Phillies' John Rogers in the Lajoie case, and the success of that suit was based on King Larry's "unique" abilities. The message of 1890 was clear: sue to enforce the reserve clause, and you lose. However, if a player tried to change teams within say, the monopolistic National League of 1895, well, all the member clubs within a single league honored each others' reserve clauses, and the presumptive contract jumper would have nowhere to jump to. So, while the Hallman case may have allowed the Players League to function in 1890, it did nothing to really free the slaves.

The 1890 Quakers were pretty much your average team, finishing third, fourth or fifth in the PL in runs, hits, doubles, home runs, batting average, slugging percentage, earned run average and runs allowed. Hallman didn't really prove to be worth suing over, as he hit .267/.338/.360 while playing the outfield, second base, catcher, third base and a couple of games at short. The offensive star of the team was shortstop Billy Shindle. Normally a pretty good third baseman, Shindle came from the Baltimore entry in the AA and moved over to make room for one of the Phillies' deserters, Joe Mulvey, at the hot corner. While Shindle did have a good year at the plate, hitting .324/.371/.483 with an Adjusted OPS of 125, and leading the Players League in total bases with 282, he also proved to be a good argument for why it's usually not wise to try and turn a third baseman into a shortstop. Although his range factor was quite good, 5.45 compared to a league average of 5.05, Shindle also set the all-time major league record for most errors in a season—a staggering 122, encompassing an incredible 119 at short.

* * *

Even after the American Association and the Athletics failed following the 1891 season, the Phillies were not really the only professional game in town. Ben Shibe re-appeared on the ownership scene in the 1890s, as the main stockholder in another team of Athletics[44] that played in the minor Eastern League (1892) and then in the minor Pennsylvania State League (1894) and then in the Atlantic League (1896).

Although these Athletic incarnations were not notably successful, the 1892 team going 12-26, and dropping out before the season was half over,[45] there were a few notable pitchers on the scene, mainly Philadelphian Matt Kilroy in 1892, and Gus Weyhing[46] and Nixey Callahan in 1894. Kilroy and Weyhing were right in the middle of their careers and happened to be between major league jobs. Callahan was just starting out, having made his professional debut for the Phillies earlier in 1894 (1-2) and then going down to the minors, where he went 10-9 for the Athletics. And, a pretty fair catcher finished up his baseball career with the 1896 Athletics. Philly native Jocko Milligan, who had a major league career adjusted OPS of 123, at the age of 35 played in 29 games behind the plate and at first, and hit .333.[47]

* * *

There would also be one final role for Philadelphia to play in nineteenth century baseball that took place outside of the "big" (National) League. With the league finding its 12-team incarnation increasingly unwieldy and unprofitable, it became an open secret around the baseball world that four of the 12 teams would be dropped after the 1899 season. A variety of heavy hitters in the baseball world, either seeing opportunity knocking, or not wishing to be shut out or kicked out of major league baseball, decided the time was ripe to re-form the American Association. Undaunted by a previous failure to do just that in 1894, work was going on behind the scenes almost as soon as the 1899 season ended to form a league with teams in Baltimore, Chicago, Boston, Milwaukee, Louisville, Providence, Detroit and Philadelphia. The movers and shakers behind this effort were some of baseball's most prominent names. Cap Anson agreed to be president of the new AA. John McGraw and Wilbert Robinson were working to keep Baltimore, one of the cities on the contraction list, in the bigs. Two of the nation's most prominent sportswriters were also involved—Alfred H. Spink of the *Sporting News* and Philadelphia Francis Richter of *Sporting Life*. Another Philadelphia newspaperman, Frank Hough of the *Philadelphia Inquirer*, was also involved as an early front man for the Philadelphia team.[48]

The new American Association was formally organized at a meeting on February 12 and February 13, 1900, in Chicago. However, the ink had barely dried on the newspapers announcing the formation of the association when President Anson announced that the organization was disbanding. It seems as if McGraw, on his way back from Chicago, had stopped by Philadelphia to check on how the team for the City of Brotherly Love was coming along. In talking to W.J. Gilmore, the principal financial backer of the Philadelphia team, McGraw was highly distressed to find out that Philadelphia didn't have a place to play, and that Gilmore's group would need another three weeks to decide whether or not they could come in to the new association at all. McGraw then wired Anson that Philadelphia couldn't be counted on, whereupon Anson pulled the plug on the whole venture. Charles Alexander, in his biography of McGraw, says this proved that Philadelphia's participation in the new AA was the key to the league.[49] And while this may have been true, the whole fiasco sounds more like—a fiasco.

First of all, in 1900, there were still places in North Philadelphia to play baseball, and to quickly build a park, which was relatively easy and cheap to do, even if Jefferson Park, Oakdale Park and Forepaugh Park were no longer around. For instance, there was a nice spot at 29th and Columbia, where Connie Mack would set up shop in Columbia Park in just over a year. So, Gilmore's problem sounds more like an excuse, either for Gilmore or Anson and McGraw. Secondly, there was the little matter of finding players. Even if you could quickly level some ground and throw up wooden bleachers to make a ballpark, you still needed players for the eight teams. A league coming together in February, and expecting to have players to play by April, would have had a lot of work to do. McGraw was quoted in the *Sporting News*, just after Anson bailed out, complaining about the "entire lack of business sagacity in the men promoting the deal."[50] McGraw was talking about Gilmore, but he could just have well have been talking about all of the new AA's prospective founders.

CHAPTER 14

War and Peace and War

It may not have been as drawn out a drama as the literary *War and Peace*, but the baseball wars that began after the 1889 season and lasted until after the 1891 season did seem to go on forever. And, if what Sherman said about war is true, then it was true in spades for the Philadelphia Athletics.

Representatives of the Players League and the American Association held a secret meeting on September 2, 1890, in Philadelphia at the Colonnade Hotel, a meeting that may well have marked a final attempt for the AA and the Brotherhood to join forces. That didn't happen, and the Philadelphia meeting didn't change the fact that, with financial losses mounting and the public and the newspapers in an uproar, there was heavy pressure on all three organizations to declare peace.[1] Into the breach at this point stepped one Allan W. Thurman, a relatively minor official with the AA's relatively minor Columbus franchise. Mr. Thurman had friends in all three camps, making him an ideal peace emissary, so ideal that he was immediately nicknamed "The White-Winged Dove of Peace." Thurman met with the National League in October 1890, and presented a peace plan that would consolidate the three leagues into two, with no city having more than two teams. While this meant that Philadelphia would lose a team, this was just as well, since the 1890 season, like the 1875 and the 1884 seasons, had pretty well shown that Philadelphia wasn't going to support three teams. Or, at least it wouldn't support three teams if one of them was no good.

Although the Players League was still proclaiming that it would operate as a six-team league in 1891 as late as mid–November 1890 (with teams in Philadelphia, Cincinnati, Cleveland, Boston, Washington and Brooklyn), the capitulation had already begun, mainly due to Al Spalding's maneuvering that played on the fear of the PL owners—the fear of losing more money. The New York PL and NL teams merged first, followed by Pittsburgh, Chicago and finally Brooklyn. This part of the dismantling of the Players League was actually pretty simple, involving the merger of teams within the same city. Such would not be the case in Philadelphia, where the Wagner Brothers (J. Earle and George) now held the PL franchise, and, by this time, the AA had expelled its original Athletics for, in Harold Seymour's understated words, "not meeting certain financial obligations."

Although Pennypacker and Whittaker had released the Athletics' players on September 17, 1890, and technically disbanded the franchise, it did still exist as a business entity. In mid–November 1890, several of the team's minority stockholders—including Bill Sharsig—filed a bill of equity to protect their investment in the now-insolvent franchise. Undaunted by this action and by the desire of the minority owners to keep the Wagner brothers out and take over a new Philadelphia AA franchise themselves,[2] Thurman and

AA vice president Billy Barnie baldly awarded the Wagner brothers the association's Philadelphia franchise in early December,[3] although some sources say this took place at the November 22 AA meeting, and some say it was in January 1891. Since the original Athletics had been expelled, that meant the Wagners would move their PL team to the AA, and that they were also awarded the name Athletics, for such was the value of the name in Philadelphia. Actually, this move took place with the approval of Spalding. In fact, it was part of a larger plan largely hatched by Spalding and Thurman to structure the settlement—more like dismantling—of the Players League.[4]

So now the AA had let the brothers Wagner into the fold, ultimately as part of the Spalding-Thurman plan to absorb the Players League, a plan that included a new National Agreement with the codicil that all players who had jumped to the PL would return to their original teams, be they in the American Association or the National League. The new National Agreement also featured a Board of Control, made up of Thurman, Louis Krauthoff (president of the Western Association) and the Phillies' John Rogers.[5] Together, the failure of the 1890 Athletics, the Wagner brothers, players supposedly returning to their previous teams, and the Board of Control would mesh into a monster controversy that would turn the peace into yet another war, one that would bring down both the Athletics and the American Association.

It all started when somebody forgot, that's the term that has been most commonly used, to reserve two of the 1889 Athletics' players. As improbable as that may sound in principle, it was even more bizarre in fact, since one of the two players involved also happened to be the American Association's best, Harry Stovey. The other was gloveman Lou Bierbauer. On the surface, the rules seemed quite specific. The new National Agreement stated that everyone was supposed to return to the teams that had reserved them in 1889. However, each team was supposed to send to the Board of Control, or National Board, a list of its reserved players. One thing that all sources do agree upon—the Athletics did not reserve either Stovey (who had played for the Boston PL club) or Bierbauer (who had been with the PL Brooklyn Ward's Wonders).

As to who failed to reserve the two, that's a matter of debate. Seymour puts the blame on the Wagners for failing to reserve Stovey and Bierbauer after they had brought their PL Quakers into the AA in the guise of the Athletics.[6] Ditto Donald Dewey and Nicholas Acocella in their brief history of the AA Athletics.[7] David Nemec, however, says that wasn't the case, and that the Wagners had every right to expect that they would regain all of the 1889 Athletics' players who had left the team for the 1890 season, and that they (the Wagners) were shocked when the Pittsburgh NL team signed Bierbauer and found out that Stovey was bound for Boston. Nemec blames the Athletics' previous administration—meaning Pennypacker, Whittaker, and maybe Sharsig—for failing to reserve Stovey and Bierbauer. However, Sharsig, the only member of the old Athletics regime who was with still with the 1891 team, claimed in 1891 that he had reminded AA president Zach Phelps in October 1890, when the association was running the Athletics, to reserve all of the Athletics' Players League participants. Phelps, in response to Sharsig's allegation, produced a collect telegram he'd received from William Whittaker that said, "Name the players as reserved that finished the season, though nearly a new nine will be got for next season."[8]

Whittaker seemed to be telling Phelps to reserve just the castoffs that finished the 1891 season for the Athletics, and that it wasn't any big deal, because they'd have a new team in 1891. But, as Phelps was probably trying to point out, that had nothing to do with reserving the 1889 players who had jumped to the PL. More importantly, Whittaker's telegram was dated October 14, 1890, almost a month after he and Pennypacker had folded the team and the AA had stepped in to allow the Athletics to finish the season. So, how much authority could Whittaker have had at that point to tell Phelps anything about whom to reserve from any list of Athletic players? In October 1890, such a directive to the AA president could only have come from Sharsig, the last man standing among the Athletics' original ownership.

October 1890 seems to be the key month in the controversy. Going to an original source, the February 15, 1891, *Philadelphia Press* (as reproduced by Dean Sullivan in *Early Innings*), while reporting on Bierbauer being finally assigned to Pittsburgh, printed this statement: "The neglect of the Athletic club to reserve Bierbauer on October 10, 1890, for the season of 1891, in accordance with the fourth section of the National Agreement, then governing the case, released him from reservation and from the jurisdiction of the National Agreement."[9] While it may have been true that the neglect to reserve Bierbauer on October 10, 1890, under the old National Agreement may have proven fatal to the Philadelphia team's attempt to keep him, in effect making him a free agent for 1891, it seems difficult to blame any management of the Athletics for this faux pas. On October 10, 1890, it had been almost a month since the September 17 fold-up. In fact, the Athletics, with Sharsig still managing the Troubadours,[10] were in the midst of their last home stand on October 10. The 1890 regular season didn't end until October 12.[11] Since Sharsig was at this point in October 1890 a front man for the AA, and since the Wagners didn't take over the AA Philadelphia franchise until November 22, 1890, at the earliest, how could the Athletics be blamed for failing to reserve Bierbauer (or Stovey)? It may well be that, as Sharsig claimed in early 1891, he had done his due diligence in reminding the AA (in the person of President Phelps) to reserve the two players, and it was the association that dropped the ball.

Finally, just to muddy the waters further, Francis Richter, another contemporaneous source on the subject, who, like the *Philadelphia Press* reporter, was on-site, said the names of Stovey and Bierbauer had been "omitted from the list handed in by the Athletic Club at the time of the reorganization."[12] Which reorganization? There wasn't one in October 1890. Was he referring to the "reorganization" following September 17, 1890, or, more likely, the one when the Wagners took over, in November 1890, December 1890 or January 1891? This statement would seem to presume that there was a second deadline for reserving 1889 players, one that fell after the Wagners took over the franchise.

Thus, the blame for the failure to reserve Stovey and Bierbauer for 1891 could rest with either the AA or the Wagners, depending on when the deadline for reserving players for 1891 actually fell. However, although the new National Agreement took effect prior to the end of calendar 1890, the reserving of players for 1891 would have come under the old National Agreement, which was still in effect in October 1890. On the weight of the evidence, the AA, and President Phelps, were the culprits.

What everybody *does* say is that the Wagners appealed Bierbauer's signing with Pittsburgh and Stovey with the Boston League club (although Seymour says the AA wanted to transfer him to the new Boston AA franchise, but that Stovey, "knowing he was a free agent" took a better offer from the Beaneaters) to the National Board, basically claiming that they were being denied Stovey's and Bierbauer's services on a technicality, and that the Pittsburgh team was a bunch of Pirates—and thus have they been named ever since. The technicality claim would also seem to support the premise that the AA, not the Wagner brothers, had failed to reserve Stovey and Bierbauer.

After two days of secret meetings in Chicago in early February 1891, the National Board ruled 2–1 against the Wagners (the action the February 15 *Philadelphia Press* was reporting upon), with Thurman casting the deciding vote against the team from his own league![13] And thus did peace become war again. The AA held an emergency meeting in New York on February 18, and kicked Thurman out of the association. Nemec even suggests that Thurman may have been a "mole" planted in the association by Al Spalding, to better extend his grasp over baseball. AA vice president Billy Barnie for certain thought so, claiming at the February 18 meeting, "It was bad enough to have Al Spalding's fingers on our throats for nine long years. Spalding says he wants war and we will give it to him." The AA then voted to withdraw from the new National Agreement.[14]

* * *

Thus began the War of 1891. How did it affect Philadelphia baseball? Well, the final outcome was obvious. When the smoke cleared, Philadelphia had only one major league team, a situation that would remain for the rest of the nineteenth century. However, for 1891, there would be two teams. First, the Athletics.

Although the Players League Quakers had been awarded that Athletic franchise and name, and although they were supposed to reserve the 1889 Athletics' players, in reality they were neither the 1889 nor the 1890 Athletics, nor even the 1890 Quakers. They also needed a place to play, since Jefferson Park had been sold at sheriff's sale after the 1890 season. They ended up staying at Forepaugh Park. Among the 13 key players on the team they had three members of the 1889 Athletics, four members of the 1889 Phillies, six members of the 1890 Quakers, five men who had never played in Philadelphia, and zero members of the 1890 Athletics.

1891 Athletics	*Previous Team(s)*
C—Jocko Milligan	1889 St. Louis AA, 1890 Quakers
1B—Henry Larkin	1889 Athletics, 1890 Cleveland PL
2B—Bill Hallman	1889 Phillies, 1890 Quakers
SS—Tommy Corcoran	Pittsburgh PL
3B—Joe Mulvey	1889 Phillies, 1890 Quakers
OF—Jack McGeachey	Brooklyn PL, Boston AA
OF—Pop Corkhill	Brooklyn, Cincinnati, Pittsburgh NL
OF—George Wood	1889 Phillies, 1890 Quakers
UT—Lave Cross	1889 Athletics, 1890 Quakers
OF—Jim McTamany	Columbus AA
P—Gus Weyhing	1889 Athletics, Brooklyn PL
P—Icebox Chamberlain	St. Louis, Columbus AA
P—Ben Sanders	1889 Phillies, 1890 Quakers

They did have for the first 17 games of 1891 the manager of the 1890 Athletics, Billy Sharsig. After going 6-11 to start the season, he was rewarded for his years of loyal service by being canned, and replaced by George Wood. Sharsig retaliated by suing J. Earle Wagner for breach of contract, claiming that the butcher wanted to run the team himself, and that Wood was a figurehead leader.[15] Although Wood would eventually get the team above .500 and finish fourth at 73-66, they were never in the pennant race and they were not among the survivors consolidated into the National League in the peace agreement following the '91 season. Indeed, pretty much all they had to offer were a few pretty good players—notably Larkin, Wood, Milligan, Cross and Weyhing.

With a lineup that finished first in doubles (182), triples (123), and second and home

The greatest left-handed catcher of all time—Philadelphian Jack Clements. Although his major league career started in 1884, he didn't start to hit until 1890 (courtesy John Thorn).

runs (55) and slugging (.375), the Athletics still had pretty good power, even without Stovey. On the other hand, if they had been able to retain the superstar, they might have been able to finish higher than fourth in runs scored (817). Proving that Jack Clements wouldn't be the only hard-hitting nineteenth century catcher produced by Philadelphia, local boy and 1890 Quaker Jocko Milligan managed to avoid returning to his 1889 team, the St. Louis Browns, and hit .303/.397/.505 for a team high 154 Adjusted OPS, leading the AA in doubles (35) and extra-base hits (58). Larkin, now 31 years old, continued his hard hitting after a year away from Philly, with a 130 OPS. Closely following Larkin was player-manager Wood at 129. And, although Lave Cross hadn't yet settled in to what would be his best-known post, third base, the combination of catching, playing the outfield and third (plus single games at second and short) didn't bother him—he had a 132 Adjusted OPS in his utility role.

Even though this was a different team of Athletics, they continued their pattern of better hitting than pitching. Outside of Gus Weyhing returning to the Athletics and pitching 450 innings for a 31-20 record and a 120 Adjusted ERA, the rest of the staff (Icebox Chamberlain, Ben Sanders and Will Calihan) was pretty average and the team finished sixth in runs allowed (794).

Meanwhile, the association, plagued by dissention, and a lack of strong leadership and cohesion, was decisively losing its second war with the league. Talk of a peace, which would almost certainly mean some form of capitulation to the league, began as early as the summer of 1891. By shortly after the end of the season most of the AA's owners were probably willing to listen to consolidation talk. By November, the word was out that plans were being made for a consolidated 12-team league.[16] Of course, the issue now was which teams from the AA would join the league, and which would be bought out? Although four AA teams were indeed taken into the National League in the consolidation (Washington, Louisville, Baltimore and St. Louis), there was apparently never any thought given to establishing two teams in Philadelphia (or any other city outside of Greater New York), despite its status as the third largest city in the nation. Maybe that's because the Wagners were the first AA owners to go for the money, being paid $56,000 for the Athletics franchise, $16,000 of which they promptly invested in buying the league's Washington franchise, which was in reality the AA's Washington franchise, transferred to the new 12-team league. This move, coming at a joint NL-AA meeting in Indianapolis on December 15, 1891, effectively killed both the Philadelphia Athletics and the American Association.[17]

While the death of the AA after 10 tumultuous years was unquestionably mourned by those who cared about baseball—Francis Richter, for instance—the loss of the Athletics, even after their up-and-down course over the past 10 years, must have been the big shock in Philadelphia. Of course, if Philadelphia baseball fans could have seen into the future, they would have been comforted to know that still to come would be the minor league Athletics of the mid–1890s and the name's final reincarnation of greatness, the Athletics of the American League and Cornelius McGillicuddy (1901–1954).

* * *

While it's possible that J. Earle and George Wagner may have ensured that there would not be a National League Athletics, it's also possible that the Phillies, aka Al Reach and John Rogers, didn't want any more competition in Philadelphia. They were by now a powerful enough force in the league to make their wishes of great significance, and they had just slipped from 78-54 in 1890 to 68-69 in 1891, and probably figured they could use a couple of extra players. In fact, author and Philadelphia baseball historian David Jordan claims that Reach and Rogers actually contributed a large share of the money used to buy out the Wagner brothers[18]—not the most far-fetched scenario of the conclusion of the second NL-AA war.

The reason for the Phillies' slippage in 1891 is easy to pinpoint. For the first, but by no means the last time, John Rogers' pig-headedness would cost the Phillies in the talent department. The general amnesty declared on behalf of the Players League jumpers after the 1890 season was a big deal, to both the players and their former teams. After all, the breach of the concept of the jumpers returning to their 1889 teams caused the second NL-AA war. In one of the great cutting-off-your-nose-to-spite-your-face moves in baseball history, Rogers declared that he didn't want any of those @*&^+XZ&*(%# jumpers back. It took all of Reach's persuasive powers to convince Rogers to make exceptions for just two players—one for basically public relations purposes, and one because apparently Reach saw something. Jim Fogarty, probably the most popular Phillie player of the 1880s outside of the late Charlie Ferguson, was, in a macabre twist of fate, also dying young. Dying of tuberculosis. He had been able to play in just 91 games in 1890 and, as the 1891 season approached, he was a very sick man. Reach, knowing it would be a disaster *not* to take Fogarty back, signed him for 1891, most likely after telling Rogers that the Californian would never play again. He didn't, dying in Philadelphia of the dread consumption, as it was known, on May 20, 1891, at the age of 27.[19]

The other prodigal welcomed back to the Phillies with somewhat less than fatted calf feast was Ed Delahanty. While it's easy to say the Phillies wanted him back because he was so good, that really wasn't the case going into the 1891 season. Or even the 1892 season. Starting with his rookie year of 1888, and including his 1890 season with Cleveland's Players League club, Delahanty had hit .228/.293/.296/.243 with slugging percentages of .293/.370/.414/.339; figures that wouldn't really scare anybody. In fact, he had a worse year with the 1891 Phillies than he'd had in the PL in 1890, falling from .296/.337/.414 to .243/.296/.339. However, Reach's apparent confidence in Delahanty would soon be rewarded.

In 1891, there were few rewards for the Phillies. Although they rather surprisingly led the National League in attendance for a second straight year, that was more probably a bad sign for the Athletics than it was a good sign for the Phillies. On the field, they were fifth out of the eight teams in both runs scored (756) and runs allowed (773). Only two-thirds of the coming Hall of Fame outfield (Hamilton and Thompson) along with Clements had good years at bat, while all the pitchers were essentially mediocre. Hamilton led the league in practically every offensive category that Harry Stovey missed.

Hamilton	*Stovey*
Batting Average (.340)	Slugging Percentage (.498)
On Base Average (.453)	Total Bases (271)
Runs (141)	Triples (20)
Hits (179)	Home Runs (16)
Walks (102)	Extra Base Hits (67)
Stolen Bases (111)	
Singles (147)	

Stovey was also in the top five in OPS, runs, doubles, RBIs, walks, steals and runs created. Hamilton was in the top five in OPS and runs created as well.

Overlooked in Hamilton's big year was the coming of age of Jack Clements. Although it must have seemed like he'd been around Philadelphia baseball forever, especially for a catcher, the lefty backstop had turned only 27 during the 1891 season. Although he'd played pretty regularly for the Phillies since the start of his tenure with them in 1885, he didn't become an offensive force until 1890, when most of the big boys were off in the Players League. However, he followed up his .315/.392/.472 1890 season with a .310/.380/.426 1891 campaign, which would end up being part of a seven-year run (1890–1896) of outstanding hitting, with Adjusted OPS numbers of 148, 131, 128, 124, 134, 171 and 156.

Since the Phillies finished fourth in 1891, 18½ games out of first, it's unlikely even the seven miscreants they were missing off their 1889 team would have helped them threaten the first place Boston Beaneaters. After all, the Phillies had also finished one game under .500 in 1889, and had finished fourth as well. As previously noted, four of the 1889 Phillies that Rogers refused to take back, namely Wood, Hallman, Mulvey and Sanders, were playing over at Forepaugh Park with the Athletics. Two of the other three, Sid Farrar and Dan Casey, were no longer in the major leagues. But, the seventh player was (along with Wood) someone they could have used—pitcher Charlie Buffington. Pitching for the AA champion Boston Reds, Buffington went 29-9 with an Adjusted ERA of 137.

* * *

As for Philadelphia, the city itself had seen some major changes in the 15 years since the Centennial. While various teams named Phillies and Athletics came and went during that period, there were two more really big teams whose fortunes from 1876 on were as indicative of the changing city as those of the Phillies and Athletics. These "teams" were, in reality, a couple of railroads, the Pennsylvania (known as the "Pennsy" to generations of Philadelphians) and the Reading. Just like in baseball, one railroad would win out, thanks essentially to strong management, while one railroad would be bought out, thanks essentially to poor management.

The period from 1876 to 1905 has been described by author Nathaniel Burt and historian Wallace E. Davies as being Philadelphia's "Iron Age." And while "iron" to Burt and Davies meant heavy industry in general (for this is when Philadelphia grew up to become an industrial giant, and not a collection of smaller industries)—industries like iron, coal, steel, oil, steam engines and steamships—its most obvious and representative manifestation was in the iron rails and iron horses of the two railroads.

While Philadelphia in the latter quarter of the nineteenth century may no longer have been the nation's political, religious, intellectual, artistic, financial or even baseball center, it was the railroad center. Burt and Davies state that the three basic industries that best typify the Industrial Revolution in Philly were iron and steel, oil, and railroads. Of the latter, they note that the steam locomotive, as produced by the Baldwin Works, was the symbol of Philadelphia. And, if the locomotive by Baldwin was the symbol, then the Broad Street Station, by Pennsylvania, was the temple.

> The Railroad was king. It was not only the most important single enterprise of the city; it also became and remained long afterward the single largest corporation in the country. Long after its great days the Pennsylvania Railroad held position as number one.[20]

A situation somewhat analogous to the baseball field in Philadelphia. From the early 1860s on, the Athletics had been king, the single most important team in the city. However, by the time 1890 rolled around, their great days were long gone, brought down by front office follies.

The Pennsy thrived around this same time because of outstanding leadership. The Al Reach and Harry Wright of the railroad business in Philadelphia were Presidents Thomas A. Scott (1874–1880), George B. Roberts (1880–1897) and Alexander J. Cassatt (1899–1906), who brought the railroad to greatness, the sweet culmination of which took place in 1910 with the opening of Pennsylvania Station—in the heart of New York City. However, the building of Penn Station was presaged by the spectacular brick castle the railroad built almost 30 years before in the heart of Philadelphia. Opening in 1882, Broad Street Station and its adjoining "Chinese Wall," a block-wide viaduct for the railroad tracks that ran a full mile west to the Schuylkill River, would dominate Center City for more than 70 years, before being torn down in 1954 to make way for modern urban renewal and Penn Center.

Ultimately playing the role of the ill-fated Athletics to the on-going Phillies in the railroad game was the Reading Railroad. Burt and Davies state that the Reading's two most notable presidents were Franklin B. Gowen and George T. Baer. However, unlike the Pennsy's leadership, and like the Athletics' later leadership, Gowen and Baer were more familiar with failure and unpleasantries. When Gowen became Reading's president in 1870, "he soon ruined the company by overinvesting in coal lands and being caught short in the depression of the 1870s. The company went bankrupt in 1880. Gowen resigned, and in 1889 shot himself."[21]

Although the Reading kept carrying coal—its' raison d'être—into Philadelphia in somewhat the same manner as the Athletics kept featuring heavy hitters in the late 1880s, it went in and out of receiverships until coming under the heavy hand of J.P. Morgan. He installed Baer as president. Baer, on his part, immediately stirred up labor troubles for the company. In the midst of all this, the Reading Terminal opened on Market Street, just three blocks east of Broad Street Station, in 1893. Reading Terminal was a facility that was almost as impressive as Broad Street Station, but, it was built by New York money, for control of the railroad was by then in New York, and, from a Philadelphia perspective, it was a failure.[22]

◆ CHAPTER 15 ◆

The 1890s Phillies—
It Was Always Something

From 1892 until the end of the nineteenth century, the Phillies were the only game in town, as far as big-time baseball was concerned. Dating from before the start of the Civil War, this was practically a unique situation in the city. Since 1860 the city had almost always had a minimum of two top level teams. Only in four years—1871, 1872, 1876 and 1882—representing the first two years of the National Association, and the first years of the National League and the American Association, had there been a single team with a clear claim to suzerainty to the baseball affections of the city. And, in each case, that organization was a team of Athletics.

But now, the Athletics were gone, and the Phillies, a group of relative newcomers were "it." However, as Al Reach and especially John Rogers were to find out over the next nine years, while being "it" was great for their attendance figures, they would not be able to match the success of the Athletics, a situation that would ultimately lead to the Phillies becoming the second team in town—to yet another team of Athletics—for the first half of the coming century. For while the Phillies were indeed "it" from 1892 to 1900, "it" was always something that kept them from greatness.

There really was no single reason what "it" was that kept the 1892 to 1900 Phillies out of first. Yes, their pitching (the most common excuse given) was by and large substandard. Yes, the right field wall at the Huntingdon Street Grounds was practically in the second baseman's hip pocket. Yes, Colonel Rogers shouldn't have talked Al Reach into canning Harry Wright. Yes, they made a couple of bad trades, most notably sending Billy Hamilton away. Yes, Rogers alienated the players. Yes, George Stallings as a manager was a disaster. Yes, those three "B" teams (Boston, Baltimore and Brooklyn) were excellent, each in their own time, with syndicate baseball also playing a role in some of their excellence. And, yes, they just had some plain old bad luck. Put them altogether, and, collectively, you have "it." No single big reason, but a multitude of little ones that kept the Gay Nineties Phillies from adding to the city's pennant collection.

* * *

The Phillies and the National League decided to celebrate the Columbian Year of 1892 by discovering that a split season didn't work. Although the World's Series was not played in 1891 due to the war between the leagues, the surviving National League recognized that some form of post-season tournament was a virtual requirement to keep fans' interest high late in the year. In casting about for a solution to not having another league to pit its champion against, the owners hit upon the idea of playing a split season, and having the first half champion take on the second half champion in a post season playoff. Like the Edsel, the Pet Rock and the intentional walk, this was not one of the great concepts in American history. In addition to leaving the league open to charges of hippodroming when the best team, the Boston Beaneaters, failed to win the second half of the split season,[1] it didn't do the Phillies much good, either. A combination of the overpowering Beaneaters, a failure to perform away from Huntingdon Street (12-22 on the road in the second half of the split season), and just plain bad luck meant the Phillies never got within hailing distance of first place, finishing the first half of the season in third (46-30) and the second half of the season in fifth (41-36), despite an excellent offense *and* excellent pitching. If you cared to put both halves of the season together, they were fourth with an 87-66 record.

It was not a season without highlights, headlined by the coming together of the greatest outfield of the nineteenth century—and a candidate for the greatest outfield of all time. Although Billy Hamilton (1890), Sam Thompson (1889) and Ed Delahanty (1888) had all been on the scene at 15th and Huntingdon for various amounts of time, this was the first time they could have been collectively called great. While they had made up the Phillies' outfield in 1891, they were not yet the unit they would become, since Delahanty hit only .243 on the year. This time, though, they posted Adjusted OPS figures of 158 (Delahanty, who led the league in slugging percentage and triples), 152 (Hamilton) and 144 (Thompson), helping the Phillies led the league in doubles (225), home runs (50), batting (.262) and slugging (.367), while finishing second in on base percentage (.328) and third in runs scored (860). And they were just getting warmed up.

As good a year as the future Hall of Fame trio would have in 1892, they weren't even the biggest gun in Harry Wright's arsenal. That would have been "Dear Old" Roger Connor, the 34-year-old former New York Giants star who would hold the career record for home runs (taking same away from Harry Stovey) prior to Babe Ruth, and who played first that one year for the Phillies with a 167 Adjusted OPS and a league-leading 37 doubles. Add it up, and the Phillies had four future Hall of Famers on the field in 1892, along with probably the second- or third-best hitting catcher of the nineteenth century in Jack Clements, who also came into his own with an Adjusted OPS of 128.

Ed Delahanty, most likely in pre-game practice during the 1890s. Check out the length of his bat. They don't make them like that anymore (courtesy John Thorn).

As for the players the Phillies picked up from the defunct Athletics, for Gus Weyhing it was a matter of returning to the Phillies, the team that had first signed him in 1887, but for whom he had never played. Lave Cross, having already played for both the AA Athletics teams and the PL Quakers, didn't have to make too much of an adjustment, either. Ditto for Joe Mulvey, who was originally a Phillie before jumping to the Players League and back and forth in the Brotherhood war. Neither Cross nor Mulvey helped much in 1892, but Weyhing had his last big year, going 32-21 with a 122 Adjusted ERA. Along with another former Giant, and future Hall of Famer, Tim Keefe (138) and Kid Carsey (101), Weyhing led the team to the third best ERA in the league (2.93).

Five future Hall of Famers (six, counting Wright), a top catcher, a pitcher who would win 264 games and was at the peak of his career, and coming in third in the league in runs scored, third in runs allowed, above-average fielding—how did this team manage to win 16 games fewer than Boston and have only the fourth best record? Part of the problem was that they were just unlucky. Given their 860 runs scored and 690 runs allowed, their Pythagorean Winning Percentage would have indicated a record of 92-61. So, with a little good luck, they would have won in the mid 90s. But, the rest of the problem was Boston. The Beaneaters combined the 1890 Boston PL champions with the existing Beaneater team, and were able to put a virtual All-Star conglomeration on the field. They even had an outfield that almost matched Philadelphia's—Hugh Duffy, Tommy McCarthy and Harry Stovey (although he was at the end of his career). King Kelly and Charlie Bennett (they were both about done, also) caught Kid Nichols, Jack Stivetts and John Clarkson (he was traded after only eight wins, but Harry Staley won 22). Herman Long, Joe Quinn and Bill Nash were in the infield. Bobby Lowe played both infield and outfield. Add that up, and you have six more Hall of Famers (Duffy, McCarthy, Nichols, Clarkson, Kelly and manager Frank Selee) plus at least two more who should be in the Hall (Stovey and Long). Even with some growing long in the tooth (as were the Phillies' Keefe and Connor), it's no wonder they went 102-48.

* * *

It's easy to assume that the Phillies expected better things in 1893. You have to think that was the case since Rogers sacked Harry Wright after they went 72-57, and finished fourth. Even the Father of Professional Baseball wasn't immune to the "failing to meet expectations" syndrome. However, looked at in retrospect, it's hard to fault the old pioneer for the team's primary shortcoming in the 1893 season—pitching. The problem was that the league moguls, fearing the pitchers were gaining too much of the upper hand, had moved the hurlers back five feet, to 60 feet, six inches, at the same time eliminating the pitcher's box and replacing it with a mound, during the off-season. And, not every pitcher was able to easily adjust to the change. Unfortunately for the Phillies, two of the pitchers who had trouble adjusting were Weyhing and Carsey, who threw 663 innings between them in 1893 (no one else on the team pitched more than 178 innings), with Adjusted ERAs of just 96 and 95. The other problem was Tim Keefe, at 36, went from old to too old, his Adjusted ERA dropping to 104 in only 178 innings. He went just 10-7 in his final year. So, the Phillies finished sixth in runs allowed and eighth in team ERA, offsetting an offense that was first in runs (1011), hits (1553), doubles (246), home runs (80), batting (.302) and slugging (.431). It was this team, along with the 1894 and 1895 Phillies, that created their blanket reputation of the 1890s for great hitting and poor pitching.

The hitting part of their rep was well earned. Delahanty (166 OPS+), Hamilton (169— he led the league) and Thompson (153) were terrors, and they hadn't even peaked as a group yet. Hamilton won his second batting title (.380—Thompson and Delahanty were second and third), and also led in on base percentage (.490) and OPS (1.014). Delahanty led in slugging (.583), total bases (347), home runs (19), RBIs (146) and runs created (144). Thompson was best in hits (222) and doubles (37). Is it any wonder they also led the league in attendance with 293,019 (the first of four times they would do so prior to 1901), a full 100,000 more than the year before?

All it got Harry Wright was a pink slip in favor of former Phillies shortstop Art Irwin, who Captain Harry had gotten rid of for being argumentative during the 1889 season.[2] So it was Irwin, not Wright, who would preside over two of the best hitting teams of all time, and who would then also get fired because the pitchers couldn't get anyone out—although Irwin may have been somewhat more responsible for that shortcoming than Wright was.

* * *

In 1894, the National League's hitters brought back the good old days of the 1860s—and nowhere more than in Philadelphia. At least, that's the popular notion. Actually, it was more a matter of Reach having put together an offensive juggernaut that would have hit as well in Yellowstone Park as it did in Philadelphia Park. Despite its fearsome reputation as a place where pitchers went to die, the grounds at 15th and Huntingdon actually played overall as a pitchers' park in 1894 and 1895. In fact, all three of the home fields the Phillies used in 1894 and 1895 were collectively pitchers' parks. Nonetheless, playing at two different versions of the Huntingdon Street Grounds, plus a few games at the University of Pennsylvania's playing field, the Phillies scored 2211 runs over the next two years.

The 1894 team had anything but a dull year. The loss of Wright, the hitting explosion (to the tune of an all-time record team average of .349) plus a spark in the wrong place all made for a hot summer in Philly. It was the hottest on the morning of August 6, 1894, when the Baltimore Orioles were in town for an afternoon game. Around 10:40 a.m., in the midst of a morning practice one of the Phillies players noticed a fire in the grandstand. Although the exterior of the park was brick, the interior was wooden, and so the Huntingdon Street Grounds was just as flammable as all the rest of the early ballparks.[3] Despite efforts by the Phillies players to stop the blaze, it soon spread to the entire structure, causing the players to realize that maybe they'd better get their street clothes and make tracks for the outside world. Two of them, third baseman Charley Reilly and pitcher George Harper, almost didn't make it, but everyone eventually reached the street safely.

It took several hours to put the fire out. When the firefighters were through, the only remains left to show that Philadelphia Park had stood at 15th and Huntingdon were a patch of badly scorched turf, the fence in dead center field and part of the brick wall running along Huntingdon Street (along the first base line). That was it. The cause of the fire, which accounted for $250,000 damage, including burning down a nearby stable, was never determined. Speculation has typically rested on a spark from a plumber's torch; apparently plumbers were in the park, making repairs of some kind that day. Another good possibility would be a spark from a locomotive engine as the Reading Railroad yards were right across Broad Street from the field. So, while Baldwin Locomotive may have given to Philadelphia, it may have also taken away. A third possible cause, an arson scenario, was bandied about by the *Philadelphia Evening Bulletin*.[4] A fourth cause might have been the Phillies themselves, except they weren't playing all that hot at the time. After bouncing in and out of second place during the early part of the season, they had fallen all the way to seventh by the end of July,[5] and were still sixth (43-38) on the morning of the fire, thanks to 16-3 (Harper actually was torched in that one) and 19-12 pastings by the Orioles just prior to the fire. Maybe it was Baltimore that was blazing. Still, possibly inspired by the pyrotechnics, the Phillies actually did catch fire, winning 10 straight from August 15 to August 25 to climb back to fourth place—which was where they pretty much stayed the rest of the year.

Remarkably, the Phillies played most of the rest of the year at 15th & Huntingdon. After playing three games in Boston, and one in Washington, the Phillies returned home with a doubleheader against the Senators on August 11, kicking off a 28-game homestand that included the 10-game wining streak, a record-setting 29-4 thrashing of Louisville and an overall mark of 21-5-2. However, they were still in fourth, 10 games out, when they went back on the road and proceeded to go 6-11 the rest of the way, finishing fourth at 71-57, 17½ games behind those red-hot Orioles.[6]

The 28-game homestand, which wasn't all that unusual in the schedules of the time, was played partly on the baseball field of the University of Pennsylvania at 37th and Spruce Streets,[7] the first time big time baseball had been played in that part of the city since the earliest clubs moved to North Philadelphia during the early stages of the Civil War. After coming back from Boston and Washington, the Phillies played their next six games at Penn's University Field, winning five, before returning to 15th and Huntingdon on August 18. The suspicion is that University Field wasn't very big (or else maybe it was very, very big, at least in the outfield) since the scores of the six games played there were 10–7, 16–4, 7–13, 14–4, 17–3, and 29–4[8]—a total of 128 runs in just six games. Even in the high-octane offense of 1894, the pitchers must have been glad for the efforts of the workers back at 15th & Huntingdon. Although the playing field was scorched at the old park, Al Reach hadn't let any grass grow under his feet. What Philadelphia baseball historian Rich Westcott describes as "an army of workers" had been toiling practically 24–7 since the last ember was put out, and had thrown up a perimeter fence and wooden bleachers seating 9,000 by the time the team returned for the August 18 game with Cleveland,[9] and the last seven games of the 10-game winning streak.

When your ballpark burning down is the highlight of the season, it's safe to say that rest of 1894 didn't go quite the way Rogers envisioned it when he disposed of Harry Wright. Art Irwin didn't prove any better at getting opposing hitters out than Wright had. In fact, his use of his pitchers might have helped undermine the efforts of Thompson, Delahanty, Hamilton, et al. The game had undergone one of its paradigm shifts during the 1893 and 1894 seasons, thanks to the change in the pitching distance which, in addition to greatly increasing offensive output, had put additional strain on pitchers' arms. No longer could a two-man rotation dominate a team's hurling efforts. However, Irwin and his immediate successor, Billy Nash, did not seem to realize this. In 1894, three pitchers shouldered practically the entire load for the Phillies—Brewery Jack Taylor (298 innings), Kid Carsey (277 innings) and Gus Weyhing (266 innings). The slightly-singed George Harper was the next most-used hurler, pitching just 86 innings in 12 games. As a means of comparison, the first-place Orioles had six pitchers who threw more than 100 innings. While the pitching of the "Old Orioles" of the 1890s has usually been pooh-poohed in comparison to the rest of the team, at least manager Ned Hanlon knew enough to spread the workload around. True, part of the 1894 Phillies' problem was that only Taylor pitched well (23-13, 122 Adjusted ERA), but you have to think that Weyhing, a proven 30-game winner in the past, might have done better at the 60½ foot distance (his Adjusted ERA was just 88 in 1894) if he'd had more rest. The same could well have been true for Carsey, who posted a 104 Adjusted ERA in 1892 (the last year at 55 feet) at the age of just 21, and then never topped 97 for the rest of his career.

With the staggering hurlers finishing 10th in the NL in ERA (5.63) and allowing a staggering 966 runs (fifth in the league), the offense that set the all-time team batting average record of .349 and scored 1143 runs (third in the league) couldn't outhit the opposition often enough to get into the pennant race, despite the famous season turned in by the outfield. Although Boston's Hugh Duffy took the batting crown with a .440 mark, the Phillies' outfield finished two-three-four-five behind him, with everyone hitting over .400. Unheralded second-year 21-year-old Tuck Turner got into enough games thanks to injuries to Thompson and Delahanty to finish second in the batting race behind Duffy at .416. Thompson and Delahanty tied for third at .407, and poor Billy Hamilton was probably ashamed to show his face in the clubhouse after hitting only .404. No, that shouldn't be true—Hamilton had no cause for embarrassment after setting an almost unbelievable record by scoring 192 runs in just 129 games, a record that is probably equally unbreakable as Levi Meyerle's .492 batting average for the 1871 Athletics. Tom Brown had scored 177 runs three years earlier for the AA Boston Reds, and Babe Ruth would also score 177 runs in 1921. And no one else has ever topped 167. It would take a tremendous change in the game for anyone to average the 1.49 runs scored per game Hamilton did—the equivalent of 241 runs scored in a 162 game season.

In addition to batting average, the Phillies also led the league in hits (1732—more than 13 a game) and on base percentage (.408) while finishing second in triples and third in slugging—and, despite the hype over the years, this wasn't the best offensive team Philadelphia would put on the field in the 1890s. In fact, Hamilton was the only Phillie to lead the league in any category (a .523 on base percentage that is still the team record, as well as runs, walks, stolen bases and singles). Still, it's pretty impressive when you can have six players above 128 in Adjusted OPS. As another comparison, the 1949 and 1950 Red Sox, possibly the two biggest offensive juggernauts since World War II, each had only two players above 128 in Adjusted OPS, and no other team in 1894 had more than two.

| Sam Thompson 176 | Billy Hamilton 157 | Jack Clements 134 |
| Ed Delahanty 158 | Tuck Turner 142 | Lave Cross 129 |

When the dust and smoke had settled at the end of 1894 season, Al Reach knew what he wanted to do. In retrospect, he might have been better off hiring a new manager or a couple of better pitchers, but it's hard to blame him for focusing on the ballpark. A man of vision, Reach was one of the first to realize just what a problem and a threat wooden parks posed. And, he was the man to do something about it, building what would be the first true baseball stadium, a structure made largely out of something other than wood. While Shibe Park would become justly famous 15 years later as the first all concrete and steel park, the new Philadelphia Ball Park was the first brick and steel baseball facility, with only the seats and the platforms the seats rested upon being made of wood. In other words, Reach set out to build, with the help of Philadelphia builders Parvin & Company, a revolutionary concept—a permanent ballpark. And, it would be a park that was as fireproof as possible. And he hit the mark. The Phillies would play in this stadium for a record-breaking 43½ years, and although the speed of design and speed of construction of the park may have led to some flaws that later caused two collapses of the grandstand, the park never burned.

In addition to these innovations, the grandstands of the new Philadelphia Park would be cantilevered, another first in stadium construction. As Reach noted in his invitation to the new park's May 2, 1895, opening day, this principle, previously used mainly in building cantilever bridges would allow "the new Pavilion [to] have no posts at all in the front two-thirds of those seated in the lower deck, and none at all in front of all those seated in the upper deck. In other words nine platforms of the upper deck project beyond any post into the air, and over the heads of those below." Reach also explained to his invitees, maybe to reassure them, but also to promote the new stadium, that Philadelphia architect John D. Allen, who designed the cantilevered grandstands, had extensively tested the design, and guaranteed its safety.

Now, as to whether Reach could guarantee that the Phillies would stop finishing fourth, as they had done in 1889, 1891, 1892, 1893 and 1894, that was a different matter. However, he tried. In the same invitation letter for the new park's opening, he noted that his players' "admitted skill and ability are foundations for their hopes (and perhaps beliefs) that they will win the Championship Pennant of 1895." Reach, sounding somewhat like the Phillies' ownership some 110 years later, also promised that said players "are always aiming for the highest place."[10]

The old Scratcher in 1898. Looking like the captain of industry he had been for some years, Al Reach nonetheless does not appear happy, probably due to the manner in which John Rogers was running the Phillies (courtesy Robert Warrington).

* * *

They didn't win the Championship Pennant of 1895, but it wasn't the fault of Messrs. Delahanty, Hamilton, Thompson, et al. Apparently taking advantage of the decreased playing field presented by the new park, they had a year for the ages, finishing first in runs (1068), hits (1664), doubles (272), home runs (61), batting average (.330), on base percentage (.387) and slugging (.450). This team had five players above 147 in Adjusted OPS: Delahanty (187), Thompson (177), Clements (171), Hamilton (154) and Turner (148). The list of individual league leaders read like the Phillies' roster:

Delahanty—on base (.500), OPS (1.117), doubles (49) and Adjusted OPS (187)
Thompson—slugging (.654), total bases (.352), home runs (18), RBIs (165), runs created (150), extra-base hits (84)
Hamilton—runs (166), walks (96), stolen bases (97)

Thompson's 165 RBIs would have been a new major league record, except that he had 166 in 1887 for the Detroit Wolverines. No one else in the nineteenth century would top the 147 Cap Anson had in 1886, and no one would top either 166 or 165 until Babe Ruth drove in 171 in 1921. Oddly enough, Hamilton, Thompson and Delahanty all missed the batting title again although the Phillies went two-three-four behind Jesse Burkett's .409 with Delahanty's .404 being tops on the team and Clements' .394 (the highest single season batting average ever for a catcher) getting him only third.

And, the Phillies didn't finish fourth. They were third. With a 78-53 record. And it was a lucky 78-53 record at that. Their Pythagorean record was just 72-59. They hung around the edges of the race all year, thanks in part to a 12-game winning streak in last August and early September, and closing to within five games of the first place Orioles on September 21, although they were still in third place. Even though it would have taken a miracle to win the pennant at that point, they didn't help their own cause by going 1-5-2 the rest of the way, particularly since they blew a four game series at Baltimore immediately after pulling within five games of the Orioles. Losing 12–4, 7–1 and 10–1 (along with a 7–7 tie), the Phillies played themselves out of the race[11] and proved pretty conclusively that this was a team that wasn't going to win if it didn't hit.

At the end of the season, they trailed the first place Orioles by nine and a half games. The second place Cleveland Spiders were up by six and a half games in the race for the late nineteenth century equivalent of the Wild Card—the Temple Cup playoff that pitted the first place team against the second place team.

Despite the fact that the construction of the new ballpark shortened the left field line to 341 feet, center field to 408 feet and the right field line from 310 feet to a cozy 272 feet, thanks to a 27-foot extension onto the playing field of the right field foul line grandstand,[12] the park, according to the Baseball-Reference.com website, still played as neutral for pitchers and hitters. The future Baker Bowl was rightly seen as a bandbox in the 1920s and '30s, but that wasn't the case in the stadium's first year although the Phillies did play and hit better at home, going 51-21 in their new park and averaging nine runs a game, against a 27-32 record and seven runs a game on the road, where their sub-standard pitching caught up with them.

Once again, a damning finger can be pointed at manager Art Irwin. Defying three years of pitching evidence at the new distance, Irwin abused pitchers Kid Carsey and Jack Taylor to the tune of 342 and 335 innings. Although these were not outrageously high figures—Carsey was eighth and Taylor ninth in the league—no other team save Cleveland had two hurlers who were put to such a test, and one of the Spiders' pitchers was old rubber arm himself, Cy Young. The first place Orioles, for instance, had five pitchers throw more than 122 innings, while only Wee Willie McGill (146) was also above 90 innings for the Phillies. By now it should have been clear that not every pitcher could handle throwing every other game from the 60 foot distance and, if you didn't have Young or one of the other rubber arms you needed to adjust your pitching strategy. One pitcher who clearly couldn't handle the strain from 60 feet was Gus Weyhing. Plagued by a sore arm, the former "Rubber Arm Gus" made just two starts for the Phillies before he was sent to Pittsburgh and then Louisville. He finished the year 8-21 with a 5.81 ERA and though he would win 32 games for Washington over the course of the 1898 and 1899 seasons, he would never be the same again (he also lost 47 for the Senators in those two years). With Weyhing hurt, only the late-season addition of rookie Al Orth (8-1, 123 Adjusted ERA) kept the pitching respectable, since Taylor (26-14, 106) and Carsey (24-16, 97) basically were living off the team's offense. As it was the pitchers gave up a whopping 957 runs, ninth in the league.

* * *

Even with one of the great offensive outfields of all time, and four of the great offensive seasons of all time, the Phillies hadn't been able to crack the Boston-Baltimore hegemony over the National League. In 1896, they would have a chance to see if they could do it without Billy Hamilton or Art Irwin. Harry Wright had disposed of Irwin for being too mouthy during the 1889 season, and he hadn't changed over the years. Too bad that the Phillies' ownership situation had. The Father of Professional Baseball had died in Atlantic City just after the close of the 1895 regular season. Captain Harry still owned a 10 percent piece of the Phillies, and Colonel Rogers wanted that piece. Under the pretext of financially helping out Wright's widow, Isabelle, Rogers went behind Al Reach's back and bought Wright's stock, making him a 53 percent owner of the team, as opposed to Reach's 43 percent.[13] John Rogers was now running the Phillies, and, since Irwin was as willing to talk back to Rogers as he was to Wright, the manager was soon on his way to baseball's late nineteenth century Siberia, New York, to manage (briefly) for the only owner worse than Rogers, Andrew Freedman.[14]

Now Rogers needed a manager, and Billy Hamilton had been asking for a modest raise.[15] Rogers saw opportunity knocking, and peddled Hamilton to the delighted Boston Beaneaters for their soon-to-be over-the-hill captain and third baseman, Billy Nash, whom Rogers promptly installed as field manager, thus also saving a salary. Although Nash had been a little better than average hitter over the past five seasons (Adjusted OPS figures of 108, 101, 114, 88 and 100) he had never led the league in any offensive category and was clearly no Billy Hamilton. He would also fail to post an Adjusted OPS above 90 in his last three years as a player. This trade, the first real stinker pulled off by the Phillies, started the team off on the only three bad years it would have between 1885 and 1902.

Still, it could have been worse. Before the season, the Phillies picked up another future Hall of Famer, Big Dan Brouthers. Playing 57 games in his final season at the age of 38, Brouthers could still swing the bat, hitting .344/.462/.455 for an Adjusted OPS of 141. However, the infirmities of old age kept Big Dan off first base a lot, necessitating moving Delahanty to that spot. This opened another hole and, with the team going nowhere in mid-season, Nash was sent off on a scouting trip to New England, notably to see the Fall River team of the New England League. Although Nash's batting eye may have gone south, he still had an eye for good players, noting Fall River outfielder Phil Geier as the man needed to fill the hole in the Philadelphia outfield. Nash was also there to check out the Fall River outfielder-first baseman-catcher, a gentleman from Woonsocket, Rhode Island, by the name of Napoleon Lajoie. Although it has been said that Nash was in Fall River just to see Geier, and that Lajoie fell into his lap by accident, that is clearly false. King Larry, as he soon would be called in Philly, was hitting .429 in his first professional season and had already been scouted by Pittsburgh and Boston. Nash just offered more money, $1500 (a goodly sum in 1896) for both players, to secure the services of yet another future Hall of Famer[16] who, in 39 games in Philly would have an Adjusted OPS of 129.

On the other hand, it could have been better, even with four future Hall of Famers in the lineup at various times. Old age was finally catching up to the potent bat of Sam Thompson. At the age of 36 he was playing his last full year, and his falloff was dramatic, from an Adjusted OPS of 177 in 1895 to 108 in 1896. Thus, the Phillies Hall of Fame brigade in 1896 was either very young (Lajoie) or very old (Brouthers and Thompson). Only Ed Delahanty was in his prime. Jack Clements, at 31, was also getting old for a nineteenth century catcher, although he did have a 156 Adjusted OPS in 57 games. Left-handed rookie shortstop Bill Hulen didn't help any either. With an Adjusted OPS of 93 he was a sub-par hitter, and with 33 errors in 73 games and a bad range factor, he proved why lefties shouldn't play shortstop.

The only player who was really OK all year was Delahanty, who led the league in slugging (.631), OPS (1.103), doubles (44), home runs (13), RBIs (126), Adjusted OPS

(190), runs created (146) and extra-base hits (74). He was never better than on July 13 in Chicago when, facing pitcher Adonis Terry, he homered in the first inning, singled in the third inning, homered again in the fifth and seventh, and then, to the cheers of the Colts' crowd, added a fourth home run in the ninth,[17] tying Bobby Lowe's record of four in a game. It would be 36 years before anyone (Lou Gehrig) would match that record.

With only Delahanty standing out at the plate all season, the offense fell off dramatically, as the Phillies led the league in only doubles (234) and home runs (49) while coming in second in runs scored with 890, one less than the pitchers gave up. Even Billy Hamilton couldn't have helped that big a fall. As for the man traded for Hamilton, Nash was the manager of record throughout the year, but sub catcher and first baseman Jack Boyle ran the team on the field during Nash's scouting trip to New England. In addition, in an arrangement that seems similar to that used by the Athletics a dozen or so years before, when administrator Bill Sharsig was often looking over the field manager's shoulder, Nash was augmented on the job to some extent by long-time club official Bill Shettsline, who had an administrative background, but had never played professionally or managed. Shettsline's job was to handle overall strategic policy,[18] though most likely *not* during the games. None of the three seemed to have learned much about pitching from Irwin's experience the two years before, or anybody's experience since 1893, since Brewery Jack Taylor (20-21) was abused to the tune of 359 innings (he was sixth in the league), with no one else throwing more than 196 (Orth, who was just 15-10) or 187 (Carsey, 11-11). By comparison, the first place Orioles had five pitchers throw more than 155 innings. Maybe it wouldn't have made any difference, since no one who pitched more than 17 innings for the Phillies had an Adjusted ERA better than Orth's 98. In all, it added up to a 62-68 eighth place finish.

* * *

The less said about 1897, the better. The Phillies fell to 10th with a dull thud, finishing 22 games under .500 at 55-77 and failing to excel in any aspect of the game, particularly at manager. What possessed John Rogers to hire George Stallings as manager is lost in the mists of time. A career minor leaguer who would play just seven games in the majors, the 29-year-old Stallings was managing Detroit in the Western League when he was chosen to lead the 1897 Phillies. As unusual as it was at that time for someone with basically no major league experience to manage a major league team, it was also pretty rare for someone with Stallings' personality to even be on the field. Although Stallings was the proverbial Southern gentleman off the field, a graduate of VMI who also took two years of medical school, he was a veritable demon on the field—profane to the extreme, highly superstitious, and a slave-driving, abusive tyrant.[19] If the Phillies players of 2004 thought Larry Bowa was a hard manager to play for, they should have seen George Stallings.

Maybe it comes as no surprise that almost no one played well. Delahanty had his typical big year (161 Adjusted OPS, although he failed to lead the league in anything) and the 22-year-old Lajoie blossomed into a star (155, and leading the league in slugging, total bases and extra-base hits) at first base, but then again, those two would have been great playing for almost anyone. Overall, the offense was unimpressive, finishing a shocking ninth in runs scored (752), actually three spots lower than their 6th place runs allowed figure. Still, the pitching wasn't great, although at least the mound work was spread out among four men, Taylor (317 innings), Orth (282), Jack Fifield (211) and George Wheeler

(191), with only Wheeler (106 and the only winning record at 11-10) having an Adjusted OPS over 99.

* * *

When 1898 started out pretty much the same way as 1897 closed, no one associated with the Philadelphia National League baseball club was very happy, least of all the players. It was bad enough to have to play for someone like George Stallings, but to do so and to lose constantly was worse. "Worse" for Colonel Rogers were the attendance figures. The Phillies had fallen to fifth in the league in 1897 after the seasons following the end of the association had provided years of growth and increasing gates.

	Attendance	Rank
1892	193,371	2nd
1893	293,019	1st
1894	352,773	2nd
1895	474,971	1st
1896	357,025	2nd
1897	290,027	5th

Thus, when the players revolted against Stallings, Rogers was willing to listen, despite the fact that he'd had the entire team sign a letter the year before (on June 23, 1897) stating their support for the manager. On June 17, 1898, with the Phillies at 19-27 and languishing in an eighth place tie with Brooklyn, the players had had enough. In what promised to be the National League's first player strike, a committee of players, headed by outfielder Duff Cooley, went to Rogers and Reach and demanded the head of George Stallings, or else. Rogers was so willing to avoid the "or else" that he canned Stallings on June 18, painfully buying out the remaining year and a half of the manager's contract.[20]

The new manager? Mr. Phillie himself, Bill Shettsline came back down from the front office to take over and to initiate a run of strong seasons that would rival the franchise's previous high point from 1886 to 1890. For just 1898, the team made as dramatic a turnaround as any Phillie Phanatic could hope for; they played .573 ball (59-44) the rest of the way, a pace that would have put them in fourth place if they could have maintained it all year. As it was, they rose up to sixth at year's end, partly by winning nine of their last 12, finishing with a 78-71 record. Maybe even better from Rogers' point of view, attendance, although still off from 1897, did rise to third in the league, at 265,414.

It helped that the team that Stallings turned over to Shettsline was pretty good. For once, the pitching had actually been bolstered with some talent, and the workload was finally beginning to be spread out. Wiley Piatt, a 23-year-old rookie from Blue Creek, Ohio, became the staff ace, leading the league with six shutouts and going 24-14 with an Adjusted ERA of 108 in 306 innings. Also bolstering the pitching staff was Red Donahue, picked up from the St. Louis Browns for a song after going 10-35 and leading the NL in losses in 1897. The Phillies' opening day starter, former Villanova hurler Donahue, would improve to 16-17 in 284 innings with a 94 Adjusted ERA. Not great, but better than 1897's 72. And, as a bonus, he would throw the team's second no-hitter on a blazing hot July 8 at the Philadelphia Ball Park, beating Boston 5–0, no small achievement against a team that would win 102 games. Donahue, who early baseball historian Ernest Lanigan said was a good hot weather pitcher, struck out just one and walked two in defeating future Hall of Famer Vic Willis.[21] Red was beginning the best stretch of his career, wherein he would win 20 three of the next four seasons and consistently post ERAs below the league average.

Unfortunately, like many other Phillies of the late 1890s, he would do most of that in the American League.

Orth, Fifield and Wheeler were still around, and, along with Piatt and Donahue, would throw 112 innings or more, with the "Curveless Wonder" (as Orth was known) going 15-13 with a 113 Adjusted ERA. Orth would win an even 100 games in his seven years with the Phillies, and he would win another 104 after jumping to the American League in 1901. With 204 wins and a career batting average of .273 (Adjusted OPS 92), Orth was a throwback to the mid–1880s, when the best players typically played some games in the field when they weren't pitching, because they could hit as well. In addition to pitching 440 games, Orth would play 55 games in the outfield, eight at short, six at second and four at first during his career. Of course, only some of those efforts were for the Phillies. The other Phillies pitcher who came up in 1898 and made a name for himself at the plate was Frosty Bill Duggleby. He would actually stay with the Phillies (except for one game with the Athletics) for his eight seasons and 93 wins, but he would be best known for starting his career with a bang. Making his first appearance in a major league uniform against the New York Giants on April 21, 1898, Duggleby got off on the right foot at the plate by hitting a grand slam in his first at-bat[22]—the first player to do so. Reports that it was a pinch-hit grand slam are incorrect, since Duggleby was the starting pitcher in the game, winning 13–4.[23] Despite the grand start, he would go only 3-3 in nine games in 1898, probably because his Adjusted ERA was 62.

The new pitchers still only managed to hold down the opponents to the tune of 784 runs allowed (seventh in the league). But, some new blood on offense was in the process of bringing that aspect of the Phillies' game back to its usually healthy status. Although the new park was still playing as neutral, it wouldn't become a hitters' park consistently until 1908, the addition of yet another future Hall of Famer, 22-year-old left-handed hitting outfielder Elmer Flick, boded well for the team's scoring potential. The Bedford, Ohio, native was mostly a speed and contact-hitting type of player who drew a good number of walks, at first blush sort of a lowercase Billy Hamilton. Even taking into account the different methods of counting steals for most of each player's career, Hamilton still looks like a much better offensive player, although Flick had a little more power.

	Batting	*On Base*	*Slugging*	*Steals*	*OPS*
Hamilton	.344	.455	.432	912	.887
Flick	.313	.389	.445	330	.834

However, Hamilton played most of his career in a high offense era, and Flick played most of his in the Deadball Era, and Flick's career Adjusted OPS was 149 to Hamilton's 141. So, Elmer Flick could hit. And, in 1898, he tied Delahanty for the highest Adjusted OPS on the team (156). Added to Lajoie's (who Stallings moved to second just before he was canned) 137, plus league-leading totals of RBIs (127) and doubles (43), and the three future Cooperstown residents helped the team finish first in doubles and slugging, and third in batting and on base percentage, even if they were still just sixth in runs scored (823).

* * *

The promise of the second two-thirds of the 1898 season under Shettsline was fulfilled in 1899 with a 94-58 record in what may have been the best all-around Phillies team of the organization's first 90 plus years. They for certain won more games than any team in the first 93 years, since the 94 W's wouldn't be topped until 1976. This team had everything; they even led the league again in attendance (388,933). As good a hitting team as the 1895 group was, the 1899 offense may have been just as good—first in runs (916), hits (1613), doubles (241), batting (.301), on base (.355) and slugging (.395). Of the seven offensive categories the '95 Phillies led the league in, they missed only home runs in '99.

Ed Delahanty had what could be considered the best year of his glittering career, with .410/.464/.582 numbers that added up to a 189 Adjusted OPS (one point less than 1896). He personally led the league in 10 offensive categories:

Batting	.410	
Slugging	.582	
OPS	1.046	
Hits	238	
Total Bases	338	
Doubles	55	(a major league record that would stand until 1923)
RBIs	137	
Adjusted OPS	189	
Runs Created	156	
Extra Base Hits	73	

In addition to his doubles mark, he also set career highs in batting average, hits and runs created. And he was far from the only big gun in Philly that year. The 1899 team had six players above 124 in Adjusted OPS:

Pearce Chiles—125
Roy Thomas—128
Elmer Flick—136
Ed McFarland—143
Nap Lajoie—169 (in only 77 games, due to injury)
Ed Delahanty—189

Although utilityman Chiles and catcher McFarland had brief starring roles—Chiles was a 32-year-old rookie who would play only one more year and McFarland, though the Phillies' regular catcher in 1898, would never again get close to his 143 mark in a Phillies' uniform—Roy Thomas was a name that was already familiar to some Philadelphia sports fans, and would remain so until 1911. A native of nearby Norristown and a former member of the University of Pennsylvania baseball team, Thomas was an early day Richie Ashburn—a little left-handed hitting outfielder who could fly. Thomas also could drive pitchers crazy by fouling off pitch after pitch until he either walked, or got something he could punch in safely for a single.[24] Although he had as little power as any long-term player in major league history (he had just 100 doubles, 53 triples and seven home runs in almost 6600 plate appearances), Thomas was an offensive force, leading the National League in walks seven times, in on base percentage twice (with a career .413 mark that is 29th all-time) and in runs scored once. His career Adjusted OPS was 123. He was also a defensive force, posting career fielding (.972 to .950) and range factor (2.43 to 1.97) marks way above the league average. As a marvelous centerfielder, Thomas, along with the graceful Lajoie and catcher McFarland, gave the team good defense up the middle (shortstop Monte Cross also covered a lot of ground), in addition to its superb hitting.

The 1899 season also saw the Phillies' best pitching staff since the days of Charlie Ferguson, finishing fifth in runs allowed (743)—a figure that could easily have been better if Shettsline had been able to better identify who his best hurlers were. Five men threw 132 innings or more for the 1899 Phillies, but it was the two least-used members of the staff, Al Orth and 28-year-old rookie righthander Strawberry Bill Bernhard, who were the best pitchers.

	W-L	ERA
Wiley Piatt	23-15	3.45
Chick Fraser	21-12	3.36
Red Donahue	21-8	3.39
Al Orth	14-3	2.49
Bill Bernhard	6-6	2.65

Although Orth (148) and Bernhard (139) posted the best Adjusted ERAs, it was the three 20 game winners who got the most work. Piatt threw 305 innings; Fraser, who was purchased from the Cleveland Spiders in December 1898 after three mediocre years with Louisville and Cleveland, had by far his best year to date in 271 innings; and Donahue, probably enjoying the hot summer the most, pitched 279. Although it's hard to argue with the success of the three 20 game winners, the fact is that, given more work, Orth and Bernhard probably would have had better won-loss records than Piatt, Fraser and Donahue. As it was, Orth tied for the league lead in won-loss percentage (.824) and would have taken the ERA title if he'd pitched more with the same success. As it was, he had two different one-month stretches between starts, and also went from mid–April to mid–June without starting. Possibly, since he had pitched 250 innings the year before, and would pitch 262 innings in 1900, he had some kind of injury. Still, his usage pattern was odd. He didn't start taking a regular turn until September. Bernhard, although he debuted on April 24, wouldn't start a game until July 6.[25]

So how did this team finish only third, nine full games behind the Brooklyn Superbas (another of those "B" teams)? The answer to this one is simple: the Phillies were facing two teams in one in the person of Hanlon's Superbas, formed from the merger of his former pennant-winning old Orioles team with the Brooklyn squad. And the Superbas ran off with the pennant, winning 101 games. The pennant race was close at the start, with the St. Louis Perfectos (another composite team), Chicago Orphans, Brooklyn, the Phillies and Cincinnati all in the hunt by mid–May, and all playing better than .650 ball in the terribly unbalanced 12-team league. By July 1, the Superbas had taken control of the race, leading by four and a half games although three other teams, in order the Beaneaters, Orphans and Phillies, were still playing better than .605 ball. A seven-game winning streak in mid–July brought the Phillies up to fourth, four and a half out, but they then lost eight of their next 10 to fall back to fourth. Against a team like the Superbas, an opponent could not afford a slump. The Phillies went 19-6 over the next 25 games, but they still couldn't get closer than second place, four games out, on August 22. All another hot streak (10-1), between September 2 and September 14, managed to do was keep them in second, and now they were eight games out, because, between August 12 and September 14, the Superbas had gone 26-3. The race was over, and Brooklyn coasted in, going 13-10 the rest of the way. The Phillies were 12-11 over that same stretch, losing second place to Boston in early October and failing to make up enough ground on the Beaneaters by going 4-3 against them as the two teams played their last seven games with each other.[26] Even if Lajoie had played a whole season, instead of half a season, it seems unlikely that they could have made up nine games.

* * *

Despite the excellence in Brooklyn, there should have been optimism in Philadelphia as the calendars turned from the 1800s to the 1900s. The Phillies had won 94 games without the services of King Larry for half the season, and the improved pitching staff was young. Bernhard, at 29 in 1900, was the oldest by two years. Furthermore, when the National League contracted early in 1900, buying out the Washington, Baltimore, Cleveland and Louisville franchises, the Phillies picked up a useful outfielder, Jimmy Slagle, from the Senators. Then, when they picked up Harry Wolverton from the Orphans to play third base a few games into the 1900 season, their lineup seemed pretty well set with, at worst, solid players, and, at best, three future Hall of Famers: Lajoie, Delahanty and Flick. The regular lineup for Philadelphia in the final year of the nineteenth century included

    C—Ed McFarland   OF—Roy Thomas   P—Red Donahue
    1B—Ed Delahanty   OF—Elmer Flick   P—Chick Fraser
    2B—Nap Lajoie   UT/INF—Joe Dolan   P—Bill Bernhard
    SS—Monte Cross   C—Klondike Douglass P—Wiley Piatt
    3B—Harry Wolverton   UT/INF—Pearce Chiles
    OF—Jimmy Slagle   P—Al Orth

Although there wasn't much of a bench, and the starters lacked a true ace, it looked like a team that could contend. However, it really wasn't to be, although they did lead the league again in attendance, drawing 301,913. The league was much better balanced now, and the Superbas couldn't dominate like they did in 1899. Nevertheless, the Phillies could come only one game closer, this time finishing eight games out in third with a 75-63 record. The hitting, though still strong, fell off some, and the pitching was worse, possibly proving the old adage that young pitchers will break your heart.

Neither Delahanty (128) nor Thomas (119) had a particularly strong year. Lajoie (140) got into only 102 games, and although he didn't have one of his great offensive years, his defense at second was so good that Charles Faber's Faber System rankings rate him as the best player in the National League.[27] Also, 1900 was the year that 24-year-old Elmer Flick became a star. Although he led the league only in RBIs (110), he was second in practically everything else, the problem being that Honus Wagner was also in the league. Flick finished second to the Flying Dutchman in batting, slugging, OPS, total bases, Adjusted OPS (172), runs created and extra-base hits. He was also second in home runs (12) to Boston's Herman Long. With a .367/.441/.545 season, Flick didn't have to apologize to anyone. And neither did the rest of the Phillies' offense. Either Flick, Delahanty, Lajoie or Thomas finished first or second in every major offensive category except for hits, triples and steals. (And Flick just missed the top two in the first two areas.) Although they couldn't match 1899's remarkable sweep, the Phillies still led the league in hits (1439) and walks (440) while coming in second in runs (810), on base percentage (.347) and slugging (.378).

Once again, the pitching was to blame. Of the team's five main hurlers, Orth (14-14), Bernhard (15-10), Fraser (15-9), Donahue (15-10) and Piatt (9-10), only Fraser had a better Adjusted ERA in 1900 than he had in 1899. And, it wasn't a matter of overuse. Orth led the team with just 262 innings pitched, while Bernhard, Fraser and Donahue were all between 219 and 240, and Piatt threw 161 innings.

	ERA +	
	1899	*1900*
Orth	148	96
Bernhard	139	76
Fraser	110	115
Donahue	109	101
Piatt	107	77

Nap Lajoie, after jumping to the American League following the 1900 season (Turkey Red).

Going from five above average pitchers in 1899 to one above average pitcher, two average pitchers, and two batting practice pitchers dropped the Phillies' runs allowed from fifth in the 12-team league to seventh in an eight-team league. However, in fairness to the pitchers, part of this problem may have been the fielders. A good defensive team for most of the decade of the '90s, the 1900 team was merely average in the field. In particular, shortstop Monte Cross died with his boots—62 in all—in just 131 games. (In addition to hitting just .202.) Fortunately for Cross' reputation, his range was so good that he still had a fielding percentage (and range factor) above the league average.

After winning 19–17 in 10 innings in Boston on Opening Day, the Phillies started hot, holding first place through the month of May. At 22-10 on May 31, they had a four game lead over the Superbas, the re-named Cardinals of St. Louis, and those Pirates in the western part of Pennsylvania. During June though, the Superbas took over the race, and were leading the second-place Phillies 35-19 to 33-23 by the end of the month. Over the course of the rest of the year, the Pirates would prove to be the up-and-coming team in the league, having been improved more than any other team by the contraction and, as a result, finishing second to Brooklyn.[28]

Possibly getting tired of there always being something standing between them and first place, the Phillies tried a new approach during the 1900 season. In mid–September, during a five-game sweep of the Reds at the Philadelphia Ball Park, a Cincinnati infielder thought he had caught his spikes on an underground vine. Now, there was a Reading Railroad tunnel under the park, but no vines like this. Closer examination showed it was an electrical wire that ran from a plate buried in the third base coaches' box to the Phillies centerfield, second-story clubhouse. Stationed in said clubhouse was backup catcher Morgan Murphy and a telescope. Since Murphy would play in just 11 games in 1900, he had plenty of opportunity to observe the opposing catcher's signals and relay them, via electrical impulse, to the coaches' box, where the third base coach could pick them up via his metal spikes.[29] While it's a good bet this device wasn't used during rainy games, it may have had something to do with the team finishing second in runs scored. Naturally, league officials requested that this new form of communication cease and desist immediately. Although manager Billy Shettsline denied all knowledge of the device, Superbas' manager Ned Hanlon called him a "crook," a classic case of the pot calling the kettle black, since Hanlon's old Orioles had specialized in such extra-legal moves as hiding extra balls in the long grass of the outfield, cutting off second or third base if the lone umpire wasn't looking, and holding on to a runner's belt when he tried to tag up and score from third base. For his part, Colonel Rogers thought this ploy was perfectly fair and legitimate.[30]

* * *

It is not really fair, though perhaps it would be fitting, to end the story of nineteenth century baseball in Philadelphia on such a note. Despite the follies of owners Rogers, Simmons, Pennypacker and Wagner, Philadelphia had played a major role in the game of baseball in the nineteenth century, so the best way to close this story is with the Philadelphia nineteenth century All-Star Team, composed of native Philadelphians and non-natives who played at least four nineteenth century seasons in Philly:

C—Jack Clements
1B—Harry Stovey
2B—Al Reach
SS—Chick Fulmer
3B—Levi Meyerle
OF—Ed Delahanty
OF—Billy Hamilton
OF—Sam Thompson

P—Dick McBride
P—Bobby Matthews
P—Gus Weyhing
P—Charlie Ferguson

MGR—Harry Wright
Front Office—Hicks Hayhurst,
   Bill Sharsig, Bill Shettsline

That's not a bad team, although only the outfield and the manager are currently in the Hall of Fame. Of course, if that august institution would consider returning to the game's roots (and revising its 10-years-in-the-majors eligibility rule), then Stovey, Reach, McBride and Matthews would be no-questions-asked Hall of Famers, and cases could be made for Clements and Meyerle. Only at short, with good field-poor hit Chick Fulmer, is this anything but an all-time All-Star team.

The strength of this team can also be judged by those who didn't make it. Although Jocko Milligan may have been a little better hitter than Clements, the old lefty catcher had a longer career and was a little better fielder. The Phillies' Hall of Fame outfield of the 1890s pushes Stovey to first, displacing another Philadelphia native who could hit and field—Wes Fisler. Thanks to the "Scratcher's" outstanding resume on and off the field, Larry Lajoie's parts of five nineteenth century seasons in Philadelphia gets left off second, as does Philly native Fred "Sure-Shot" Dunlap. The competition at third is especially fierce—Cap Anson played there in less than half of his games during his four years with the Athletics, and Philly native Ned Williamson (who largely played for Anson in Chicago) was often said to be the best in the business there. Another AA star, Denny Lyons, gets left off, as does his teammate, outfielder Henry Larkin.

Perhaps this is the best way to remember baseball in Philadelphia in the nineteenth century—since what really matters in baseball is what's on the field.

PART II

A Biographical Dictionary

A Note on Sources

Thanks to the Society for American Baseball Research (SABR) and the Internet, biographical information on nineteenth century baseball figures has never been more accessible. Also available on an unprecedented scale are post–1870 statistics, mainly from Baseball Research (www.baseball-research.com). The career statistical lines for each of the players in this section, listing his career statistics from 1871 on, are from Baseball-Reference (www.baseball-reference.com). In addition, Retrosheet (www.retrosheet.org), Baseball Almanac (www.baseballalmanac.com), Baseball Library (www.baseballlibrary.com), The Deadball Era (www.thedeadballera.com), The Church of Jesus Christ of Latter-day Saints (www.familysearch.org) and the SABR (www.sabr.org) websites are invaluable biographical resources, although the best resource for hard copy historical baseball information is still the National Baseball Library (NBL) in Cooperstown, New York.

Among individuals, author-historians such as John Thorn (who supplied some of the information herein from the NBL), David Jordan, Rich Wescott, David Nemec, William Ryczek, Marshall Wright, Donald Dewey and Nicholas Acocella, among others, have produced invaluable works of reference containing information on many of Philadelphia's nineteenth century baseball figures. Even more significant in this undertaking are two compendiums of nineteenth century biographies, published by SABR, *Nineteenth Century Stars* and *Baseball's First Stars*. Providing a lot of the basic information on many of the following individuals, they also provide a good ground rule for whom to include in the following biographies—those players whose careers were primarily in the nineteenth century.

Most of the content of these biographies is based upon the work of those who have gone before. Rather than try and footnote every reference used in every biography herein, the major sources that each biography is drawn from are listed, along with the authors, where appropriate, at the end of each individual biography, just after each player's career statistical summary.

Adrian Anson

Long before he became possibly the most controversial figure in nineteenth century baseball; long before he became possibly the most popular figure in nineteenth century baseball, the incomparable "Pop" Anson; long before he was "Cap" Anson, but after he was "The Marshalltown Infant" or "Baby" Anson, he was just plain Adrian Anson, third baseman for the Philadelphia Athletics. And, while Anson may have established himself as both a phenom and one of the towering figures of baseball in Illinois, earning induction to the Hall of Fame in 1939, he first became a star in Philadelphia.

The first white child born in Marshalltown, Iowa (on April 17, 1852), and the son of a ballplaying mayor, Henry Anson, Adrian Anson first came to prominence with the Rockford Forest Citys in the first year of the National Association. Having previously played at Notre Dame—which was closer to a high school at that time in its history—and for the local Marshalltown Stars, young (18) Anson came to the attention of the Forest Citys when the Stars held the pros to a 17–3 win on September 16, 1870, at a time when Rockford was beating small town teams by scores of 72–3 and 97–13. Anson was invited to try out for the 1871 Rockford team, which would play in the first year of the NA, though not with most of its stars, including ace pitcher Albert Spalding. They had all gone on to greener pastures—without any kind of a reserve clause, this happened all the time. In fact, it happened again after the 1871 season, during which Anson hit .325 with a league-leading 11 doubles for Rockford. The Forest Citys wanted to keep him, but the Athletics, already boasting just about the longest history of paying players, outbid the small town crew, offering Anson $1250 for the 1872 season, a good bit more than Rockford's $50 a month contract. Although Anson went back to Illinois and told the Forest Citys he would stick with them for $100 a month, they couldn't afford him; in fact, the team actually disbanded shortly thereafter.

Anson became a hero in the big city of Philadelphia. He was the best hitter on the second-best team in the association, hitting .415, .398, .336 and .325 for Athletic and leading the association in on base percentage (.455) in 1872. A third baseman for Rockford, he played mostly third (82 games) and first (92 games) for Athletic, starting at the former position and moving more and more across the diamond during his four years in Philadelphia. This transition was also not surprising, for although Anson was, by many standards, the best hitter of the nineteenth century, he was far from the best fielder. At least 6-0 and 227 pounds, he was much larger (and less mobile) than the average player of the time, and the move to first was certainly a natural.

With a salary that grew to $1800, he cut a large swath through Philadelphia, an exciting place for a veritable boy—he was still only 23 during his last season in Philly—from, if not the Wild West, at least the sticks of Iowa. He took up billiards and boxing in Philly, as well as the night life, the latter apparently during the Red Stockings-Athletic tour of London in 1874. This led to some serious barhopping and fighting back in Philly, but Anson soon saw the error of his ways, thanks to a young lady, Virginia M. Fiegal, the daughter of a Philadelphia hotel and restaurant owner. They eventually married during the 1876 season, but not after a few adventures.

Adrian Constantine Anson—he might have been wearing a Philadelphia uniform if William Hulbert hadn't banished the Athletics in 1876 (Library of Congress photograph).

About the time Anson was cleaning up his act, the NA was falling apart, thanks in part to a couple of great nineteenth century robber baron-types, William Hulbert and Al Spalding. However, the NA's troubles wouldn't be a bother to Anson. First of all, he was already a star, and stars have a way of landing on their feet. Secondly, he was off to Chicago to join Hulbert's and Spalding's White Stockings. The scenario for this deal seems to be that Hulbert first out-bid the Athletics for Anson's services in 1876, and then demanded the Philadelphia team relinquish any claim to Anson as the price for allowing the Athletics into his new National League. Making this story more likely is the fact that Anson had found himself in a utility role in 1875 after the Athletics bought George Bechtel from the Philadelphia Centennials. Even though the Athletics' directors made him captain (manager) in the middle of the team's October 9 game, he was off to play in Chicago—which was closer to both of his hometowns anyway—for the price of a $2000 yearly contract.

Not so fast. Virginia didn't like the idea of Adrian playing on the shores of Lake Michigan, and Anson subsequently tried to buy his contract back from Hulbert, so he could return to Philadelphia and Virginia. He might as well have tried the same thing with Jay Gould or J.P. Morgan for all the success he had. In protest, Anson, who had more than a fair amount of ham in him, actually appeared in a Chicago National League game wearing a Prince Albert and striped trousers—the dress of an *eastern* gentleman. That ploy didn't work, so Anson wrote back to Philadelphia to Virginia's father, asking for her hand. They were married in a Philadelphia church during the White Stockings' first 1876 visit to play the Athletics.

Nonetheless, it may be that Virginia wasn't entirely placated. Research by SABR member Frank Vaccaro has shown that the April 1, 1894, *Chicago Tribune* reported that Anson signed an 1877 contract to return to the Athletics, very possibly at Virginia's urging. However, when the Athletics were conveniently booted out of the National League after the 1876 season, Anson had to return to National League and Chicago president William Hulbert's suzerainty, at least if he wanted to play major league baseball for 1877.

Anson's career in Chicago has been much-documented and discussed. He became Cap Anson in 1879 when he was named manger of the White Stockings. In that role, the burly, loud, innovative, larger-than-life Anson cut an even larger swath through baseball, eventually playing a total of 27 major league seasons, and running up 3418 hits and 52 points in the Black Ink Test, while leading Chicago to five pennants between 1880 and 1886 as a dictatorial, puritanical (if he didn't drink anymore, neither should anyone else) intimidator of players, opponents, umpires, executives, etc., who would try anything to get a win or gain an advantage. Picture a much larger John McGraw with a much longer playing career, and you'll get a pretty good idea of Cap Anson.

At the time Anson was playing and managing, that was the image of the Chicago leader. It was not until some 80 years after the fact that the events of the mid–1880s brought Anson and his legacy into the controversial category. Anson's actions and statements in regard to African Americans playing professional baseball in the mid–1880s were *not* greatly remarked upon in his time because, while Anson was a racist, so was almost everyone else in any kind of position of authority. This was an era when Jim Crow laws were being enacted all over the country. In this climate, baseball's drawing of the unofficial Color Line, which was firmly in place by the mid-1890s, was inevitable, no matter what Anson did or did not do.

Let go as Chicago's manager after the 1897 season, the widely-admired and praised Anson retired as a player at age 45, having hit .285 in his final year. After three weeks as the Giants' manager in 1898, he never held another job in major league baseball, though it wasn't for a lack of effort on his part. At various times during the final 24 years of his life, he tried to re-start the American Association, performed on stage, served as city clerk of Chicago (leaving under the cloud of a financial scandal), and managed a semi-pro team (and also played, at nearly 60 years of age)—always looking for a way to market his name. He was forced into bankruptcy, lost his house, and generally spent his last two decades down on his luck financially, thanks mainly to a string of bad business deals in everything from bowling alleys to bottling ginger beer. Having worked with Al Spalding in baseball, he figured he could match him in business as well. He couldn't, and when he died on April 14, 1922, he left no estate and the National League paid for his funeral expenses.

G	AB	R	H	2B	3B	HR	RBI	BA	OBP	SLG	OPS+
2523	10277	1996	3418	581	142	97	2076	.333	.393	.445	141

Sources: *The Baseball Book 1990* (Bill James), *The Ballplayers* (Mike Shatzkin, editor), *Blackguards and Red Stockings* (William Ryczek), *Baseball's First Stars* (SABR), Capanson.com, AllGamesBaseball.com, *Chicago Tribune*.

Octavius Catto

If you were to take a poll of historians, sociologists, civic and civil rights leaders as to the identity of the two most influential and notable African Americans of the twentieth century, the odds are good that the first two names would be Martin Luther King, Jr., and Jack Roosevelt Robinson. Now, imagine combining these two great Americans into one, and you have Octavius Valentine Catto—civil rights leader, educator, radical, martyr and baseball pioneer—of the nineteenth century. And one of Philadelphia's great men, for all-too-short a time.

Octavius Catto was born in Charleston, South Carolina, on February 22, 1839, the son of Sarah Isabell Cain and the Reverend William T. Catto, a Presbyterian minister who later became a bishop in the African Methodist Episcopal Church. William Catto was a free man, a rare thing for a black man in South Carolina in 1839. But then, William Catto was a rare man for his time. Originally a millwright, he was also an inventor of an improvement to the threshing machine and then he turned to the clergy. The Catto family's free and relatively affluent status allowed the senior Catto the opportunity to get his family out of the South when the Presbyterian Church called him to a pulpit in Philadelphia in 1844—a good thing for both Philadelphia and the Catto family, since South Carolina had a law at that time that prohibited teaching blacks to read and write, another reason for Reverend Catto to want to move his family

So, at the age of five, Octavius Catto became a Philadelphian. He was educated in the city's grammar schools, the Academy in Allentown, New Jersey, and the new Society of Friends–sponsored Institute for Colored Youth (the future Cheyney University) at 715 Lombard Street in Philadelphia, where he enrolled in 1854. According to Catto biographer, Temple University professor and Civil War historian Andrew Waskie, this last organization was, from the beginning, a teacher's college, and one of the finest of its type in the land, providing a free, college-level education to "colored" youth so that they could go out and teach in black schools. Furthermore, according to Catto biographers Daniel Biddle and Murray Dubin (both reporters for the *Philadelphia Inquirer*), the institute was also the intellectual hub of Philadelphia's black community (the largest free black population in the country) and modeled after Philadelphia's already-prestigious Central High School which was, at this time, all-white. Catto graduated from the institute in four years as the valedictorian, and was soon thereafter added to the teaching staff as assistant to the principal, Professor E.D. Bassett, one of the foremost black scholars in the country. As Biddle and Dubin summarized the developing Octavius Catto in their July 6, 2003, *Inquirer Magazine* cover story on Catto, "He was 20 and a teacher, a respected man." That status would only grow over the next dozen years.

Despite offers from around the nation, Catto stayed with his alma mater and his adopted home town, becoming more and more involved in intellectual, political and athletic pursuits, founding the Banneker Library Institute, the Equal Rights League and, in 1866, the Philadelphia Pythian Club. Indeed, Catto was founder, captain, manager, promoter and second baseman-shortstop for Pythian, which although not the first black ball club, was one of the first Philadelphia black clubs. A top amateur club, either black or white, Pythian played several other local black clubs, most notably the Excelsior club of Philadelphia, in their first year of games, 1867. Typically batting second in the powerhouse Pythian lineup, it was not uncommon for Catto to score a half dozen or more runs a game, according to the Pythian scorecards preserved at the Historical Society of Pennsylvania.

It is ironic then, that in the fall and winter of 1867, both the Pennsylvania Convention and the National Association of Base Ball Players (NABBP) refused Pythian membership in their growing fraternity of clubs, the first drawing of baseball's color line. Part of the irony came from the fact that Pythian's captain was himself a member of numerous civic, literary, patriotic and political groups, including the Franklin Institute, the Philadelphia Library Company, the 4th Ward Black Political Club, the Pennsylvania State Equal Rights League, the Social, Cultural and Statistical Association of Colored People of Philadelphia, and the Union League. This last membership may well cause current members of that very Republican organization mild cardiac distress; however, in the 1860s, the Republican Party was the party of the Great Emancipator, Abraham Lincoln. Even more ironic, Catto had spent most of the Civil War joining with other black leaders like Frederick Douglass in an effort to raise black troops to support the very Union whose victory helped spread the game of baseball, and helped the NABBP prosper. Of course, major league baseball wouldn't be dragged, kicking and screaming, into the integrated era until Jackie Robinson came along 80 years later.

The rejections by the Pennsylvania and national groups notwithstanding, Catto continued to play for, lead and promote Pythian, even designing the club's blue uniforms. In a letter (noted by Biddle and Dubin) to a teammate during the 1867 season, Catto proclaimed that Pythian's success was attracting "considerable interest, and not a little anxiety among the White Fraternity." According to historian Christopher Threston, that anxiety was mostly financial, since the "White Fraternity" wasn't playing Pythian at that time. Undeterred by the NABBP's snub, Pythian carried on, with all the trappings of the other top-level amateur clubs, including their own office at 718 Lombard Street—across the street from the institute.

The 1868 season saw Catto recruiting a couple of top players from Excelsior—something all the white teams did amongst themselves as well, but for a unique reason. "Especially in view of the probability of our meeting our white brethren.... We can put a conquering nine in the field." Yes, this man was a competitor, and one who had a unique relationship between baseball and his other civic responsibilities. As Threston points out in *The Integration of Baseball in Philadelphia*, Catto was doing a lot more than playing and captaining a baseball team, he was also using Pythian as part of his efforts to chip away at the massive roadblock of segregation that marked American society as a whole at the time. Although it's problematic as to whether Catto became famous in Philadelphia in the late 1860s because he was a civil rights pioneer, or because he was a well-known baseball player, there's no doubt he was famous, and, on the baseball diamond, he did accomplish one small step in his efforts to fight Jim Crow. On September 18, 1869, history was made when Pythian beat NABBP member City Item 27–17 in what may have been the first interracial baseball game among two top-level clubs.

A leader in the years-long fight to integrate Philadelphia's horsecars, Catto had been a battler against Jim Crow, in what would later be called the civil rights movement, from before the start of the Civil War. On July 4, 1859, he pre-empted Lincoln by publishing a pamphlet that predicted that someday, "slavery will be only known in history." As Biddle and Dubin put it, "Catto wanted to fight." And fight he did, in the streetcar battle. Although he was closely connected with many white Republican Quakers, he chose a more militant course. In other words, he was pushy, or as the whites he left back in the South would have said years later, "uppity." Or maybe he was just a competitor, like Jackie Robinson. Whatever you want to call it, Catto's style proved to be the successful course, after Erie state senator Morrow Lowry introduced a bill in the State House to integrate public transportation. Catto went to Harrisburg to lobby for the ultimately successful, on March 22, 1867, bill.

Even before the Civil War ended, a war in which Catto was commissioned a major in the First Division of the state's National Guard, and then in between his teaching profession and thrashings of other ball clubs, Catto threw himself into the very basic goal of establishing full and equal rights for blacks—a fight that Martin Luther King would still be pursuing 100 years later.

An educator first and foremost—fittingly, an elementary school is now named after him in East Camden, New Jersey—Catto was, according to Dorothy Gondos Beers, writing in *Philadelphia: A 300 Year History*, "the most magnetic and perhaps the most promising leader the Philadelphia black community had yet produced." Waskie refers to Catto as "an eloquent, persuasive and powerful speaker, with an upright, intelligent and charismatic bearing, possessed of impeccable academic credentials." He also refers to Catto as "Philadelphia's Renaissance Man." Another irony, since very few white top-level baseball players around 1870 could be said to possess *any* academic credentials worth mentioning. And he was more. According to Biddle and Dubin, he also wrote romantic verses for the young ladies he courted, was a major league clothes horse—once spending $113 at one time at Wanamakers (a fortune in those days)—and a classical philosopher who could quote Aristotle and Martin Luther.

Like Martin Luther King and the passage of the Voting Rights Act, Octavius Catto lived long enough to see his greatest crusade succeed. In 1869, Pennsylvania passed the 15th Amendment, guaranteeing voting rights for black males, the amendment going into effect in 1870. Although the minor election in Philadelphia in 1870 was relatively quiet, white backlash would prove fatal to the great educator and leader the next year. Election Day in 1871 was on October 10, and Catto, who was now head of the boys school at the institute and was generally called "Professor Catto," had been unceasing in his attempts to get out the black vote, raising much enmity among the Democratic Party in Philadelphia. Actually, he'd already raised the hackles of South Philadelphia Democratic Party boss William "Squire" McMullen during the streetcar fight. However, this was a much more serious matter. In fact, the mobocracy of the earlier part of nineteenth century Philadelphia returned that day, with street violence, disturbances at polling places, and even murder.

After casting his ballot, most likely for Republican district attorney candidate Colonel William Mann, Catto went by the institute and then proceeded towards his home at 814 South Street. As he passed 822 South Street, he exchanged remarks with Frank Kelly, a Democratic Party operative and associate of McMullen who had already attacked one black voter that day. Kelly turned after passing Catto, and shot him in the back. In a final irony, Octavius Catto ran behind a streetcar, one of the streetcars he had helped integrate, to try and get away. Kelly followed him, and shot him through the heart. Octavius Catto died in the arms of a Philadelphia policeman, and was carried to the nearby 5th Ward Police Station, where his fiancée, Caroline Le Count, formally identified his body. Frank Kelly was acquitted of all charges.

"Strong men wept like children when they realized how much had been lost in the untimely death of the gifted Catto," wrote his friend, black journalist William C. Bolivar. His funeral, the city's largest public funeral since Lincoln's, and, at that time, the largest funeral ever held in America for a black man, was held six days later, complete with a parade that included his fellow members of the Pythian club. City offices and businesses closed as he lay in state, in full dress military uniform, in the City Armory at Broad and Race. Octavius Catto was 32 years old, and Philadelphia would not see his likes again until a young man named King came from Atlanta to enroll as a seminary student in Chester in the middle of the next century.

Sources: *Philadelphia Inquirer Magazine, American Negro Historical Society Papers (Historical Society of Pennsylvania), Philadelphia: A 300 Year History, Dr. Andrew Waskie, John Thorn, Afrolumens, The Integration of Baseball in Philadelphia (Christopher Threston), Dr. Daniel Rolph.*

Jack Clements

He probably wasn't the best catcher of the nineteenth century. That would have been Buck Ewing. He probably wasn't the best all-around catcher born in Philadelphia. That would have been Roy Campanella. He wasn't even the best-hitting catcher from Philadelphia. That would be Mike Piazza. And he wasn't the first (or the last) left-handed catcher, either. But, he sure was the best. And he can stand as second to Buck and Campy and Mike in the other three categories.

John James "Jack" Clements was born in Philadelphia on July 24, 1864, the only child of James and Margaret Clements. (Some sources give his birth date as June 24 and his middle initial as T). There would be few of Philadelphia's nineteenth century heroes who would be more closely identified with the city or the game. A 5-8½, 204 pound brick wall of a man, Clements was one of the few Union Association rookies to have a long major league career. He was the best player to start his major league career in the UA. Appearing in 41 games for his hometown Keystones as a 19- and 20-year-old rookie, Clements hit a respectable .282 with 18 extra-base hits in 177 at-bats. Although it would be another five years before he really made his mark as a hitter, Clements' first turn gave some indication of the power he would show from ages 25 to 31.

His short term with the Keystones also brought another distinction, although this was one of those "firsts" that are so hard to prove. Almost all sources say that Clements was one of the first catchers to wear a chest protector. Some, however, claim that he was the

Jack Clements, without his chest protector and a glove on his right hand (Library of Congress photograph).

first. Or maybe the Detroit Wolverines' Charlie Bennett was. Either way, he most certainly threw (and batted) left-handed, and one thing that all the sources say is that he was quite a gate attraction as a result of his unique catching and throwing style, an indication that, by the late 1880s, left-handed catchers (he also played four games each at third base and shortstop) had become as rare as catchers who can hit .394.

When the Keystones folded, Al Reach and Harry Wright, always on the lookout for talent, signed Clements to a Phillies' contract. And there he would stay for the next 13 seasons. Although he struggled some at the plate at first, Clements could hold his own with any right-handed catcher defensively. A good handler of pitchers, he also led the NL in fielding average in 1888, 1892 and 1898. Overall, for the 1890s, he ranked fourth in putouts and fielding average (.950) and fifth in total chances and games caught. In 1898 (he was with the St. Louis Browns by then) he became the first man to ever catch in 1000 games.

Still, it was ultimately his hitting that made him a star. He became the Phillies' regular backstop in 1887 and, after a couple of ordinary years, he took off as a hitter in the somewhat weakened National League of the 1890 season. Since there were now 24 major league teams, thanks to the Players League, he was in effect playing in an expansion situation— a circumstance that has historically led to an overall jump in hitting. Even so, his .315/.392/.472 figures, while by far the best of his career to date, were well above the league norms for regular players, to say nothing of catchers. His adjusted OPS of 148 placed him second in the league, as did his raw OPS of .864 and his slugging percentage of .472. He was also in the top 10 in batting, doubles and home runs.

When the Brotherhood players returned to the National League, Clements kept right on hitting, posting adjusted OPS figures of 131, 128, 124, 134, 171 and 156 over the course of the next six years. Some highlights along the way include finishing second in the league in home runs in 1893 with a career high 17, and then third in 1895 with 13. He also finished in the top 10 in slugging percentage five times. His 1895 season was a whopper—his adjusted OPS and batting averages would place him third in the league, and that .394 batting average is still a record for full-time catchers. In fact, all his averages that year were numbers that another pretty good hitting Philadelphia-area catcher, Mike Piazza, would gladly have taken in his prime.

Batting	On Base	Slugging	OPS	OPS+
.394	.446	.612	1.085	171

Clements might have had almost as good a year in 1894, but he broke his ankle and played in only 45 games, hitting .346/.455/.503. In 1896, he had another big year, hitting .359/.427/.543. However, by the end of the year he would turn 32, and even with his chest protector he had taken a lot of physical abuse over the years; he was the Phillies' reserve catcher in '96 and '97. After 14 years with the Phillies, the unsentimental Colonel Rogers sent him to the St. Louis Browns for 1898 and then the Robison brothers, figuring he was about through, sent him to their Cleveland Spiders as part of their dual team syndicate. Fortunately for Clements, he had to play only four games for the 20-134 1899 Spiders. His remarkably long, 17-year major league career ended with 16 games for the 1900 Boston Beaneaters (he still hit .310).

After a year with Worcester in the Eastern League, he retired back to Philadelphia, and a second job with his old boss, Al Reach, this time working in the A.J. Reach plant. When that facility closed, he went to work in another baseball factory in nearby Perkasie, Pennsylvania. He died in Norristown, Pennsylvania, of heart disease on May 23, 1941, a couple of months short of his 77th birthday, and a little more than 27 years before another pretty good catcher would be born in the same Montgomery County town—Mike Piazza.

G	AB	R	H	2B	3B	HR	RBI	BA	OBP	SLG	OPS+
1157	4283	619	1226	226	60	77	687	.286	.347	.421	117

Sources: *Nineteenth Century Stars (SABR), The Ballplayers (Mike Shatzkin, editor),Occasional Glory (David Jordan), Encyclopedia of Major League Baseball Teams (Donald Dewey and Nicholas Acocella), The Phillies Encyclopedia (Rich Westcott and Frank Bilovsky), Family Search.*

Lave Cross

He was named after one of Philadelphia's favorite adopted sons of the Revolution (the Marquis de Lafayette), and became almost as popular an adopted Philadelphian as the city's most famous adopted Revolutionary son, Benjamin Franklin. Certainly, few Philadelphians of any sort, except maybe Franklin, could claim to have worn as many hats in the city as Lafayette Napoleon Cross. Although he is the answer to one of those classic trivia questions—what player represented the same city in four different leagues—Lave Cross was anything but a trivial player. And, although at one time he held several other moderately obscure records—most career hits by a third baseman (2645), most assists in a game by a second baseman (15), most RBIs in a season without a home run (108 in 1902), most consecutive games played (447—although it hasn't been positively established that this was a record)—he was also anything but an obscure player. At least, not in Philadelphia around the turn of the previous century.

A tremendous favorite of Philadelphia baseball fans from 1889 to 1897 and from 1901 to 1905, Cross was born, the second of three ballplaying sons, to parents of Czech descent in Milwaukee, on May 12, 1866. His parents had arrived from the Old World only within the previous five years, since his older brother, Amos, was born in what later became Czechoslovakia in 1861. At that time, it was part of the Austro-Hungarian Empire, and Cross is almost certainly an Americanization of a longer Slavic name. The family soon moved to Cleveland, where younger brother Frank was born in 1873. Lave Cross moved to the Toledo area at the age of 18 when he started playing professional ball with a team in Sandusky in 1884. By 1887, he had followed Amos (who came up in 1885) to the American Association's Louisville Eclipse. In fact, he and Amos both caught some games for Louisville in 1887. However, Amos became sick after the season ended, and died in July 1888.

Lave carried on as a part-time catcher and outfielder for Louisville in 1888, and then hit the City of Brotherly Love for the first time in 1889, catching 55 games for the Athletics, despite the fact that his legs were so bowed that anything that got by his hands must have rolled all the way back to Toledo. Undaunted by his physique (he was also 5-8 and weighed 155), and his .482 and .553 OPS for the '88 and '89 seasons, the Philadelphia Quakers of the Players League took him on for the 1890 season. Playing in 63 games as a catcher-outfielder, the right-handed hitting Cross rewarded the Quakers with a .298/.331/.429 season—and, he was just getting started, both as a hitter and as an honorary Philadelphian.

When the PL folded, Cross was back with the "new" Athletics for 1891, this time mostly as an outfielder-catcher, although he did play for the first time at the position he would become best known for—third base. And, he had his best year to date, finishing fifth in slugging (.458), eighth in triples (14) and 10th in OPS (.823). However, for the second year in a row, a team and a league folded underneath him, and Cross found himself out of a job when 1891 ended. Not for long, though. He stayed in Philadelphia, this time beginning his six year tenure as sort of a super utility man for the Phillies. Although he got into more than 100 games in four of his six years with the Phillies, he seldom had a regular position. With the exception of 1895, when he played only third, Cross played all over the field at Philadelphia Park, playing every single position except pitcher. He also gained some notoriety by keeping his catcher's mitt on when he played third base. Hard to believe? Well, first of all, there was no rule prohibiting such a seemingly-strange move—although a rule was soon passed because of Cross' practice. Secondly, recall what most baseball gloves were like at that time—they were hardly more than what a batting glove would look like now. They didn't offer much protection for the hands at the hot corner and they weren't much help in flagging down the hard shots that are a way of life at third.

Hence, Cross figured he had a better chance of fielding the position better while wearing his better-padded catcher's mitt. Whatever he was wearing, it must have worked, for Cross' career fielding percentage at third was .938—far above the league average of .902. He also got to a few more balls than the average third sacker—his range factor at third was 3.49, compared to the league's 3.36. For that matter, as the numbers show, Cross was a good fielder wherever he played more than 50 games, although his range factors in the outfield, at short and at second were a little sub-par.

Position	Games	Field%	League F%	Range	League/RF
3B	1721	.938	.902	3.49	3.36
C	324	.932	.916	5.84	5.58
OF	119	.914	.909	1.70	1.91
SS	65	.936	.900	5.14	5.47
2B	60	.963	.934	4.83	5.53

If your legs were that bowed, and your name wasn't Honus Wagner, you might have trouble getting to those balls in the outfield and at the keystone, although Cross did steal 301 bases for his career. Oddly enough, his most noted fielding feat came at a position he played very little, and with a sub-par range factor—second base. On August 5, 1897, playing second base for the Phillies, Cross had 15 assists in a 12-inning game—a record for second basemen that stands to this day.

Along with the rest of the Phillies, Cross had another big year at the plate in 1894, finishing sixth in the NL in hits (204), eighth in batting average (.386) and eighth in RBIs (125), while posting a career-high .945 OPS. Still, he couldn't get a regular job until he went to St. Louis for the 1898 season. As the Perfectos' regular (149 games) third baseman he was seventh in the league in hits (191), eighth in doubles (28) and ninth in total bases (244). Unfortunately, all this got him was a trip back to Cleveland, and the job managing the worst team in major league history—the 1899 Cleveland Spiders. Now a 33-year-old veteran of 12 major league seasons, Cross was tabbed by the manipulative Robison brothers to take over the shell of the Spider franchise after all of Cleveland's good players were shipped to the Robisons' other team—St. Louis. However, when he started out hitting .286 in the Spiders' first 38 games, the Robisons figured he still had some value as a player, and besides, the Perfectos still needed more help. So he was transferred back to St. Louis, to pick up his old job at third. He had gone 8-30 as Cleveland's manager, which was far better than their record after he left—12-104.

He then split the 1900 season between St. Louis and Brooklyn, after which the soon-to-be 35-year-old Cross was called "home," to Philadelphia and Connie Mack's American League Athletics, his fourth Philly team in his fourth league. Mack, no fool when it came to both assessing talent and marketing, rightly figured that Cross might be tired of the National League's syndicate baseball scheme, rightly figured that Cross still had a lot of good baseball at third, and rightly figured that he was getting a popular name in his battle for the hearts and wallets of Philadelphians. Cross was, if anything, an even bigger hit as an American League Philadelphian, serving as the A's first captain (he was joined in the AL by brother Frank for one game with Cleveland in 1901), an important position since Mack couldn't go on the field in his street clothes. He was practically the A's only third baseman for those five years, playing 447 straight at third between April 23, 1902, and May 8, 1905, and leading the team to two pennants. Fred Lieb, in *Connie Mack: Grand Old Man of Baseball*, characterizes Cross as an aggressive leader, who had to be the first one on the horse-drawn buses that took the A's from their hotel to the ballpark. "Anyone trying to scramble in ahead of Lave had a fight on his hands," is how Lieb puts it. Along the way, he finished in the top 10 in the AL in hits (four times), doubles (four times), RBIs (four times), batting (three times), extra-base hits (twice), total bases (twice), slugging (once), and OPS (once). In short, he had his five best years between the ages of 35 and 39.

When Mack decided the old favorite had slowed down too much to cover third after the 1905 World's Series—Lieb says Mack decided that on the spur of the moment, after Cross had a grounder go through those bowed legs in the fifth game; however, that sounds like one of Lieb's fables—he sold him down the river to the Washington Senators, where he played his last two seasons at third in 1906 and 1907 at the ages of 40 and 41, retiring only after he broke an ankle on June 6, 1907. He had played 2275 games, made 2645 hits, and scored 1333 runs—all of which ranked him high among career leaders at that time, and all of which still rank him in the top 100 in those categories after 98 years. Although he never led his league in any hitting category, he was regularly among the leaders in average, hits, power and RBIs, and was an excellent fielder, especially at what were, at the time, true "defensive" positions—third and catcher. In fact, Charles Faber's Faber System, which produces a comprehensive numeric figure for a player's offense, defense and overall value, makes Cross the best fielding third baseman of the nineteenth century, and the best overall third baseman of the nineteenth century.

Although his career OPS+ was just 100, since third base was a defensive position in his era, his offense for a third baseman was actually quite good. Cross did gain some support in the voting for the Hall of Fame when it began in 1936, but, like some other deceased old-timers, he was soon forgotten by the voters, and the Veterans Committees.

After he retired, Cross returned to his home on Post Street in Toledo, was a charter member of the Toledo Pigeon Club, and became a machinist for Willys-Overland, eventually to be the Jeep Corporation. He died of a heart attack on the way to work on September 6, 1927, at the age of 61. Connie Mack said he was one of the last of the old crowd of players that really loved to play. In other words, the type of player that Philadelphia fans have always loved.

G	AB	R	H	2B	3B	HR	RBI	BA	OBP	SLG	OPS+
2275	9072	1333	2645	411	135	47	1371	.292	.328	.382	100

Sources: *Connie Mack: Grand Old Man of Baseball* (Fred Lieb), *Occasional Glory* (David Jordan), *The Athletics of Philadelphia* (David Jordan), *Baseball's First Stars* (SABR), *Phillies Encyclopedia* (Rich Westcott and Frank Bilovsky), *The Beer & Whiskey League* (David Nemec), *Baseball Pioneers* (Charles Faber), Family Search, The Baseball Page, Baseball Library, The Deadball Era.

Ned Cuthbert

Although Edgar Edward Cuthbert wasn't one of the best players produced by Philadelphia, he had one of the most interesting careers, starting with the Keystone club in 1863 and stretching all the way to 1884 and the Union Association.

Cuthbert, who went by both "Ned" and "Edward," "Eddie" or "Ed," was born in Philadelphia. The date usually given is June 20, 1845, however, he told the 1880 census taker he was born in 1847, and that is possible from his playing record—a 16-year-old could have been playing with the Keystone club in 1863 (when Cuthbert is credited with stealing the first base in a game against Atlantic of Brooklyn), especially if some of their other players were still off fighting the Civil War. Besides, Dick McBride was playing for the Athletic club in 1861 at the age of 16. After four years with Keystone, playing everywhere but pitcher, Cuthbert moved over to the West Philadelphia club for the 1867 season. But not for long. It was around this time that the Athletic club, while vying for the title of the best baseball team in the land, starting getting serious about paying all its players, and not just the Al Reaches and Dick McBrides. By the end of 1867, Cuthbert was with Athletic, and probably getting paid as well. Except for a sojourn to Chicago with the original White Stockings in 1870, he would stay with Athletic through the 1872 season, after which he would play for six different teams in four different leagues. Even his relatively long stretch with Athletic was marked with controversy, when he signed both Athletic and White Stockings contracts for the 1871 season. Even in the loosely-configured NA, this was considered bad form, and a fuss ensued that eventually resulted in the Athletics winning him back.

What were his employers paying for, other than a reputation for revolving? It was mostly his fielding in the outfield and his base running. Except for his 1872 season, he was never even an average hitter in his time in the NABBP, the National Association, the National League, the American Association and the Union Association. In the four pro leagues he played in, his career adjusted OPS was just 90.

His offensive shortcomings to the contrary, counting his time prior to his NA years, Cuthbert played baseball at its highest level for 13 straight years (from 1865 to 1877), plus three more years (1882–84) after he thought he had retired. While he is sometimes also credited with being the first player to slide head-first into a base—while he was with Keystone in 1865—Cuthbert's real claim to fame was his fielding. His career fielding percentage in the outfield was .841, enough above the league norm of .823 that, in this era when good fielding was so highly-prized, he would have stood out.

As would happen with many other players in the future, Cuthbert had his big batting year at the age of 27, hitting .338/.353/.388 for the 1872 Athletics and posting a 128 adjusted OPS. This fluke year made him a tempting target for the great 1873 raid on the Athletics by the new Philadelphia White Stockings, wherein the newcomers took five of the Athletics' eight regulars from 1872. Despite losing 101 points off his OPS from 1872 to 1873, Cuthbert was, for the 1874 season, a tempting target for another team of raiders called White Stockings. This time, he jumped back to his old Chicago White Stockings team, reconstituted in the wake of the Chicago Fire of 1871. However, he stayed back in Chicago only one year, before revolving to St. Louis and Cincinnati, where he played only a dozen games in 1877 before retiring at the age of either 30 or 32.

Having moved to St. Louis in 1875, he would spend the rest of his life there, opening a saloon in the Mound City after his erstwhile 1877 retirement. However, he kept playing baseball for local club teams until 1881, when he helped persuade Chris Von der Ahe that he should back a team in the new American Association. For his part, Von der Ahe announced that Ned Cuthbert would be the playing manager for the Browns for the 1882 season. He would also be Von der Ahe's top personal baseball advisor for the year. Realizing something that his former managers hadn't, manager Cuthbert batted himself seventh in the Browns' lineup. Still, after a fast start, St. Louis ended up fifth in the six-team league and Cuthbert's managing career was over. After playing 21 games for the Browns in 1883, he finished up his career a second time with Baltimore of the Union Association in 1884.

Returning to St. Louis, he again took up bartending, except for a brief sojourn as an American Association umpire in 1887. Meanwhile, his life away from baseball was no less interesting than his travelogue career on the diamond. While the 1880 census taker did indeed find him living in St. Louis as a saloon keeper, he was living with the John Bucher family and his wife, Mary E. Cuthbert (known as Maggie) was listed as "away, visiting" on the part of the census form that described occupation. That hardly seems like an occupation, and, in fact, Ned and Maggie would be divorced at some point in the future. Skip ahead to August 1904, when Cuthbert suffered a stroke that left him paralyzed. In the ensuing years, Maggie had married someone else and had subsequently been widowed. Hearing of Ned's illness, she returned to the old ballplayer to take care of him, and they were remarried on February 2, 1905, just four days before his death.

G	AB	R	H	2B	3B	HR	RBI	BA	OBP	SLG	OPS+
452	2113	453	537	74	17	8	179	.254	.276	.317	90

Sources: *Baseball's First Stars (SABR), Blackguards and Red Stockings (William Ryczek), The National Association of Base Ball Players (Marshall Wright), The Beer & Whiskey League (David Nemec), The Baseball Timeline (Burt Solomon), Baseball in the Afternoon (Robert Smith), Family Search.*

Ed Delahanty

Despite the fact that he was one of the great hitters in baseball history, despite the fact that he's been in the Hall of Fame since 1945, despite the fact that he's fifth all-time in career batting average (.346) and 29th in adjusted OPS (152), despite the fact that he was the second player to hit four home runs in a major league game, despite hitting .400 three times, despite the fact that he was the eldest and best member of the largest baseball family, despite the fact that he jumped teams six times, and would have gladly done so a seventh time—despite all this, Edward James "Big Ed" Delahanty is best known for the manner in which he died.

At the start of the 1903 season, Delahanty was coming off a year where he had finished second (.378–.376) to fellow Phillie-expatriate Nap Lajoie in the American League batting race. Having jumped from the Phillies to the Washington Senators at the start of the 1902 season, and with the National and American leagues still busily engaged in a trade war, Big Ed was in demand before the 1903 season started, most notably by the aggressive new manager of the New York Giants, John McGraw, who signed Delahanty to a lucrative contract prior to the season. Unfortunately for the 6-1, 170 pound right-handed slugger, the National and American leagues settled their differences between Delahanty's signing with the Giants and the start of the season, and part of the peace treaty was that all players would stay with their 1902 teams. Thus, Big Ed was stuck in Washington.

This did not sit well with the former pride of 15th and Huntingdon. He was drinking heavily throughout the 1903 season, and although there have been some reports it was because he was losing heavily at the race tracks, the more likely cause is that he was brooding over the unfairness of having to play for less money in Washington. As David Jordan writes in his history of the Phillies, teammate Jack Boyle noted that all Delahanty really cared about was taking it easy during the winter on the money he made during the summer. However, he was stuck in Washington (and still hitting .333, although his power was down), and the American League, making less money, until George Stacey Davis, like Delahanty a future member of the Hall of Fame, jumped his contract with the AL Chicago White Stockings, and joined McGraw's Giants. This happened in late June 1903, when Big Ed was already under suspension by the Senators (for whom he played his last game on

June 25, in his home town of Cleveland) for drinking. With Davis, who had been sitting out the entire year previously, having joined the Giants, Delahanty figured his turn had come, and hopped a train to from Detroit (where the Senators were now playing) to New York, a good week after he'd last played for Washington.

Delahanty apparently decided to start celebrating his move to the Giants early. He was drinking heavily on the train, which might not have been that big a problem if he hadn't started brandishing a straight razor in the sleeper as the train approached Niagara Falls. As might be expected, this action got him put off the train at Ft. Erie, Ontario, which happened to be the last stop on the Canadian side of the train bridge that ran across the Niagara River above the falls. Actually, he should have been turned over to the Canadian authorities, who would have arrested him, but that didn't happen and, a week later, his mangled body, minus a leg, was found in the river below the falls. And so began the Legend of Ed Delahanty and his "Mysterious" Death.

The only mystery involved with Delahanty's death is how could he have been so dumb as to try and walk across a train bridge in the middle of the night while he was drunk? For years, the mythmakers would insist that Big Ed might have met with foul play on the bridge, that he was pushed to his death, or mugged and then thrown off the bridge. Although his relatives "hinted" at foul play, there was nothing to bear out such a theory, according to the July 9, 1903, *New York Times*. Common sense would also refute that option, since very few people hang around train bridges in the middle of the night. Furthermore, a story in the July 8, 1903, *New York Times* makes it pretty clear what happened. Once he was put off the train, he started to follow it, coming to the bridge. He started to walk across the bridge, and the bridge's night watchman, Sam Kingston, told him to return to the shore. Why? Because the drawbridge was open. Well, Big Ed (who was not positively identified until his body was found), after wrestling a little with Kingston, then started to run towards the American side of the bridge. Maybe a not-surprising action, since his suitcase was still on the train. (That helped identify the body on July 9.) Kersplash!

Part of this fable comes from the fact that he reportedly had $200 in cash and $1500 in diamonds on his person, and that they weren't found on his body. Even outside the unlikely possibility that Sam Kingston was a thief and murderer, this is not hard to explain. If you fall off a bridge into a river, go over Niagara Falls, spend a week in the water, and probably get run over by the Maid of the Mist excursion boat, it's unlikely you'd have much in your pockets, either. There has also been speculation that Delahanty committed suicide (although his family discounted this theory), because he had taken out a large insurance policy shortly before his death. Interesting, but illogical, since he thought he was on his way to play for the Giants, and more money. So why would he jump off a bridge, drunk or otherwise?

No, Ed Delahanty died dead drunk, a victim of high living and low judgment, to use historian Norman Macht's phrase, ending a remarkable baseball career at the age of 35. Born on either October 30 or October 31, 1867, in Cleveland, to Irish-born parents originally with the name Delahunty, Ed was the eldest of James (a gas company employee) and Bridget's seven sons, five of whom would play major league baseball, the others being Tom, Jim, Frank and Joe. Ed was by far the best, starting out as a second baseman-catcher with Mansfield of the Ohio State League in 1887. After about a month with Wheeling in the Tri State League in 1888, he was bought by the Phillies, since he was hitting .408 and the Phillies needed a second baseman to replace the late Charlie Ferguson. Although he didn't hit right away, and lost the second base job to Al Myers in 1889, Delahanty was a good enough outfielder that John Rogers was enraged when he became a triple jumper in

1890. In this case, Delahanty's hop-step-jump was from Philadelphia to Cleveland to Philadelphia to Cleveland: he jumped his Phillies contract, signed with his home town Cleveland Infants of the Players League, and then broke his Brotherhood contract to re-sign with the Phillies. Rogers didn't mind that part too much, except that the Brotherhood came calling with more money, and Delahanty jumped back to the PL, where he eventually played in 1890. It most likely took all of Al Reach's persuasive powers to get Rogers to accept Delahanty back in the Phillies fold for 1891—the only player from the 1889 Phillies who left for the PL who would play for the team in 1891.

Despite having been in such high demand at this point in his career, Delahanty wasn't yet much of a hitter. His adjusted OPS for his first four years (1888 to 1891) were 72, 89, 107, 82. Then he absolutely exploded, with an average adjusted OPS of just over 166 for the last 12 years of his major league career. During the rest of his career, he would lead either the National League or the American League in every single major offensive category except walks and runs scored, tallying 55 on the Black Ink Test as the premier power hitter of the '90s and the first two years of the new century, leading the league in doubles and slugging percentage five times each. Although he only won two home run crowns, his biggest and best-known day came on July 13, 1896, in Chicago when he hit four home runs and a single off Adonis Terry in a 9–8 loss—a microcosm of the Phillies' difficulties during most of the '90s.

If this is how Ed Delahanty played second, it's no wonder the Phillies moved him to the outfield (Library of Congress photograph).

While Del was a great

hitter, his fielding is almost never remarked upon. It should be. As good a center fielder as his teammate Billy Hamilton was, Delahanty was a better left fielder. Compare these career numbers for both....

	Field%	L Field%	Range Factor	L R Factor
Delahanty	.951	.927	2.38	2.05
Hamilton	.926	.923	2.29	2.03

In fact, Delahanty was as good an all-round player as the nineteenth century produced. Charles Faber's system's total player rating has him as the fourth best overall player of the century, behind Bid McPhee, Cap Anson and Jack Glasscock. Faber's system also makes him the National League Player of the Year (in effect, the numeric MVP) for 1893 and 1899.

Although Connie Mack offered Delahanty $4000 to jump to the Athletics for the 1901 season, Rogers managed to keep him by matching the American League offer. Another double jump for Big Ed. However, after leading the National League in OPS (.955), doubles (38) and extra-base hits (62) in 1901, Rogers was unwilling to match Washington's offer for 1902, and Delahanty jumped for a sixth time. It was the attempted seventh jump that would end up being a long jump off a short bridge, and would cost him his life.

G	AB	R	H	2B	3B	HR	RBI	SB	BB	BA	OBP	SLG	OPS+
1835	7505	1599	2596	522	185	101	1464	455	741	.346	.411	.505	152

Sources: *Baseball's First Stars* (SABR), *Phillies Encyclopedia* (Rich Westcott and Frank Bilovsky), *Occasional Glory* (David Jordan) *The Historical Baseball Abstract* (Bill James), *Biographical History of Baseball* (Donald Dewey and Nicholas Acocella), *Early Innings* (Dean Sullivan), *Baseball Pioneers* (Charles Faber), *Baseball in the Afternoon* (Robert Smith), *Family Search*, *The Deadball Era*.

Fred Dunlap

They called him "Sure Shot," an indication that his peers sure considered him one of the nineteenth century's best second baseman. In fact, as late as 1910, the year Nap Lajoie won his fifth batting title, *The Sporting News*' Al Spink said Fred Dunlap was the greatest second baseman of all time. And, while the stats fail to support that claim, he was pretty good, and he also had a year that was quite comparable to Lajoie's renowned 1901 campaign.

Dunlap was born in Philadelphia on May 21, 1859, and was orphaned before he was 10 years old. The German couple that took him in apparently were not the best foster parents in the world, paying little attention to his education or care; the only item on his daily agenda was fetching a bucket of beer, after which he was free to do as he pleased. Usually, that meant playing baseball, sometimes by himself. It did not mean school. He grew up to be a fine, though illiterate, baseball player, since he was blessed with remarkable physical talents, and he was living in the right city to make use of them. Possibly to escape from his "home" life, he soon took to baseball as a career, appearing for four local clubs, Gloucester of New Jersey, Cregar of Camden, Kleinz of Philadelphia and Acme of Philadelphia between 1874 to 1877. According to Robert Smith in *Baseball in the Afternoon*, he actually signed a contract as a professional with Acme. He would join the National League Cleveland Blues (from minor league Albany) in 1880 at the age of 21. He was a star right from the start, a highly intelligent, in a baseball sense, player who posted Adjusted OPS figures of 141, 155, 120 and 146 in his four years for the Blues. He led the league in doubles in 1880, and posted fielding averages and range factors well above the norm, while "never" throwing to the wrong base or being caught out of position. He was by far the best established player lured to the Union Association in 1884 by Henry Lucas. And, since Lucas was running the whole show, Dunlap ended up playing for Lucas' St. Louis Maroons for a salary of $3400 (some sources say $5000)—the highest in baseball.

As was the case with Lajoie playing for the Athletics in the American League in 1901, Dunlap was able to utterly dominate the weaker UA, leading the league in batting, on base percentage, slugging percentage, OPS, runs (160—a major league record at the time), hits, total bases, home runs, adjusted OPS, runs created and extra base hits. Taking into account that Lajoie played 30 more games and had almost 100 more at-bats in 1901, their two years are very similar.

	AB	R	H	2B	3B	HR	RBI	BB	BA	OBP	SLG	OPS
Lajoie 1901	544	145	232	48	14	14	125	24	.426	.463	.643	1.106
Dunlap 1884	449	160	185	39	8	13	n/a	29	.412	.448	.621	1.069

And, like Lajoie, Dunlap never quite matched any of those numbers again, his problem being that the UA folded after the 1884 season, and Lucas took his Maroons into the National League. Back in the NL, Dunlap was again a fine player, but not a superstar. He also managed the Maroons in 1885, as he had done in 1884. Although he played another seven years in three leagues, he never again led a league in any offensive category, although he did lead the National League in all second base fielding categories, as he did the Union Association, at one time or another.

Sold to Detroit in 1886, he was the Wolverines' regular second baseman in their pennant-winning year of 1887, and the star of the 1887 World's Series, after which he was sold to Pittsburgh. He didn't appreciate this move, and held out for a piece of the purchase price. Given his status, this ploy worked, and he received a total of $6000 in salary and bonuses for 1888, a record-breaking sum of money. Released by the Pirates during the 1890 season, he played one game with the Players League New York Giants, and then closed out his career with the American Association's Washington team in 1891, breaking his leg on April 20.

How good was Fred Dunlap? His 1884 season skews all of his offensive numbers, so it's a little hard to tell on his hitting. Except for that 1884 season, he never was a dominant hitter, although he did finish in the top 10 in various non–UA offensive categories a total of 22 times over his 12 seasons in the majors. And, he did post a solid 133 adjusted OPS for his career. As to his fielding, there the record would seem to indicate that he was well above average. He was ambidextrous and, although he always batted right-handed, he could throw superbly or catch with either hand. For his career at second base, his fielding percentage was .924, well above the league average of .902. His range factor was also excellent, 6.28 versus a league standard of 5.82. In other words, he got to 8 percent more balls than the average second baseman. Suffice it to say that, along with Bid McPhee (who was an even better fielder) and Hardy Richardson, he is a candidate for the honor of the best second baseman of the 1880s.

Dunlap was quite the fashion plate when he was in the game, to the extent that no less a Beau Brummel than King Kelly said he was the best-dressed man in the world. Despite his meager upbringing, he was also charming and outwardly cultured. He was, however, sadly lacking in skills for life after baseball, despite his native intelligence and the negotiating skills he showed with Henry Lucas and the Pittsburgh Alleghenys. He went into the building business when he retired, getting a good start since he was quite well off when he left baseball—supposedly, he had $100,000 in the bank. He was reputed to have lost his fortune in the stock market when he died in poverty in a seedy Philadelphia rooming house on December 1, 1902, 11 years after he retired from the game. Since he had no family, his body went unidentified until a policeman who was a baseball fan recognized him and persuaded Lave Cross, then a star with the American League Athletics, to identify him. Fred Dunlap was buried in a pauper's grave in Philadelphia.

Philadelphia native Fred "Sure-Shot" Dunlap. He couldn't read or write with either hand, but he could play baseball with the best of them with both (Library of Congress photograph).

G	AB	R	H	2B	3B	HR	RBI	BB	BA	OBP	SLG	OPS+
965	3974	759	1159	224	53	41	366	283	.292	.340	.406	133

Sources: *Nineteenth Century Stars (SABR), Baseball in the Afternoon (Robert Smith), The Beer & Whiskey League (David Nemec), Baseball Library.*

Charlie Ferguson

Without question, the biggest "might have been" in Philadelphia baseball history was Charlie Ferguson. And the most tragic as well. He was better than Kenny Hubbs, Harry Agganis, Austin McHenry. He was Jim Creighton, dying young before his immense potential was fulfilled. He was, in fact, on a career track that could have made him Babe Ruth, several years before the Babe was born.

Charles J. Ferguson was born on April 7, 1863, in Charlottesville, Virginia, in the midst of the Civil War. By the time he was 19, he was playing for his hometown team, the University of Virginia. That's not to say Ferguson had matriculated at UVA, he was just playing there. Since eligibility rules were somewhat looser in college sports in the nineteenth century than they would become later on, this was neither frowned upon, nor even particularly unusual. From UVA, Ferguson moved on to pitch and catch for the independent Richmond club, which is where Al Reach and the Phillies found him during the 1883 season. He probably wasn't too hard to find, since he had shut out the Boston Red Stockings on four singles while pitching for Richmond. After Reach promised he could finish out the season with Richmond, Ferguson signed a Phillies contract for 1884. Since it was already obvious that Charlie Ferguson could literally do it all on a baseball field, this caused the Richmond club to protest that this was the greatest attack by those northern Yankees since the Confederate capitol was taken by U.S. Grant 19 years before—a protest that was just about as successful as the Confederacy.

Although Ferguson's experience was limited to playing for UVA and Richmond, he took to Philadelphia and the National League quite nicely. On opening day of the 1884 season, he defeated Detroit 13–2 and personally accounted for two singles and a triple. Over the course of the next four years, he quickly became the most popular professional athlete in Philadelphia, even surpassing hometown hero Harry Stovey, along with everyone else who had previously played professional baseball in Philly. And with good reason. As a pitcher, he relied on tremendous speed and control, although some accounts say he could throw a good breaking ball as well. After a so-so rookie year (21-25, 84 adjusted ERA, 99 adjusted OPS), he became the Phillies' ace, their answer to the Athletics' Bobby Matthews, for the next three years, winning 26, 30 and 22 with adjusted ERAs of 125, 166 and 140. Among his highlights as a pitcher were the Phillies' first no-hitter on August 29, 1885, 1–0 against the Providence Grays (he'd shut out the Grays on three hits in his previous start); closing the 1886 season with 11 straight wins, including a 5–1, 6–1 doubleheader victory over Detroit on October 9 that has been claimed to be the first instance of a major league pitcher winning two games in one day; and a 16 game winning streak that he put together when he won his first five decisions in 1887. His 30-9, 166 1886 season also earned him John Thorn and John Holway's Jim Creighton Award as the top pitcher in the NL in 1886, as well as the National League Pitcher of the Year award from the Faber System.

Away from pitching, Harry Wright increasingly used him in the outfield; five games in 1884, 15 in 1885 and 27 in 1886, with good results. A 6-0, 165 pound switch-hitter at the plate (he threw right-handed), Ferguson was an average hitter in 1884 and 1886, but posted adjusted OPS figures of 144 and 140 in 1885 and 1887. Wright, who had himself been an exceptional center fielder in the 1850s and 1860s, considered Ferguson outstanding in center, with good ball instincts and, not surprisingly, a good arm. Actually, his range factor in center was better than his fielding percentage—he was very fast with long legs that covered a lot of ground.

Then, in 1887, Wright had a moment of inspiration, and moved Ferguson to second base when he wasn't pitching. And he was good there, too, posting a .924 fielding average for the year, against the league average of .911. However, his range factor was sub-par, probably because he was still learning the position. He seems to have gotten better as the year went on, and was at his best during the team's 16 game winning streak that closed out the 1887 season and brought the Phillies so close to a pennant. He was even hotter than at the end of 1886 and the beginning of 1887, going 7-0 with a 1.75 ERA while fielding .963 at second and hitting .361, at which point he probably could have been elected mayor of Philadelphia.

After such a finish to 1887, optimism was riding high in Philadelphia in 1888. Part of this optimism was based on the statement, made at the beginning of spring training by Harry Wright, that Ferguson would play second base whenever he wasn't pitching, for the simple reason that, according to Wright, Ferguson was the best second baseman in the league. And, Ferguson played regularly in the exhibition games up until April 11. On April 13 though, the club made an announcement that Ferguson was ill. In reality, he was more than ill, he had contracted typhoid fever, and was confined to bed in teammate Arthur

Irwin's home at 2512 North Broad Street, right down the street from the Huntingdon Street Grounds. There he was attended by no less than the most famous doctor in Philadelphia, the University of Pennsylvania's renowned Dr. William Pepper. Although several reports over the next two weeks, including one from Harry Wright, seemed to be optimistic as to his eventual recovery, he was deathly ill, and, with unseasonable warm weather making his condition more serious, he suffered a turn for the worse on April 28. That day, virtually the entire team visited the failing star, with Jack Clements, Sid Farrar and trainer Tom Taylor remaining on what became a death watch. Charlie Ferguson died the next night at 10:30 p.m. at the age of 25.

Every account you read of this tragedy says the same thing: the passing of the most popular athlete in Philadelphia was mourned throughout the baseball world, including at Princeton University, where he coached the baseball team in the off-season, but especially on the streets of Philadelphia. Such was the interest in Ferguson in Philadelphia that his obituary in the *Philadelphia Inquirer* went into extensive detail on his treatment, including the fact that Pepper and his fellow doctors had given Ferguson four hours of hypodermic injections to reduce his pulse from 160 to 84. He left a young wife of two years who had, along with her late husband, buried an infant daughter the year before. His body was returned to Virginia for burial.

The ill-fated Charlie Ferguson. This picture would have been taken during his last year, 1887, when he pitched and played second (Library of Congress photograph).

Trying to look back objectively at his too-short career, Charlie Ferguson had not yet become a superstar or a future Hall of Famer as either a pitcher or a field player, despite twentieth century claims—one by former National League president John Tener, who played against Ferguson—that he might have become the greatest baseball player of all time. Another knowledgeable source from the early twentieth century, *The Sporting News'* Al Spink, claimed he was perhaps the greatest pitcher ever. According to the statistics he left behind, that's a bit over done. He never led the National League in any significant pitching or offensive category. He was, however, an unusual balance of skills at both pitcher and second base, with a career adjusted ERA of 121 and a career adjusted OPS of 122. In other words, he was more than 20 percent better than the average hitter, *and* more than 20 percent better than the average pitcher—a player without a weakness, what would now be called a five-tool player. Plus, the final few weeks of the 1887 season would seem to give at least the hint that he was on his way to doing what Babe Ruth would do in 1919 and 1920, transitioning from a top pitcher to a superb hitter and fielder. Certainly his contemporaries thought so. Wright, Tener, Spink and Al Reach's son George were just a few among the many who said he was a wonderful player.

The Phillies would wear black armbands in his memory in 1888, but the *Philadelphia Inquirer* said it best: he was one whose services the Philadelphia club could not replace.

G	AB	R	H	2B	3B	HR	RBI	BB	BA	OBP	SLG	OPS+
257	963	191	277	37	13	6	157	113	.288	.364	.372	122

W	L	G	SHO	IP	H	BB	SO	ERA	ERA+
99	64	183	13	1515	1402	290	728	.263	121

Sources: *Nineteenth Century Stars* (SABR), *Occasional Glory* (David Jordan), *Phillies Encyclopedia* (Rich Westcott and Frank Bilovsky), *The Neyer/James Guide to Pitchers* (Bill James and Rob Neyer), *The Pitcher* (John Thorn and John Holway), *Baseball Pioneers* (Charles Faber), *The Deadball Era*.

Wes Fisler

The patrician-sounding Weston "Wes" Dickson Fisler was in some ways as much an anomaly in the rough-edged world of nineteenth century professional baseball as Morris "Moe" Berg was in the hard-scrabble world of 1930s professional baseball—and for some of the same reasons. Like the mysterious Mr. Berg (a spy for the OSS in World War II), the also mysterious Mr. Fisler was a refined, genteel intellectual in a roughneck game. And, although Fisler may not have possessed the super intellect of Berg, he was a better ballplayer and had a better nickname, Icicle. Always cool and collected, even long after he had retired, Fisler picked up his distinctive nickname while playing for Philadelphia club teams during the Civil War. While an active player, it was said that he was so cool under pressure that icicles would form on his immaculate collars and cuffs. When he was living in retirement in Philadelphia and attending the games of Connie Mack's Athletics, he once told an interviewer that he would not think of going out to a game without white cuffs, collar and necktie. Very cool. In fact, former teammate Cap Anson, quoted in Joseph Overfield's profile of Fisler in *Nineteenth Century Stars*, opined that Fisler was "a fine all-around ballplayer, remarkable for his coolness and nerve." "I was a cool sort of player, and never saw the necessity for getting all mussed up and covered with dirt. I never got excited about anything," Fisler told the *Philadelphia Press* in an interview more than 40 years after he retired.

Fisler wasn't born a Philadelphian. Rather, he was originally a native from right across the river, having been born in Camden, New Jersey. His father, Dr. Lorenzo Felix Fisler, was the five-term mayor of Camden, having himself been born in Fislertown, New Jersey, in 1797. As to exactly when Wes (or West, as he was also called) was born, well, that's the first mystery associated with him. Most baseball records state his birth date—he was the youngest of six children of Dr. Fisler and Anna Maria Somers—as July 5 or July 18, 1841. However, genealogical records give an 1843 birth date, with the 1841 birth date going to his brother, Lorenzo. If the 1843 date is correct, then Wes Fisler was young indeed when he broke into club baseball in Philadelphia with Equity in 1860 (he also played in Camden before that), and he would have just passed his 17th birthday (assuming one of the July dates is correct) when he faced Jim Creighton and the NABBP champion Excelsiors as part of the Philadelphia picked nine during the former's 1860 tour.

Whatever the year of his birth, Fisler moved from his private school upbringing to the top level of baseball quickly and successfully, thanks in part to a teacher who used to take the boys at his school out to play on Wednesday afternoons. After Equity disbanded due to the Civil War, Fisler spent several years as a baseball mercenary, playing for other Philadelphia clubs, Camden, and, according to one (probably incorrect) source, Eckford of Brooklyn. After the war ended, in 1866 Fisler came into his own, and gained most of his fame, with Athletic, thanks to the persistence of Athletic vice president Colonel Thomas Fitzgerald, who badgered the little Camdenite for so long that Fisler finally gave in and joined up with the first name in Philadelphia baseball. Although Fitzgerald's interest in Fisler makes it seem unlikely, the Icicle was not one of the first Athletic players to be paid. As he told it, he played for Athletic for free for three years, 1866 to 1868, until the rest of the players persuaded him to go to Fitzgerald to ask for a salary. He got $1500 a year (which was the most he ever made for a single season) and proclaimed that, at the time, it seemed like an enormous sum.

Primarily a first baseman and second baseman throughout his career, the 5-6, 137 pound Fisler was small for an initial sacker, even 140 years ago. However, he was a smooth operator around the bag and was actually better known as a fielder than as a hitter—another case that illustrates how highly regarded good fielders were in this gloveless era. The *New York Clipper* said he never had a superior, and few equals, at first. It should be pointed out though that the fielding statistics we have for Fisler, dating from the second half of his career, do not bear this out. From 1871 to 1876, Fisler split his time with the NA and NL Athletics equally between first and second, posting fielding averages above the league norm (.955 to .934 at first, and .867 to .832 at second), but range factors below the league averages (9.65 to 10.25 at first, 5.39 to 5.40 at second). At this point in his career, Fisler was a smooth fielder, but not a particularly wide-ranging one. Since his style of play has been described as "deliberate," this should not be a surprising conclusion.

His hitting was certainly not bad, although it isn't known if he was right-handed (he threw right) or left-handed. He was one of nine players awarded a gold medal by the *Clipper* (the premier baseball reporting paper at the time) for excellence in hitting in 1868, and, four years later, he finished in the top ten in the National Association in batting average (.350), on base average (.360), slugging (.428), OPS (.788), hits (85), doubles (13) and RBIs (48). Even in his final major league season with the Athletics in 1876, he was still ninth in the National League in doubles. His NABBP stats weren't bad, either. Although his runs average and over of 5,5 for Athletic in 1866 put him last among the regulars, it must be remembered that the club's top six hitters all broke the old NABBP mark for total and average runs. In 1867 he moved up to 5,14 which was about the middle of the pack for the high-scoring Athletic, and then earned his gold medal from the *Clipper* in 1868, finishing third in the NABBP in runs scored with 231, and leading the NABBP in a new stat, total bases average and over. For the 1868 season, Fisler averaged about six and a half total bases per game (6, 21 was his average and over). Although the rampaging Red Stockings set all the batting records in 1869, Fisler still increased his total bases to 7,26. Finally, in professional-only games in 1870, we find that the Icicle led all pro players in hits (85), total bases (139), average hits (2.36) and average total bases (3.86).

When the National Association was formed, Wes Fisler was there, along with his Athletics, helping lead the team to the first official pennant, and hitting a respectable .279, .350, .344, .328 and .276 for the five years of the association. After the Athletics' disastrous 1876 year in the National League, he played one more year with the independent Athletics, playing first and second and scoring 83 runs in 96 games. Although he was initially supposed to play for the 1878 Athletics, he instead retired and opened a haberdashery in Philadelphia. He continued to be an Athletic at heart, taking time out to journey from his home at 2134 North Park Avenue to see Connie Mack's team play, or to shoot some billiards at a pool hall on Market Street. He also worked as a law clerk in the firm of Baird & Hopkinson up until two weeks before he died of pneumonia at Presbyterian Hospital on Christmas Day 1922, apparently, like Moe Berg, unmarried. He had remained somewhat shy and reclusive, although he was interviewed a couple of times by local newspapermen who wanted to know about the good old days, and the Icicle.

G	AB	R	H	2B	3B	HR	RBI	BA	OBP	SLG	OPS+
273	1334	258	414	72	14	2	189	.310	.318	.390	119

Sources: *Nineteenth Century Stars (SABR), The National Association of Baseball Players (Marshall Wright), Philadelphia North American, Philadelphia Press, National Baseball Library/John Thorn, Family Search.*

Jim Fogarty

James G. Fogarty can be seen in a historical perspective as both a throwback player and a player who was ahead of his time. Fogarty, whose fatal illness-shortened career ran from 1884 to 1890, was a throwback to the 1860s, when superlative defensive players would draw kudos based solely on their defense. And, he was ahead of his time, maybe 90 years ahead of his time, in that he was a fast, top flight defensive outfielder who was judged as being a better hitter than he really was—a common model in the 1980s and 90s.

One of the early Californians in the major leagues, Fogarty was born on February 12, 1864, in San Francisco. He originally played both the outfield and third base for the Haverly club in his hometown, apparently while attending St. Mary's College of California, before coming east to join the Phillies. Although some sources say the Phillies purchased his contract from a minor league team, that would seem unlikely, unless he stopped somewhere along the way between California and Philadelphia. The original plan was for the 20-year-old to play for the Phillies' reserve team—an anachronism left over from the club structure of the 1860s—in 1884. When the reserve team failed to materialize, Wright gave the 5-10½, 180 pound right-hander a shot with the varsity. He made his major league debut in the same 1884 opening day win over the Wolverines as Charlie Ferguson, in what would later prove to be an eerie coincidence.

Now, while another Fogarty (John) would later sing about *Centerfield*, this Fogarty initially played right for Wright, and played it well. He soon did move to center though, and his defensive figures in the outfield for his seven-year major league career were superlative.

	Fielding %	Range Factor
Fogarty	.940	2.50
League	.893	1.90

Forty years after his death in 1891, sportswriters were still praising his defense, claiming that no outfielder, and that included Tris Speaker, had ever outshone him. Earlier, in the 1892 *Reach Guide*, he was memorialized by noting his ability to cover the outfield and his amazing catches. He led all outfielders in putouts, total chances per game, fielding percentage and double plays twice each, and his 42 outfield assists in 1889, though not a Phillies' record, was still pretty good, and in the top 10 single seasons all time for outfielders.

As to his hitting, that's more of a mixed message. Although his speed led Wright to typically bat him either leadoff or third, he finished in the top 10 in on base percentage

Just three years after the death of Charlie Ferguson, the Phillies' second most popular player—Jim Fogarty—would also die young (Allen and Ginter).

only once, although he did lead the National League in walks in 1887 with 82. His career adjusted OPS was just 98, he finished over 100 only one time (140 in 1886), his career batting average was just .246, and his career on base percentage was just .335. He just didn't get enough hits to be a really good offensive player, even though, under the different scoring rules of the time, he stole 102 bases in 1887, becoming the second major leaguer to top 100, and also took a league-leading 99 in 1889.

In addition to his popularity for his defensive skills—and he was very popular among Philadelphia fans—Fogarty was famous as an early baseball unionist. His involvement with the Brotherhood began during Al Spalding's 1888-89 around the world tour. Fogarty was chosen to be the center fielder for the "all–American" team that would oppose Spalding's Chicago White Stockings on the tour and he got an earful on the Brotherhood and the owners' mistreatment of the players from Phillies teammate and Brotherhood stalwart George Wood. When Fogarty, Wood, et al., arrived back in the U.S. to start the 1889 season, he was a full-fledged unionist. Although Fogarty was named the Phillies' captain in June 1889, there seems to have been no doubt as to what action he would take when the Players League was formed.

Jim Fogarty, supposedly doing what he did best— chasing down a fly (Library of Congress photograph).

At the start of the 1890 season, at the age of just 26, he became the player-manager-captain, and one of the biggest gate attractions, of the Philadelphia Quakers.

His final season in baseball would not prove to be a happy one, due to dissension within the leadership ranks of the Quakers and, at least according to one account, his own failing health. He quarreled with Quakers president H.M. Love, claiming Love was interfering and resigned as manager and captain after just 16 games (7-9). Although he shortly did come back to play for the Quakers, he got into a total of only 91 games, hitting just .239 but fielding at a remarkable (for this era) .963 percentage. The reason for his limited play? Most likely it was the onset of the tuberculosis that would take his life in 1891.

Jim Fogarty returned to California during the winter of 1890-91, most likely a sick man. It was his condition, along with his immense popularity with Philadelphia fans, that seems to have enabled Al Reach to persuade an otherwise adamantly anti-union John Rogers to take Fogarty back with the Phillies when the Players League collapsed. However, Rogers then sold Fogarty's contract to Pittsburgh, the assumption herein being that Rogers knew Fogarty's condition, but Ned Hanlon at Pittsburgh didn't. Either way, it made no difference. Fogarty never got to western Pennsylvania, and he died in Philadelphia on May 20, 1891, at the age of 27.

G	AB	R	H	2B	3B	HR	RBI	BB	BA	OBP	SLG	OPS+
751	2880	508	709	110	55	20	320	351	.246	.335	.343	98

Sources: *Baseball's First Stars* (SABR), *Phillies Encyclopedia* (Rich Westcott and Frank Bilovsky), *Occasional Glory* (David Jordan).

Chick Fulmer

Charles John "Chick" Fulmer may not have been one of Philadelphia's greatest players, but he had a knack of being present at some important events. Maybe it ran in the family. His great-grandfather Michael served in the French and Indian War. His grandfather John fought in the Revolution. Father Michael was a major in the Civil War before coming back to Philadelphia to make his living as a butcher. While his dad was in the army of the Union, 14-year-old Charles was enlisting as a drummer boy with the Southwark Guards, although he was sent home when they found out how young he was. Charles would later at least witness, if not fight in, two baseball wars.

His long—he lived to the age of 89—and adventurous life began in Philadelphia on Lincoln's birthday, February 12, 1851. A six-foot, 160-pounder who both batted and threw right, Chick Fulmer was, like Dick McBride, another example of a highly skilled player appearing at both shortstop and pitcher. He certainly must have been skilled to have been playing in fast company with the Philadelphia Olympic club during the 1868 season at the age of 17. Most probably Olympic's youngest Civil War veteran, Fulmer appeared in five games at shortstop—the position he would be best known for throughout his career—and had a runs average and over of 2,0. He moved over to another of Philadelphia's top clubs, Keystone, for the 1869 season, undoubtedly due to the lure of a professional salary, for this was the season that Keystone would field a professional team. He pitched in 11 games for Keystone, mainly behind George Bechtel, and had a hands average and over of 2,1. Early on in his career, Chick Fulmer's path was established. He wasn't much of a hitter, but many teams—he would play for a dozen or so during his 17-year career as a top baseballist—would covet him for his defensive prowess.

When Keystone returned to amateur status for 1870, Fulmer went to the Forest City club of Cleveland, where he played some outfield and pitched a little, compiling the fewest number of hits per game (1.50) on the team. It was with the Rockford Forest Citys that he joined the National Association in 1871, a 20-year-old, three season veteran. Although he made a few more errors than average at short for Rockford, he covered a lot of ground—his range factor was 5.88, compared to the league average of 5.18. Continuing to revolve, he jumped to the New York Mutuals for 1872, proving to be a fine shortstop and a not-so-good third baseman. Although it must have seemed to the fans that he had his bags packed constantly, his first two years in the NA were his best offensively, adjusted OPS of 105 and

108. Still, for his professional career in the NA, the National League and the American Association, he was a .261 hitter with no power and a career 89 adjusted OPS.

Fulmer returned home to Philadelphia with the new White Stockings in 1873—one of the few players the Philadelphias didn't pilfer from the established Athletics—his sixth team in six years. However, Fulmer stayed at home through the 1875 demise of the National Association and the Philadelphias—a case wherein he was a witness to the brief NA-NL struggle and his Philadelphias team being aced out of the new league by the Athletics, whereupon he resumed his career as a travelling man, sometimes in the major leagues, sometimes with independent teams.

Even though the Philadelphias lost out on joining the National League, Fulmer himself was still in demand for 1876, joining Louisville. After one year in the Falls City, he played a couple of months with the 1877 independent Athletics, before moving on to first Pittsburgh (1877) and then Buffalo (1878) of the International Association. When the Bisons joined the National League for the 1879 season, he went along, now playing second base, and playing it well. However, he played only 11 games with Buffalo in 1880 before returning to Philadelphia during the season and entering the most important role of his career—one of the key players in the founding of the American Association.

Fulmer captained (managed) Bill Sharsig's "new" Athletics for the last two months of the 1880 season, then played shortstop for the team in 1881, also taking part in that Athletic club's tour through the Midwest. When the AA held its first formal meeting on November 2, 1881, in Cincinnati, Fulmer was there, again as the Athletics' shortstop-manager, and taking part in a territorial dispute between his team and Horace Phillips' Philadelphias. Due to the importance of Philadelphia to the new league, and the persuasiveness of O.P. Caylor, the two Philadelphia teams ostensibly merged. As a result, the next day Fulmer, who also held stock in the Athletics, was elected to the AA Board of Directors as a representative of the Athletics. The Philadelphia merger lasted only until the spring of 1882, with the Athletics getting the nod to join the AA, because Sharsig had secured a playing grounds. One thing Sharsig hadn't secured were the happy feet of Chick Fulmer. He was off again, this time to the AA's Cincinnati team, which had offered him a better contract.

In the highlight of his playing career, Fulmer was the starting shortstop on the first American Association pennant winner in the 1882 "war year" with the National League. Although he was beginning to slow down a bit in the field (about a league average range factor), he still picked up far more balls than the average, an .897 fielding percentage, compared to the league's .859. He also had career highs for home runs (5) and adjusted OPS (112). His combined offense and defense, notably the latter, made him the '82 AA MVP, at least according to the Faber System rankings. However, this was his last hurrah. Although he was still the Reds' shortstop in 1883, he slumped at the plate (he hit .168) and in the field, and lost his job in 1884, being shipped off to St. Louis for one game before finishing his baseball career in the Eastern New England League in 1885.

Off the field, Fulmer had no less an interesting life than he had on the field. During his final year with the Philadelphias (1875) he married a young (19) woman from Delaware named Anna. Better known as Annie, she and Chick would, unlike many of the rough-hewn baseball players of the time, have an extremely long-lasting marriage—65 years. To help make ends meet during the off-season, Chick held at least four other professions. In 1880 he was working with his father (Michael was living with his son, daughter-in-law and grandsons John and Charles at the time) as a butcher. The next year, while playing with the Athletics, he was also managing a traveling acting company that was putting on *Uncle*

Tom's Cabin, possibly through a connection with Athletics' owner and theatrical producer Billy Sharsig. After his playing days were over, Fulmer returned to Philadelphia and served as a magistrate, despite the fact that he never went to college and certainly didn't have a law degree. His last job was with one of the Philadelphia landmarks of the publishing business—he was a doorman in Center City Philadelphia for the Curtis Publishing Company. His long and full life came to an end three days after his 89th birthday, on February 15, 1940.

G	AB	R	H	2B	3B	HR	RBI	BA	OBP	SLG	OPS+
583	2440	360	636	70	30	8	261	.261	.273	.324	89

Sources: *Nineteenth Century Stars* (SABR), *The National Association of Base Ball Players* (Marshall Wright), *Blackguards and Red Stockings* (William Ryczek), *The Beer & Whiskey League* (David Nemec), *Baseball Pioneers* (Charles Faber), National Baseball Library/John Thorn, Frank Vaccaro, Family Search.

Billy Hamilton

Head first sliding may have been popularized by Pete Rose, but the first significant proponent of this means of going into a base was Sliding Billy Hamilton, who was if not the greatest leadoff hitter of all time, at least one of the candidates for that title. There are innumerable ways of measuring offensive greatness in baseball, but, looking at adjusted OPS as a simple and fairly accurate yardstick, the commonly-acknowledged greatest leadoff hitter of all time, Rickey Henderson, has a career adjusted OPS of 127. Billy Hamilton's was 141. And while it's true that adjusted OPS doesn't measure contributions on the basepaths, Hamilton has no reason to hang his head in comparison to Rickey. Although Henderson has a record 1406 stolen bases, Hamilton wasn't called Sliding Billy for nothing. He's still third in career steals with 912.

While the scoring rules for steals changed to the present standards in 1898, Hamilton was still the best base stealer of his era, even if that era did count extra bases taken on other player's hits, or sacrifice flies, or infield outs, as steals. He stole 54 bases under the present scoring rules in 1898, second in the league and only a dozen fewer than he'd had under the old rules in 1897. Even if his stolen base totals were inflated by a dozen or so during each of his nine big stolen base years (1889 to 1897) under the old rules, it seems safe to postulate that he actually stole in excess of 750 bases. Even this modest adjustment may be too

Billy Hamilton, one-third of a Hall of Fame outfield, in his AA days with the Kansas City Cowboys (Library of Congress photograph).

great—Hamilton was originally credited with 117 steals in 1889 and 115 in 1891. Modern research using the present-day rules has revised both of those figures down to just 111 each, seemingly indicating that scorers were loathe to give "cheap" steals for advancing on an infield out or the like.

He was born William Robert Hamilton in Newark, New Jersey, on February 16, 1866, to Irish parents. Samuel and Mary McCutchin Hamilton were both born in the Emerald Isles and came to the United States sometime before Billy's birth. Soon thereafter, the family moved to Worcester, Massachusetts, where daughter Mary was born (in 1869) and father and son worked in a cotton mill. It's a good bet that young Billy must have seen the Worcester Ruby Legs play a couple of times during the team's three-year (1880 to 1882) stint in the National League, because although he was only five and a half feet tall, this little speedster—who was also a top sprinter in high school—was a great ballplayer.

A left-handed slap hitter who threw right-handed, Hamilton got his start with Waterbury of the Eastern League in 1887 at the age of 21. Moving to his hometown team—Worcester was now in the New England League—in 1888, Hamilton soon became the best and most famous player on the short-lived Kansas City Blues franchise of the American Association. Although KC fans must have wondered about the squat, 5-6, 165 pound Hamilton when he first appeared in the Wild West, they were sold in his second year when he posted a 125 adjusted OPS and led the league in steals while scoring 144 runs. However, the directors of the Kansas City team weren't sold on trying to stay in the AA for the Brotherhood war, so they took their team into the Western League, while putting some of their players up for auction to teams in the three major leagues for 1890. Sharp-eyed Al Reach paid $5000 for Hamilton, certainly to the delight of Harry Wright and Phillies' fans, for whom Hamilton was a crowd-pleaser with his daring base running. He was great right off the bat, with his hitting earning the Faber System's NL Hitter of the Year honors in each of his first three seasons in Philly, as well as the Faber System's NL MVP in 1891 and 1894. No less an authority than Sam Thompson, who would play in the same outfield with both Hamilton and a young and reckless Ty Cobb, said that Hamilton was even more daring on the base paths than Cobb.

While that judgment is subjective, the numbers don't lie when it comes to measuring what is ultimately the most important skill of a leadoff man—scoring runs. A .344 career hitter playing in a very high-scoring era who led the National League in walks and on-base percentage five times each, Hamilton was, and is, still the best run-scorer in baseball history. His 1894 season was remarkable.

AB	R	H	2B	3B	HR	RBI	SB	W	BA	OBP	SLG
544	192	220	25	15	4	87	98	126	.404	.523	.528

His runs scored eclipsed Tom Brown's old record by 15, and it would be 27 years before Babe Ruth would also score 177 runs. And no one else has ever gone above 167, so a paradigm shift that would allow someone to score 193 runs in a season is still far off. For his career, he scored 1690 runs in 1591 games—another major league record (runs scored per game) that also looks fairly safe for the immediate future, since the most runs anyone has ever scored in a 162-game season is significantly below one run per game—the 152 scored by the Houston Astros' Jeff Bagwell in 2000.

Hamilton roamed center field, and roamed it well, for the Phillies from 1890 to 1895, when he foolishly asked John Rogers for more money and was shipped off to Boston for over-the-hill Billy Nash. Apparently Hamilton thought two batting titles, leading the league in runs scored three times and four stolen base crowns (in addition to his other statistical accomplishments) merited a raise. He continued to star for the Beaneaters through the 1901 season, when maybe because his breakneck style of play started to wear down his legs, he returned to the minor leagues at the age of 35.

Part of his hell-bent-for-leather play was seen in the outfield, where he covered a lot of ground, a 2.29 range factor, as opposed to the league's 2.03, including running up the curved walls of the bicycle track that Colonel Rogers had installed in the Huntingdon Street Grounds outfield. He would stand facing Ed Delahanty in left and watch the batter over his left shoulder—an odd fielding stance to be sure, but apparently an effective one.

When Hamilton returned to the minors, he still had enough get up and go to play nine more years, mostly in the New England League, hitting as high as .412 with 74 steals in 1904. Maybe his legs came back, although it's more likely he suffered from the "old" age prejudice of this era of baseball—players over 35 were typically just considered too old to play in the majors. The fact that he hit .332 with 23 steals in 1909 (when he was 43 years old) with Lynn would seem to refute that theory, and it's not hard to imagine him still playing well enough in the majors through 1909 to pile up another 600+ major league hits, another 100 steals or so, and reaching 2000 runs scored long before Cobb was the first to reach that milestone.

A baseball lifer, Hamilton finally quit playing in 1910, at the age of 44, and then managed in the minors until 1916. Leaving his uniform behind, he scouted for the Boston Braves and also owned a piece of the Worcester team. It was during this time that his accomplishments, particularly in base-stealing, began to be discounted. Because of the change in rules, he was left out of the record books, something he protested vehemently in letters that he signed "the greatest base stealer of all time." He never really received the credit he was due while he was living, dying at home in his adopted home town of Worcester on December 16, 1940. He left behind a widow, Rebecca Carr Hamilton, four daughters, Ethel, Mildred, Ruth and Dorothy, and two grandchildren. He had spent 50 years in baseball, and was one of the game's top 10 players for 10 years, but he missed seeing his election to the Hall of Fame by 21 years.

G	AB	R	H	2B	3B	HR	RBI	SB	BB	BA	OBP	SLG	OPS+
1591	6268	1690	2158	242	94	40	736	912	1187	.344	.455	.432	141

Sources: *Baseball's First Stars (SABR), Occasional Glory (David Jordan), Phillies Encyclopedia (Rich Westcott and Frank Bilovsky), Encyclopedia of Major League Baseball Teams (Donald Dewey and Nicholas Acocella), Baseball Pioneers (Charles Faber), Family Search, The Deadball Era.*

Hicks Hayhurst

In another lifetime, in another circumstance, he could have been celebrated as the Branch Rickey of the nineteenth century. Or, if history had taken a different path, Branch Rickey might have been known as the Hicks Hayhurst of the twentieth century.

He was Elias Hayhurst, almost universally known as "Hicks." To his fellow members of the Athletic Club, to the 1880 U.S. census taker who came to his door, to the other members of the National Association of Base Ball Players, possibly to his fellow members of the Philadelphia City Council, and maybe even to his wife, Elizabeth, he was Hicks Hayhurst—star baseball player, early baseball executive, Philadelphia civic leader, businessman and pioneer for the attempted integration of the National Game.

He was born Elias Hayhurst, most likely on January 6, 1827, and most likely in Pennsylvania. However, as is often the case with the records of early baseball players, there are other possibilities. According to the 1870 U.S. Census, he was born in the state of Delaware, and, according to the 1880 Census, he was born in 1828. Intriguingly enough, in the 1880 Census, Elias Hayhurst is listed as Hicks E. Hayhurst, leading one to believe that even the census-taker knew him as Hicks. In either case, he was the fifth of Thomas Hayhurst and Martha Croasdale's 10 children. A good Dutchman from Lancaster, Pennsylvania, Thomas Hayhurst was born in 1789 and married Martha, who was born in Middletown, Pennsylvania, in 1797, on October 22, 1818. Unlike his parents, Hicks did not have any children.

He wasn't quite old enough to have been one of the young men who first formed the Olympic Club in the early 1830s. However, he did eventually join up with the mother club. His early years in the sport were spent as a town ball star for years prior to 1860, according to his obituary in the *New York Clipper* (provided by John Thorn), which places the start of his baseball career that same year. The *Clipper* says he was affiliated with both the Winona and Excelsior clubs in 1860. The Winona club is obvious—they were the club given credit by Charles Peverelly in *American Pastimes* for playing Philadelphia's first baseball game, an intramural affair, on May 18, 1860. However, the only Excelsior club on the record in 1860 is the Brooklyn Excelsior club, the unofficial NABBP champs. Other than his obit, there seems to be no evidence that Hayhurst was affiliated with the Brooklyn Excelsior club. Marshall Wright does not list Hayhurst among Excelsior's players in 1860, and Peverelly does not even mention his name in *American Pastimes*. Although Hayhurst would later be closely associated with black baseball in Philadelphia, it seems a bit of a stretch to assume that the Excelsior reference in his obit refers to Philly's black Excelsior club, since there is no evidence that this organization was founded prior to 1866. It is, however, intriguing to speculate on the presence of a white baseball–town ball star on the roster of a black organization. Such a circumstance would be, to say the least, unique.

It was with the Athletic club that Hayhurst's name would be mostly associated during his years as a baseball pioneer. His affiliation with Winona was brief, just the 1860 season and maybe part of 1861, since the *Clipper* says he was induced to join Athletic in 1861, playing his first game for them on June 19 of that year (a 41–13 win over Mercantile), and becoming a loyal Athletic up until 1875. While holding down a dual role in the management of the club, he would usually appear as the club's center fielder. Hayhurst also would act as a "change" pitcher for young Dick McBride, in a fashion very similar to the role Harry Wright would play in relieving Asa Brainard for the 1869 Cincinnati Red Stockings. Like Brainard, McBride was a fastball pitcher in a game where curves were technically illegal. When Athletic (or the Red Stockings) wanted to give McBride (or Brainard) a rest, and throw off the opposition, they brought in a slowballer (the term used at that time)—Hicks Hayhurst (or Harry Wright).

Thus, on the day in 1865 when Athletic had its team picture taken on the porch of their clubhouse, a photo reproduced in the spring 1984 *The National Pastime*, there was 20-year-old Dick McBride, sitting front and center, holding a bat roughly the size and shape of a small pillar, and there was Hicks Hayhurst, with his rather Lincolnesque beard framing his face and his high forehead, easily recognizable in a spiffy tan vest, standing two rows behind McBride and slightly to the left of the still-young phenom. At the time, Hayhurst was almost twice McBride's age, however, these two were already well on their way to making Athletic not only the first name in Philadelphia baseball, but a name of no little renown throughout the baseball world.

Old Hicks was still a very effective player at the age of either 36 or 37, as the substitute outfielder and change pitcher for the 1864 8-1 Athletic club, a fairly notable accomplishment if you consider that, in this era, very few men were able to remain as top-level players far into their thirties, either because of the physical demands of the primitive game, or because they had to get on with their lives, and stop playing kids' games. Hayhurst must have been a kid at heart, because for the seven games he appeared in in 1864, his runs average and over was 3,6, just behind team leader Dan Kleinfelder's 3,7. His active playing career for Athletic continued through the club's first glory years, up until 1869, when he was at least 41 years old. If the Athletics caused a stir by bringing Nate Berkenstock out of retirement at 40 to play the final game of the 1871 season, imagine what people must have said when they saw old Hicks out there for five games in 1869, especially when his runs average and over (6,0) led the team.

And those weren't his only highlights while he was playing for Athletic. In 1866, at either 38 or 39, his 6,4 figure for runs average and over set a new NABBP record. Well, it would have been a new record if McBride hadn't topped him in the same year, going for 6,10.

Thus, the evidence suggests that Hicks Hayhurst was a fine player, and an unusually good player, at an advanced age. Finally retiring as a player after the 1869 season, he continued on in club management, acting as a "virtual" (the *Clipper's* term) director for 13 years. The *Clipper* also clears up the issue of who was running Athletic on the field, and in the office, during the National Association years, stating that Hayhurst was especially good at the position of manager, which the *Clipper* defines quite clearly as a job requiring executive qualities and business acumen. Hayhurst had both in abundance, thus leading to the club's "pecuniary" success. Obviously, Hayhurst was club secretary, what we would now call a business manager, counting the till, scheduling games, etc.

Off the field, Hayhurst did even more for Athletic than he had done as a player. In addition to in effect serving as a member of the board of directors from 1861 to 1874, Hayhurst was chairman of the board for seven straight years, vice president from 1866 to 1868, president in 1872 and 1873 and the club's representative at the meetings of the NABBP and the National Association from 1862 on.

It is for a contribution to the game he made off the field in this last capacity that he deserves to be feted above and beyond his hitting and longevity. While he was playing for the Athletic club, Hicks Hayhurst was a well-known citizen of Philadelphia, and a mover and shaker in the NABBP, in addition to being a top player. Hayhurst was additionally Athletic's captain in the mid–'60s, a friend of Philadelphia Pythian club founder and Philadelphia civil rights pioneer Octavius Catto, and an umpire at many black games in and around Philadelphia. He was, in short, one of the game's prominent figures, undoubtedly helping him to at least get his foot in the door in an attempt to integrate both the Pennsylvania Association and the NABBP. Just as it took someone of the stature of Branch Rickey to get a single black player into the game in the 1940s, so would it take someone of Hayhurst's stature to try and get an entire team into the NABBP.

The American Negro Historical Society Papers, now located at the Historical Society of Pennsylvania, make it quite clear: the delegate from the Philadelphia Pythian club (most likely a Pythian player named Raymond Burr) was present at the October 16, 1867, Harrisburg, Pennsylvania, meeting of the Pennsylvania Base Ball Association through the good offices of Athletic club vice president Hicks Hayhurst, who was canvassing other convention delegates, introducing Burr to all the right people, and otherwise lobbying for the

Pythian delegate to be seated—an action that would have both made the Pythian club a member of the Pennsylvania Association and, thanks to the rules of the NABBP, also a member of that national body. Alas, despite Hayhurst's best efforts, the Pennsylvania Association sidestepped the entire issue and, when the matter was brought before the entire NABBP in Philadelphia in December 1867, that august body drew baseball's first color line. Nonetheless, the Pythian club appreciated Hayhurst's efforts. "Your delegate cannot speak too highly of the kind attentions which these gentlemen showed him and their expressions of friendship for our club," said Burr.

Although Hayhurst retired as an active player a couple of years after the Pythian episode, he remained a major figure in Philadelphia and Philadelphia baseball for some years thereafter. Although he listed himself as a "bookkeeper" on the 1870 census (wife Elizabeth worked in millinery), he was far more than that, holding a much-needed front office position for what was now a professional sports organization. Indeed, Athletic had been a professional team since at least 1868, leading one to believe that, while Hayhurst may not have been a full-time professional baseball player, he was, along with Harry Wright, one of the first professional baseball administrators. And, as someone with close ties to the city tax collectors, Hayhurst was, as the *Clipper* suggested, a pretty good business manager.

When the Athletics joined the National Association, Hicks Hayhurst came along as the top day-to-day administrator for the team, also continuing his umpiring duties in the NA. He was part of a number of key association committees, and was embroiled in a number of big controversies during the first professional league's five years. In 1872, he was offered the vice presidency of the NA under President Bob Ferguson, but declined. If you were a significant part of the NA, you pretty much had to be involved with Harry Wright. Hayhurst, who was several years older than Wright, knew the Red Stockings boss from way back, and knew him well enough that Wright wrote Hayhurst a chummy letter in the midst of the 1873 season, suggesting that the Red Stockings and the Athletics could both catch the front-running (and vacationing in Cape May) Philadelphias. Significantly, Wright and Hayhurst had the opportunity to actually rule on the final outcome of the 1873 pennant race some four months after the former's letter to the latter. They were both members, along with the Philadelphias' Frank McBride, of the NA's Championship Committee that ruled on the Philadelphias' protest that Wright's Boston Red Stockings should forfeit the games in which Bob Addy had appeared—an action that would have given the 1873 flag to the Philadelphias. Hayhurst sided with Wright—the Philadelphias' claim was very weak, anyway—and the pennant stayed in Boston.

As far as Philadelphia was concerned, another major flap took place in November 1874 when Hicks Hayhurst left the Athletics after some 13 years. Having seen the simultaneous success of both the Athletics and the Philadelphias, Hayhurst left his old team to form a third NA team in Philadelphia, the Centennials. It was a move that would prove to be his only real mistake in baseball. A couple of mistakes, that is. First, the city really couldn't support three professional teams. Second, he should have known better than to sign a lot of bad apples like Bill Craver, John Radcliff and George Bechtel, all of whom had been accused or suspected of hippodroming in the past.

Even though Hayhurst's judgment was off in forming the Centennials—the team would fold in late May 1875, after just 16 games—he was still an important figure in the association as a member of the Judiciary Committee. As part of that august group he also ruled on the Davy Force case, sending the shortstop to Hayhurst's old team, the Athletics. When the Athletics were invited into the new National League in 1876, Hayhurst apparently did not come along, although he was back with the team in his old job as "manager" for the 1877 season in the League Alliance.

Hayhurst would keep busy for the remaining six years of his life, having served on the Philadelphia City Council in the early 1870s, and then working as an "agent" (according to the 1880 census). He also wasn't done with baseball. Now, 25 years after he first became involved with grown-up kids' games, Hicks Hayhurst joined the mother club, the still-amateur Olympics, in 1880, coming full circle. He had started out in amateur baseball, made a name for himself in professional baseball, and then, late in life returned to the amateur game, this time as an "active member," and subsequently the president of the oldest ball-playing organization in the country.

One of the great men of not just Philadelphia baseball but early baseball, Elias Hayhurst was, according to the *Clipper*, held in high esteem by all, and was a genial and trustworthy associate as well as a supporter of the national pastime. In early December 1882, he fell ill with the dreaded typhoid fever, the same scourge that would take the life of Phillies' star Charlie Ferguson in less than five and a half years. Hayhurst died just a week later, on December 18, 1882, at his home at 1126 Marlborough Street near the riverfront in Philadelphia's Fishtown section (Ben Shibe's neighborhood), less than a year before the name he did so much to bring to prominence in baseball would win another championship for the city where he was known as "Hicks."

Sources: *The New York Clipper, American Negro Historical Society Papers (Historical Society of Pennsylvania), The National Association of Base Ball Players (Marshall Wright), Blackguards and Red Stockings (William Ryczek), American Pastimes (Charles Peverelly), The Great 19th Century Encyclopedia of Major League Baseball (David Nemec), The National Pastime Spring 1984 (SABR), Baseball The Early Years (Harold Seymour), John Thorn, Family Search, 1870 Census.*

Matt Kilroy

Although there never was a sign posted outside the deep right field corner of Shibe Park at 20th and Lehigh Streets that said, "Kilroy was here," there could well have been. While he never pitched in the major leagues in his home town, Matthew Aloysius Kilroy, also known as "Matches," probably in tribute to a blazing fastball, did achieve a certain notoriety in Philadelphia, albeit for his actions long after he had retired as one of the first notable left-handed professional pitchers. Some 15 years after his playing career ended due to arm problems in Hartford in 1899, Kilroy opened a bar and grill—Kilroy's Bar—across the street from Shibe Park at 20th and Lehigh. In the great tradition of John McGraw's Diamond Café in Baltimore and Al Reach's cigar shop at Fourth and Chestnut in Philadelphia, Kilroy's place became the local hangout for the baseball crowd. In fact, rumor has it that it also became a hangout for bored or thirsty pitchers—including Mack ace Lefty Grove—during games. So well-entrenched was the establishment that it lasted far longer than either Kilroy or the original tenants of Shibe Park. Although Kilroy sold the place in 1935, it continued to be run for the baseball trade as Charley Quinn's Deep Right Field Café, and was still there when the old park closed in 1970. In fact, it's *still* there to this day, although it closed a few years back as Bobo's Lounge, probably because being across the street from a 5000-seat church made it seem a little out of place.

In terms of his contribution to baseball in Philadelphia, Kilroy's friendship with Mack—they were about the same age and had played against each other 25 years before—

The corner of 20th and Lehigh in 2005, the site of the former Kilroy's Café (on the first floor corner). Shibe Park once stood to the left of this shot and looking north up 20th Street are the two-story row houses that Connie Mack built his spite fence in front of (Matthew J. Coyne photograph).

his close proximity to the home of the Athletics, and a resume that included a major league record 513 strikeouts in 1886, and a major league record for left-handed pitchers of 46 wins in 1887, led the shrewd Mack to enlist his help as an unofficial pitching coach for the Athletics.

A lifelong resident of the City of Brotherly Love, Kilroy pitched major league baseball in an up-and-down career that took him to Baltimore, Boston, Cincinnati, Washington, Louisville and Chicago. A two game (0-1) stop in Philadelphia in 1892 for Ben Shibe's Eastern League Philadelphia Athletics marked the only time the home town fans had a chance to cheer for the holder of the all-time single season major league strikeout record.

Born on June 22, 1866, in Philadelphia, Kilroy was a 5-9, 175 pound 19-year-old when he started his professional career with Augusta (some sources say he also pitched for Nashville) of the Southern League, going 29-22 and catching the eye of manager Billy Barnie of the American Association Baltimore Orioles, although he managed to do so without having a reputation as a strikeout pitcher. That changed in his rookie year (1886) in Baltimore, when, thanks in part to the rules at the time that allowed him to take a running start while pitching from only 55 feet away, he posted one of the most unusual records in baseball history.

W-L	G	GS	CG	SHO	IP	H	BB	SO	ERA	ERA*
29-34	68	68	66	5	583	476	182	513	3.37	101

Although as his Adjusted ERA shows, Kilroy was basically an average AA pitcher in 1886, that's anything but an average record. Only Toad Ramsey, who had 499 strikeouts pitching for Louisville in the AA that same year, has ever come really close to Kilroy's record of 513 K's in a single season. What's more, in the 68 games that the Orioles played and Kilroy did not pitch, the team went an awful 19-49, for an overall record of 43-83, good for dead last in the eight-team AA. Although he did lead the association in losses in 1886, that was at least partly because the Orioles hit a staggering .204 as a team, the lowest figure ever achieved by a major league team in a full season. One the other hand, Kilroy was also sixth in the AA in wins, second in innings, first in appearances, third in shutouts, and tied with Ramsey for the lead in complete games, while being responsible for 67 percent of the Orioles' wins. He threw 21 games of less than six hits, including one-hitters on April 26, August 20 and September 10. Having been narrowly denied no-hitters three times, he went out on October 6 and no-hit Pittsburgh 6–0. And, those strikeouts weren't solely a function of his high innings total; he struck out 10 or more batters in a game 21 times. Is it any wonder that, according to Ernest Lanigan, who also noted that he was "the best man in the country at picking men off the bases," Kilroy picked up another name, The Phenomenal Kid? Remarkably, he was even better in 1887.

Although the rules makers, in one of their many back-and-forth swings of the 1880s and 1890s, changed the strikeout rule to "four strikes and you're out" for the 1887 season, and also cut out the running start for pitchers—they were now allowed to take only a single step—Kilroy was the best pitcher in the AA on the season, going 46-19 and finishing second in the league in ERA (3.07) as he led the O's to a third place finish. John Thorn and John Holway award Kilroy their Jim Creighton Award for the AA for 1887, and the Faber System ranks his year as the best single season for a pitcher in the entire nineteenth century.

While the extra strike rule helped drop his strikeout total to 217 in 1887, that was still second in the AA, and he led the league in wins, games, innings, complete games and shutouts. Although he injured his shoulder in a collision at third base with the St. Louis Browns' Arlie Latham during the year, it wasn't until 1888 that there was any noticeable fall-off, as he went 17-21 in "only" 321 innings, missing most of early May and late July. Still, he bounced back with a 29-25, 217 strikeout, 481 inning season in 1889 that included another one-hitter and a seven inning no-hitter called because of darkness.

Unquestionably the biggest name in Baltimore baseball for the last four years of the 1880s, the handsome Kilroy had a remarkable run, winning 121 games in those four years, and striking out 1082 in a monumental 1974 innings. That's an average record over those four years of 30-25 with 271 strikeouts in 494 innings. Kilroy was a hero to baseball fans young and old throughout "Ballmer," including a young Henry Louis Mencken, whose father, August, a noted local cigar maker, went so far as to name a stogie after the local hero—despite being a stockholder in the AA's Washington franchise. However, as would be the case time and again throughout baseball history, especially in the latter part of the nineteenth century, an overly-heavy workload greatly shortened his career, though not before he ran up a record that led the AA's leading twentieth century historian, David Nemec, to proclaim him one of the best four pitchers in association history.

Jumping to the Boston Reds of the Players League in 1890, Kilroy was anything but a good signing, as his arm problems became acute and he went 9-15 in only 218 innings, making just five mound appearances from July 31 on as the Reds won the PL crown without him. After the Brotherhood War ended, he bounced around baseball for nine more years, never winning more than six major league games in a season, and never pitching more than 100 innings—both with Chicago in 1898. After winning 121 games in four years, he would win just another 20 thereafter, finishing his career 141-133 with 1170 K's in 2436 innings and an Adjusted ERA of 109. Despite winning 32 games for Syracuse in the Eastern League in 1894 and 1895, he retired for the 1896 and 1897 seasons, in the hope that his arm would come back. It never did, and, as a .222 hitter for his career, and a good base runner, he actually played right field and led off for the '98 Orphans in as many games as he pitched, hitting .229 and scoring 20 runs in 26 games while going 6-7 on the mound.

After dropping back to the Eastern League with Hartford in 1899, where he was strictly an outfielder, hitting .246, Kilroy retired at the close of the nineteenth century, to await the start of his second baseball career, a few years after Ben Shibe opened his spectacular new ballpark at 21st and Lehigh. Even after Kilroy sold the taproom, his name was carried on in Philadelphia. Son Elmer, while helping his father run the café, was active in both the construction business and Democratic politics, some years before that had much significance in a Republican-dominated city. In fact, that was Elmer's problem—timing. Although he rose to be speaker of the Pennsylvania House of Representatives in 1941, he was a Democrat about 10 years too early, and a series of electoral defeats dimmed his star just before his party—largely in the person of old foe Richardson Dilworth—took over Philadelphia in the early 1950s. Dilworth's ascendancy must have irritated Elmer no end, because, as a resident of North 20th Street, he had battled with Dilworth, who was the Athletics' mouthpiece in the legal battle over Connie Mack's spite fence.

Another battler in the family was Matt's great-nephew, Bucko Kilroy, who may have been even more famous than the pitcher. He was a bruising football lineman, first for Temple University and then for the Philadelphia Eagles during their original glory years in the late 40s—when they played at Shibe Park.

As for Matt Kilroy, he died on March 2, 1940, in his hometown and with a name that would be carried on in his city, and with two records that it is pretty safe to say will never be broken without a major paradigm shift in the game.

W	L	G	SHO	IP	H	BB	SO	ERA	ERA+
141	133	303	19	2436	2445	754	1170	3.47	109

Sources: *Nineteenth Century Stars (SABR), The Beer & Whiskey League (David Nemec), To Every Thing a Season (Bruce Kuklick), The Pitcher (John Thorn and John Holway), Baseball Cyclopedia (Ernest Lanigan), Connie Mack: Grand Old Man of Baseball (Fred Lieb), Baseball Pioneers (Charles Faber), Baseball Library.*

Henry Larkin

Henry Larkin could hit. He may not have been much of a fielder, which may be why he played only 10 years in the major leagues, but he could hit. Even in his final season, with the awful (40-89) 1893 Washington Senators, he was one of the National League's top hitters; his 131 adjusted OPS (.317/.422/.436) put him ninth in the league in that category, and that wasn't even a good year for him. For his 10-year career, seven of which were spent with the American Association Athletics, his adjusted OPS was 141, or the same as Billy Hamilton's.

Larkin was born in the fine little baseball town of Reading, Pennsylvania, not in 1860, as the encyclopedias will tell you, but in 1862—at least according to the 1880 census. His Irish-born parents, Henry and Margaret, though 40 years old at the time of his birth, were busy producing seven children, of which Henry was the second youngest. His father was a heater in a steam forge, and young Henry was apprenticed in a similar line, to a boilermaker. However, after he hit .355 for Reading in the Interstate League in 1883, he got into a cooler line of work, playing the outfield for the Philadelphia Athletics starting in 1884. He was a star at the plate from the start—his adjusted OPS figures for his first six years with the Athletics were 136, 174, 162, 122, 134, 144. The 1885 and 1886 seasons were his best; he led the AA in doubles both years (37 and 36) while finishing in the top five in on base percentage, slugging percentage, OPS, runs, home runs, total bases, adjusted OPS and runs created. He also led the AA in extra-base hits in 1885 with 59. Starting out playing mostly center field, the right-handed hitting and throwing Larkin was moved in stages to left field and then gradually to first base by 1888.

One of the players who jumped to the Players League in 1890, Larkin managed the Cleveland Infants, including Ed Delahanty, for the first part of the year, going 34-35. He also finished in the top 10 in a dozen hitting categories, coming in fourth in Adjusted OPS (148). Returning to the AA and the Athletics, who were in reality the PL Quakers for 1891, he finished up his playing time in Philadelphia with a career-high 10 home runs—fourth in the AA—in 1891. Larkin was a valuable enough property that the Wagner brothers took him to Washington with them when they sabotaged the Athletics and the AA following the 1891 season. He had two more good seasons there, although he played only 81 games in 1893, and he was not retained for the 1894 season, despite his big bat and the

A great hitter for the AA Athletics, Reading's Henry Larkin (Library of Congress photograph).

fact that he was only 32 years old. In fact, he was back playing for Reading in the Pennsylvania State League in the latter part of the 1893 season, hitting .338. He hung around in the Pennsylvania State League with Allentown, Altoona and Reading in 1894 and 1895, hitting .339 and .358 before heading back to Reading in retirement, where he died on January 31, 1942.

Why didn't he stick in the majors? David Nemec has suggested Larkin's lack of speed kept him from being a top star. However, he stole as many as 37 bases in a season, including 21 as late as 1892, and was in double figures in triples for seven straight years, finishing in the top 10 in that category six times. He also had a better than league average range factor as an outfielder. Maybe it was his inability to catch the ball—he was sub-par in the outfield, at first, and at second.

	Fielding %	League Fielding%	Range Factor	League Range Factor
1B	.971	.975	9.94	10.23
OF	.877	.879	1.93	1.80
2B	.860	.911	5.48	5.73

That's not great, but it's not Levi Meyerle, either. As shown by his last major league season, and his two years in the Pennsylvania State League, Larkin could still hit in his early 30s. It seems odd that he wasn't given a chance to stay in the National League, especially for a team as bad as the Senators.

G	AB	R	H	2B	3B	HR	RBI	SB	BB	BA	OBP	SLG	OPS+
1184	4718	925	1429	259	114	53	836	129	484	.303	.380	.440	141

Sources: *Nineteenth Century Stars (SABR), The Beer & Whiskey League (David Nemec).*

Charlie Mason

He is the least-known of the founders of the American Association Athletics. In reality, Charles E. Mason was a better baseball player than his compatriots, and was initially better known by nineteenth century baseball fans than either Lew Simmons or Bill Sharsig. He was also one of the rare significant nineteenth century baseball figures from the south.

Mason was born in New Orleans on June 25, 1853, and grew up playing with amateur teams in the Crescent City and for Williams College (as a pitcher). By 1874 he was playing with the amateur Americus club of Philadelphia, leading to speculation that he must have moved to the Quaker City for other reasons sometime before 1874—baseball players did not revolve sectionally among amateur teams. While playing with Americus as a first baseman-catcher, he caught the practiced eye of Hicks Hayhurst, who signed him to his first professional contract as a right fielder-catcher for his new Philadelphia Centennials for the 1875 season. When the Centennials failed early in the final National Association season, Mason was picked up by the NA's Washington team, jumping that squad during a swing through the Midwest to hook up with the independent Ludlow club of Cincinnati as their captain-manager and second baseman.

Mason returned to Philadelphia, and the now-independent Philadelphias, for the 1876 season, playing right field again. He would change positions as often as he changed teams, although neither was uncommon at this time. When this version of the Philadelphias disbanded during the 1876 season, Mason and most of his teammates joined a professional club in Harrisburg, Pennsylvania. After a year at first and the outfield for the Lynn Live Oaks in Massachusetts, he returned to Philadelphia for a third time, now playing first base with the 1878 independent Athletics, and replacing Wes Fisler.

After a brief trip to Davenport, Iowa, to play for a pro team there, Charlie Mason finally found a home back in Philly (his fourth time through) and, according to the *New York Clipper*, he was instrumental in the re-organization of the Athletics—lending credence to the theory that Sharsig bought into the pieces of the Athletic team that folded during the 1880 season. Mason had played for the first 1880 Athletics, and then played for Sharsig's 1880 Athletics in the months of September and October. Every source says that

Sharsig and Mason were the two main men in the Athletics' late 1880 re-organization—a supposition that makes sense from an organizational standpoint, since Sharsig had the money and Mason the baseball background. Given that background, Mason was Sharsig's main scout in assembling the team that would win the 1883 American Association pennant—while the now former player wasn't running a Philadelphia saloon and bookie joint on the side.

While most sources list Lew Simmons as the third partner along with Sharsig, who is universally recognized as the leader of the trio, and Mason, it may well be that that the former minstrel didn't come along until a year or so after the formation (or reformation of the Athletics), when Horace Phillips left the team to join a new version of the Philadelphias under Al Reach's ownership. This version also makes sense in that the canny Sharsig would have been more likely to enlist the aid of two baseball men (Mason and Phillips) in his initial venture into the game. Then after Hustling Horace hustled off, Sharsig turned to a former associate from the entertainment field, Simmons, as a fall back position.

A tall, heavily built (about 175 pounds) right handed thrower and hitter, Mason was a good base runner and hitter who would eventually find homes in both Philadelphia and at first base, where he was reputed to have good hands. He was probably indicative of a very common player type of the 1870s and '80s; he was good enough to play for just about any top-level team, he just didn't happen to find many jobs with the teams that would later become recognized as "major league." Only 30 years old in 1883, and still in shape since he worked out regularly with the team, Mason would go on to play one game in the outfield on the Fourth of July for the pennant-winning Athletics, going one for two with an RBI.

In other aspects of the game, he has been given credit, probably inaccurately, for inventing Ladies Day and for suggesting the rule that a batter take his base after being hit with a pitched ball. He also managed the Athletics, certainly in 1887, and maybe in 1884 as well, eventually leaving the team in 1888 when he and Simmons sold out their shares to H.C. Pennypacker and William Whittaker.

Charlie Mason appears to have left baseball at that point, dying on October 21, 1936, in Philadelphia at the age of 83 and being buried just north of the city in Roslyn, Montgomery County. Even though he had been out of baseball for some time, he was still remembered in Philadelphia at the time. His *New York Times* obituary quotes no less a source than Connie Mack as saying that "Pop" Mason did a lot for old-time baseball.

G	AB	R	H	2B	3B	HR	RBI	BA	OBP	SLG	OPS+
21	82	7	15	0	0	0	5	.183	.183	.183	30

Sources: *National Baseball Library/John Thorn, The Beer & Whiskey League (David Nemec), Brock Helander, Frank Vaccaro, Encyclopedia of Major League Baseball Teams (Donald Dewey and Nicholas Acocella), The Deadball Era, The New York Times, The New York Clipper, The Great 19th Century Encyclopedia of Major League Baseball (David Nemec), Baseball Almanac.*

Bobby Mathews

Winning 300 games is supposed to be a pitcher's sure ticket to the Hall of Fame. It's been almost 120 years since Robert T. "Bobby" Mathews retired from top-level baseball, and he may well spend another 120 years on the outside of Cooperstown, looking in. Without rehashing the argument about whether or not Cooperstown should, or can, honor such forgotten heroes, what are we to make of the baseball career of the little man from Baltimore who is the biggest major league winner outside of the Hall?

Although Mathews pitched in Philadelphia only at the end of his long (19-year) career of battling the game's best batters, it is as a Philadelphia Athletic that he is best known, due to his having pitched the Athletics to the 1883 American Association championship in the first of his three consecutive 30-win seasons.

Mathews was born in the Monument City of Baltimore on November 21, 1851. He grew up during the war, and first appeared on the baseball scene in 1867 at the age of 15 with the Maryland Juniors—sort of the JV club of the Maryland club of Baltimore. And he was indeed a junior, in both age and size. Although there is no absolute consensus on just how small Mathews was, a good guess would place him at around 5-6 and 140 pounds. That was little, even just after the Civil War, and provides a pretty good indication that he must have been some pitcher, even as a teenager with an 1869 Baltimore team that finished a respectable 14–13 in NABBP action. Mathews was also a good fielder who played the outfield some when he wasn't pitching.

Given the limited individual records from that era, it's impossible to know exactly what the little right-hander's record was as a hurler in 1869. Mathews appeared in 15 Maryland games, while the team's other pitcher, former Keystone Elias Cope, appeared in 14—clearly an indication that there were a couple of relief appearances in there somewhere. It would seem reasonable to assign Mathews a record of 7-7 for the season, since Maryland was a .500 team and he appeared in 15 games. Mathews then came back in 1870, at the ripe old age of 18, and pitched in at least 14 more games for a less-successful (9-18) Maryland club. Since the box scores are missing for nine of the team's 1870 games, figuring out Mathews' record is a little trickier. If we assume he again pitched in about half the team's games, and that his individual record was pretty similar to that of the team, then we can figure he went maybe 4-9 in 1870. Not a great record (11-16) for his pre–National Association years, but not bad, considering his age, size and the rest of his team. How did he do it?

Mathews had a trick pitch, even at the age of 15 and 16. Bobby Mathews was the

Along with Harry Stovey, little (5-6) underhand spitballer Bobby Mathews carried the 1883 Athletics to the American Association pennant. Here Mathews is apparently preparing the throw overhand (card from Larry Fritsch, Stevens Point, WI, photograph by Leigh G. Wills).

first to, at the very least, throw an effective spitball. Claims on Mathews' behalf have been filed by some notable historians, including claims based on nineteenth century testimony. Donald Dewey and Nicholas Acocella in *The New Biographical History of Baseball* say Mathews was loading them up as early as 1867. John Thorn and John Holway, in *The Pitcher*, say it was in a Maryland–Ft. Wayne game in 1868, and quote Mathews' contemporary Phonnie Martin as saying the youngster was throwing a pitch that was a "revelation." Since there was hardly anyone even throwing a regular curveball at this time—and Mathews is sometimes given credit for inventing the curve, too—an underhand pitch that either outcurved (away from a right-handed batter), or incurved and dropped, must have been a sensation. The source book on pitchers, *The Neyer/James Guide to Pitchers*, quotes both Hank O'Day, a pitcher whose career overlapped Mathews,' and *The Sporting News'* Alfred Spink to the effect that Mathews threw a spitball. In fact, O'Day's recollection—from 1908, when he was a National League umpire—is quite specific. Mathews would spit on the palm of his hand and rub the ball in the saliva.

Martin's and O'Day's comments make it sound like Mathews was throwing a pitch no one had ever seen before. The Neyer/James book also quotes a *Baseball Magazine* article from 1931, telling about an Eckford-Maryland game with the same details as the Martin anecdote used by Thorn and Holway. Mathews was throwing a pitch the Brooklyn team had never seen before and the ball would outcurve at times, and also act like Christy Mathewson's fadeaway at other times. Despite this evidence, Neyer and James will only go so far as to state that Mathews "might have been the first to throw a good spitball."

And good it was. And so was his curve. Although it's possible that his spitter broke like a latter-day curveball he was also apparently one of the first purveyors of the breaking pitch supposedly invented a year or two before him by Candy Cummings. Mathews was at the least one of the first to throw an effective curve.

When the National Association was formed, Matthews was pitching for the Fort Wayne Kekiongas. In fact, he won the first professional league game 2–0 on May 4, 1871, over the Cleveland Forest Citys on a five-hitter that would prove to be the NA's lowest scoring game in its first four years. From Fort Wayne he went next back to the Lord Baltimores and then spent three years with the second team he would be widely associated with, the New York Mutuals, peaking with a 42-22 record in 1874. In all, he won 131 games in the National Association, trailing only Al Spalding and the Athletics' Dick McBride in that category. In 1876, when the Mutes joined the National League, Mathews went with them and went 21-34, only to find himself without a team when the Mutuals were unceremoniously tossed out of the NL after the 1876 season. Mathews now entered the gypsy portion of his career, pitching in Cincinnati, Columbus, Lynn, Worcester, Providence, San Francisco and Boston in a variety of leagues between 1877 and 1882. By the time the 1883 season rolled around, his major league record since leaving the Mutuals was just 39-41, and he most likely was considered over the hill at 31—a lot of pitchers were just that in that era.

However, having somewhat paralleled Dick McBride for a few years, he now became a successor to McBride with a team of Philadelphia Athletics. Winning 30 games in each of the 1883, 1884 and 1885 seasons, Mathews became the toast of Philly—and, apparently he did a lot of toasting, as his tastes were well-suited for the Beer and Whiskey League and he found Philadelphia a lot more exciting than Baltimore. He went 30-13, 30-18 and 30-17 in those three years, also pitching 1234 innings with adjusted ERAs of 141, 101 and 142 and becoming, along with Will White, one of the two last great underhanded pitchers of the nineteenth century. The classic photo of Mathews, taken in this era, shows a little man with a huge, brushy mustache, giving the camera a suspicious look, like maybe he was afraid the photographer would find out the secret of his spitter.

His arm finally gave out in 1886, when he went 13-9 in only 198 innings. His last season as a pitcher was 1887, when at the age of 35—he was the fourth oldest player in the AA—he went 3-4 in seven games with the Athletics, concluding his five years in Philadelphia with a 106-61 record. He had become the only pitcher to win at least 50 games in three different leagues, pitching 578 games, winning 297 of them in the National Association, the National League and the American Association, losing 248, and posting an adjusted ERA of 107. If you add in his estimated record of 11-16 from the NABBP—which was certainly the equivalent of the major leagues—then he had a career record of 308-264 with mostly bad teams. And Bobby Mathews was a 300-game winner.

Like many of his fellow professional ballplayers of the nineteenth century, Mathews found himself at loose ends after his playing days were over. He did serve as an American Association umpire in the 1888 and 1891 seasons, and he umped in the Players League as well. However, soon afterwards he was suffering from paresis, and his last job before his mind failed was in 1897 as a greeter in Joe Start's Providence roadhouse. Mathews, who never married, was moved to the Maryland University Hospital, to Spring Grove Asylum, and then to his parents' house in Baltimore before dying at the age of 46 on April 17, 1898. Despite the fact that the had won 300 games, and had, if not invented, then at least helped pioneer, the spitball and the curve, he was basically forgotten when the Hall of Fame started inducting his peers some 40 years later, and he remains largely so today.

W	L	G	SHO	IP	H	BB	SO	ERA	ERA+
297	248	578	19	4956	5591	533	1366	2.89	107

Sources: *Nineteenth Century Stars* (SABR), *The Beer & Whiskey League* (David Nemec), *Blackguards and Red Stockings* (William Ryczek), *The Pitcher* (John Thorn and John Holway), *The Neyer/James Guide to Pitchers* (Bill James and Rob Neyer).

Dick McBride

He was Philadelphia's first superstar. James Dickson McBride was so good that he made Athletic's first nine in June 1861, when he was about 16 years old. He was so good that he had been a top-shelf cricket bowler in a city where cricket was still a big game. He was so good that, in the simpler, less talent intensive baseball of the mid-nineteenth century, he played shortstop when he wasn't pitching—just like high school superstars do today. In fact, he was so good that, in 1862, at the age of 17, he was named shortstop for the Philadelphia Picked Nine that would face a similarly select squad from Brooklyn. He was so good he led the Athletics in runs average and over in 1865 as a 20-year-old pitcher who also went 11-3 in the box, and the next year, he set NABBP records for runs scored with 160 (in 25 games) and runs average and over (6,10). He was so good that Tom Pratt, the national champion Brooklyn Atlantics' pitcher, twice failed to beat him out of the starting pitching job with Athletic. He was so good that Harry Wright filed a complaint with the NABBP that McBride was getting paid, contrary to NABBP rules. He was so good that the *New York Clipper* awarded him a gold badge as the top-hitting pitcher of 1868. He was so good that John Thorn and John Holway picked him as one of the top seven pitchers of the 1860 to 1879 era, despite the fact he never won a game in what are classically referred to as the "major" leagues. He was so good that when he left baseball after appearing in just four games during the 1876 season, when he was still just 31 years old, he most likely held the record for most games won by a top-level pitcher. Although his records for 1862, 1863, 1864 and 1866 are largely estimates, it's still quite a record—and all with the Athletic club of Philadelphia, except for his last four games in 1876 with the National League Boston Red Caps.

Dick McBride's Career

Year	Record
1862	1-1
1863	3-2
1864	6-1
1865	11-3
1866	21-2
1867	27-2
1868	33-3
1869	17-4 (3-3 in pro games, 14-1 in amateur games)
1870	56-10 (21-10 in pro games, 35-0 in amateur games)
1871	18-5
1872	29-14
1873	24-19
1874	33-22
1875	44-14
1876	0-4 (Boston)
Total	323-106 (.753)

Even just taking his National Association and National League marks (149-78, .656, 114 ERA+), he was a fine pitcher. And, if judging pitching records against the best competition in the nation is your standard, Dick McBride was better than George Zettlein. Better than Asa Brainard. Better than Phonny Martin. Better than Candy Cummings. He was the first 300-game winner in baseball history. Brainard won about 200 games in his career, around 120 of them with the Cincinnati Red Stockings. Al Spalding, although he won more games than McBride, didn't get to 300 until the 1876 season, a year after the Athletics' ace made it, as noted below.

Al Spalding's Career
(*estimates)

Year	Record
1866	*10-5
1867	*10-5
1868	11-4
1869	20-4
1870	37-14 (7-14 in pro games, *30-0 in amateur games)
1871	19-10
1872	38-8
1873	41-14
1874	52-16
1875	54-5
1876	47-12
1877	1-0
Total	340-97 (.778)

Born in Philadelphia some time in the latter part of 1845, Dick McBride, though an unimposing 5-9 and 150 pounds, was a star baseball and cricket player while still a teenager. He continued to play cricket regularly through the 1864 season, even while becoming Athletic's baseball ace, with his right-handed bowling being a key factor in an upset win that season over the famed St. George Dragonslayers of New York and their star bowler, Harry Wright.

By the time he was in his early 20s, or about the time Athletic became a yearly contender for the mythical title of the best team in the nation, he was certainly more notable in appearance, having raised an impressive set of sideburns—his particular style was known as Dundreays at that time. He was always notable in the box, even though he apparently did not resort to the rule-bending of the curveball. McBride got by with just a fast ball and excellent control. He was also what was even then referred to as a pitcher who used his head even though, unlike Martin or Harry Wright, he didn't resort to throwing a slow ball, or what we would now call a change-up. McBride was sort of a primeval Walter Johnson or Lefty Grove in their early years.

At the same time, up until the game's specialization demanded more concentration on behalf of the pitcher—around the time the National Association was formed in 1871—he was also one of the best hitters in the nation. He displayed the same dual skill set of Babe Ruth, together, from about 1864 to 1870. The April 2, 1911, *Philadelphia North American*, in quoting an unnamed article that was contemporary to McBride's and the Athletic club's heyday, notes that McBride's skill as both a pitcher and hitter was such that he was like the numeral "1" in the number "10," that is, without him, Athletic would be a big zero, and with him, they were more than an ordinary "nine."

By 1863, at the age of 18, he was already the third best hitter on Athletic, with a runs average and over of 2,5. In 1865, in addition to going 11-3, he equaled Mike Smith for the best offensive mark on the team, a runs average and over 4,0. From 1866, when he set the two NABBP records, to 1868, he was one of the best hitters in baseball, to say nothing of being the best-hitting pitcher. In 1869, despite missing part of the year due to illness, he tied Al Reach in leading the team in hits average and over (5,12) for the approximate equivalent of a .470 batting average. And in the final pre–National Association year of 1870, he hit around .370 and was second on the team to Fergy Malone in hits per game (3.19) and third in total bases per game (4.64).

Then, as the game changed and became more sophisticated and the burden upon the pitchers became greater, his hitting became more like a pitcher's. Although they were still throwing underhanded from 45 feet, the number of games and number of innings against top competition increased greatly, beginning with the second year (1872) of the National Association. In 1872, '73, '74 and '75, McBride threw 419, 383, 487, and 538 innings—just in NA competition. There's no telling how many innings he threw outside of NA play. With that kind of workload, it's no wonder he hit only .259 in the Association and the National League.

While the game changed so that McBride was forced to put all his efforts into pitching, he didn't change, either his style of pitching or his style of play. Although pitching styles started to sneak up towards sidearm hurling, and curveball pitchers came into demand, McBride stuck to the underhand fastball as his weapon. Along with Al Spalding and Tommy Bond, he became known as one of the three greatest all-underhand pitchers, at least according to David Voigt. The boy, and then the man, throwing all those fastballs was not an individual to mess with. He was the owner of an explosive temper and a sharp, sarcastic tongue that did little to make him a favorite among opposing batters—sort of an early-day Gil Gamesh, Phillip Roth's supremely cocky and unhittable pitching creation from *The Great American Novel*. In Philadelphian terms, McBride had an attitude. He also wasn't afraid to take on his own team's management. When Dave Eggler was hired away from the Philadelphia Philadelphias for the 1875 season with a $2200 contract as incentive, McBride, in what may have been the first holdout on record, demanded $2200 himself, or he wasn't playing. He got the money.

He was nonetheless a cool performer in the box when the chips were down, as evidenced by his 4-1 throttling of the Chicago White Stockings in the 1871 pennant clincher, a victory that made him the manager of the first official professional pennant winner. McBride had been running the team on the field as the captain for some years prior to 1871, with responsibilities more in keeping with a present day manager. He continued to star and manage Athletic for the remainder of the NA era and, even though they couldn't break the resultant stranglehold the Boston Red Stockings had on the association, McBride was one of the leading lights of the NA. That was never more the case than in 1874, when Athletic and the Red Stockings took their joint trip to England. Since Al Spalding had arranged for a tour of both baseball games and cricket matches, the three Wright brothers were more than glad to have another first-rate cricketeer along on the trip.

The final chapter in McBride's brilliant career came in 1875, when the immense strain of the past five years on his right arm must have caught up with him. Although he went 44-14 with six shutouts over his 538 innings, Athletic was losing money and the club's directors brought in Lon Knight as a potentially cheaper alternative—since McBride was still making around $2200. During the season's last month McBride was struggling in the box. Then, on October 9, McBride was getting battered by the Red Stockings—something that happened to all pitchers the Boston team faced in 1875—when one of the most bizarre incidents in Philadelphia baseball history took place. In a move that would have made Lew Simmons or John Rogers blanch, the club's directors stopped the game in the fifth inning, came down on the field, and, in effect, fired McBride in mid-game, removing him as captain-manager of the team. Adrian Anson was appointed captain-manager on the spot and, showing the lack of tact for which he would become famous, removed McBride from the game, forthwith. Except for those four games with Boston in the National League in June 1876, he never pitched again, although McBride himself later claimed he had retired in 1875. While it seems clear that McBride's arm must have been permanently damaged by his extreme workload prior to the October 9 game, the scene on the Jefferson Street Grounds that day was a disgrace to Athletic and Philadelphia baseball, one that unquestionably wouldn't have happened if McBride's old friend, teammate and class act Hicks Hayhurst, was still running Athletic at the time.

After baseball, Dick McBride becomes hard to follow. Census records would seem to indicate that McBride and his 22-year-old Pennsylvania-born wife, Emma (both first generation Americans), were living in Philadelphia's Germantown section in June 1870. McBride (he was James McBride to the census-taker) was working in Philadelphia's predominate industry, textiles, as a carder. Since he was listed as 24 years old at the time, his 25th birthday must have been in the last six months of the year. Dick, now through with baseball though still not 35, and Emma were also living in Philadelphia during the 1880 census, with nine-year-old daughter Anna, and sons Francis (6) and James R. (1). Dick was now an engineer, with his birth date listed as 1847—most likely an incorrect date.

After 1880, the trail grows colder. Philadelphia's first superstar at some point went to work as a clerk in the post office, a job he held for some years before dying in Philadelphia on October 10, 1916, at the age of approximately 71. When the *North American* interviewed him in 1911, the paper found he was still an ardent fan of the game. And, he had an interesting perspective of the game in the 1860s and 1870s, noting that the reason the

Athletic club won so much was their excellent fielding—the most difficult skill of that era. Perhaps he was too modest to say that Athletic's pitcher had something to do with those 300+ wins as well.

W	L	G	SHO	IP	H	ERA	ERA+
149	78	237	10	2082	2420	2.85	114

Managerial Record

W	L	PCT
161	85	.654

Sources: *Baseball's First Stars (SABR)*, *The National Association of Base Ball Players (Marshall Wright)*, *The National Pastime Spring 1984 (SABR)*, *Blackguards and Red Stockings (William Ryczek)*, *Richter's History and Records of Baseball (Francis Richter)*, *National Baseball Library/John Thorn*, *Philadelphia North American*, *Philadelphia Press*, *American Baseball (David Voigt)*, *The Great 19th Century Encyclopedia of Major League Baseball (David Nemec)*, *The Pitcher (John Thorn and John Holway)*, *American Pastimes (Charles Peverelly)*, *1870 Census*, *A.G. Spalding and the Rise of Baseball (Peter Levine)*, *Family Search*.

Levi Meyerle

They called him "Long Levi." Levi Meyerle may have been the first "born DH," but, except for Harry Stovey, he was also the best hitter to come out of Philadelphia prior to Reggie Jackson. And yet, just 50 years after posting the highest batting average in major league history, he died forgotten in and by his hometown, despite also holding the distinction of playing for four different Philadelphia teams.

Most sources list Levi Samuel Meyerle's birth as coming in July 1845 in Philadelphia, to Jacob and Margaret Meyerle. However, should you check the records of The Church of Jesus Christ of Latter-day Saints, you'll find 1849 as his birthdate. Ditto, if you have a copy of the original, 1969 version of the *Macmillan Baseball Encyclopedia*. If this latter date is true, then Long Levi (he was 6-1 and weighed close to 180 in his prime) was a precocious 17-year-old pitcher for the 19-6 Geary Club in 1867, scoring 110 runs in 25 games for a team-leading average and over of 4,1. Geary, however, was playing only local competition in 1867, so Meyerle was a small fish in a big pond.

The 1868 season was pretty much the same, though a little less successful—Geary played only 18 local games, going 7-6 in their recorded contests and getting whomped twice by Athletic. However, Athletic must have liked what they saw in Geary's young pitcher, because, by 1869, he was wearing the blue and white and had also become a professional. Meyerle appeared in only 10 of Geary's 1868 games, for another team-leading average and over of 4,1.

Playing as a utility man, Meyerle got into 34 of Athletics' 49 NABBP 1869 games as a catcher, pitcher, third baseman and right fielder—a season that would prove to be typical of most of his career—because, although nominally a third baseman, his teams kept moving him around from position to position, trying to get his bat in the lineup while hiding his hands. Moving up in class from the local Geary competition to the national-level Athletic, Meyerle's hitting suffered—he was last among the regulars in both hits (3,26) and runs (3,33) average and over, although he did have one of the better hands lost average and over figures (2,30).

Although he had not been a star in his first big-time season, Meyerle was in demand,

and on the move, to the Chicago White Stockings. Chicago placed an ad in the *New York Clipper*, asking players to apply. Proving that it pays to advertise, Chicago soon had Meyerle and Ned Cuthbert signed up. A salary of $1500—not bad for that time—lured Meyerle to Chicago, for whom he limited his efforts to third, with a few turns in the pitcher's box. Chicago went 22-7 in its pro games, 65-8 overall, with Meyerle now starting to show his power in the 63 games he played. Although he was next to last among the regulars in hits per game (3.38), his 5.19 total bases per game put him in the middle of the team's sluggers.

However, Levi Meyerle's 1870 was just a prelude to 1871, one of the best years any hitter would ever have in any league. As would also prove to be the case later in his career, the young slugger didn't stay away from home for long. Athletic brought him back to Philadelphia for the 1871 season, to play third base while living with his parents, and to set an all-time record in the first season of the National Association. Admittedly, this was only a 26-game season, but Meyerle led Athletic to the championship of the first true professional league with a batting mark that not only has never been topped in the 135 years since, but which has never even been approached. Here then, was Levi Meyerle's historic 1871 season.

G	AB	R	H	2B	3B	HR	RBI	BA	SLG
26	130	45	64	9	3	4	40	.492	.700

A small sample of at-bats, but what a sample it was. For lack of a single hit, Long Levi would have batted .500. He led the association in home runs, batting average, slugging average (also a record), total bases (91) and runs created (46) while finishing second in hits, third in RBIs and singles (48), sixth in runs and eighth in doubles. Under the rules of the time, it was almost impossible to draw a walk, so it's not of much significance that he led the NA in on base percentage (.500) and OPS (1.200). What is significant is that this latter mark stood as a major league record for an incredible 49 years, until finally topped by Babe Ruth's 1.379 in 1920.

Although Meyerle hit a fair number of triples, that would seem to be because of the huge spaces in the outfields in those days—faster runners would have turned those blows into home runs. And while the big and not overly mobile Meyerle may have batted .492, he fielded .646 at third (the league fielding percentage at third was .701) with 45 errors in 26 games. It may be that Meyerle's problems on the rough fields of his day were, as his biographer James D. Smith III said in *Nineteenth Century Stars*, due largely to his size and relative lack of mobility. However, Long Levi's problems in the field were not mirrored a similarly large, and heavier, teammate of his from his NA days—Cap Anson. Although not thought of as a great fielder, Anson's fielding percentages at third—mostly compiled during his NA career—were well above the league standard (.813 to .783), Furthermore, Anson's range factor at third was a little above the league mark (3.88 to 3.81), while Meyerle's range factors at every position where he played more than 20 games were below the league mark.

Oddly enough, given Meyerle's fielding troubles, those positions included 82 games at second and 24 games at shortstop. Not until late in his career was he really hidden at what would later become the classic spot to stash such poor fielders: first base. And, he would have made an excellent target at first. Maybe his hands were so bad that he had trouble catching the ball, and he did make 18 errors in 18 games at first during his career. His travelogue of the diamond after 1871 looked like this: Athletic moved him to the outfield for 1872, after which he went back to third, and then started to wander the diamonds of the 1870s; he played mostly second and third in 1874, second, third and first in 1875, back to third for the first NL season in 1876, and then finished up as a shortstop-second baseman.

While in search of a home on the field, Meyerle played for five more teams, including a third stint with Athletic. Although 1874 was his only other truly outstanding season—he led the NA in batting (.394), on base (.401) and OPS (.889)—he was still a feared hitter throughout his career. He returned to Athletic for 1872 and had an off year, reaching the top five in the league only in slugging (.486) and triples (5), one of the reasons, along with Boston's dominance, that Athletic did not repeat in 1872. In 1873, as part of their raids on Athletic, the Philadelphia White Stockings persuaded Meyerle to jump ship. He finished second in the NA in home runs (3), fourth in slugging (.479), eighth in doubles (14) and ninth in batting (.349) for his third Philadelphia team, thus leading the Chicago White Stockings to bring him back to the midwest for 1874 where, as noted, he thrived, and actually posted better-than-average fielding (.833 to .805) and range factor (5.32 to 5.19) numbers at second base. Contrarily, the less said about his fielding at third that year, the better. Not only was his fielding percentage at third .671, but, on May 16, 1874, in a game against Athletic, he made six errors at third, causing some observers to suggest he was hippodroming (throwing the game) in favor of his old team. However, Smith comes to Meyerle's defense in this case, quoting a contemporary source that "Levi could field this way most any time he got a bit rattled," suggesting that maybe he choked, as opposed to throwing the game.

Away from the hazards of the diamond, his 1874 stay in Chicago also produced a bonus: a wife. Meyerle married Ella Miller in Chicago on November 5, 1874. However, the marriage seems to have been short lived. According to Smith, he was back to living with his parents in Philadelphia by the end of the decade, and there is no record in the 1880 census of Ella Meyerle, or Jacob or Margaret Meyerle, or Levi Meyerle, for that matter, either in Philadelphia or anywhere else, despite Levi playing baseball in Baltimore and Rochester that year. Perhaps the census taker came looking for him when he was in transit between Baltimore and Rochester.

Whatever the circumstances of his marriage to Ella, Levi was back in Philadelphia, with the Brotherly Love version of the White Stockings, in 1875. After a so-so year for him (he just made the top 10 in batting, slugging, OPS and triples), Meyerle re-joined Athletic for the third time, just in time for the first season of the National League. He had averaged .353 for his five years in the National Association, winning two batting and two OPS titles. His adjusted OPS figures for those five seasons were 241, 147, 141, 181 and 150.

Although Athletic stumbled through a 14-45 season in the National League in 1876, it couldn't be blamed on Long Levi's hitting. It was a classic Meyerle season: fourth in triples (8), fifth in OPS (.797) and slugging (.449), seventh in batting (.340) and singles (79). His adjusted OPS of 164 placed him fourth in the league. Of course, he also fielded .790. When Hulbert expelled Athletic from the NL following the 1876 season, Meyerle stayed with the team as their third baseman for the start on the 1877 campaign in the League Alliance. However, the Cincinnati Reds were in need of a professional bat, and Meyerle returned to the NL, playing 27 games at short and second while hitting .327 and slugging .430; if he'd played enough to qualify, he would just have missed the top five in the league in both categories. A sprained ankle ended his season early, and probably limited his already-limited mobility even more. Now pretty much restricted to playing first base, he played outside of the major league for Springfield, the Washington Nationals, Baltimore and Rochester over the next three seasons. Even though his playing days in Philly were over, he must have still been popular—both the 1878 Athletics and the 1880 Philadelphias (who never actually played at all) hoped to add him to their squads.

A long-time worker in the construction trades as a lather, plasterer and carpenter, Meyerle finally gave up baseball for good following the 1880 season, and returned home to Philadelphia. However, baseball wasn't finished with him. When the Union Association Philadelphia Keystones were casting around for warm bodies to fill up their team for the 1884 season, manager Fergy Malone, knowing his old teammate (on the 1871 Athletics) was still in town, and knowing that Long Levi had been a tremendous fan favorite in his salad days, asked him to come play first base in the UA. Coming out of a four-year retirement at the age of either 34 or 38, Meyerle played three more major league games, going one for 11 with a double before calling it quits in April. Counting all his professional years starting in 1869, Meyerle had played 10 seasons of top level baseball, hitting .356 with a .479 slugging percentage for the seasons when such averages were obtainable. Although he was only really a dominant player in two years (1871 and 1874), and he was clearly a sub-par fielder, only Ty Cobb and Rogers Hornsby, among current Hall of Famers, posted higher career batting averages, and Meyerle was also a good power hitter for his era, finishing in the top 10 in slugging six straight years. There are far worse hitters now in the Hall of Fame than Levi Meyerle who, among other accomplishments, drove in .909 runs per game and scored .997 runs per game—just below the figures of Sam Thompson and Billy Hamilton. Further, his career OPS+ was 21 points higher than Harry Stovey's. There is just too much evidence, in too many offensive categories, to ignore Meyerle's credentials as one of his era's great hitters.

According to Smith, Meyerle married a woman named Anna following his brief comeback (she died in 1905; there were no children in this marriage and, apparently, none in his marriage to Ella) and continued to work in the construction trades, while reliving some of the glory days of Philadelphia baseball with Wes Fisler, before dying of chronic heart trouble on November 4, 1921. Considering his popularity in his home town 50 years before, and that he was one of the main reasons there were glory days in Philadelphia baseball in the 1870s, it is odd indeed that not a single newspaper published anything about his death in the sports pages.

G	AB	R	H	2B	3B	HR	RBI	BA	OBP	SLG	OPS+
307	1443	306	513	86	31	10	279	.356	.360	.479	164

Sources: *Nineteenth Century Stars* (SABR), *The Beer & Whiskey League* (David Nemec), *The National Association of Base Ball Players* (Marshall Wright), *Blackguards and Red Stockings* (William Ryczek), Brock Helander, Family Search.

Jocko Milligan

John "Jocko" Milligan was Irish and at least the second-best hitting catcher produced by the city of Philadelphia prior to Roy Campanella. If you care to put their standard historical profiles into an analogy, Jocko Milligan would be to Jack Clements as Henry Larkin was to Harry Stovey, the common knowledge being that both Milligan and Clements were catchers and hard-hitting, close contemporaries. Clements was a little bit better hitter, and a lot better fielder. Actually Milligan was a decent enough defensive catcher and, as an offensive player, he was very comparable to Clements.

A big for his time, 6-0, 192 pound right-handed catcher and hitter, Milligan was born about three years before his left-handed counterpart, on August 8, 1861. He broke in with the Phillies' local rivals, the American Association Athletics, on May 1, 1884, after spending a couple of years catching in the minors in Pennsylvania's coal country. Having caught the eye of Athletics' president Billy Sharsig, the 23-year-old Milligan was a part-time catcher-first baseman with the team through the 1887 season, sharing the backstopping job with first Jack O'Brien and then Wilbert Robinson. Sharsig then shipped him to the St. Louis Browns in a big trade following the 1887 season. Although it's been said the deal was done because Sharsig didn't have a place to play him—his other position was first, and Stovey and Larkin were both there—it is more likely that Sharsig, a good judge of talent, dangled Milligan as his extra catcher in front of Chris Von der Ahe because he needed an outfielder, in this case, Curt Welch. The deal was Milligan, shortstop Chippy McGarr and sub outfielder Fred Mann for Welch (one of the best defensive outfielders of his time), shortstop Bill Gleason and $3000. The shortstops were a wash, and Mann was done with his major league career, so the deal came down to Welch and $3000 (a lot of money in those days) for Milligan. That's not exactly giving him away. And, there was good reason why Sharsig wouldn't give Milligan away. Look at the stats for the Athletics' three catchers for Milligan's four years with the team.

	OPS+	Fielding%	Range Factor
1884			
Milligan	129	.939	8.83
O'Brien	123	.930	7.07
1885			
Milligan	104	.935	8.25
O'Brien	111	.903	5.84
1886			
Milligan	112	.919	7.05
O'Brien	110	.918	6.22
Robinson	61	.893	6.13
1887			
Milligan	109	.966	8.98
Robinson	51	.901	6.24

These numbers would seem to go a ways towards disproving that Milligan had an iron glove. For his career, his fielding percentage was .930 against a league percentage of .916, and his range factor was 6.93 to the league's 6.04. While there may be many ways to slice and dice these numbers, that doesn't look like a bad defensive catcher. And, he could hit. Maybe only as good as O'Brien for the three years they played together, but, overall, he was Clements' equal. The famous lefty's career adjusted OPS was 117, while Milligan's was 123. Clements may still get the nod as a better peak hitter, thanks to his seven fabulous years in the 1890s, but Milligan was consistently good throughout his shorter career.

In his two years with St. Louis, he was still a part-timer, despite hitting .366 in 1889. When the Players League was formed, he came back home to Philadelphia and caught for the Quakers, now sharing the job with Lave Cross. When the Quakers moved over to the AA as the Athletics in 1891, Milligan had his only season as a regular catcher, and quite a season it was, .303/.397/.505. In the AA's final season, he led the league in doubles (35) and extra-base hits (58), and was second in slugging, OPS, home runs (11) and adjusted

OPS (154). He also had a better-than-average fielding percentage and range factor, although he did lead the league with 40 passed balls.

As was the case with Larkin, he moved along to Washington with the Wagner brothers for the 1892 season, and went back to sharing the catcher's spot, this time with Deacon McGuire, whose adjusted OPS was 20 points lower than Jocko's 134. Milligan also fielded significantly better than the Deacon. All that performance did was buy him a ticket to New York and Baltimore for 1893, where he had his one and only bad season, a 75 adjusted OPS. That earned him a trip back to the coal country and the minors, where he played for Allentown, Reading and Shamokin, hitting over .400 twice and managing during the 1895 season, He closed his career back with the Athletics, only this time in the Atlantic League in 1896 (he hit .333).

Another Jocko Milligan puzzle, in addition to his inability to impress his bosses enough to play more often (in his 10-year major league career, he averaged only 77 games a season), was his home life. Although his bio in *Baseball's First Stars* indicates that his wife's name was Isabella, that would be a coincidence, since his sister's name was Isabella, and he was living with her in 1880, just prior to starting his baseball career. The Milligan family's Irish parents must have died relatively young, because two sisters and two brothers were living together in the same household in 1880. Oldest sister Isabella, then 27 and single, was the head of the household and employed in Philadelphia's biggest industry — textiles. She worked in a cotton mill. Nineteen-year-old John, and his twin sister, Margaret, both lived with Isabella, John working as a carpenter and Margaret keeping house for her siblings, who also included 15-year-old Thomas, who worked in a brickyard. Thus, it's not sure when or if John "Jocko" Milligan married before he died in Philadelphia on August 29, 1923.

G	AB	R	H	2B	3B	HR	RBI	SB	BB	BA	OBP	SLG	OPS+
772	2964	440	848	189	50	49	497	41	210	.286	.341	.433	123

Sources: *Baseball's First Stars* (SABR), *The Beer & Whiskey League* (David Nemec), Family Search, SABR Biography Project.

Horace Phillips

He was known as "Hustling Horace," a great nickname that fit the man, the man who was, along with O.P. Caylor, the seminal figure in the founding of the American Association. And yet, as has been the case with so many of the AA's main figures, his story is seldom told, and is incomplete as well.

Horace B. Phillips was born in Salem, Ohio, although two completely different dates have been given for his birth — May 14, 1853, and May 20, 1856. His family moved to Philadelphia when he was just three months old, and he grew up a Philadelphian, and was closely identified with the city throughout his baseball career, despite travelling all over the northeast, midwest and even out to California in pursuit of baseball success. In other words, in the same vein as Bill Veeck referred to himself, he was a hustler. Phillips began playing baseball in 1870 (which would seem to make the 1853 date for his birth more likely) as a catcher with the Philadelphia Girard club. In 1871 and 1872 he was a left fielder and catcher for the Zephyr club, and then moved on to the Syracuse Stars for a few games in 1873. He first showed up as a professional player in 1877 when he joined the independent Philadelphias as Fergy Malone's left fielder. He took Malone's job as on-the-field manager—

the occupation he would be most commonly identified with for the rest of his baseball career—during the 1877 season, although that engagement lasted only until late July, when the Philadelphias folded and he jumped to the professional Hornellsville (New York) Hornells. He stayed there a year before going back to the Stars as manager. From there it was a short jump to Troy, New York, where he first became a major league manager, leading the National League Troy Trojans before resigning in August (a 12-34 record).

The rest of the 1879 season saw him managing in Baltimore and then playing winter ball in San Francisco. He then managed again in Baltimore in 1880, despite newspaper reports early in the year that he was organizing a professional team in Philadelphia. He then moved on to the Rochester Hop Bitters later in 1880, getting enmeshed in a lawsuit against the team due to a disappearance of funds. Although he lost the suit in April 1881, and had to pay $1463 to the Hop Bitters, the 1881 season wasn't all bad—he also hooked up with Billy Sharsig's Philadelphia Athletics as manager.

Hustling Horace went through most of the 1881 season leading the Athletics—and also playing a little—including leading the team on its St. Louis trip. However, at this stage of his career he never stayed anywhere very long—he was always looking for a new hustle. As a result, he ended up calendar 1881 hustling for Al Reach and the Philadelphias. It was in this role as Philadelphias' manager that, along with O.P. Caylor, he helped get the ball rolling to start the American Association. During a series of organizational meetings in September, October and November 1881, the 28-year-old Phillips and Caylor were the main players. The success of the 1881 Athletics' tour had given Phillips the bright idea of sending out postcards to prominent baseball figures in the cities the Athletics had visited, inviting them to a meeting in Philadelphia. Although only Caylor showed up in Philly, a subsequent November 2, 1881, meeting at the Gibson House in Cincinnati became the first formal meeting of the American Association. However, Hustling Horace wasn't the only Philadelphia representative there. Also in attendance from his old team was shortstop-manager-stockholder Chick Fulmer. At the persuasion of Caylor, the two Philadelphia teams called a temporary truce, or maybe a consolidation, which lasted until the next spring when the new league's principals re-assembled in Philadelphia. Sharsig and the Athletics now had the upper hand since he had a lease on the Oakdale Grounds, and they got the Philadelphia AA franchise. Thus was Horace Phillips outhustled and aced out temporarily from his brainchild.

Phillips remained with Reach and the still-independent Philadelphias as manager through July 1882, when he joined St. Louis's AA team as a "confidential agent." Before the year was out, the AA would hire him as an umpire (although he never served as such) and as a special front office assistant for the Pittsburgh Alleghenys. Finally, the AA sent him to Columbus to organize, from scratch, a new AA franchise for that city. When the 1883 season started, he was also the Columbus Colts' manager, finishing sixth with a 32-65 record, at least in AA games. The Colts, thanks to Phillips' hustling, ended up scheduling 175 games in 183 days—an unprecedented feat of scheduling at this time. Apparently feeling unfulfilled, he was part of the December 1883 Union Association organizational meeting in Philadelphia. Still, when the 1884 season started he was in Grand Rapids, Michigan, before being called back to the AA to take over as manager of the Pittsburgh Alleghenys late in their 10th place campaign. Since the Columbus team would fold at the end of the 1884 season, Phillips signed up some of his better Colts players for Pittsburgh in 1885, notably pitcher Ed Morris and right fielder Tom Brown. Almost an amalgamation of the Columbus and Pittsburgh teams, the Alleghenys jumped all the way to third in 1885 (56-55) and second in 1886 (80-57), thanks largely to Hustling Horace.

The Alleghenys' success, plus the desire of the National League to establish more eastern franchises, led the entire Pittsburgh organization to declare free agency for 1887, and jump, lock, stock, barrel and manager, to the older league, where they would eventually help cause the AA's downfall in 1891 and be re-named the Pirates. However, that latter development would be without Horace Phillips. He managed Pittsburgh's NL club with mediocre results in 1887 (55-69—except for one or two teams, the league was usually stronger than the association), 1888 (66-68) and 1889 until July 25, when he was relieved as manager and replaced by Philadelphian Fred Dunlap under very unusual circumstances. Some sources say it was fatigue; however, David Nemec and Brock Helander both tell a much more dramatic story of Phillips having, if not a mental breakdown, serious mental problems—imagining he was a wealthy tycoon, and trying to buy, among other things, the B& O Railroad, diamonds, jewelry, and all the other major league baseball franchises. The doctors believed he was suffering from paresis, the last stage of syphilis, and he was committed, with his wife, Anna's, approval, to an insane asylum in Merchantville, New Jersey, on August 1, 1889. In the late nineteenth century, paresis meant a fairly quick death. However, according to Helander, a "thoroughly rational" letter from Phillips appeared in the *Chicago Daily Tribune* in March 1890. Written from Grand Rapids, he said he was feeling fine, but that he was through with baseball. Nemec also reports that Phillips was supposedly still alive in 1894, thus leading to the conclusion that he was suffering from some sort of mental illness. Whatever it was, as Nemec puts it, he was never heard from again.

Sources: *National Baseball Library/John Thorn, The Beer & Whiskey League (David Nemec), Encyclopedia of Major League Baseball Teams (Donald Dewey and Nicholas Acocella), Richter's History and Records of Baseball (Francis Richter), Brock Helander, Frank Vaccaro, Boston Daily Globe, Washington Post, Family Search, Baseball Library.*

Tom Pratt

One of the true pioneers of baseball in the City of Brotherly Love, Thomas Jefferson Pratt followed Ben Franklin's path from Massachusetts to Philadelphia, after which he would often prove that a strike in time saves the nine. Along with Dick McBride, he was one of the city's two premier pitchers of the very early days.

Pratt was born in Massachusetts. That much is certain. It's the where and the when that are a little fuzzy. Most sources say he was born on January 26, 1844, in Chelsea, Massachusetts. However, LDS Church records also have him born on March 25, 1844, in Roxbury, Massachusetts. Wherever he was born in Massachusetts, his parents, Thomas and Fidelia Pratt, soon moved to Philadelphia, where young Tom became, like Dick McBride, a cricket player. Like McBride, he joined a baseball club when they started popping up all over the city in 1860. And, like McBride, he was very young, just a year older than the precocious Athletic ace in 1860 when he joined Winona as an outfielder, first baseman and right-handed pitcher.

Even at this early point in its development, the Athletic club was looking for good players. As a result, the 17-year-old Pratt and not the 16-year-old McBride—he played left field—was pitching for Athletic in 1861, and splitting four decisions. By 1862, Pratt and McBride were splitting Athletic's work in the pitchers' box, McBride playing short when he wasn't pitching and Pratt second. However, what seemed to be developing as a pretty good two-man rotation was broken up midway through the 1863 season, when the now–19-

year-old Pratt jumped to the team that would become Athletic's arch-rival, the Brooklyn Atlantic club. On the year, he appeared in seven games for each club, pitching and playing the infield (he was just an average hitter at best) when he wasn't in the box. Why did he do it? Although there is no evidence that a salary was involved, the inducement may have been an easy paying job in Brooklyn.

The 1864 and 1865 seasons were the peak of Pratt's career. He went undefeated as a pitcher (19-0 and 13-0) as Atlantic was the undisputed champion of the NABBP. Although he jumped back to Athletic briefly in 1866, he couldn't take the pitcher's job away from McBride, and ended up back with Atlantic in September, just in time to replace George Zettlein in the box as the Brooklyn club was attempting to defend its title. Although he lost 31–12 to his old Athletic teammates, he beat enough of the right teams (Eureka, Irvington and Mutual) to keep the whip pennant in Brooklyn under the NABBP's obtuse "take-two-out-of-three-from the-previous-champs" system of deciding its champion.

He played the 1867 season back in Philadelphia, but not with Athletic. A new club, Quaker City, had been formed to try and take Philadelphia supremacy away from Athletic, most probably by bringing in hired guns. Pratt (14-7 as a pitcher) and Quaker City gave Athletic a run for their money, but fell short, going 28-9 to Athletics' 44-3. Back in Brooklyn for 1868—most likely for more money—he had another undefeated season in the box, going 11-0, despite taking some time out to play the infield for the Tri-Mountain club of Boston.

Even though he was still just 25 years old, Tom Pratt's career as a baseball player was coming to an end. He pitched in just six games with Atlantic in 1869 (3-1) and then returned to Philadelphia for a fourth and final time in 1870 and 1871. Still unable to supplant McBride as Athletic's main pitcher, he played third base in 1870 (getting 2.87 hits per game, tied for last among the regulars), and one game at first (going two for six) for the 1871 National Association pennant winners. Although he would play a lot of cricket from then on, and still be involved in baseball, Tom Pratt's playing career was over after 12 years at the age of 27. Although no great shakes as a hitter, he had gone an estimated 80-19 as a pitcher. Like McBride, he was strictly a fastball pitcher, maybe faster than renowned speedballer George Zettlein. Also like McBride, Pratt was known for his headwork, his ability to deceive batters, despite throwing nothing but fastballs.

Pratt kept his hand in the game, in the management of Al Reach's 1882 Phillies, and as an umpire in the National Association and the National League, through the 1886 season. His most notable role though was with the Union Association. Pratt was Henry Lucas' main man in Philly, putting up the funds to establish the UA Philadelphia Keystones and becoming president of the team. Since Pratt's involvement in Philadelphia baseball dated back to before the Civil War, he knew what sort of names might attract fans in 1884. Since Athletic and Philadelphias were taken already, he went with Keystone, after the city's second pro team. Unfortunately, the name alone wasn't good enough to make a go of it; the Keystones went under, and Pratt lost his shirt on the deal.

Away from the diamond, Pratt was part of the family business, Pratt Bros., a paint and whitewash distributor and manufacturer in Philadelphia. In fact, his success with Pratt Bros. provided him with the funds to invest in the Keystones. Pratt and his wife, Georgie, had four children, daughters Emma and Addie and sons Thomas and Emmert. The second best Philadelphia pitcher-cricketeer died in Philadelphia on September 28, 1908, at age 64.

Sources: *Baseball's First Stars* (SABR), *The National Association of Base Ball Players* (Marshall Wright), *Encyclopedia of Major League Baseball Teams* (Donald Dewey and Nicholas Acocella), *Blackguards and Red Stockings* (William Ryczek), *American Pastimes* (Charles Peverelly), Brock Helander, Family Search.

Al Reach

Of all the individuals who could be said to have been *the* seminal figure in the development of baseball in Philadelphia, and the other candidates might include Thomas Fitzgerald, Hicks Hayhurst, Ben Shibe, Bill Sharsig, John Rogers, Billy Shettsline and Connie Mack, the man with the best claim to that title was born Alfred James Reach in London, England, on May 28 (or maybe May 25), 1840. Perhaps if we substitute the word "great" for "seminal" in discussing the evolution of the National Pastime in Philly, a clearer picture of Reach's importance to the city and the game may be obtained. That's because, when talking about true greatness among individuals, one way to separate the very head of the class from the merely remarkable is to use a broad definition of great in that, when talking about the pinnacle, great not only means skilled to an extraordinary degree, but also possessing the ability to create a paradigm shift in the individual's appointed field of endeavor.

Al Reach was not, as has been claimed, the first professional baseball player. This fallacy may date from his *New York Times* obituary on January 15, 1928, which stated as much. In reality, the weight of the evidence clearly indicates that Jim Creighton earned that distinction, either after he revolved from Niagara of Brooklyn to Star of Brooklyn during the 1859 season, or perhaps when he then revolved to Excelsior for the 1860 campaign. What does appear more likely is that Reach was the first openly professional baseball player—Creighton, and maybe others, having been paid under the table—as well as the first player paid a salary to change cities to play baseball. Since he was moving from Greater New York to Philadelphia, that makes him very important indeed to the game in the Quaker City. When Reach, who was previously a regular for Eckford of Brooklyn, joined Athletic for the 1865 season at a salary of $25 a week (some sources state this as $1000 a year or season), it marked both the start of Philadelphia getting serious about national-level baseball, and the city's first real challenge to New York's hegemony of the game—both of which were clearly seminal moments in the game's development in Philly.

A classic rags to riches story, Reach was the son of a trading agent and cricket player, Benjamin Reach, who brought his family to Brooklyn in 1841. There, Al earned money selling newspapers, and working as a ship caulker and iron molder in a foundry—some of his work went into building some of Fifth Avenue's finest hotels. In between helping his family make ends meet, and no doubt influenced by his father's cricket background, young Al took up the New York game, as the Knickerbocker version of the bat-and-ball sport was commonly known, in the mid–1850s.

At first playing as a left-handed catcher for the Jackson Juniors of the Williamsburg section, Reach moved to the Eckford club for the 1861 season, playing first, third and shortstop as Eckford went 8-4. The 5-6, 155 pound Reach quickly established himself as a hard hitter, and a sure-handed fielder, known as "Scratcher" for his ability for "digging" out ground balls. In 1862, Eckford not only won a tie-breaking third game following a home-and-home series from defending NABBP champion Atlantic, but they even had the most wins (14) and the best won-loss percentage (a 14-2 record) in the NABBP, thus establishing themselves as indubitably the 1862 title holders. Reach played just about everywhere—first, outfield, third and short—except the position he would become famous for, second base. At the plate, the scanty stats available for this season place his runs average at 4,1, placing him fifth among an Eckford regular nine that boasted the NABBP's top three scorers for the year. Eckford continued to hold the NABBP title in 1863, going 10-0, as Reach played only first base and scored a modest 16 runs in eight games. Eckford then had a disappointing season in 1864, playing just five games (a war-related slowdown?) and going 1-4. Reach played first again this year, and posted an average and over runs scored of 2,3—once again, about the middle of the pack in the Eckford lineup.

Although, at age 24, Reach was established as a regular on one of the NABBP's best teams, he also was not an offensive power, leading to the conclusion that his early reputation was based more on his fielding prowess. Jerrold Casway in his brief bio of Reach and Ben Shibe in the 2003 edition of SABR's *The National Pastime*, indicates that Reach made the first move, having been attracted by the "integrity and business acumen" of Athletic president Colonel Thomas Fitzgerald. Eckford, while Reach was on the club, had played Athletic twice, in October 1862 and June 1863, so it is possible that the ambitious Reach might have observed, or otherwise known, something about Fitzgerald and Athletic. However, it seems more likely that baseball historian Joseph M. Overfield, writing in SABR's *Nineteenth Century Stars*, had a better answer for Reach's appearing in the "A" uniform in 1865. "It was while playing for the Eckfords that he received an offer of $25 in 'expense money' to join the Athletics of Philadelphia." In other words, Fitzgerald was attracted to Reach's athletic ability, and offered him a salary to commute (because that's just what he did at first) the 100 miles to the south to play baseball. Since Eckford was apparently suffering from war-related blues, and Athletic was not, it shouldn't have been too hard a sell for a young man who wanted to get ahead. And that's a scenario that is more in keeping with the direction baseball, and baseball teams, would take—contact a top player, and pay him to play for you.

Either way, Reach got to Philadelphia for the 1865 season, and never looked back, establishing himself as the premier individual name in Philadelphia baseball for the next 40-odd years, or at least until Connie Mack started winning pennants with regularity. For his $25 a week in 1865, he did commute back and forth from his home in Brooklyn to Philadelphia for games—a do-able feat since Athletic played only 18 games over five months (June to November) in 1865. With Reach playing second base in 15 of those contests, posting a 3,12 average and over, good for third on the 15-3 team, Fitzgerald must have been pleased with the results of the original "business arrangement" the club had with Reach. At the start of the 1866 season, Fitzgerald set his second baseman up with a cigar and tobacco store in the heart of Center City, at 404½ Chestnut Street. This move proved just as popular in Philly as bringing Reach to town in the first place. His operation soon expanded to include ticket brokering and selling baseball gear, while establishing itself as *the* place for the city's sporting crowd, even though it was a distance from Athletic's field at 17th and Columbia. Given that circumstance, it's not surprising that Reach moved to Philadelphia's Frankford section after an 1866 season that saw Athletic go 23-2 and Reach increase his average and over to 5,19 on 134 runs scored—third in the NABBP behind Dick McBride's association record 160.

In 1867 Al Reach really became a star, starting a five-year run of offensive years that matched his defensive reputation. Although it's questionable that he was, as is sometimes claimed, the first second baseman to actually play between first and second, he apparently had a good enough arm to play his position very deep, and to be chosen as the second baseman on the 1871 *New York Clipper* All-Star team—the first ever media pronouncement of its type. What little fielding stats exist for Reach date from the end of his career, in the professional National Association, when he posted good fielding averages in the outfield (.857), second (.841) and first (.962), and a cumulative range factor better than the league mark.

His offensive peak started with his best year, 1867, and a new NABBP record of 270 runs scored, and a team-leading average of exactly six runs a game—figures that were helped somewhat by hitting 37 home runs in 47 games. He followed that up with 216 runs and 5,6 (tied for third in the NABBP) in 1868, and 248 and 5,18 (George Wright's 5,54 led the NABBP) in 1869. He was back in the middle of the Athletic team in offense in 1870 (3.03 hits per game) and then, when Athletic took the first official professional title in 1871, he still had enough left to post a .353 batting average and a 149 Adjusted OPS, finishing among the association's leaders in runs (10th), triples (8th) and RBIs (5th). His last season as a regular was 1872; as the fifth-oldest player in the association, he hit just .195. He played a little with the Athletics in 1874 and 1875, finishing his playing career in 1877 at 37 with the independent Athletics, scoring 85 runs in 94 games as a right fielder, although he originally considered coming back for the 1878 campaign. However, his influence on baseball in Philadelphia had barely begun.

During his 12-year playing career in Philadelphia, Reach was one of the city's best-known sporting figures, partly because he was a top player for the city's top team, but also because of his business ventures. In a fashion similar to the John McGraw–Wilbert Robinson-owned Diamond Café in Baltimore, which made those two worthies the biggest names in Baltimore baseball, Reach's multi-faceted store helped make its owner the key figure in Philadelphia baseball. It also didn't hurt that he displayed the tokens of the many Athletic victories—gilded game balls—in his store.

Having gotten his start from Colonel Fitzgerald, Reach used his popularity, his own business acumen, his personality—he was most commonly lauded for his integrity and described as respected by others—and his foresight to build a successful sporting goods empire, in a fashion exceeded only by his future partner, Albert Spalding. He promptly established a larger retail outlet for sporting goods just a few doors south of another key Center City Philadelphia intersection, Eighth and Market. This operation, at 6 South Eighth Street, so was successful that Reach had to move to larger quarters at 23 South Eight Street by 1881. This led to Reach getting into the manufacture of sporting goods, three years after he retired from play. It was this move that brought Reach into his best-known partnership, a relationship that would shape Philadelphia baseball for even longer than the lifespan of the two principals.

By the time Reach decided he needed to expand into manufacturing, Ben Shibe had long-since taken his father's modest harness-making business, combined it with his own impressive mechanical and inventive prowess, and turned it into a key player in the manufacture of leather sporting goods—especially baseballs. Instead of butting heads with the longer-established Shibe, Reach saw within a year that an alliance would be best for both companies. Shibe, who had been around baseball in Philadelphia long enough to know who Al Reach was, and what he represented, agreed. The new company, formed to wholesale sporting goods, was named for Reach and was located across Eighth Street from Reach's old store. The new company was run by Shibe as president and featured, as its headline product, the Shibe baseball.

At about this same time—the middle of 1881—Reach decided to make a foray into bringing major league baseball back to Philadelphia. Since Athletics was already taken by Bill Sharsig, Reach gave his team the other well-known local name—Philadelphias, or Phillies. Although Shibe was not involved in this venture, it may well be that Reach had a base in the Shibe semi-pro club to help build the Phillies.

As the American Association was being formed during the fall and winter of 1881,

Reach was one of two applicants for a Philadelphia franchise in the new loop, the other being Sharsig. This was one time when Reach's good name was not quite good enough, and his team lost out to Sharsig's Athletics because the latter had a guaranteed place to play, Sharsig having secured a lease on Oakdale Park. The history of Philadelphia baseball would have been much different if Reach had obtained the AA franchise. It is easy to speculate that his name, and business and leadership skills would have kept the franchise afloat a lot better, ensuring its survival during the Brotherhood War and maybe even its inclusion in the 1891 buyout of the AA by the National League. It is interesting to speculate what might have happened had the Phillies had entered the AA. Who knows what would have happened in either the great 1891 or 1900 shakeouts—would Philadelphia have been able to keep two teams in the NL, as did New York? Would Ban Johnson have even considered trying to move the American League into Philadelphia? Would Philly still have two teams to this day?

Al Reach's timing, either through luck or insight, was always good. First, his family moved to the U.S. to the epicenter of baseball when the game was first developing. Then, he moved to Philadelphia when baseball was on the verge of exploding in the Quaker City. Next, he joined with Shibe to market, among other things, the most indispensable product of the game, just as the National League was looking to re-enter the Philadelphia market. The 1882 season was a successful one for the team Reach established, and for which he served as treasurer. With the help of another old time Philly baseball star, Tom Pratt, he brought in such talent as Arlie Latham and Charlie Buffington, and even stole away the Athletics' 1881 manager, Horace Phillips, to manage the Phillies for part of the year.

After the 1882 season ended, National League president A.G. Mills contacted Reach to let him know that the NL wanted to move out of little Worcester, Massachusetts, and into big Philadelphia. Reach jumped at the opportunity, along with the team's other prominent investor, Philadelphia lawyer Colonel John Rogers, a highly irritating man who was in baseball for the money. This partnership would prove to be the only serious mistake of Al Reach's career. Although Reach and Rogers were initially minority partners, the Reach name had sufficient cachet in Philly so that he was named the first president of the Philadelphia Phillies.

To commemorate the occasion, and to add another product to the A.J. Reach Company product line, Reach began publishing the Reach Official Baseball Guide at this time. It provided a service for which he was eminently well-qualified, and which also helped the advance of the game by popularizing baseball statistics. Helped by the growth of the sporting goods business, and good attendance, first at Recreation Park and later at the new stadium at Broad and Lehigh—like Shibe, Reach was a stadium pioneer, building the first concrete stadium—Reach and Rogers eventually took over majority ownership of the Phillies. However, market pressures from the Spalding Company, plus the looming baseball labor issue posed by the Brotherhood, caused the businessman in Reach to suggest to his sporting goods partner that they sell their retail outlets to the Spalding Company. This was accomplished in December 1889, to the tune of $100,000, as part of Spalding's consolidation of his holdings into the growing sporting goods giant, A.G. Spalding Brothers. The deal with A.G. included Reach getting 600 shares of stock in the new corporate structure—but, more importantly, he also retained his company's name and the production side of the business, notably the business of wholesaling Shibe's baseballs. Shibe and Reach's brother Robert then set up a full-fledged factory at Palmer and Tulip Streets in the city's Frankford section. This move, along with the sale of Reach's high-value Center City properties, enabled the old second baseman to survive the Players League Brotherhood War in good financial shape—which, along with Spalding, made him the exception to the rule in the baseball world of 1890.

Unfortunately for Reach, Rogers was still his partner in the Phillies, with both holding equal shares of what was now the only major league game in town. The jealous attorney went back on his word to Reach, supposedly helping Harry Wright's widow after the long-time Phillies manager died in October 1895. Rogers bought out Isabelle Wright, and became majority owner with 53 percent of the stock. This despite an agreement he had with Reach that neither would upset the balance of the stock-holding. Reach's 43 percent now made him a figurehead president. It was this action that started the schism between Reach and Rogers, a break that would ultimately lead to Reach offering Rogers $150,000 for his shares in 1899, and then selling out in 1903, but not before he had helped his other partner—Ben Shibe—establish the American League Athletics as a direct competitor to the Phillies.

This latter move has long puzzled baseball followers. Why in the world would Shibe, whose flourishing primary source of business was in partnership with Reach—they'd opened another plant in Brantford, Ontario, and moved their wholesaling storefront operation to a large building at 1820 Chestnut Street—invest in a new venture that was in direct competition with his partner's other business—the Phillies? As Casway points out in his Reach-Shibe article, the answer is eminently simple. Reach was, if not financially a part of Shibe's American League move, at least highly supportive of same. That's because Reach and Shibe, long before the 1901 advent of the American League, had become far more than business partners. In 1894, Shibe's daughter, Mary, married Reach's only son, George. A pretty neat story, since the wedding was actually the product of the two families' closeness, not the cause of the relationship. It was said during the late nineteenth century that Reach and Shibe were like brothers, and, neither one made a business move without consulting the other. They also invested money together outside the Reach Company, and spent most of their social time in each other's company. Consequently, there should be no doubt that Shibe consulted with Reach before investing with Connie Mack and Ban Johnson in the American League.

Why then would Reach willingly give Shibe his blessing to create competition for the Phillies? There are two very easy answers. First, recalling Reach's legendary integrity, he obviously could not abide by the actions of the devious Rogers, and, having already had his 1899 offer to buy out the colonel rejected, he was looking to get out of the Phillies as soon as possible. Of course, the businessman in Reach—by this time he was well on his way to being a millionaire—also probably liked another part of Shibe's deal with Johnson. Part of the sweetener to get Shibe to sign on with the AL was Johnson's promise that the Reach baseball would be the official baseball of the American League.

It took a couple of years for Reach and Rogers to agree on selling the Phillies; however, the inevitable finally happened on February 28, 1903, when they sold the team for $170,000 in a deal mediated by Pittsburgh Pirates' owner Barney Dreyfuss. However, Reach and Rogers did not sell their park to the new owner, Philadelphia socialite James Potter. Instead, they kept the title to Philadelphia Park and leased it back to the new owners. Afterwards, Reach and Shibe carried on the sporting goods biz, highlighted by the Reach Company being granted an August 31, 1909, patent for a cork-centered baseball that would replace the rubber-centered baseball and help end the Deadball Era, ultimately allowing Babe Ruth to make his paradigm shift in the game.

Just prior to this, Reach took part in another baseball-related venture that, in hindsight, did little to advance the game, but did add more prestige to the name Reach. When, at A.G. Spalding's behest, baseball formed the 1907 A.G. Mills Commission to determine the origin of baseball, Reach, as both an associate of Spalding and Mills, and as a true baseball pioneer, was asked to join the commission. This was not Reach's finest hour, since the commission went in the tank to Spalding's wishes and proclaimed Abner Doubleday the inventor of baseball, and Reach, who was playing baseball in New York within 10 years of the Knickerbocker rules having been promulgated, must have known better.

Still, there was no doubt as to the identity of the towering figure in baseball in Philadelphia. "The establishment of Mr. Reach has grown to larger proportions, and the name is synonymous with baseball," opined the *Philadelphia Ledger* in 1915. Shortly thereafter, Reach, who was also an ardent golfer, retired to Atlantic City, leaving the Reach Company in the good hands of son George. He died on January 14, 1928, exactly six years to the day after his long-time partner and friend Ben Shibe died. Close in life and in death, Reach and Shibe, and their families, are all buried within a few hundred yards of each other at West Laurel Hill Cemetery, just outside of Philadelphia.

Perhaps the final word on Al Reach should belong to long-time Philadelphia sportswriters Frank Bilovsky and Rich Westcott, in *The Phillies Encyclopedia*: "Practically everything Reach did was done well and with good results." Both for him and the game he served so well in Philadelphia for so many years.

G	AB	R	H	2B	3B	HR	RBI	BA	OBP	SLG	OPS+
80	393	89	97	15	7	0	57	.247	.264	.321	73

Sources: *Nineteenth Century Stars* (SABR), *The National Pastime 2003* (SABR), *Phillies Encyclopedia* (Rich Westcott and Frank Bilovsky), *Occasional Glory* (David Jordan), *To Every Thing a Season* (Bruce Kuklick), *Encyclopedia of Major League Baseball Teams* (Donald Dewey and Nicholas Acocella), *The Ballplayers* (Mike Shatzkin, editor), *Biographical History of Baseball* (Donald Dewey and Nicholas Acocella), *Blackguards and Red Stockings* (William Ryczek), *Philadelphia North American*, *Brock Helander*, *Chicago Tribune*, *Baseball Library*, *The Deadball Era*.

Francis Richter

Before there was a *Sporting News*, there was *Sporting Life*. And there was Francis C. Richter. And, although it is for his Philadelphia-based baseball weekly that Philadelphian Francis Richter is best known, there are manifest other reasons he was one of the seminal figures of the professional game, from the early 1880s to his death in 1926.

Born in Philadelphia on January 26, 1854, Francis Charles Richter was one of the many young men in the city in that era that fell in love with baseball. An amateur player of some note in Philly as a young man, he was also one of the first baseball players who, figuring out that he wasn't quite good enough to make a career playing the game, turned to another aspect of baseball. In 1872, at the tender age of 18, he became a sportswriter for the *Philadelphia Day*. The paper's 26-year-old managing editor when the *Day* folded in 1880, Richter moved on to the *Sunday World* and *Public Ledger* where, it is claimed, he instituted the first complete sports department in any U.S. newspaper, or at least the first in Philadelphia. Whether or not that supposition is true, what is true is that the young editor and reporter was a close observer of the Philadelphia baseball scene in the late 1870s and early 1880s.

Although he referred to himself as a "printer" when the 1880 census came calling to his Philadelphia home—he was married to the former Helen Dwyer, 20, at the time, and they had a one-year-old daughter, also named Helen—Francis Richter was a writer, and an activist. He would play a role in the founding of the American Association in 1882 and the entry of the Philadelphia Athletics into same, and the founding of the NL Philadelphia Phillies in 1883. He was also a major supporter of the Players League in 1890, to the extent that, when John Montgomery Ward held his "wake" following the dissolution of that ill-fated venture in communal capitalism, Richter was one of the "mourners" he invited to Nick Engle's place in Manhattan. Obviously a proponent of competition in baseball, believing it to be good for the essential survival of the game, he also, in 1894 and 1900, tried to revive the American Association after it failed following the 1891 season. Despite efforts that may have seemed to the sport's moguls to be bent on tweaking organized baseball's collective nose, he was offered the presidency of the National League in 1907, possibly an indication that the baseball hierarchy understood that his basic motive was to improve the game. To baseball's loss, since Harry Pulliam's subsequent NL presidency was somewhat less than successful, Richter turned down the offer.

Richter always seemed to be on the scene when something important was happening in nineteenth century baseball because he was also the 1883 founder and editor of the weekly *Sporting Life*, the original bible of baseball. Richter published *Sporting Life*, which he started three years before *Sporting News*, until 1917, when the economic pressures associated with World War I drove him out of business. Such a fate did not befall the St. Louis–based *Sporting News*, because the Spinks were getting a subsidy from major league baseball. An unfair practice? Absolutely. The first time Richter had faced an unfair practice? Absolutely not. Back in 1890, in conjunction with the Brotherhood walkout that Richter supported, the National League had subsidized the start-up of O.P. Caylor's rival *Sporting Times* magazine. Even though the National League was willing to make Richter its president in 1907, you have to wonder if that gesture wasn't a case of trying to co-opt a thorn in its side, or an attempt to muzzle the independent newspaperman.

As much as Richter was identified with *Sporting Life* and new ventures, those were hardly his only contributions to baseball. After becoming a father for the second time in 1893—daughter Gladys would subsequently live to 1972 and see two major rounds of expansion in baseball, something her father surely would have approved of—Richter made unsuccessful 1894 and 1900 runs at reviving the AA, joining with such notable figures as Al Buckenberger, Billy Barnie, Fred Pfeffer, John McGraw, Cap Anson and Chris Von der Ahe. Yet, the one baseball pioneer he didn't ally with was Ban Johnson. Apparently, Richter did not understand the depth of Johnson's financial backing and initially withheld his support of the American League. Nonetheless, the AL made him editor of the *Reach Guide* in 1902, a job he would hold for the rest of his life.

And an eventful life it was. He would be a World's Series official for many years. As part of that role, he originally claimed the 1919 World's Series was on the up-and-up, proving no one's perfect. He helped persuade the Reds' Garry Herrmann to take a flyer at night baseball in 1914. In 1917 he wrote and published *History and Records of Baseball*, the first really comprehensive history of the game. Although Al Spalding and Spink had also published baseball histories, Richter's was the first arranged topically like a reference book and could also be said to be the first written without an axe to grind. Thus, going back to 1883 and going through 1926, was Francis Richter the publisher or editor of no less than three of the most important publications in baseball.

Richter would have one final distinction. Showing a good newspaperman's respect for deadlines, he finished the 1926 edition of the *Reach Guide* on February 11, 1926, one day before he died of bronchial pneumonia at his home in Philadelphia.

Sources: *Baseball's First Stars* (SABR), *Richter's History and Records of Baseball* (Francis Richter), *Baseball: The Early Years* (Harold Seymour), *American Baseball* (David Voigt), *The Beer & Whiskey League* (David Nemec), Family Search.

John Rogers

The Phillies' history of chief executives is not a glittering one. Horace Fogel was banned from baseball for impugning the integrity of the 1912 National League pennant race, several umpires, a couple of managers and league president Thomas Lynch. William Baker and Gerry Nugent became notorious for running shoestring operations that sold or traded off their best players to keep the team afloat. William Cox was banned from baseball after only one year (1943) for betting on the Phillies—a practice that was both dumb (they were 64-90 that year) and historic, since Cox thus joined Fogel as the only two NL CEOs ever permanently banned from the game.

Before all of them there was Colonel John Ignatius Rogers. Although no one banned him from the game, the Phillies might have been better off otherwise. Although Al Reach is usually recognized as the Phillies' president from the team's founding in 1883 until the team was sold to socialite James Potter in 1903, in fact John Rogers was the man running the team from just after Harry Wright's death (at the end of the 1895 season) until the Potter sale. And while Reach was, with good reason, widely revered in Philadelphia, Rogers was, also with good reason, as big a problem to the team as Reach was an asset. Read any account of the Phillies' first 20 years, and you'll see adjectives attached to various aspects of the colonel and his career in Philadelphia baseball, adjectives like self-promoting, stubborn, arrogant, overbearing, enraged, gloating, litigious, bitter, mean-spirited, long-winded meddler, suspicious, strident and manipulative.

John I. Rogers was born on May 27, 1844, in Philadelphia. The son of Irish-born parents who most likely were fleeing the potato famine, Rogers made his way up in the world quickly, earning a law degree from the University of Pennsylvania, and going into practice specializing in corporate and real estate law. As the proverbial Philadelphia lawyer, he became involved in politics, a connection that some have claimed attracted him to Reach who, it is also claimed, needed political clout to get the Phillies up and running in 1883. However, given Reach's long term high profile presence in Philadelphia, first as a player, then as a sporting goods entrepreneur and promoter, it seems unlikely that he needed much help, especially since he attempted to place a team in the better-established National League. Besides, Philadelphia was not New York, where a lack of Tammany Hall connections could get a streetcar line run through the property where you wanted to build your ball field. It does not seem as if the Phillies had many political problems getting established in Philadelphia, although Rogers' political connections couldn't have hurt. He had served a term in the state legislature and was also appointed judge-advocate of the state national guard. This legal position entitled him to the rank of colonel, a title he would use the rest of his life.

When the team was formed, Reach (20 shares) and Rogers (10 shares) were minority partners with Reach, thanks to his baseball experience, being named president and Rogers being named secretary, an indication of his importance from the beginning. Although some accounts state that Reach and Rogers each put up half the money to fund the new team, they didn't become the majority owners until near the end of the 1880s.

Despite his various faults, or maybe because of them, Rogers eventually stepped out of the shadow of the high-profile Reach, partly because he became a leading legal advocate for the National League. With both the Brotherhood and American Association disputes, and later the American League brouhaha, to litigate, Rogers' experience in corporate law came in handy for the league as a whole. Handy, but not always successful, since he lost the suit to keep Bill Hallman with the Phillies in 1890, just like the National League lost various other suits at the same time.

Rogers married a Philadelphia girl, 19-year-old Elizabeth H. Henkels, in Germantown on January 20, 1876. The colonel and Elizabeth would have four sons, John, Frank, Karl and Edmund, none of whom seem to have been involved in baseball in any significant way. This shouldn't be too surprising, since dad was in the game strictly for profit and prestige. There is no evidence that he cared much about baseball for the game's sake. One indication of that was the 15-foot-wide bicycle race track built around the edges of the new Huntingdon Avenue Grounds in 1887, an action that reeks of Rogers and his hunt for the almighty dollar. He would do anything to maximize profits, squeezing out every last cent, a fault that would come back to haunt the Phillies time and again in the future.

Rogers' increasing importance in National League circles led to his taking a more active role with the Phillies, especially during the Brotherhood war and its aftermath. This was clearly manifested after the Players League collapsed. Reach wanted to let most, if not all, of the Phillies' defectors back in the fold, while Rogers was violently opposed to such a move. Indicating Rogers' growing power within the franchise, only the dying Jim Fogarty and Ed Delahanty came back — most of the rest of the ex–Phillies stayed ex–Phillies and played elsewhere in the NL or AA.

Rogers next threw his weight around after the 1893 season, when, by all accounts, he persuaded Reach that the Father of Professional Baseball, Harry Wright, had to go as Phillies' manager. Although Rogers' questions about the Phillies' relative lack of success despite having such a ferocious offensive attack were quite germane, and would continue to be for the next few years, it is less certain just how much Wright could have done about the pitching shorts, or how much the composition of the pitching staff was his fault. It was just as true then as it is now that you can't make a silk purse out of a sow's ear, and the Phillies' pitchers were largely a bunch of pigs.

If Rogers was on-target in his criticism of the Phillies' pitching, he was way off base in his next move. Under the guise of helping out Isabelle Wright after her husband died in October 1895, Rogers went behind Reach's back and bought the Wrights' share of the Phillies, giving him, for the first time, a clear and sole majority interest in the team. From then on until they sold out to Potter, et al., John Rogers was running the Phillies. He also took advantage of this move to make himself secretary-treasurer and, as such, to award himself a healthy raise.

When someone like this takes over a baseball team, he often proceeds to run said team into the ground. And yet, through several contretemps with Reach, his players, some of the other owners in the National League, and the American League, that's not really what happened in Philadelphia under John Rogers. In the period from 1899 to 1901, the Phillies finished third, third and second. Now maybe Rogers was listening to Reach on baseball matters, or maybe Rogers really was pretty good at recognizing baseball talent — although his trade of Billy Hamilton for the washed up Billy Nash would argue against that. Or maybe Billy Shettsline was a great manager. Whatever the reason, the Phillies bounced back from bad years in 1896 and 1897 and were generally a good team in the turn of the century years under Rogers' control, despite his terrible relations with the players.

The Reach-Rogers era started to come to an end in 1901, when the former, rightly believing the latter had violated his trust in the Wright stock deal, started to pull away from the Phillies, and to support his sporting goods partner and friend, Ben Shibe, in the establishment of the American League Athletics. Besides, Reach was probably tired of warring with Rogers. As a result, the colonel had one more battle to fight, first losing (in 1901) and then winning (in 1902) a suit against the American League and the Athletics, a suit to regain the services of the Phillies players, notably Nap Lajoie, who had jumped to the AL. This time Rogers won several battles, but lost the war. By winning round two in the Pennsylvania Supreme Court in April 1902, he forced pitchers Frosty Bill Duggleby and Chick Fraser back to the Phillies from the A's. However, Rogers then blew the negotiations with Lajoie for his return by playing hardball—a not surprising development, since Lajoie had no love for Rogers. The Frenchman ended up with the AL Cleveland Blues along with fellow future Hall of Famer Elmer Flick and Strawberry Bill Bernhard.

Even while he was doing battle in the courts with the AL, John Rogers was warring with his own league, or, at least, some of the owners. His most famous tete a tete within the National League took place at the league meeting in December 1901, when Andrew Freedman and John Brush were trying to turn the National League into one big trust. Rogers engineered a rump election of Al Spalding as league president, effectively turning back the syndication scheme for good.

Despite his legal victory over the AL in 1902, and the attendant crowing over same, Rogers ultimately lost the war, as the NL and the AL buried the hatchet on January 11, 1903, about six weeks before Reach and Rogers finally sold the team. Exactly how much effect the NL-AL peace had on the sale, or what Rogers thought about the whole matter, is strictly conjecture. However, it's pretty easy to speculate that the man who sued to keep his players in 1901 wouldn't have been thrilled to realize that he probably wouldn't be getting his players back in 1903. While Reach had been willing to get out for a long time, it's not hard to believe that the NL-AL peace was the last straw for Rogers.

John Rogers' last connection with baseball was still with Al Reach. When they sold the Phillies, they kept the Philadelphia ballpark, and leased it to the new owners for $10,000 a year, a contract that would get Rogers sued following the August 1903 collapse of part of the stands that killed 12 and injured more than 200 fans.

The litigious life of John I. Rogers came to an end at the age of 65 on March 13, 1910, just before the start of the baseball season.

Sources: *Phillies Encyclopedia (Rich Westcott and Frank Bilovsky), Occasional Glory (David Jordan), Encyclopedia of Major League Baseball Teams (Donald Dewey and Nicholas Acocella), The National Pastime 2003 (SABR), Family Search.*

Bill Sharsig

If Hicks Hayhurst was the first great professional baseball executive in Philadelphia, then William A. "Bill" Sharsig was the second—despite the fact that he was originally a theatrical producer.

Born in 1855 in Philadelphia with a very supportive mother, Sharsig was precocious on both the stage and in baseball. Before he was 25 years old he was already a theatrical producer, though clearly one with interests and designs beyond the floorboards of the

Chestnut Street Theater. Although there are a couple of different versions of the story, young Sharsig decided to go into baseball as an executive and promoter in 1880, in effect stepping into the leadership vacuum left by Hayhurst's retirement from the pro game, and the organizational vacuum left by the Athletics' failure in the summer of 1880. A promoter with a vision, Sharsig saw that there was plenty of room in a major city like Philadelphia for professional baseball to flourish, as indeed it had already done since 1868. As a result, Sharsig funded the September 1880 re-organization of the Philadelphia Athletics that had folded a couple of months before. The money to build a baseball team with pretensions of national stature came from the young promoter's mother. Mom Sharsig proved to be most helpful, donating her life's savings so that son Bill could bring the name Athletics back into the forefront of the national sporting scene.

When Sharsig first got involved with baseball, William Hulbert was still running the only major league, the National League, which meant there was no place for a Philadelphia team. Undaunted by this, Sharsig sent his Athletics out on a national tour in 1881, through Pittsburgh, Columbus, Louisville and Cincinnati, and going as far as St. Louis, playing other independent teams—a venture that helped illustrate how much interest there was in professional baseball in cities that did not have National League franchises.

Sharsig's partners in this venture were former player Charlie Mason and former major league manager Horace Phillips. Eventually, Phillips jumped to Al Reach's Philadelphias, and a character that Sharsig presumably knew from show biz, minstrel Lew Simmons, took his place. It is probably accurate to say that Sharsig would end up wishing that Simmons had stayed in blackface.

The success of the Athletics' tour, and the ambition of Sharsig's 1881 manager, Hustling Horace Phillips, were a direct cause of the creation of the American Association in late 1881 and early 1882. However, just because Sharsig had sowed the seeds didn't mean his Athletics were automatic members; another local team, the Philadelphias, were also applying for the Philly spot in the AA. However, Sharsig and company won out, thanks to his foresight in keeping his existing lease on the Oakdale Park grounds. And so, starting with the first AA season in 1882, and lasting partway into the 1891 season, Bill Sharsig would ride a roller coaster with his Athletics.

Although the Athletics won the 1883 AA pennant, and were profitable up until the Players League war, no team has ever had a more confused managerial record than Sharsig's Athletics. Some sources even say that Billy Martin's five tours of duty as Yankees manager broke Sharsig's own personal record of managing the Athletics four different times. Suffice it to say that, due to a variety of circumstances having to do with the instability of the rest of the team's ownership, Bill Sharsig had more than one occasion to come on to the field and manage his team, even though this was contrary to Athletics' policy, which stated that the uniformed captain had complete suzerainty during the games. Historian Norman Macht says that Sharsig took over as Athletics manager at the end of every season from 1884 to 1887, before becoming the full-time manager in 1888. Francis Richter actually gives Sharsig credit for being the manager of the 1883 team, instead of Simmons, who is more often given credit. Actually, Sharsig was more of a general manager and traveling secretary than a field manager, a job that was handled by captain Lon Knight. Donald Dewey and Nicholas Acocella give Sharsig credit for taking over in the latter part of the 1884 and 1886 seasons, and for running the team on the field by himself from the start of 1888 through the beginning of 1891.

Some of the managerial musical chairs may have been a function of the general administrative chaos of the Athletics, as Sharsig, Simmons and Mason seemed to rotate through the various team leadership functions. Sharsig, who was essentially the senior partner among the three from at least the start of the team's AA days until 1888, served as president from 1882 to 1886, and then as secretary in 1887. Simmons had a short term as manager in 1886, and served as president in 1887. Mason also seems to have managed, or at least held the managerial title, in 1884 and 1887. Following the 1887 season, Sharsig, possibly tiring of the revolving door approach to management, engineered buying out Simmons and Mason, and selling their shares to H.C. Pennypacker and William Whittaker. Sharsig remained on as secretary until 1890, while also serving as manager.

However often or seldom Sharsig managed the Athletics—Old Judge issued an 1888 baseball card of him, dressed in a natty three-piece suit, overcoat and bowler, and identifying him as the Athletics' manager—he became a popular figure among Philly baseball fans. That was partly because, according to Macht, he was a fine handler of men and a kind, but firm, disciplinarian—traits that would also come in handy in his dealings with Simmons and future partners H.C. Pennypacker, William Whittaker, J. Earle Wagner and George Wagner. Indeed, Sharsig's one great failing as a baseball executive seems to have been in his choice of partners—not that those choices were always his.

Although Sharsig turned down several offers to sell his team at a profit, he outlasted all but the Wagners and the Players League war. After he finally dropped Simmons and Mason at the start of the 1888 season, he did, by all accounts, a good job managing until the Players League war, when Pennypacker's and Whittaker's hefty salaries bankrupted the franchise late in the 1890 season. Sharsig was then unsuccessful in rallying the Athletics' minority partners, one of who was Ben Shibe, to keep the team out of the hands of the Wagner brothers. When the AA awarded the Philadelphia franchise to the Wagners, part of the deal must have been a settlement of some kind with the minority partners who had sued to keep the Wagners out. It was a settlement that, in effect, finally forced Sharsig to sell his piece of his team. The Wagners then kept him on as just the manager for the start of the 1891 season, before firing him 17 games into the season. Even though Sharsig would then sue J. Earle Wagner for breach of contract—presumably his managerial contract—his association with the Athletics was over.

But not his association with baseball. By the start of the 1892 season, he was managing the Indianapolis Hoosiers of the Western League. Of more importance, he was still a significant enough figure in baseball that, in March 1893, he was a prominent delegate at the historic meeting of the National League that increased the pitching distance to 60 feet, six inches. This despite the fact that he'd never had any direct association with the NL. In such an august group, including such luminaries as Francis Richter, Frank Selee, Harry Wright, John Montgomery Ward and Billy Barnie, Bill Sharsig fit right in.

For the rest of the 1890s, he managed other minor league teams in Pennsylvania, including the 1897 Atlantic League Athletics, although his most significant managerial job came with the Indianapolis Hoosiers in 1894. By that point, the Western League was being run by Ban Johnson, and was on its way to becoming the American League. When that organization came to Philadelphia in 1901, Bill Sharsig wasn't forgotten. Connie Mack, possibly thanks to a word from Johnson, or possibly thanks to Ben Shibe, hired the old Athletic as early as January 1901 as the new Athletics' business manager. Sadly enough, one of the under-rated contributors to the game of professional baseball died in his 47th year on February 1, 1902, and was buried in Mt. Vernon Cemetery in Philadelphia, just eight months before he would have seen another Athletics' pennant raised.

Managerial Record

W	L	PCT
238	216	.524

Sources: *The Beer & Whiskey League (David Nemec), Encyclopedia of Major League Baseball Teams (Donald Dewey and Nicholas Acocella), Brock Helander, Brooklyn Eagle, Baseball Library.*

Bill Shettsline

While Lave Cross had the unique distinction of playing for four different Philadelphia professional baseball teams, William Joseph Shettsline, also known as "Mr. Phillie," had the unique distinction of working in an administrative capacity for three different Philadelphia professional baseball teams, and in just about every aspect of the sport, over a period of 44 years.

Bill Shettsline was born on October 25, 1863, in Philadelphia to Jonathan and Elizabeth Shettsline. His parents had been married since 1854, and Billy was the fourth of five children. Where some baseball executives, like Andy McPhail, come from baseball families, Bill Shettsline came from a family of coach painters. An 1880 U.S. Census taker reported that Jonathan Shettsline and his two oldest sons, James and John, were employed as coach painters. Youngest son Bill was at school at the time, and he was about to embark on a much different career path.

Starting in 1884, Bill Shettsline became a baseball man, with the Union Association Philadelphia Keystones. A sandlot player as a kid, Shettsline was involved in the short-lived Keystones franchise, although the nature of his involvement is uncertain. Donald Dewey and Nicholas Acocella state that Shettsline, along with Tom Pratt, "backed" the Keystones. Did a 20-year-old son of a coach painter have the money to back a professional baseball team? More likely, UA president Henry Lucas, who had a hand in virtually everything that went on in the UA during its one year, was involved in some fashion behind the scenes, maybe making the well-known Pratt the front man. Or maybe Shettsline, a painter, knew Pratt, a paint distributor. Shettsline's role is subject to conjecture, although historian Norman Macht probably has it right—Shettsline was a ticket seller at Keystone Park.

After the Keystones folded, the Phillies picked up the 21-year-old Shettsline, who has been described as a protégé of Colonel John Rogers and an aspiring attorney himself. Shettsline started at the bottom with the Phillies as a handyman–office boy and ticket taker, before moving up to assistant secretary and then secretary. He was serving in the latter role when he was the choice of Rogers and Reach to take over the manager's job when the players revolted against George Stallings, resulting in his firing on June 18, 1898. This was a move that reeked of Rogers' penchant for squeezing nickels, since it represented a way of saving a salary by bringing in someone who was already on the payroll.

The person Rogers brought in to manage was surely familiar with the administrative side of baseball after 14 years in that sector. But you can imagine the fans saying, "He never played the game!" Shettsline did have some experience with baseball strategic policy. In 1896, when Rogers canned Art Irwin as manager and traded Billy Hamilton for Billy Nash, the lesser Billy became the team's game manager, and Shettsline, for the 1896 season, was made responsible for overall strategic policy. Exactly what that means is hard to say; it sounds a bit like he was made what we would now call the general manger.

Even with that experience, it would still seem as if Shettsline was poorly equipped to manage the Phillies on the field in 1898. But, he had one tremendous asset. His cheery, kindly, easy-going, likeable personality was just what the team needed after the inflammatory Stallings. The pride of Glenolden, Delaware County, was an immediate hit as manager, taking over the '98 club at 19-27 in eighth place and leading them to a 59-44 record the rest of the way, and a sixth place finish.

Shettsline would go on to lead the Phillies to their late-century renaissance, finishing third, third and second before the results of two years of American League raids dropped the team to seventh in 1902. As to whether the single most notable event of this period—the electrical sign-stealing gimmick the Phillies were caught with in September 1900—was Shettsline's doing, the manager claimed innocence, and such a trick does sound much more like the work of the devious Rogers than it does of the easy-going Shettsline.

The team's 56-81 record in 1902, which left Shettsline with an overall 367-303 mark as a manager, was hardly the manager's fault, but it did cost him his managerial job indirectly, mainly because it was also part of the straw that broke the camel's back in the deteriorating relationship between Reach and Rogers. With attendance dropping 50 percent from 1901 to 1902, both of the team's main owners decided it was time to get out, selling the team in March 1903 to a group led by socialite James Potter. Despite Shettsline's success as a manager, he was kicked back upstairs to the front office, with Chief Zimmer coming over from Pittsburgh—Pirates owner Barney Dreyfuss mediated the sale—to take his place as manager.

Shettsline, who being of Taftian proportions, had managed in street clothes, then became the team's business manager just in time to suffer along with park owners Reach and Rogers when the stands at Philadelphia Park collapsed on August 8, 1903. Shettsline was in charge of park operations at the time and was reported to be so upset by the disaster that he could hardly talk. He could, though, issue a statement from Potter the next day, saying the club's owners had no liability in the matter.

The August 1903 disaster turned out to be the worst in Philadelphia baseball history. And yet, such was the popularity of Shettsline that he not only did not suffer bad fallout from the affair, but he was also a popular choice to succeed Potter as club president in 1905, serving in that capacity through to 1908, when Philadelphia Republican political bosses Israel Durham and James McNichol bought the team. The highlights of Shettsline's tenure as president included signing Sherry Magee, trading for Kitty Bransfield, and setting club attendance records in 1905 (317,932) and 1908 (420,660).

Some sources say Shettsline stayed on as club president through 1915, but this seems unlikely, since the Durham-McNichol ownership, the Horace Fogel ownership, the Albert Wiler presidency and the William Lock ownership came and went before William Baker took over the team after Wiler died in July 1913. Most likely, Shettsline went back to being business manager in 1908, and was something like an interim president between the various 1908 to 1913 administrations.

Shettsline survived as business manager under the grossly-undercapitalized Baker until 1927. How poor were the Phillies in those days? For a number of years in the '20s, the grass at what was now called Baker Bowl was "cut" by two ewes and a ram as a cost-saving measure. In 1925 though, the ram took umbrage at Shettsline's presence on the field, and charged the ponderous executive, leading to the ultimate banishment of the sheep. Although Shettsline survived the ram's attack, he couldn't survive nepotism after 42 years with the Phillies. Gerry Nugent joined the team's front office in 1925 and married Mae Mallon, who happened to be Baker's secretary. Following the 1927 season, Nugent took Shettsline's job as business manager. When Baker died in 1930, Nugent succeeded him as president.

As for Billy Shettsline, he joined the Athletics front office for the 1928 season before finally retiring. Only Connie Mack would end up serving in the administrative end of a Philadelphia baseball team for longer than Shettsline, who died in Philadelphia on February 22, 1933, at the age of 69.

Managerial Record

W	L	PCT
367	303	.548

Sources: *Phillies Encyclopedia (Rich Wescott and Frank Bilovsky), Occasional Glory (David Jordan), Encyclopedia of Major League Baseball Teams (Donald Dewey and Nicholas Acocella), Philadelphia's Old Ballparks (Rich Westcott), Family Search.*

Ben Shibe

Any Philadelphia baseball fan over the age of about 60 can never forget Shibe Park, the glorious old ballpark that stood at 21st and Lehigh from 1909 until the Bicentennial. In fact, it would probably not be incorrect to say that most older Philly fans still refer to that now-long demolished stadium as Shibe Park, and not by its second incarnation, Connie Mack Stadium. Some of those fans, like the author's father, still even have a piece or two of old Shibe Park, in some cases bought from the owner of the salvage rights, George Berdine, and in some cases lifted from Connie Mack Stadium during the riotous final game in 1970.

Those fans may also know the name Benjamin Franklin Shibe, but the details of this notable Philadelphian's life, and his many contributions to the game, have largely been forgotten in the 80-some years since his death. And that's a shame, because, Benjamin Franklin Shibe, named after Philadelphia's most glorious adopted son, was, like his namesake, an inventor of some note and a man worth remembering.

Born on January 28, 1838 (although the 1880 census has him born in 1839), in the working class Fishtown section of Kensington, Ben Shibe had neither a great deal of formal education, nor much of a pedigree as a baseball player, the latter handicap being due to a leg injury. However, he did have a brilliant sense of all things mechanical, and would go on to hold, in his own name, many patents, of which his most famous, in a baseball sense, was his invention of a machine for making (more accurately, winding) baseballs. Described by Bruce Kuklick in *To Every Thing a Season* as "the most prolific technical innovator in the sport," and by Bill James in *The Bill James Historical Baseball Abstract* as "one of baseball's great innovators," Shibe was originally a horse car driver in the city. However, his mechanical genius soon led him to gravitate to his father's small harness-making business and hardware business, also located in Kensington.

Along with his brother John, Shibe took over the business and expanded its product line to include baseball and cricket bats, as well as leather sporting goods, most notably, the baseballs whose four-part covers were originally hand-sown by neighborhood women, and later wound with an ingenious two-part cover—that Shibe popularized—on Ben's ground-breaking winding machine. He also developed a machine that cut out and punched the holes in the baseball covers. The business was already thriving in 1880, when Shibe

Baseball's great inventor, Ben Shibe (left), looking crusty and dour, on December 16, 1910, with nineteenth century Hall of Fame player Hugh Duffy (Library of Congess photograph).

described himself as a "Baseball Manufacturer" to the census taker. Living in Philadelphia's 31st Ward after moving his family back to the city from New Jersey sometime after 1872, Shibe and wife Josephine Fritz Shibe had three children, son Thomas and daughters Alice and Mary. Younger son Jack, who along with Tom would later help run the American League Athletics, hadn't been born yet. And, youngest daughter Mary, then eight, was still a little young to show any interest in Al Reach's son, George.

A *Sports Illustrated* study in the 1950s found that, at that time, there were 65 patents held by people trying to improve the baseball, and that Ben Shibe held more than anyone else. So, it should come as no surprise that Shibe's success in this market led to his partnership with the ambitious and canny Al Reach in 1881, as both men realized the benefits of an alliance, as opposed to a competition between Shibe's manufacturing efforts and Reach's retail-wholesale efforts. It was, in fact, a match made in baseball heaven.

Shibe's interest in baseball for many years had extended beyond making the game's equipment. He had a long history in Philadelphia baseball as a fan and an Athletic club supporter. Even before forming his own team in the late 1870s, he was a fan of the original Athletic club and its star second baseman, Al Reach. So, it wasn't too big a jump for Shibe to become the main stockholder in one of the city's top semi-pro clubs, known as the Shibe Ball Club. He also later became a minority partner in the American Association Athletics. However, he lost both that position and his investment when the first AA Athletics franchise collapsed near the end of the disastrous 1890 season. Undeterred, he personally brought the Athletic name back to Philadelphia baseball in the minor leagues by backing a team called Athletics in the Eastern League in the 1890s.

Of course, Shibe is best known outside the sporting goods world as the key founder, along with Connie Mack, of the American League Athletics. Shibe had been making baseballs for Ban Johnson's league when it was still the minor Western League. Johnson, having made the decision to expand into Philadelphia after the 1900 National League consolidation, and in light of the fact that there was only one major league team in a city the size of Philadelphia and the city bore such a distinguished baseball pedigree, suggested to Connie Mack that he look up Ben Shibe, by this time quite a rich captain of the sporting goods industry. Both Kuklick and Fred Lieb, in *Connie Mack: Grand Old Man of Baseball*, claim that Shibe was always a supporter of the two-league concept, making him a natural for an American League franchise, despite his partnership with then–Phillies president Reach. And, he may have been. However, it's more likely that the businessman in Shibe played a big role in his interest from the start, since he was also attracted from his December 1900 meeting with Mack to the offer to make the American League's baseballs.

Either way, "Uncle Ben," as he was known at this time, came on board—most likely after consulting with Reach, who undoubtedly also knew a good business opportunity when he saw one—as a 50 percent stockholder in the Athletics, and the team president. In fact, Kuklick claims that Reach *recommended* Shibe as an owner of the new team. Kuklick also says that Shibe wanted the social standing that came with being a team owner—having enjoyed said status previously—and that he wanted to foster the sport's good name, something that would have also benefited his various baseball-related investments. Just how much money Shibe put up, and when he put it up, is unknown—he may well have both purchased his half-share of the total $50,000 in stock, and also put up the money for the quarter-share owned by Philadelphia sportswriters Frank Hough and Butch Jones. Kuklick also states Shibe didn't actually buy in to the Athletics until after April 26, 1901—the opening day sellout at Columbia Park. As for the development of the new team, Lieb tells the story, probably apocryphal, that Shibe was appalled when Mack told him they would probably go after the Phillies' players. Ben Shibe was no fool, and he knew very well, from his past experiences in baseball, how new leagues obtained their players. And Al Reach, himself the first player to change cities for money, knew this as well when he approved his partner's move.

Thanks in part to Hough and Jones' support in print, and several ex–Phillies, the Athletics were a big hit, both at the box office and on the field from the start, leading Mack (who held the other quarter share) and Shibe to realize that their little Columbia Park was way too small. Thus was born in 1909 Shibe Park, at a location chosen by Shibe, and under Shibe's direction, providing the man's most enduring physical legacy and being the first iron and concrete stadium. A close second to Shibe Park as a monument to Uncle Ben was his invention, patented in the same year the park opened, of the cork-centered baseball, which would swing the delicate balance of offense and defense back to the batters and ultimately help put an end to the Deadball Era.

Soon after the edifice bearing his name was erected, the humble and basically retiring Shibe—although he was often referred to in print as being both dour and crusty—turned the daily management of the franchise over to Mack, Tom, Shibe and playboy-socialite Jack Shibe—both of whom had been big supporters of their father's return to major league baseball from the start. This, however, may well have been a mistake, this being one of the cases where the sons couldn't match up to the father's business acumen.

Still, when Ben Shibe died in his native Philadelphia on January 14, 1922, his name was indeed known throughout the region as one of the original pillars of baseball management in the City of Brotherly Love.

Sources: *The National Pastime 2003 (SABR), Connie Mack: Grand Old Man of Baseball (Fred Lieb), Occasional Glory (David Jordan), The Athletics of Philadelphia (David Jordan), The Historical Baseball Abstract (Bill James), To Every Thing a Season (Bruce Kuklick), Family Search.*

Harry Stovey

Let's get one thing about Harry Duffield (Stow or Stowe) Stovey out of the way, right from the very start. Harry Stovey should have been an inductee into the National Baseball Hall of Fame back when they first were choosing nineteenth century players to honor. Because Harry Stovey is, by any reasonable measure, a Hall of Famer. This guy could hit. And yet, the Quaker City's best baseball playing native son of the nineteenth century has been left out of the Hall—an egregious failure that has played a role in his present anonymity. The most common reason given to explain his absence is because he played half of his 14 major league seasons (1880–1893) for the Philadelphia Athletics of the American Association, and the Hall has traditionally treated AA stars shabbily. It may also be that, like many old-time, and even present day, stars, he suffered from bad timing and relative anonymity after leaving the game.

Stovey's Philadelphia pedigree is as good as they come—he was born Harry Stow(e) in Philadelphia on December 20, 1856, and was related to one of the 1753 recasters of the Liberty Bell, John Stow. Stow and fellow foundry worker John Pass actually melted down the cracked bell and recast it twice that year. Most sources list Harry's birth name as Stowe, however, the name engraved on the Bell is "Pass and Stow." Either way, from the very beginning, the gentlemanly and articulate Harry Stow played under the nom de diamond Stovey so his mother wouldn't find out about his being a professional baseball player.

Before he turned pro, he was a product of the Philadelphia club system, starting out as a right-handed pitcher for the Defiance club in 1877. The Athletics, though having been evicted from the National League following the 1876 season, were still playing top-level professional baseball as an independent team in 1877, and signed the local boy away from Defiance. Stovey made his professional debut on September 4, 1877, beating Chicago 6–5, the first of several successful performances on the mound for the 1877 Athletics. The next year, famed baseball executive Frank Bancroft signed Stovey for New Bedford of the International Association and moved him more regularly to first and the outfield. After two years, Stovey followed Bancroft to Worcester and the National League.

Stovey's move to Massachusetts would have long-lasting implications for the young Philadelphian. He liked New Bedford so much that he moved there, and ultimately retired from baseball to nearby Fall River. Of course, Stovey did have an ulterior motive, a young woman named Mary, born in 1862, that he met and married while playing minor league ball in the Bay State. By the time of the 1880 census, the Stowes (that's how Harry gave his name to the census taker—Stowe) had a three month old daughter, Elizzia.

Starting out with the Worcester Ruby Legs as a 5-11, 180 pound, 23-year-old outfielder–first baseman in 1880, Stovey played his first three seasons in the National League as the best player for that short-lived franchise, breaking in with a bang by leading the NL in triples (14) and home runs (6) as a rookie. When Worcester's franchise was terminated by the NL both the new Phillies and the one-year-old AA Athletics wanted Stovey to return to his home town to play for them. He chose the better-established

The best eligible player not in the Baseball Hall of Fame, Philadelphia's Harry Stovey (Library of Congress photograph).

Athletics, beginning his seven-year reign of terror in the AA. He started off by leading the Athletics to the 1883 AA pennant, and setting a major league record for home runs with 14 in the process. And, he would only get better over the next couple of years.

Throughout the remainder of the 1880s, Stovey was, along with Pete Browning, the dominant hitter in the AA. A SABR poll of nineteenth century baseball experts taken in 1983 showed that these two AA stalwarts were the nineteenth century players most deserving of admittance to Cooperstown. Not George Davis, not Bid McPhee, both of whom have been since enshrined, but Harry Stovey and Pete Browning.

Stovey's best year was probably 1884, although the Faber System's total player ranking has him the best player in the AA in 1885, when his adjusted OPS peaked at 186 on the strength of a .326/.368/.545 year that saw him lead the loop in runs (124), triples (23—the equivalent of 35 triples in a 162 game season), runs created (89) and extra-base hits (55). Although he would run afoul of volatile part-owner Lew Simmons after the 1884 season—Simmons making the absurd claim that Stovey was responsible for the team's fall from first to seventh—co-owners Bill Sharsig and Charlie Mason supported Stovey, and actually made him captain-manager for 1885. Although his adjusted OPS was still 163, the Athletics actually had a worse won-loss record (55-57) than they had in 1884, though the team did move up to fourth place. Stovey returned to just playing the outfield, plus a little first base, after 1885.

After four more fine years in Philadelphia, he joined the exodus from the foundering Athletics to the Players League, helping Boston win that league's title in 1890. When the Players League folded after a single year, he returned to the National League, also with Boston, and became enmeshed in one of the biggest controversies of his era. Somebody in the AA, most likely a league official since the AA had taken over the Philadelphia franchise late in the 1890 season, failed to reserve Stovey (and Lou Bierbauer) for the 1891 AA Athletics, thus precipitating a crisis that ultimately spelled the end of the line for the association. Back in the NL, he helped the Beaneaters win the pennant—his third title in three leagues—by leading the NL in slugging (.498), triples (20) and home runs (16), among other things. He then finished his major league career with Boston, Baltimore and Brooklyn in 1892 and 1893.

Although he made his name as an offensive player, Stovey was also a better than average fielder, at least in range factor, where he was above the league norms at both first (10.70 to 10.31) and the outfield (2.08 to 1.91). He was noted for having sure hands—although his fielding percentage was merely average for his positions for his era—a strong arm (a legacy of his pitching days), and excellent range. Under the different scoring rules of the 1880s, he was credited at one time with as many as 156 (1888) and 143 (1887) steals. Some of his other statistics have been called into question in the past, mainly because, as David Nemec suggests in *The Beer & Whiskey League*, AA officials may have padded his stats to make the National League jealous of having lost Stovey to the AA in 1883.

During Stovey's tenure as a major slugger and runner—he has been credited, maybe falsely, with inventing sliding pads—he dominated the AA in multiple offensive categories, notably as a power hitter. When he retired after 1893, he was the career home run leader and even during the higher-scoring late 1890s, only Roger Connor and Sam Thompson would eventually pass his 122 home runs among nineteenth century players. Overall, he led his league in home runs (five times), triples (four times), runs scored (four times—and he scored a remarkable 1492 runs in 1486 career games, placing him third all-time in runs scored per game), slugging percentage (three times), stolen bases (twice) and doubles and RBIs once each. Addressing the issue of the quality of AA play, as opposed to that of the National League, Stovey was not strictly an AA hitter; he led the National League in home runs (twice), triples, slugging percentage, extra-base hits and total bases, and led the Players League in steals as well. He also amassed 56 points in the Black Ink Test, to the average Hall of Famer's 27 points.

So how is it that Stovey has been neglected by the Hall? When he retired from baseball at the relatively advanced age of 36 he reverted back to his original name and returned to live in Fall River, Massachusetts, and worked as a policeman in New Bedford. The gentlemanly and low-key "Stovey" walked a beat as "Officer Stowe" for 40 some years, proving to be as accommodating in private life as he had been in public life. In what was undoubtedly a typical gesture, he gave a young man named Warren Goff 30 cabinet card-style photos of himself, just because Goff was dating Stovey's granddaughter, Beatrice.

While following the Red Sox and American League Athletics as a fan, he built a fine career of public service, but hardly one that would keep his name in front of the baseball world. Still, in the Hall of Fame voting in 1936, the year before he died, he received six votes—that's twice as many as Kid Nichols and six more than Jim O'Rourke, both of whom would later be inducted as "no-questions-asked" Hall of Famers. Stovey, on the other hand, never received another vote, dying on September 20, 1937, at the age of 80 while the Hall was still trying to induct the rest of the game's unquestioned superstars. In other words, his omission also became a case of out of sight, out of mind, as he was overlooked in the rush to induct the living and better known.

While it is hard to argue with Stovey's Hall of Fame–like dominance, there is another side to the issue of whether or not Stovey should now be added to the Hall of Fame. Many deep baseball thinkers have come out against adding to the Hall's membership any more nineteenth century, or early twentieth century players, all of whom are long dead. They are, indeed, largely forgotten, and the argument runs that you cannot honor dead people, you can only honor a line of statistics and it's impossible to honor someone's memory if no one remembers them. But, those objections beg the real question: what is the Hall of Fame supposed to be about? Isn't a Hall of Fame also supposed to be a repository of historical accuracy? A roster of the greatest of their type? By that definition, it is never too late to induct a great figure from the past to the Hall of Fame, and, by that measure, Harry Stovey deserves enshrinement. By doing so, the Hall can provide for a more accurate portrait of the game and its players—a goal worth pursuing.

G	AB	R	H	2B	3B	HR	RBI	SB	BB	BA	OBP	SLG	OPS+
1486	6138	1492	1771	347	174	122	908	509	663	.289	.361	.461	143

Sources: *Nineteenth Century Stars (SABR), The Beer & Whiskey League (David Nemec), Encyclopedia of Major League Baseball Teams (Donald Dewey and Nicholas Acocella), The National Pastime Winter 1985 (SABR), The Ballplayers (Mike Shatzkin, editor), Baseball Pioneers (Charles Faber), Baseball Library, Family Search.*

Sam Thompson

The third member of the Phillies' All-Hall-of-Fame outfield of the 1890s, big Samuel Luther Thompson was, like teammate Big Ed Delahanty, big (at 6-2, 207, he was somewhat bigger than Delahanty) and a power hitter. Although he was the last of the three to join the Hall of Fame, waiting until 1974, there is no reason to think of him as the lesser of the three.

Born on March 5, 1860 (or 1861), in Danville, Indiana, he was the son of cabinet maker Jessie and Rebecca McPheeters Thompson, who moved north from North Carolina and Kentucky, respectively. The eldest of five children (two sons and three daughters), he didn't start his baseball career until quite late in life, working originally as a laborer and then as a carpenter and roofer while playing for local teams in Danville. Legend has it that a scout for the Detroit Wolverines had to talk Thompson down from a roof to get him to sign a contract, although he had played 35 games in the minors with two Indiana teams, Evansville and Indianapolis, before ending up in the future Motor City midway through the 1885 season at the advanced age of 24 or 25.

He was a .300 hitter right from the start, hitting .303, .310 and .372 with adjusted OPS' of 170, 139 and 168. In 1887, he led the Wolverines to the National League pennant and a win in the World's Series against the American Association St. Louis Browns. His 166 RBIs that year was not only a major league record, but a nineteenth century record, and a mark that would last until Babe Ruth edged the mark up to 171 in 1921. His 203 hits in 1887 were also the first time the 200 mark had been topped in the National League.

Thompson missed more than half of the 1888 season, due to illness and a sore arm, thus contributing to both the Wolverines' fall to fifth place and the team's dissolution after the season. With Detroit holding a going-out-of-business sale, the first great left-handed slugger ended up in Philadelphia with the Phillies at the cost of $5000. Beginning in 1889, and running through 1895, Thompson had a streak of sustained brilliance that would be topped only by outfield mates Delahanty and Hamilton. Thompson was merely very good for his first five years in Philly (1889 to 1893), with adjusted OPS' of 125, 134, 122, 144 and 153. Then he caught a second wind, thanks possibly to the rule that moved the pitchers' mound back five feet for the 1893 season. After a real good 1893 campaign of .370/.424/.530 (leading the league in hits with 222 and doubles with 37) he was even better in 1894 and 1895.

	AB	H	R	2B	3B	HR	RBI	W	BA	OBP	SLG
1894	437	108	178	29	27	13	141	40	.407	.458	.686
1895	538	131	211	45	21	18	165	31	.392	.430	.654

He missed some time with a hand injury in 1894 or else his totals would have been just as impressive as they were in 1895. The hand injury was so severe—a "dead bone" in his little finger—that he had to have some small bones in his finger removed as an alternative to having the finger amputated. Nevertheless, he came back in 1895 and won the home run, RBI and slugging crowns and also led the league in runs created (150) and extra-base hits (84)—leading to the Faber System ranking him the top NL hitter that year.

Despite his hand problems, he was a remarkably sure-handed fielder, although his range was not good (1.74 to a league 1.97). He went 50 straight games in '94 without dropping a fly ball, and made just seven errors in 1896. For his career in the outfield, almost entirely in right field, his fielding percentage was a sterling .935, well above the league average of .909.

While Big Sam was terrorizing National League pitchers, he also became a popular and respected member of the Phillies. The quiet and restrained type, who seldom argued with umpires in an era when "kicking" was a national pastime, he wasn't afraid to tell off Colonel Rogers in 1894 for providing substandard traveling accommodations for the team. Maybe that was one of the reasons he won a Phillies' popularity contest in 1895 and was, as was the custom of the day, often presented with bouquets of flowers at home plate before games.

Thompson would play one more season as a 36- (or 35-) year-old regular in 1896, but his hitting slipped to a 108 adjusted OPS, and back problems limited his action to 17 games over the next two years, after which he retired to Detroit. He had played in 14 major league seasons, but as a full-time regular in only nine, missing parts of four seasons with injuries and another in the minors. He left behind a remarkable record, with RBIs his specialty, despite the fact that he sometimes batted second behind Hamilton. Of course, Hamilton was on base almost half the time. In 1407 major league games he drove in 1299 runs, and average of .923 per game, a figure that has never been topped.

Back in Detroit, he worked as a deputy U.S. marshal, a crier (bailiff?) in the court of U.S. District Judge Arthur J. Tuttle, and as an election inspector. He also kept in shape playing amateur baseball around Detroit, and struck up an acquaintance with American League Tigers owner Frank Navin. Then, in 1906, when he was at least 45½ years old, he came out of retirement at the request of Navin. The Tigers were suffering from a severe shortage of healthy outfielders, including young Ty Cobb, who had suffered some kind of physical and possibly emotional breakdown, leading to stomach surgery. The old Wolverine played eight games in right field during 1906 Tiger home games, playing alongside relative youngsters who probably had no idea just who he was. And, wouldn't you know it, he picked up three more RBIs.

The third member of the Phillies' Hall of Fame outfield, Sam Thompson, before he was sold from Detroit to Philadelphia. Thompson remains the all-time leader in RBIs per game (Library of Congress photograph).

Big Sam died of two heart attacks on Election Day, November 7, 1922, while serving as an election inspector. He would wait 47 years for the *Macmillan Encyclopedia* to bring him back from obscurity, and 52 years for his ticket to Cooperstown.

G	AB	R	H	2B	3B	HR	RBI	SB	BB	BA	OBP	SLG	OPS+
1407	5984	1256	1979	340	160	127	1299	229	450	.331	.384	.505	146

Sources: *Baseball's First Stars* (SABR), *Phillies Encyclopedia* (Rich Westcott and Frank Bilovsky), *The Ballplayers* (Mike Shatzkin, editor), *Occasional Glory* (David Jordan), *Ty Cobb* (Charles Alexander), *The Numbers Game* (Alan Schwarz), *Baseball Pioneers* (Charles Faber), Family Search, *The Deadball Era*.

Gus Weyhing

One of the hardest and wildest throwers of the 1880s and 1890s, August Weyhing was the Tommy Byrne of Philadelphia baseball from 1887 to 1894—hard to hit, but easy to get a walk off of. Starting out with the Athletics before his 21st birthday, he pitched three years in Philly before jumping to the Players League. After a year in Brooklyn, he went back to the Athletics and then, when the AA folded, he ended up with the Phillies until early in the 1895 season. During his slightly more than seven seasons in town, Weyhing won 186 games, losing 140, and threw 2860 innings—408 per season. And, although he never led his league in any significant statistical category, he was always among the leaders during his tenure in Philadelphia, along the way earning the nicknames Cannonball, Rubber Arm Gus and Rubber-Winged Gus. Ernest Lanigan also called him the Human Hatpin—a tribute to his physique. Although he would seem to have been more of a fastball pitcher, an 1899 *Washington Post* article referenced in *The Neyer/James Guide to Pitchers* states that Weyhing's best two pitches were a curve and a drop curve. Of course, there have also been many other hard curve throwers over the years, and the deuce is generally harder to control than a fastball.

Weyhing gave up just 2764 hits in those 2860 innings, but he also walked a whopping 1566, finishing in the top five in bases on balls four times and passing an impressive 212 in 1889. After all these years, he's still ninth in career walks. Just for good measure, he also led the AA in hit batters in 1887 with 37. John Thorn and John Holway in *The Pitcher* give Weyhing credit for holding the career record for plunking batters, with a painful 286—most of them from just 55 feet away.

Born in Louisville on September 29, 1866, he grew up in a family run by his widowed German (born in Wurtenberg) mother, Katherine, three brothers and two sisters. Originally a house painter as a teenager, the right-handed throwing Weyhing first played on a team sponsored by the M.J. Latterle Company in 1884. He entered organized ball in 1885 with Richmond in the Virginia League, moving to Charlotte in the Southern League in 1886, and pitching against the Phillies in a spring exhibition game. This contest brought him to Philadelphia's attention, and the Athletics tried to purchase his contract during the season. Charleston raised his salary to $75 a month, but, he left the team in July, claiming that he had a sore arm. That winter, he signed with the Phillies, who decided they had too many players at the start of the 1887 season, and allowed the Athletics to purchase his contract. After Weyhing started off the season with several good games, the Philadelphia sportswriters jumped in the fray, ripping the Phils for letting him go. Weyhing would win 84 games for the Athletics in his first three years, topped by 30 in 1889 and including a July 31, 1888, no-hitter against Kansas City.

After picking up 30 wins for Brooklyn, and having the Players League fold, he was back with the Athletics in 1891, this time winning 31 and ranking as the Faber System's AA Pitcher of the Year. When a second straight league folded on him after the 1891 season, he finally ended up with the Phillies, and won 30 for a third straight year, going 32-21 in 1892. Having won 30 in four straight seasons, becoming the only pitcher to win 30 or more games in three different major leagues, he won 39 more in 1893 and 1894, after which the Phillies released him just two games into the 1895 season. From that point on, he became a journeyman, never winning 20 again, though losing 20 three times, and bouncing from Pittsburgh to Louisville to Washington to St. Louis to Brooklyn to Cleveland to Cincinnati, with several minor league stops thrown in, including his final regular gig in the Southern League in 1903.

With the exception of a very few nineteenth century iron men like Kid Nichols or Cy Young, most pitchers who threw the immense number of innings that Weyhing put in at the start of his career succumbed to sore arms that short-circuited their careers. However, Weyhing was a different case. Despite being just 5-10 and 145 pounds, there's no record of his actually having a serious arm injury, and, in fact, he came back to throw almost 700 major league innings in 1898 and 1899 at the age of 32. Rather, it seems as if his downfall was the change in the pitching parameters that went into effect in 1893. Not only was the pitching distance increased five feet, but pitchers were no longer allowed to roam a pitcher's box, being confined to keeping one foot on a rubber slab. Note his key stats in the years from 1892 to 1895.

Year	W-L	GS	CG	IP	H	ERA*
1892	32-21	49	46	470	411	122
1893	23-16	40	33	345	399	96
1894	16-14	34	25	266	365	88
1895	8-21	28	23	231	318	80

Prior to 1892, Weyhing's worst Adjusted ERA after his rookie season (101) was 120. His Adjusted ERA of 96 in 1893 would be his best for the rest of his career, which ended with a 264-232 record and an Adjusted ERA of just 102. Still, for the first six years of his career (1887 to 1892, all but one of them in Philly), he was one of the best.

Weyhing later returned to his hometown of Louisville, operating a cigar store and tavern, both of which were favorite old ballplayer pastimes of past centuries. He also came back to baseball briefly in 1910, in the Western and Texas leagues, even pitching four games at the age of 43 before finishing the season as an umpire. Later, he became a policeman in Louisville. Four years after being one of several old-timers honored by the Boston Red Sox during their 50th anniversary celebrations, Weyhing died in Louisville just short of his 89th birthday, on September 3, 1955.

W	L	G	SHO	IP	H	BB	SO	ERA	ERA+
264	232	538	28	4324	4562	1566	1665	3.89	102

Sources: *Nineteenth Century Stars (SABR), The Beer & Whiskey League (David Nemec), The Ballplayers (Mike Shatzkin, editor) Occasional Glory, (David Jordan), The Pitcher (John Thorn and John Holway), The Neyer/James Guide to Pitchers (Bill James and Rob Neyer), Baseball Cyclopedia (Ernest Lanigan), Baseball Pioneers (Charles Faber), Family Search.*

Ned Williamson

Edward Nagle Williamson, better known as Ned, is another nineteenth century player who received a lot of praise from his contemporaries. His long-time manager, Cap Anson, said in 1900 that he was the best all-around player, ever. Heady praise, and while it's not true, he was a better-than-average hitter and a very good third baseman in an era when third basemen weren't expected to hit much. Williamson is also still known among the cognoscenti as the individual whose single season home run record Babe Ruth broke in 1919.

He was born in Philadelphia on either October 24, 1857 (the more common date), or on October 24, 1855 (according to LDS Church records). He played amateur ball with the Neshannock club of New Castle in 1876, where his teammate was future catching star Charlie Bennett. Late that same year he became a professional with the Pittsburgh

Allegheny club in the International Association, moving up to the National League in 1878 with the Indianapolis Blues. Except for his rookie year in Indy, and his final year with the Chicago Pirates in the Players League, Williamson spent his entire major league career playing for Anson and the Chicago White Stockings, a rarity among nineteenth century players.

The 5-11, 175 pound (early in his career) Williamson was the third baseman on the "Stonewall Infield," with Anson, Fred Pfeffer and Tommy Burns, that won National League pennants in 1880, 1881, 1882, 1885 and 1886. In 1886, he switched positions with Burns, and became Chicago's shortstop. He stayed with the White Stockings through the 1889 season, jumping to the Players League Chicago team for his last season. That, in brief, was Ned Williamson's career, one that produced a nice, though not exceptional, 113 adjusted OPS and some pretty good fielding stats at third—an .866 fielding percentage (the league average was .849) and a 3.63 range factor (the league's was 3.33).

There were also some interesting sub-plots to Ned Williamson's career. First, the home run record. Although Williamson had decent power, and drew a goodly number of walks, he did

Philadelphia native and one-time single-season home run champ Ned Williamson (Library of Congress photograph).

not hit for a high average. And, he wasn't normally a home run hitter. Then, prior to the 1883 season, the White Stockings' Lake Forest Park was renovated, reducing the distance down the right field line to 196 feet and down the left field line to 180 feet. For the 1883 season, balls over either fence counted as doubles, and the right-handed Williamson set a major league record with 49 doubles. In 1884, and only in 1884, the ground rule double rule was taken off in Chicago, and any ball hit over either fence was a home run. While Williamson's record of 27 home runs has been widely dismissed as a fluke, the fact is he still had to be able to get the ball over the short part of the fence, and that no one else on the Stockings hit 27 home runs that year. Hitting 25 at home and two home runs on the road, Ned Williamson, who had never hit four home runs in a season previously, set a major league single season record that would last for 35 years, a year longer than the Babe's record would stand and just two years less than Roger Maris' record would hold up.

Williamson was also a key player in the Brotherhood dispute—a rallying point, in fact. A member of the 1888 White Stockings team that Al Spalding took around the world, Williamson tore up his knee sliding on uneven and rocky ground in a game in the vicinity of the Eiffel Tower. Confined to bed for the rest of the trip and given incorrect treatment by French and English physicians, Williamson had to pay for his own medical care when all that Spalding would pony up was his fare home—$150. This blatant mistreatment of a fellow union member helped rally the troops after the 1889 season, a year in which Williamson, trying to rehab his knee, was able to play in only 47 games, and hit .237. Although he joined the Players League struggle, he was able to play in only 73 games in 1890, and hit just .195. After the PL folded, he begged Spalding to take him back. Not being interested in a now-overweight infielder who hadn't hit his weight in 1890, and not being famous for his forgiveness, Spalding said no. Williamson then opened a Chicago saloon with another disabled (he'd lost a leg to infection) former ballplayer, Jimmy Wood, and died of either a kidney infection or dropsy on March 3, 1894, in Willow Springs, Arkansas, where he'd previously gone to try and rehabilitate his bad knee.

All accounts of Ned Williamson say he was a pretty good guy—well-read, observant, articulate, good-natured, kind-hearted, hard-working, fair-minded. He even supported blacks being able to play major league baseball, a very unpopular stance at this time. He was also a skilled and acrobatic fielder who was quick on his feet and had a fine arm. Remarkably, in a poll of a dozen baseball stars taken in 1894, Ned Williamson was the number one choice as the greatest player of all time. Maybe nice guys don't always finish last.

G	AB	R	H	2B	3B	HR	RBI	BB	BA	OBP	SLG	OPS+
1201	4553	809	1159	228	85	64	667	506	.255	.332	.384	113

Sources: *Nineteenth Century Stars (SABR), The National Pastime 2001 (SABR), Biographical History of Baseball (Donald Dewey and Nicholas Acocella), The Ballplayers (Mike Shatzkin, editor), Family Search.*

Harry Wright

Nineteenth century baseball cannot be said to be lacking for figures that could, for one reason or another, be considered heroic. Jimmy Creighton was probably the first. But, so were Al Spalding. And King Kelly. Al Reach. Cap Anson was, in his own time, thought to be heroic. In many ways though, the most notable hero of early baseball, and the game's most influential figure, except maybe for Henry Chadwick, was Harry Wright. He's been given credit—in some cases rightly, in some cases wrongly—for inventing or developing practically every innovation you can think of. The change of pace (maybe), relief pitching (quite possibly), the first national-scope all-professional team (unquestionably), baseball knickers and colored stockings—the first really distinctive uniform (you bet), the first professional league (sort of), the first dynasty (without a doubt), the first international baseball tour (yes, along with Spalding), signs (maybe), fielders backing up each other (possibly), teamwork in general (sportswriter Tim Murnane thought so), batting and fielding practice (highly doubtful), platooning (not likely), the hit and run (who really knows?), and heckling (no way, though one source says he was good enough at it that the National League considered banning managers from the players' bench to keep him quiet, a claim that's a little hard to believe).

Along the way, Wright picked up almost as many nicknames as he had supposed innovations. Cap'n Harry. Bearded Boy in Bloomers and Captain of the Bloody Calves. Uncle Harry. Dew Drop (after his junkball pitching). Dear Old Harry (when he was managing the Phillies in the 1890s). The Father of Professional Baseball. This last appellation was unquestionably the truest.

There are a multiplicity of possible dates for his birth. Although January 10, 1835, is the most popular, and likely, it is far from a unanimous choice. The 1880 census places his birth in 1836. Different records on file with The Church of Jesus Christ of Latter-day Saints give birth dates in 1831, 1832 and 1835. His death certificate puts his birth date on December 13, 1834. It appears as if it's possible that he could have been born in any year from 1831 to 1836. It does seem pretty likely that the location was Sheffield, England, that his parents were Samuel Wright, Sr., and the former Ann Tone and that he had an earl and a grand master in the Knights Templar in his ancestry. Samuel Wright brought his family to New York City sometime shortly after William Henry Wright was born. Like many others, the elder Wright was seeking opportunity in the New World. Unlike almost anyone else, it was as a professional athlete, since Samuel Wright came to America for a spot as the star of the famous St. George's Dragonslayers cricket team. Harry's brothers Dan (the only non-baseball player), George and Samuel, Jr., were born in America, along with a sister, Mary.

In 1849, Harry dropped out of school, and apprenticed as a jeweler at Tiffany's. However, that was the nineteenth century version of flipping burgers for Harry. He was born to play ball and, a year later, he would join his father on the Dragonslayers, although it took him until 1857 to get paid for it. Legend has it that, about this same time, Harry happened to check out an adjoining area nearby the Dragonslayers' Elysian Fields, and saw his future—his first baseball game, possibly being played by the Knickerbockers, who he joined up with shortly thereafter. At first pitching and catching for Knickerbocker, he was already an all-star in his first year, playing center field in the famous 1858 Fashion Course Matches against the best of Brooklyn. By 1863, he was playing for Gotham and, by 1864, he either tired of baseball, or got a better offer from Cincinnati, and left the Big Apple to play cricket with the Union Cricket Club. Ultimately, he would start his legend in baseball with the Cincinnati Base Ball Club. Despite the fact that he batted ninth for New York in the Fashion Course games, what few individual records there are for this era would seem to indicate he was a pretty good hitter, leading Knickerbocker in 1858 and Gotham in 1863 in runs average and over.

Wright went west in 1865 with his wife, Mary Fraser, and their three children. However, at some point after arriving in Cincinnati, Mary died, and Harry re-married, this time to Ohio native Caroline "Carrie" Wright, with whom he would eventually have seven children. Unfortunately, as would be the case with Connie Mack's family many years later, the two sets of children from the two marriages fought like cats and dogs. Harry thought the world of Carrie, at least according to Darryl Brock, the author of the historical novel on the 1869 Cincinnati Red Stockings, *If I Never Get Back*. Although Brock was writing fiction, he is one of the foremost scholars on the team that Harry Wright would become most linked to. "Carrie ... why she's the truest wife a man could have, a servant in my home and a queen in my heart. To my mind, she embodies the noblest elements of the human spirit. She promises the highest I can hope. She purges what is dark within me, strengthens what is failing," Brock has Wright say at one point. It's also clear that Brock considers Harry Wright a true hero, portraying him as a man of quiet nobility, morality and immense strength of character. A man with very few dark or failing moments. "I was impressed by his calm authority. And by a sense of integrity in the wise brown eyes that seemed to promise he would recognize and respect one's best qualities. I found myself wanting to earn the man's respect right away," Brock has his time-traveling narrator, Sam Fowler, say of his first meeting with Cap'n Harry.

With the Red Stockings, Wright was the general manager, traveling secretary, scout, manager, captain, center fielder and relief pitcher. And, it could be said he did a pretty good job. Starting in 1867, the first time Cincinnati appears in NABBP records, Wright's charges ran up the following records.

<pre>
1867 — 16-1
1868 — 36-7
1869 — 57-0
1870 — 67-6-1
</pre>

The Father of Professional Baseball, Harry Wright (Library of Congress photograph).

That's a composite mark of 176-14-1, or a .924 winning percentage that included winning 89 straight games from October 4, 1868, to June 13, 1870. While the figure of 57 straight is the number most commonly associated with the Stockings, in addition to winning all 57 of their games in 1869, Cap'n Harry's boys also won their last eight games in 1868 and their first 24 in 1870. However, just to prove that nineteenth century baseball fans were as fickle as twenty-first century fans, the Red Stockings followers, and their financial backers turned on them after they had the audacity to go 67-6-1 in 1870. The team folded and went back to all-amateur club status shortly after the season ended.

Undaunted, Wright took his act, and several of his best players, to Boston, where, in addition to reprising the same roles he filled in Cincy, he also was one of the founders of the National Association. After falling short of Athletic in 1871, the Boston Red Stockings swept the next four NA titles in dominating fashion, to the extent that the NA became widely known as "Harry Wright's League," an appellation unique in sports.

As a player, Wright, although he may have been as old as 40 in 1871, was a regular in the Red Stockings' outfield for the first three years of the NA, hitting .299, .250 and .252 and proving to be one of the better players at working a walk, finishing second, fourth and fifth in base on balls. He also continued to serve as a "change" pitcher for Spalding, appearing in 34 games, starting seven, from 1871 to 1874 and going 4-4 with a 93 Adjusted ERA. Using modern scoring methods, he also had eight saves, theoretically leading the league three times.

Having helped sink the NA with his own team's success, Wright moved on with his team to the National League, in the process helping William Hulbert and Spalding found the new league. At this point, Harry Wright had been a seminal figure in the first all-professional baseball team, and the first *two* professional baseball leagues. Although Boston came up short in 1876, thanks to the player raids by Hulbert's White Stockings, they won the 1877 and 1878 NL titles, giving Wright seven championships in 10 years—a feat not topped until Casey Stengel won 10 in 12 years from 1949 to 1960—in three different organizations. He stayed with Boston until 1881, when he moved south to manage Providence. Given his success over the years, and his long-term status as a professional athlete, it is perhaps telling of the social status of baseball to note that, in the 1880 census his occupation is listed as "sporting goods dealer." While it is true that brother George was in the sporting goods business with his Wright & Ditson firm, and while Harry may have worked for George, the man was not a salesman of gloves, balls and bats—he was a professional athlete, and had been one since 1857.

Harry Wright finally reached Philadelphia in 1884, when old friend and Phillies' co-owner Al Reach brought him to the City of Brotherly Love to take over the team after its awful first year. In an era where major league franchises came and went with regularity, Wright may well have saved the Phillies from extinction, as, after he spent 1884 righting the ship, they finished as low as .500 only once during his 10 years (1884 to 1893) as manager. Dressed in a manner somewhat similar to Connie Mack 20 years later—a coat, tie and top hat—Wright directed the Phillies to a 636-566 record (.529), despite personal hardship and tragedy. In late May 1890, Wright suddenly went blind, and was forced to miss most of the season, coming back only late in the year, still with just partial vision. This ailment, which has been described in the general terms as a catarrh, or inflammation of the mucous membranes, could have been similar to the sinus infection that almost ended George Sisler's career in the 1920s, or, it could even have been a side effect of a more serious problem, like diabetes or meningitis. It's also been suggested that, as a devoted studier of box scores, Wright had strained his eyesight by reading too much agate type. Whatever it was, it was a painful time for both Wright and his many admirers in baseball.

Even worse, Carrie Wright suffered a nervous breakdown of some kind shortly after Harry went blind. She died less than two years later on February 5, 1892. Although heartbroken, Harry continued to manage the Phillies for the 1892 and 1893 seasons, after which Colonel Rogers, going against public opinion, decided not to renew his contract. At about the same time (January 1894), he married for a third time, apparently to his first wife's sister, Isabelle.

To this day, no one has managed the Philadelphia National League franchise for as many seasons as Harry Wright, and only Gene Mauch has won more games (646-636). Overall, in his 27 years managing baseball teams at the very highest level of the sport, Wright rang up a record of 1401-899-36, a .607 winning percentage for 2336 games.

Such was the respect Harry Wright had earned in his 35 years in baseball that, for the last two years of his life, he was chief of umpires for the National League, a post the league created specifically for him for the rest of his life, with the understanding that it would be abolished when he died. That end came in Atlantic City on October 3, 1895, where he had gone to try and recover from a lung disease. He was buried in Philadelphia's West Laurel Hill Cemetery, under the inscription, "The Father of Baseball." In many ways, a truism.

G	AB	R	H	2B	3B	HR	RBI	BA	OBP	SLG	OPS+
180	816	183	222	24	9	4	111	.272	.303	.338	89

W	L	G	SHO	IP	H	ERA	ERA+
4	4	34	0	99	149	3.81	93

Managerial Record

W	L	PCT
1225	885	.581

Sources: *Baseball's First Stars (SABR), If I Never Get Back (Daryl Brock), The Biographical History of Baseball (Donald Dewey and Nicholas Acocella), Phillies Encyclopedia (Rich Westcott and Frank Bilovsky), Occasional Glory (David Jordan), The Ballplayers (Mike Shatzkin, editor), Encyclopedia of Major League Baseball Teams (Donald Dewey and Nicholas Acocella), American Baseball (David Voigt), Baseball: The Early Years (Harold Seymour), Family Search, SABR Biography Project.*

Chapter Notes

Chapter 1

1. Block, David, *Baseball Before We Knew It* (Lincoln: University of Nebraska Press, 2005), p. 153.
2. *Proceedings from Philadelphia's Baseball History* (Philadelphia: The Historical Society of Pennsylvania, 1990), pp. 6, 7.
3. *Ibid.*, p. 7.
4. Peverelly, Charles A., *The Book of American Pastimes* (New York: Charles Peverelly, 1866), p. 337.
5. *Ibid.*, p. 472.
6. *Philadelphia Daily Evening Telegraph*, March 25–26, 1908.
7. Richter, Francis C., *Richter's History and Records of Base Ball* (Jefferson, NC: McFarland, 2005), p. 219.
8. Charlton, James, ed., *The Baseball Chronology* (New York: Macmillan, 1991), p. 50.
9. *New York Clipper*, December 23, 1882.
10. Peverelly, p. 472; *Philadelphia Daily Evening Telegraph*, March 25–26, 1908.
11. *Philadelphia Daily Evening Telegraph*, March 25–26, 1908.
12. E-mail correspondence with John Thorn, January 4, 2006. Thorn specifically points to long-time baseball author Robert Smith, in his 1993 book, *Baseball in the Afternoon*, stating that the "Philadelphia game" was played on a diamond-shaped field that was smaller than that laid out by the Knickerbocker committee.
13. Block, p.158, 159, and e-mail correspondence with David Block, August 14, 2006.
14. *Philadelphia Daily Evening Telegraph*, March 25–26, 1908.
15. George Thompson, writing in the 2001 edition of SABR's *The National Pastime*, notes an organized association of young men playing ball in New York in April 1823. However, this sole organization seems to be ephemeral at best.
16. Peverelly, pp. 472, 473.
17. Wright, Marshall D., *The National Association of Base Ball Players, 1857–1870* (Jefferson, NC: McFarland, 2000), pp. 44, 63.
18. Seymour, Harold, *Baseball: The Early Years* (New York: Oxford University Press, 1960), p. 15.
19. *Philadelphia Daily Evening Telegraph*, March 25–26, 1908.
20. Peverelly, p. 474.
21. Seymour, p. 29; Richter, p. 7.
22. Peverelly, p. 474.
23. *Philadelphia Daily Evening Telegraph*, March 25–26, 1908.
24. Sullivan, pp. 5–8. Having personally handled this latter task for the Penn-Jersey League champion Germantown Friends School baseball team in 1970, I can attest that the coach, and especially the players, will get surly if the scorebook is not properly attended.
25. *Ibid.*, pp. 5–8.
26. *Philadelphia Daily Evening Telegraph*, March 25–26, 1908.

Chapter 2

1. Lieb, Fred, *Connie Mack: Grand Old Man of Baseball* (New York: G.P. Putnam's Sons, 1945), p. 68. Long-time Athletic Wes Fisler, in a 1918 or 1919 interview with the *Philadelphia Press*, apparently told the reporter that the Athletic Club was founded as a town ball club on May 31, 1859. Francis Richter, in *The History and Records of Baseball* (p. 221), also places Athletic's formation, as a town ball club, in May 1859. According to Richter, Athletic announced its preference for the new game in June 1860. However, Fisler was interviewed 60 years after the fact, and didn't join Athletic until 1866. Richter, though a Philadelphian, was six years old in 1860 and was writing 55 years after the fact. The best evidence, from Al Reach and several other sources, points to the April 1860 founding date.
2. *Proceedings from Philadelphia's Baseball History* (Philadelphia: The Historical Society of Pennsylvania, 1990), p. 7.
3. Peverelly, Charles A., *The Book of American Pastimes* (New York; Charles Peverelly, 1866), pp. 475–477.
4. Richter, Francis C., *Richter's History and Records of Baseball* (Jefferson, NC: McFarland,

2005), p. 220. Richter's "Base Ball Records" section, from which this excerpt is taken, apparently is based on information originally kept by William Rankin, the official scorer of the New York Mutual Club "as far back as 1868."
  5. Weigley, Russell E., et al., *Philadelphia: A 300 Year History* (New York: Norton, 1982), p. 378.
  6. Peverelly, p. 477.
  7. *Proceedings from Philadelphia's Baseball History*, p. 8.
  8. Undated, unidentified clipping from the National Baseball Library, supplied by John Thorn.
  9. *Ibid.*
  10. Peverelly, p. 488.
  11. Undated, unidentified clipping from the National Baseball Library, supplied by John Thorn.
  12. Peverelly, pp. 485, 486.
  13. Richter, p. 401.
  14. Peverelly, pp. 479–483.
  15. Westcott, Rich, *Philadelphia's Old Ballparks* (Philadelphia: Temple University Press, 1996), p. 10.
  16. Peverelly, pp. 486–488.
  17. *Baseball's First Stars* (Cleveland: Society for American Baseball Research, 1996), p. 129.
  18. Peverelly, pp. 486–488.
  19. *Ibid.*, p. 410.
  20. Wright, Marshall D., *The National Association of Base Ball Players, 1857–1870* (Jefferson, NC: McFarland, 2000), p. 44. This intercity All-Star game was notable enough that both Peverelly and Wright report on it.
  21. Tiemann, Robert L., and Rucker, Mark, *Nineteenth Century Stars* (Kansas City: Society for American Baseball Research, 1989), p. 32.
  22. Warner, Sam Bass, Jr., *The Private City* (Philadelphia: University of Pennsylvania Press, 1996), pp. 49–62.
  23. *Ibid.*, pp. 49–62.
  24. Weigley, et al., pp. 361, 377, 379.
  25. *Ibid.*, pp. 272–274.

Chapter 3

  1. Peverelly, Charles A., *The Book of American Pastimes* (New York: Charles Peverelly, 1866), pp. 487, 488.
  2. *New York Clipper*, December 23, 1882.
  3. Wright, Marshall D., *The National Association of Base Ball Players, 1857–1870* (Jefferson, NC: McFarland, 2000), pp. 67–73.
  4. *Ibid.*, p. 66.
  5. *Ibid.*, p. 67.
  6. *Ibid.*, pp. 75, 77, 81.
  7. Peverelly, p. 486.
  8. Wright, p. 54.
  9. Ivor-Campbell, Frederick, Tiemann, Robert L., Rucker, Mark, eds., *Baseball's First Stars* (Cleveland: Society for American Baseball Research, 1996), p. 129. Pratt's jumping to Atlantic, though probably not for a straight salary, was a year and a half before Al Reach was lured from the Brooklyn Eckford club to Athletic.
  10. Wright, pp. 86–93.
  11. Weigley, Russell E., et al., *Philadelphia: A 300 Year History* (New York: Norton, 1982), p. 396.
  12. *Ibid.*, pp. 414–416.
  13. *Ibid.*, pp. 419, 427, 430, 447, 448.
  14. Weigley, et al., pp. 359–361, 363.
  15. Kuklick, Bruce, *To Every Thing A Season* (Princeton: Princeton University Press, 1991), p. 21.

Chapter 4

  1. Tiemann, Robert L., and Rucker, Mark, eds., *Nineteenth Century Stars* (Kansas City: Society for American Baseball Research, 1989), p. 32.
  2. Seymour, Harold, *Baseball: The Early Years* (New York: Oxford University Press, 1960), p. 47; Voigt. David Quentin, *American Baseball: From Gentleman's Sport to the Commissioner System* (Norman: University of Oklahoma Press, 1966), p. 15.
  3. Richter, Francis, *The History and Records of Baseball* (Jefferson, NC: McFarland, 2005), p. 221.
  4. E-mail correspondence with Matthew J. Coyne, December 9, 2005.
  5. Seymour, p. 43.
  6. Thorn, John, ed., *The National Pastime* (Cooperstown, NY: Society for American Baseball Research, 1984), pp. 14, 15.
  7. Westcott, Rich, *Philadelphia's Old Ballparks* (Philadelphia: Temple University Press, 1996), p. 2.
  8. Peverelly, Charles, *The Book of American Pastimes* (New York: Charles Peverelly, 1866), p. 483.
  9. Westcott, p. 4.
  10. E-mail correspondence with Matthew J. Coyne, December 9, 2005.
  11. Richter, p. 218. William Ryczek, in *Blackguards and Red Stockings*, confirms this astronomical score, and adds that it was a relatively close game until Niagara scored 58 runs on Columbia in the eighth inning! Richter also mentions a game that Athletic played against a junior squad in Philadelphia. After holding their opponents scoreless for eight innings—an incredible feat in any baseball game at this time—Athletic decided to allow "junior" 27 outs in the ninth inning. No less than 16 of the outmatched opponents were put out in succession. Finally they scored three runs on what Richter terms Athletic's "careless fielding."
  12. Peverelly, p. 476.
  13. Peverelly, p. 488.
  14. Wright, Marshall D., *The National Association of Base Ball Players, 1857–1870* (Jefferson, NC: McFarland, 2000), pp. 138, 183, 232.
  15. Ivor-Campbell, Frederick, Tiemann, Robert

L., and Rucker, Mark, eds., *Baseball's First Stars* (Cleveland: Society for American Baseball Research, 1996), p. 129.
    16. Peverelly, pp. 483–485.
    17. Richter, p. 219.
    18. Wright, p. 112.
    19. *Proceedings from Philadelphia's Baseball History* (Philadelphia: The Historical Society of Pennsylvania, 1990), p. 8.
    20. Richter, p. 8. Harold Seymour, in *Baseball: The Early Years*, gives the 40,000 figure and adds the details of businesses closing and the like.
    21. Westcott, p. 3.
    22. Richter, p. 8.
    23. *Philadelphia North American,* April 2, 1911.
    24. Westcott, p. 3.
    25. Telephone conversation with Dr. David Quentin Voigt, February 28, 2005.
    26. Wright, p. 112.
    27. Seymour, p. 48. David Voigt, quoting from Henry Chadwick's scrapbooks, also reports on this scandalous behavior in *American Baseball*.
    28. Voigt, p. 19.
    29. Seymour, pp. 42–45.
    30. Wright, pp. 141, 143.

Chapter 5

    1. E-mail correspondence with John Thorn, June 2, 2005.
    2. Stone, Tanya Lee, *Abraham Lincoln* (London: DK Publishing, 2005), p. 56.
    3. Freedman, Russell, *Lincoln, a Photobiography* (New York: Clarion Books, 1987), p. 5.
    4. E-mail correspondence with John Thorn, June 2, 2005.
    5. Sullivan, Dean A., *Early Innings: A Documentary History of Baseball, 1825–1908* (Lincoln: University of Nebraska Press, 1995), pp. 68, 69.
    6. Threston, Christopher, *The Integration of Baseball in Philadelphia* (Jefferson, NC: McFarland, 2003), p. 9.
    7. *New York Clipper*, December 23, 1882. In this obituary Hayhurst, clearly a friend of black baseball, was reported to have been a member of an Excelsior team in 1860. Little of substance is known about the black Philadelphia Excelsior team, even by an expert like Threston.
    8. Sullivan, p. 34.
    9. *Ibid.*, p. 68.
    10. Peterson, Robert, *Only the Ball Was White* (New York: McGraw-Hill, 1970), p. 17.
    11. Threston, p. 9.
    12. E-mail correspondence with Christopher Threston, May 23, 2005.
    13. E-mail correspondence with Dr. Andrew Waskie, February 8, 2005.
    14. Thorn, John, and Palmer, Pete. *Total Baseball.* 4th ed. (New York: Warner Books, 1995), p. 516.
    15. http://en.wikipedia.org.
    16. Threston, p. 8.
    17. American Negro Historical Society Papers (The Historical Society of Pennsylvania). Threston says that, like Octavius Catto, many of these players were former Union Army officers from the Civil War period.
    18. Thorn and Palmer, p. 516. In *Only the Ball Was White*, Peterson says the score of this game was 42–37, Excelsiors, in seven argument-laced innings.
    19. Threston, p. 8.
    20. Thorn and Palmer, p. 516.
    21. *Proceedings from Philadelphia's Baseball History*, p. 8.
    22. Wright, Marshall D., *The National Association of Base Ball Players, 1857–1870* (Jefferson, NC: McFarland, 2000), p. 141.
    23. *Philadelphia Inquirer Magazine*, July 6, 2003.
    24. Threston, p. 9.
    25. Solomon, Burt, *The Baseball Timeline* (New York: DK Publishing, 2001), p. 61.

Chapter 6

    1. Telephone conversation with Dr. David Quentin Voigt, February 28, 2005.
    2. Voigt, David Quentin, *American Baseball: From Gentleman's Sport to the Commissioner System* (Norman: University of Oklahoma Press, 1966), p. 15.
    3. Telephone conversation with Dr. David Quentin Voigt, February 28, 2005.
    4. Wright, Marshall D., *The National Association of Base Ball Players, 1857–1870* (Jefferson, NC: McFarland, 2000), p. 190.
    5. Seymour, Harold, *Baseball: The Early Years* (New York: Oxford University Press, 1960), p. 52.
    6. Wright, p. 42.
    7. Telephone conversation with Dr. David Quentin Voigt, February 28, 2005.
    8. Voigt, *American Baseball,* pp. 24–26.
    9. Wright, p. 253.
    10. *Proceedings from Philadelphia's Baseball History* (Philadelphia: The Historical Society of Pennsylvania, 1990), p. 8.
    11. Brock, Darryl, *If I Never Get Back* (New York: Crown, 1990), pp. 158, 159.
    12. Seymour, p. 51.
    13. Undated, unidentified clipping from the National Baseball Library (courtesy of John Thorn).
    14. Wright, p. 240.
    15. *Ibid.*, pp. 284, 285.
    16. Ivor-Campbell, Frederick, Tiemann, Robert L., and Rucker, Mark, eds., *Baseball's First Stars* (Cleveland: Society for American Baseball Research, 1996), p. 129.
    17. Westcott, Rich, *Philadelphia's Old Ballparks* (Philadelphia: Temple University Press, 1996), p. 3.
    18. Wright, pp. 287, 288.

Chapter 7

1. Voigt, David Quentin, *American Baseball: From Gentleman's Sport to the Commissioner System* (Norman: University of Oklahoma Press, 1966), p. 35.
2. Sullivan, Dean A., *Early Innings: A Documentary History of Baseball, 1825–1908* (Lincoln: University of Nebraska Press, 1995), pp. 84, 85. According to Francis Richter, the NABBP hung on in a diminished form until 1874.
3. Ryczek, William J., *Blackguards and Red Stockings* (Wallingford: Colebrook Press, 1992), pp. 12, 13.
4. *Ibid.*, pp. 12, 13; Sullivan, pp. 85, 86. Ryczek was working from the same source documents, namely the *New York Clipper* and Henry Chadwick's scrapbooks, that Sullivan reproduces in his book.
5. Westcott, Rich, *Philadelphia's Old Ballparks* (Philadelphia: Temple University Press, 1996), pp. 4, 5.
6. Financially, reports are mixed; Voigt says they made $150, Ryczek says they lost $2,000, and Seymour says they wiped out a $5,000 debt.
7. Nemec, David. *The Great Encyclopedia of 19th Century Major League Baseball* (New York: Donald I. Fine Books, 1997), pp. 9, 29.
8. Ryczek, pp. 45, 46.
9. *Ibid.*, pp. 53–62.
10. *Ibid.*, p. 63.
11. Seymour, Harold, *Baseball: The Early Years* (New York: Oxford University Press, 1960), p. 72. Why they didn't hang the pennant in Al Reach's store, where they had previously displayed their game balls, is unknown.
12. www.retrosheet.org. Retrosheet is the source used herein for the rest of the 19th Century standings and game-by-game results.
13. *Proceedings from Philadelphia's Baseball History* (Philadelphia: The Historical Society of Pennsylvania, 1990), p. 9.
14. Ryczek, p. 97.
15. *Ibid.*, p. 113.
16. *Ibid.*, p. 115.
17. *Ibid.*, pp. 116–118, 125.
18. *Ibid.*, pp. 126, 127.
19. *Ibid.*, p. 134.
20. *Ibid.*, p. 132.
21. *Ibid.*, pp. 130, 131, 145.
22. *Ibid.*, pp. 147.
23. David Block's *Baseball Before We Knew It* makes this abundantly clear.
24. Voigt, p. 49.
25. Ryczek, p. 162.
26. Voigt, p. 48.
27. Ryczek, p. 161.
28. *Ibid.*, pp. 163, 164. Al Reach was the one Athletic player who stayed home as he had to tend to his sporting goods business.
29. Westcott, pp. 9, 10.
30. Ryczek, pp. 192, 193.
31. Richter, Francis, *The History and Records of Baseball* (Jefferson, NC: McFarland, 2005), p. 47. Craver had been crooked for a long time, since at least 1869 according to Darryl Brock in *If I Never Get Back*, so Richter may have been indulging in some Monday morning quarterbacking.
32. Ryczek, pp. 187–189.
33. *Ibid.*, pp. 213.
34. Ivor-Campbell, Frederick, Tiemann, Robert L., and Rucker, Mark, eds., *Baseball's First Stars* (Cleveland: Society for American Baseball Research, 1996), p. 104.
35. Solomon, Burt, *The Baseball Timeline* (New York: DK Publishing, 2001), p. 32.

Chapter 8

1. Weigley, Russell E., et al., *Philadelphia: A 300 Year History* (New York: Norton, 1982), pp. 417, 419.
2. *Ibid.*, pp. 419–421.
3. *Ibid.*, p. 421.
4. *Ibid.*, p. 429.
5. *Ibid.*, p. 432.
6. Richter, Francis, *The History and Records of Baseball* (Jefferson, NC: McFarland, 2005), p. 49.
7. Voigt, David Quentin, *American Baseball: From Gentleman's Sport to the Commissioner System* (Norman: University of Oklahoma Press, 1966), p. 60.
8. Ryczek, William J. *Blackguards and Red Stockings* (Wallingford: Colebrook Press, 1992), pp. 216, 217. Voigt, Alexander, Seymour and practically everyone else who has written a history of the National League tells this story about Hulbert's pirating of the Big Four of Boston. Ryczek adds the key detail that it was accomplished by the early part of the summer of 1875.
9. Voigt, p. 62.
10. Sullivan, Dean A., *Early Innings: A Documentary History of Baseball, 1825–1908* (Lincoln: University of Nebraska Press, 1995), pp. 95, 96. Harold Seymour notes Hulbert's expressed desire to reform existing abuses.
11. Seymour, Harold, *Baseball: The Early Years* (New York: Oxford University Press, 1960), p. 78.
12. Voigt, p. 61.
13. Frommer, Harvey, *Primitive Baseball* (New York: Atheneum, 1988), p. 20.
14. Voigt, p. 62. Seymour says that Hulbert "never forgave" the association for awarding Force to the Athletics, instead of his White Stockings.
15. Seymour, p. 80.
16. Dewey, Donald, and Acocella, Nicholas, *Encyclopedia of Major League Baseball Teams* (New York: HarperCollins, 1993), p. 410.

17. James, Bill, *The Baseball Book 1990* (New York: Villard Books, 1990), p. 249.
18. Weigley, p. 470.
19. Idell, Albert E., *Centennial Summer* (New York: Holt, 1943), pp. 74, 75, 244–247.
20. Weigley, et al., pp. 460–470.
21. Westcott, Rich, *Philadelphia's Old Ballparks* (Philadelphia: Temple University Press, 1996), p. 5.
22. *Baseball Research Journal* (Cooperstown: Society for American Baseball Research, 1976), p. 115.
23. Seymour, p. 88. The Athletics' debts were exacerbated by attendance falling off even more, due to competition from two free public events, the Regatta and the Fireman's Parade. At least that's what Thompson told Hulbert in his letter to the NL president.
24. www.AllGamesBaseball.com.
25. Voigt, p. 70.
26. *Chicago Daily Tribune*, April 1, 1894.

Chapter 9

1. E-mail correspondence with Jerrold Casway, February 4, 2005.
2. Richter, Francis C., *Richter's History and Records of Base Ball* (Jefferson, NC: McFarland, 2005), p.117.
3. Seymour, Harold, *Baseball: The Early Years* (New York: Oxford University Press, 1960), p. 136. Richter tells the same story, that this western tour was the key act in arousing interest in starting a new league to compete with the National.
4. Dewey, Donald, and Acocella, Nicholas, *Encyclopedia of Major League Baseball Teams* (New York: HarperCollins, 1993), p. 411; e-mail correspondence with Jerrold Casway, February 4, 2005.
5. Nemec, David, *The Beer & Whiskey League* (Guilford: The Lyons Press, 2004), p. 192.
6. *Brooklyn Eagle*, September 1, 1880. SABR member Brock Helander gets credit for discovering that there were two Athletic teams in 1880.
7. Richter, p. 119.
8. Nemec, pp. 19, 20.
9. Seymour, pp. 137, 138. Seymour says that Phillips instigated the October meeting in Pittsburgh, but that he forgot about the whole matter after sending the postcards because he had been deposed as the Philadelphias' manager and then quit baseball (clearly not the case.
10. Nemec, pp. 21, 22.
11. *Washington Post*, May 9, 1880; e-mail correspondence with Brock Helander, February 18, 2006. Helander notes that Sharsig took a five-year lease on Oakdale Park in July 1881. Historian and author Norman Macht, writing on the Baseball Library website (*www.baseballlibrary.com*) also says that Sharsig's Athletics had already been playing at Oakdale Park since he "organized" the team in 1880.

12. Nemec, p. 25; e-mail correspondence with Frank Vaccaro, February 10, 2006. Vaccaro, quoting an article from Richter's June 21, 1913, *Sporting Life* says the Reds offered Fulmer, at the time a shareholder in the Athletics, a large bonus.
13. *The National Pastime* (Cleveland: Society for American Baseball Research, 2003), p. 124.
14. Nemec, p. 35.
15. Westcott, Rich, *Philadelphia's Old Ballparks* (Philadelphia: Temple University Press, 1996), pp. 4–6.
16. Nemec, p. 31.
17. *Ibid.*, p. 53.
18. Seymour, pp. 140, 141.
19. Nemec, p. 83.
20. *Ibid.*, p. 38.

Chapter 10

1. Westcott, Rich, *Philadelphia's Old Ballparks* (Philadelphia: Temple University Press, 1996), p. 6.
2. *www.baseball-reference.com*.
3. Nemec, David, *The Beer & Whiskey League* (Guilford: The Lyons Press, 2004), pp. 45, 46.
4. Westcott, p. 5.
5. Nemec, p. 46.
6. *Ibid.*, p. 48.
7. *Ibid.*, pp. 44, 45.
8. *Ibid.*, pp. 45, 53.
9. *www.retrosheet.org*.
10. Voigt, David Quentin, *American Baseball: From Gentleman's Sport to the Commissioner System* (Norman: University of Oklahoma Press, 1966), p. 129. The Athletics definitely had the city's attention in 1883. One of Voigt's favorite stories, which he has told on numerous occasions, involves a sleepy Athletic fan in church, who, upon hearing the pastor's rhetorical question about the 10 lepers—"Where are the nine?"—answers out loud that the nine are all right, and that the Browns aren't going to down them.
11. Nemec, p. 53.
12. Jordan, David M., *Occasional Glory* (Jefferson, NC: McFarland, 2002), p. 8.
13. Voigt, p. 129. Nemec says the post-season series never got beyond the talking stage.
14. Tiemann, Robert L., and Rucker, Mark, *Nineteenth Century Stars* (Kansas City: Society for American Baseball Research, 1989), p. 144.
15. Nemec, pp. 53, 54.
16. Dewey, Donald, and Acocella, Nicholas, *Encyclopedia of Major League Baseball Teams* (New York: HarperCollins, 1993), p. 412. Although he doesn't give any figures, Francis Richter says the Athletics set a Philadelphia attendance record in 1883.

Chapter 11

1. Tiemann, Robert L., and Rucker, Mark, *Nineteenth Century Stars* (Kansas City: Society for American Baseball Research, 1989), p. 65.
2. Seymour, Harold, *Baseball: The Early Years* (New York: Oxford University Press, 1960), p. 143.
3. Nemec, David, *The Beer & Whiskey League* (Guilford: The Lyons Press, 2004), p. 44.
4. Voigt, David Quentin, *American Baseball: From Gentleman's Sport to the Commissioner System* (Norman: University of Oklahoma Press, 1966), p. 70.
5. Dewey, Donald, and Acocella, Nicholas, *Encyclopedia of Major League Baseball Teams* (New York: HarperCollins, 1993), p. 588.
6. Jordan, David M., *Occasional Glory* (Jefferson, NC: McFarland, 2002), p. 6.
7. Dewey and Acocella say this took place in 1881. Rich Westcott, in *Philadelphia's Old Ballparks*, says this happened in 1882. Most likely, it was after the end of the 1881 season.
8. *The National Pastime* (Cleveland: Society for American Baseball Research, 2003), p. 123. Shibe and Reach consulted each other on all their business dealings, thus Shibe probably felt the same way as Reach.
9. Dewey and Acocella, p. 413.
10. Jordan, p. 6.
11. Westcott, Rich, *Philadelphia's Old Ballparks* (Philadelphia: Temple University Press, 1996), p. 12.
12. Dewey and Acocella, p. 413.
13. Dewey, Donald, and Acocella, Nicholas, *The New Biographical History of Baseball* (Chicago: Triumph Books, 2002), p. 127.
14. Tiemann and Rucker, p. 43.
15. Jordan, p. 7.
16. Bilovsky, Frank, and Westcott, Rich, *The Phillies Encyclopedia* (New York: Leisure Press, 1984), p. 323.
17. Nemec, p. 45.
18. Westcott, p. 12.
19. Nemec, p. 54.
20. Westcott, pp. 12, 13.
21. Nemec, p. 54.
22. Jordan, p. 8.
23. Dewey and Acocella, *Encyclopedia of Major League Baseball Teams*, p. 414.
24. Ryczek, William J., *Blackguards and Red Stockings* (Wallingford: Colebrook Press, 1992), p. 115. "Let us get our and your second wind, then look out Philadelphias," said Wright.
25. Voigt, p. 45.
26. Tiemann and Rucker, p. 42.
27. Ivor-Campbell, Frederick, Tiemann, Robert L., and Rucker, Mark, eds., *Baseball's First Stars* (Cleveland: Society for American Baseball Research, 1996), p. 63.
28. Jordan, p. 8.
29. Bilovsky and Westcott, pp. 12, 13.
30. Jordan, p. 9.
31. Westcott, pp. 11, 28–32.
32. www.retrosheet.org.
33. Bilovsky and Westcott, p. 14.
34. Jordan, p. 10.
35. Smith, Robert, *Baseball in the Afternoon* (New York: Simon & Schuster, 1993), pp. 48, 49.
36. Bilovsky and Westcott, p. 14.
37. *The National Pastime*, p. 123.
38. Jordan, p. 12.
39. *Ibid.*
40. Shatzkin, Mike, and Charlton, Jim, *The Ballplayers* (New York: William Morrow, 1990), p. 1204.
41. www.retrosheet.org.

Chapter 12

1. Dewey, Donald, and Acocella, Nicholas, *Encyclopedia of Major League Baseball Teams* (New York: HarperCollins, 1993), p. 412.
2. Richter, Francis C., *Richter's History and Records of Base Ball* (Jefferson, NC: McFarland, 2005), p. 126.
3. Nemec, David, *The Beer & Whiskey League* (Guilford: The Lyons Press, 2004), p. 192.
4. Dewey and Acocella, p. 412.
5. Nemec, p. 192.
6. Richter, p. 117.
7. Seymour, Harold, *Baseball: The Early Years* (New York: Oxford University Press, 1960), pp. 234, 235.
8. Nemec, p. 66.
9. Lanigan, Ernest J., *Baseball Cyclopedia* (Jefferson, NC: McFarland, 2005), p. 138.
10. Seymour, p. 191.
11. Nemec, p. 93.
12. *Ibid.*, p. 115.
13. Lansche, Jerry, *Glory Fades Away* (Dallas: Taylor Publishing, 1991), p. 234.
14. Lieb, Frederick G., *Connie Mack: Grand Old Man of Baseball* (New York: Putnam, 1945), p. 70.
15. Nemec, pp. 142, 154.
16. Lanigan, pp. 139, 140.
17. Nemec, p. 156.
18. www.retrosheet.org.
19. Dewey and Acocella, p. 412.
20. Nemec, pp. 193–195.
21. Dewey and Acocella, p. 412.
22. Nemec, p. 243.
23. *Ibid.*, p. 197.
24. Dewey and Acocella, p. 412.
25. www.retrosheet.org.
26. Nemec, p. 197.

Chapter 13

1. Wright, Marshall D., *The National Association of Base Ball Players, 1857–1870* (Jefferson,

NC: McFarland, 2000), pp. 229–237, 280–283, 324–327.
2. Ryczek, William J., *Blackguards and Red Stockings* (Wallingford: Colebrook Press, 1992), pp. 52, 179, 187.
3. Weigley, Russell E., et al., *Philadelphia: A 300 Year History* (New York: Norton, 1982), pp. 424, 425.
4. Gordon, Robert, and Burgoyne, Tom, *Movin' On Up* (Moorestown: Middle Atlantic Press, 2004), p. 171.
5. Ivor-Campbell, Frederick, Tiemann, Robert L., and Rucker, Mark, eds., *Baseball's First Stars* (Cleveland: Society for American Baseball Research, 1996), pp. 117, 147, 182.
6. *Brooklyn Eagle*, September 14, 1882.
7. Seymour, Harold, *Baseball: The Early Years* (New York: Oxford University Press, 1960), p. 136.
8. *Brooklyn Eagle*, January 9, 1877; e-mail correspondence with Frank Vaccaro, February 6, 2006.
9. Tiemann, Robert L., and Rucker, Mark, eds., *Nineteenth Century Stars* (Kansas City, MO: Society for American Baseball Research, 1989), pp. 44, 49, 94, 106, 119.
10. Ivor-Campbell, Tiemann, Rucker, pp. 9, 57, 167.
11. *Chicago Daily Tribune*, April 1, 1894.
12. E-mail correspondence with Frank Vaccaro, February 6, 2006.
13. *Proceedings from Philadelphia's Baseball History* (Philadelphia: The Historical Society of Pennsylvania, 1990), p. 28.
14. Tiemann and Rucker, p. 22.
15. *Proceedings from Philadelphia's Baseball History*, p. 28.
16. *Chicago Daily Tribune*, March 31, 1878.
17. Tiemann and Rucker, pp. 44, 94, 106.
18. *Chicago Daily Tribune*, March 31, 1878.
19. *Washington Post*, July 8, 1878; April 23, 1879; May 31, 1879. The April 23, 1879, *Boston Globe* also reports on Defiance.
20. *Brooklyn Eagle*, July 27, 1879.
21. E-mail correspondence with Frank Vaccaro, February 6, 2006.
22. *Washington Post*, May 9, 1880; e-mail correspondence with Frank Vaccaro, February 6, 2006.
23. E-mail correspondence with Brock Helander, February 18, 2006.
24. *Brooklyn Eagle*, September 1, 1880.
25. Despite the fact that both the *Chicago Tribune* and the *Boston Globe* reported in late March 1880 that Phillips was organizing a Philadelphia team.
26. Tiemann and Rucker, p. 76.
27. Westcott, Rich, *Philadelphia's Old Ballparks* (Philadelphia: Temple University Press, 1996), p. 10.
28. E-mail correspondence with Frank Vaccaro, February 6, 2006; correspondence with Brock Helander, February 13, 2006.

29. Westcott, p. 11.
30. Ivor-Campbell, Tiemann, Rucker, pp. 6, 62, 100.
31. Threston, Christopher, *The Integration of Baseball in Philadelphia* (Jefferson, NC: McFarland, 2003), p. 11.
32. Peterson, Robert, *Only the Ball Was White* (New York: McGraw-Hill, 1970), pp. 34, 38. *Sporting Life* also indicated that the St. Louis Black Stockings or Baltimore Atlantics might have been pros at this time as well.
33. Nemec, David, *The Beer & Whiskey League* (Guilford: The Lyons Press, 2004), pp. 77–80.
34. Ivor-Campbell, Tiemann, Rucker, p. 129.
35. Dewey, Donald, and Acocella, Nicholas, *Encyclopedia of Major League Baseball Teams* (New York: HarperCollins, 1993), p. 433.
36. Westcott, p. 6.
37. Nemec, p. 213.
38. Voigt, David Quentin, *American Baseball: From Gentleman's Sport to the Commissioner System* (Norman: University of Oklahoma Press, 1966), p. 164.
39. Dewey and Acocella, p. 434.
40. Lowry, Philip, *Green Cathedrals* (Manhattan, KS: AG Press, 1986). p. 69.
41. Westcott, p. 6.
42. Dewey and Acocella, p. 434.
43. Voigt, p. 163.
44. *The National Pastime* (Cleveland: The Society for American Baseball Research, 2003), p. 124.
45. *1893 Philadelphia Record Almanac*, p. 82.
46. Tiemann and Rucker, pp. 71, 134.
47. Ivor-Campbell, Tiemann, Rucker, pp. 20, 113.
48. *Baseball Research Journal* (Kansas City: The Society for American Baseball Research, 1987), p. 19. Although his efforts failed, he would be back in another year in a similar role for Connie Mack in the founding of the American League.
49. Alexander, Charles, *John McGraw* (New York: Viking Penguin, 1988), p. 69. According to Bill Wagner, writing in SABR's 1987 *Baseball Research Journal*, Pittsburgher George Stoer was, as of February 2, the financial backer of the Philadelphia franchise.
50. *Ibid.*, 69.

Chapter 14

1. Nemec, David, *The Beer & Whiskey League* (Guilford: The Lyons Press, 2004), p. 213.
2. Seymour, Harold, *Baseball: The Early Years* (New York: Oxford University Press, 1960), pp. 240, 241, 245, 246.
3. Nemec, p. 220.
4. Seymour, pp. 245, 247.
5. Nemec, p. 221.
6. Seymour, p. 251.
7. Dewey, Donald, and Acocella, Nicholas, *En-

cyclopedia of Major League Baseball Teams (New York: HarperCollins, 1993), p. 412.

8. Nemec, p. 221.

9. Sullivan, Dean, *Early Innings: A Documentary History of Baseball, 1825–1908* (Lincoln: University of Nebraska Press, 1995), p. 211.

10. Nemec, p. 192. The late 1890 Athletics were called the Troubadours because they were masquerading as a major league team; this is also a possible reference to Sharsig's theatrical background.

11. *www.retrosheet.org*.

12. Richter, Francis C., *Richter's History and Records of Base Ball* (Jefferson, NC: McFarland, 2005), p. 130.

13. Seymour, pp. 249, 251, 252. Rogers' vote against the Athletics would have been a given as he certainly didn't want Stovey playing back in Philadelphia and competing for fans against the Phillies.

14. Nemec, p. 222.

15. *Ibid.*, p. 227.

16. Seymour, pp. 257, 260.

17. Dewey and Acocella, p. 412.

18. Jordan, David M., *The Athletics of Philadelphia* (Jefferson, NC: McFarland, 1999), p. 9.

19. Jordan, David M., *Occasional Glory* (Jefferson, NC: McFarland, 2002), p. 14.

20. Weigley, Russell E., et al., *Philadelphia: A 300 Year History* (New York: Norton, 1982), pp. 471, 474, 475.

21. *Ibid.*, pp. 475, 478.

22. *Ibid.*, p. 478.

Chapter 15

1. Voigt, David Quentin, *American Baseball: From Gentleman's Sport to the Commissioner System* (Norman: University of Oklahoma Press, 1966), p. 246.

2. Bilovsky, Frank, and Westcott, Rich, *The Phillies Encyclopedia* (New York: Leisure Press, 1984), p. 17.

3. Solomon, Burt, *The Baseball Timeline* (New York: DK Publishing, 2001), pp. 79, 80. Early baseball stadia all over the country had a strong tendency to burn down, even as late as the great Polo Grounds fire of 1911. In fact, two other wooden ballparks—in Boston and Chicago—also burned in 1894.

4. Westcott, Rich, *Philadelphia's Old Ballparks* (Philadelphia: Temple University Press, 1996), pp. 74, 75.

5. Bilovsky and Westcott, p. 17.

6. *www.retrosheet.org*.

7. Westcott, p. 75.

8. *www.retrosheet.org*.

9. Westcott, p. 75.

10. *Baseball Research Journal* (Cooperstown, NY: The Society for American Baseball Research, 1982), pp. 4, 5.

11. *www.retrosheet.org*.

12. Westcott, p. 49.

13. *The National Pastime* (Cleveland: The Society for American Baseball Research, 2003), p. 124.

14. Bilovsky and Westcott, p. 291.

15. Jordan, David M., *Occasional Glory* (Jefferson, NC: McFarland, 2002), p. 17.

16. *Ibid.*, p.19.

17. *Ibid.*, p.18.

18. Dewey, Donald, and Acocella, Nicholas, *Encyclopedia of Major League Baseball Teams* (New York: HarperCollins, 1993), p. 416.

19. Bilovsky and Westcott, p. 292.

20. Jordan, p. 20.

21. Lanigan, Ernest J., *Baseball Cyclopedia* (Jefferson, NC: McFarland, 2005), p. 146.

22. Dewey and Acocella, p. 416.

23. *www.retrosheet.org*.

24. Jordan, p. 22.

25. *www.retrosheet.org*.

26. *www.retrosheet.org*.

27. Faber, Charles F., *Baseball Pioneers* (Jefferson, NC: McFarland, 1997), p. 70. The Faber System produces a single number for a player's offensive, defensive and total production (obtained by adding the other two figures together.) The latter is sort of a "total player ranking" such as Pete Palmer and John Thorn use in *Total Baseball*.

28. *www.retrosheet.org*.

29. Jordan, p. 22.

30. Seymour, Harold, *Baseball: The Early Years* (New York: Oxford University Press, 1960), p. 289.

Bibliography

Alexander, Charles. *John McGraw*. New York: Viking Penguin, 1988.
_____. *Our Game*. New York: Holt, 1991.
_____. *Ty Cobb*. New York: Oxford University Press, 1984.
The Baseball Encyclopedia. New York: Macmillan, 1969.
Bilovsky, Frank, and Westcott, Rich. *The Phillies Encyclopedia*. New York: Leisure Press, 1984.
Block, David. *Baseball Before We Knew It*. Lincoln: University of Nebraska Press, 2005.
Brock, Darryl. *If I Never Get Back*. New York: Crown, 1990.
Charlton, James, ed. *The Baseball Chronology*. New York: Macmillan, 1991.
Davids, L. Robert, ed. *Insider's Baseball*. New York: Scribner's, 1983.
Dewey, Donald, and Acocella, Nicholas. *Encyclopedia of Major League Baseball Teams*. New York: HarperCollins, 1993.
_____. *The New Biographical History of Baseball*. Chicago: Triumph Books, 2002.
Durso, Joseph. *Baseball and the American Dream*. St. Louis: The Sporting News, 1986.
Faber, Charles F. *Baseball Pioneers*. Jefferson, NC: McFarland, 1997.
Freedman, Russell, *Lincoln, a Photobiography*. New York: Clarion Books, 1987.
Frommer, Harvey. *Primitive Baseball*. New York: Atheneum, 1988.
Gordon, Robert, and Burgoyne, Tom. *Movin' On Up*. Moorestown, N.J.: Middle Atlantic Press, 2004.
Hynd, Noel. *The Giants of the Polo Grounds*. New York: Doubleday, 1988.
Idell, Albert E. *Centennial Summer*. New York: Holt, 1943.
Ivor-Campbell, Frederick, Tiemann, Robert L., and Rucker, Mark, eds. *Baseball's First Stars*. Cleveland: Society for American Baseball Research, 1996.
James, Bill. *The Bill James Historical Baseball Abstract*. New York: Villard Books, 1985.
_____. *The New Bill James Historical Baseball Abstract*. New York: The Free Press, 2001.
_____. *The Politics of Glory*. New York: Macmillan, 1994.
_____, and Neyer, Rob. *The Neyer/James Guide to Pitchers*. New York: Simon & Schuster, 2004.
Jordan, David M. *The Athletics of Philadelphia*. Jefferson, NC: McFarland, 1999.
_____. *Occasional Glory*. Jefferson, NC: McFarland, 2002.
Kaese, Harold, and Lynch, R.G. *The Milwaukee Braves*. New York: Putnam, 1954.
Kuklick, Bruce. *To Every Thing A Season*. Princeton, NJ: Princeton University Press, 1991.
Lanigan, Ernest J. *Baseball Cyclopedia*. Jefferson, NC: McFarland, 2005.
Lansche, Jerry. *Glory Fades Away*. Dallas: Taylor, 1991.
Levine, Peter. *A.G. Spalding and the Rise of Baseball*. New York: Oxford University Press, 1985.
Lieb, Frederick G. *Baseball As I Have Known It*. New York: Grosset & Dunlap, 1977.
_____. *Connie Mack: Grand Old Man of Baseball*. New York: Putnam, 1945.
Lowry, Philip. *Green Cathedrals*. Manhattan, KS: AG Press, 1986.
Nemec, David. *The Beer & Whiskey League*. Guilford, CT: The Lyons Press, 2004.
_____. *The Great 19th Century Encyclopedia of Major League Baseball*. New York: Donald I. Fine Books, 1997.
Peterson, Robert. *Only the Ball Was White*. New York: McGraw-Hill, 1970.
Peverelly, Charles. *The Book of American Pastimes*. New York: Charles Peverelly, 1866.
Proceedings from Philadelphia's Baseball History. Philadelphia: The Historical Society of Pennsylvania, 1990.

Richter, Francis C. *Richter's History and Records of Base Ball.* Jefferson, NC: McFarland, 2005.

Roth, Philip. *The Great American Novel.* New York: Holt, Reinhart and Winston, 1973.

Ryczek, William J. *Blackguards and Red Stockings.* Wallingford, CT: Colebrook Press, 1992.

Schwarz, Alan. *The Numbers Game.* New York: St. Martin's Press, 2004.

Seymour, Harold. *Baseball: The Early Years.* New York: Oxford University Press, 1960.

Shatzkin, Mike, and Charlton, Jim. *The Ballplayers.* New York: William Morrow, 1990.

Smith, Robert. *Baseball in the Afternoon.* New York: Simon & Schuster, 1993.

Solomon, Burt. *The Baseball Timeline.* New York: DK Publishing, 2001.

STATS All-Time Major League Handbook. Morton Grove, IL: STATS Publishing, 2000.

Stone, Tanya Lee. *Abraham Lincoln.* New York: DK Publishing, 2005.

Sullivan, Dean. *Early Innings: A Documentary History of Baseball, 1825–1908.* Lincoln, NE: University of Nebraska Press, 1995.

Thorn, John. *A Century of Baseball Lore.* New York: Galahad Books, 1980.

Thorn, John, and Holway, John. *The Pitcher.* New York: Prentice Hall Press, 1987.

Thorn, John, and Palmer, Pete. *Total Baseball.* 4th ed. New York: Warner Books, 1995.

Threston, Christopher. *The Integration of Baseball in Philadelphia.* Jefferson, NC: McFarland, 2003.

Tiemann, Rober, and Rucker, Mark. *Nineteenth Century Stars.* Kansas City, MO: Society for American Baseball Research, 1989.

Voigt, David Quentin. *American Baseball: From Gentleman's Sport to the Commissioner System.* Norman, OK: University of Oklahoma Press, 1966.

Warner, Sam Bass, Jr. *The Private City.* Philadelphia: University of Pennsylvania Press, 1996.

Weigley, Russell E., et al. *Philadelphia: A 300 Year History.* New York: Norton, 1982.

Westcott, Rich. *Philadelphia's Old Ballparks.* Philadelphia: Temple University Press, 1996.

Wright, Marshall, D. *The National Association of Base Ball Players, 1857–1870.* Jefferson, NC: McFarland, 2000.

Websites

Afrolumens Project
 www.afrolumens.org
All Baseball
 www.all-baseball.com
All Games Baseball
 www.AllGamesBaseball.com
Cap Anson
 www.capanson.com
Baseball Almanac
 www.baseball-almanac.com
Baseball Archive
 www.baseball1.com
Baseball Immortals
 http://totk.com/baseballimmortals
Baseball Index
 www.baseballindex.org
Baseball Library
 www.baseballlibrary.com
Baseball Page
 www.baseballpage.com
Baseball Primer
 www.baseballprimer.com
Baseball Prospectus
 www.baseballprospectus.com
Baseball Reference
 www.baseball-reference.com
Baseball Think Factory
 www.baseballthinkfactory.org
Billy-Ball
 www.billy-ball.com
The Church of Jesus Christ of Latter-day Saints
 www.familysearch.org
Deadball Era
 www.thedeadballera.com
Historical Society of Pennsylvania
 www.hsp.org
Major League Baseball
 http://mlb.com
Mudville Magazine
 www.mudvillemagazine.com
National Baseball Hall of Fame
 http://baseballhalloffame.org
Retrosheet
 www.retrosheet.org
Society for American Baseball Research
 www.sabr.org
Wikipedia
 http://en.wikipedia.org

Newspapers and Periodicals

The Baseball Book
Baseball Research Journal
Beadle's Dime Base Ball Player
The Bill James Baseball Abstract
Boston Globe
Brooklyn Eagle
Chicago Daily Tribune

The National Pastime
New York Clipper
New York Times
Nine
Philadelphia Daily Evening Telegraph
Philadelphia Inquirer
Philadelphia Inquirer Magazine
Philadelphia North American
Philadelphia Press
Philadelphia Record Almanac
Sporting Life

The Sporting News
Washington Post

Collections

1870 United States Census (National Archives and Records Administration Southeast Regional Archives).

American Negro Historical Society Papers (The Historical Society of Pennsylvania).

Index

No fewer than six distinct organizations in Philadelphia have born the name "Athletics" and two different organizations fielded teams known as "Philadelphias." (Not counting the present-day Phillies.) To differentiate between them, they are identified parenthetically in this Index, i.e., Athletic Club (1)—the original Athletic Club; Athletic Clubs (2)—the independent, professional Athletics; Philadelphia Athletics (3)—the first American Association Athletics; Philadelphia Athletics (4)—the 1891 AA Athletics; Philadelphia Athletics (5)—the 1890s minor league Athletics; Philadelphia Athletics (6)—Connie Mack's Athletics. Similarly, there were two different American Associations (one still-born) in the 19th century. They are designated American Association (1) and American Association (2) herein. Numbers in ***bold italics*** indicate pages with photographs.

A.G. Mills Commission 14, 242
A.J. Reach Company 114, 149, 189, 239–242
Acocella, Nicholas 91, 97, 153, 181, 223, 247, 249
Addy, Bob 78–81, 214
African-American clubs: Cuban Giants 146, 147; Excelsior 58–60, 185, 212; Keystone Athletics 146; Mutual 146, 147; Orion 60, 146, 147; possible NABBP membership 57–59; Pythian 37, 55–61, 67, 83, 146, 185–187, 213, 214; Washington Manhattan 146
Allen, Bob 128
Allen, John 167
Allison, Doug 65, 66, 69
Altherr, Thomas 3
Altoona Mountain Citys 33, 147
American Association (AA) (1) 98–100, 102, 105, 139, 152–155, 157, 208, 234, 239, 240, 243, 247
American Association (2) 150, 151
American League 144, 150, 157, 172, 191, 194, 196–198, 240, 241, 243, 245, 246, 248, 250, 253, 257, 259
American Negro Historical Society 213
Andrews, Ed 124
Anson, Adrian (Cap) 56, 76, 80, 84, 85, 91, 92, 94–96, 144,
151, 167, 178, 181–184; 197, 202, 227, 229, 243, 261–263
Anson, Henry 181
Athletic Club (1): advancing popularity of baseball 33, 34; Camac Woods grounds 18, 21, 25, 27, 29, 39, 41–44, 49, 64, 72, 106; 1860 season 25; 1861 season 31, 32; 1862 season 32; 1863 New York tour 33; 1863 season 33, 34; 1864 season 36; 1865 games with Atlantic 42, 43; 1865 season 41–45; 1865 tournament in Washington 42; 1865 trips to Western Pennsylvania 44; 1865 trip to New York 44; 1866 season 47–50; 1867 season 51, 52, 54; 1867 lineup 52; 1868 season 62–64; 1868 tour 64; 1869 lineup 66; 1869 season 66, 67; 1870 lineup 68, 69; 1870 season 67–70; 1871 directors 73; 1871 injuries 74, 75; 1871 lineup 73; 1871 pennant race 74, 75; 1871 season 72–75; 1872 turnover 76; 1872 season 76, 77; 1873 season 77, 78; 1874 season 82, 83; 1874 trip to England 81, 82; 1875 debts 86; 1875 team 85; 1876 lineup 94, 95; 1876 pitching 94; expulsion from National League 95, 96; first pennant 72–75; first player transaction 84; first playing grounds 41;
founding 24; importance to National Association 72; Jefferson Park 39, 72, 74, 77, 79, 80, 93, 95, 100, 106, 107, 111, 124, 132, 134, 135, 137, 139, 140, 227; joining the National League 90–92; loss of 1869 players 65, 66; managers/captains 50, 66, 73, 78, 133, 213. 227; mythical national titles 42, 47, 60, 91; *New York Clipper* Gold Medals 63–65; October 1866 series vs. Atlantic 48, 49; October 30, 1871 game vs. Chicago 75; paying players 41, 44, 50, 52, 62, 63, 66, 203, 237; playing grounds 29, 41–43, 49, 72, 77, 93; professional first nine 62, 63; rivalry with Philadelphia White Stockings 77, 78, 95
Athletic Clubs (2) 97–100, 142–146, 204, 208, 215, 220, 230, 234, 239
Atkinson, Al 132, 134

Baer, George 160
Bakely, Jersey 108, 109, 148
Baltimore Monumentals 103, 147
Baltimore Orioles 101–103, 134, 164, 165, 168, 170, 174, 177, 216, 217
Bancroft, Frank 255
Barnes, Ross 89
Barnes, Samuel 22

281

Barnie, Billy 145, 146, 153, 155, 216, 243, 248
baseball: amateur to professional transition 62; baseball manufacturing 17, 240, 251, 254; during the Civil War 31, 32, 37, 38; evolution of 3, 4, 13, 14, 16, 17, 141; first professional season 62–65; Philadelphia's 19th century role 3, 4, 13–19, 33, 34, 41, 44, 51, 52, 55–59, 63, 71, 72, 76, 81, 82, 84–86, 90–92, 97–100, 113, 114, 141, 146–150, 152–155; pitching distance changes 163; professionalism in 41, 42, 47, 50, 51, 53, 61–64, 66, 67, 69–75, 89, 123, 146, 147; in the south 38, 74
Bastain, Charlie 125
Battin, Joe 82, 142
Bechtel, George 54, 68, 69, 73, 75–77, 79, 81, 83–85, 94, 144, 183, 207, 214
Beers, Dorothy Gondos 92, 186
Benedict Club 27, 31
Berg, Moe 203, 204
Berkenstock, Nate 45, 75, 213
Bernhard, Bill 77, 174, 175
Berry, Tom 49, 52, 62, 63, 66, 68, 73
Biddle, Daniel 184–186
Bierbauer, Lou 4, 131, 134, 153, 154, 256
Bierbauer/Stovey case 4, 153, 154
Birchall, Jud 101, 109, 131, 144–146
Blakiston, Bob 101, 102, 109
Blanchard, William 20
Block, David 3, 16
Bolivar, William 187
Borden, Joe 86, 95
Boston Beaneaters 112, 124, 154, 159, 162, 163, 169, 174, 189, 211, 256
Boston Red Stockings 25, 71, 72, 81, 90, 95, 114, 119, 199, 214, 227, 265
Bowa, Larry 170
Bowlby, Edward, Jr. 20
Bowlby, Samuel 20
Boyle, Jack 170
Bradley, George 108–111, 132, 142, 144
Branson, Samuel 20
Brenner, John 20
Brock, Darryl 66, 264, 265
Brooklyn Atlantic Club 22, 32–34, 36, 42, 47–54, 63, 64, 66, 67–69, 76, 79, 80, 87, 90, 98, 116, 142, 150, 192, 224, 233, 236, 237

Brooklyn Eckford Club 32, 33, 41, 45, 52–54, 64, 66, 203, 223, 237, 238
Brooklyn Excelsior Club 27, 33, 41, 44, 53, 72, 203, 212, 237
Brooklyn Superbas 174, 175, 177
Brotherhood of Professional Baseball Players 126, 127, 130, 137, 148, 149, 152, 163, 189, 196, 206, 210, 217, 240, 241, 243, 245, 263
Brouthers, Dan 169
Brown, Tom 166, 234
Buffington, Charlie 123–127, 146, 149, 159, 240
Burns, Tom 145, 262
Burr, Raymond 56, 57, 213, 214
Bushong, Doc 142, 146

Callahan, Nixey 150
Camac Woods Grounds (17th & Columbia) 18, 21, 25, 27, 29, 39, 41–44, 49, 64, 72, 106
Camden 14, 15, 17–19, 27, 38, 47, 51, 60, 74, 88, 125, 186, 203
Campanella, Roy 187, 231
Campbell, John 92
Carpenter, Samuel 20
Carsey, Kid 163, 165, 168, 170
Casey, Dan 121, 123–127, 149, 159
Cassatt, Alexander 159
Casway, Jerrold 97, 238, 241
Catto, Octavius *58*; as baseball player 37, 57, 60, 61, 185; bio 184–187; integration of horse cars 37, 55, 88, 186; murder of 55, 61, 187; passing of 15th Amendment 61, 186, 187; reasons for applying to NABBP 57
Catto, William 184
Carr, William Hart 20
Caylor, O.P. 98–100, 105, 111, 208, 233, 234, 243
Centennial Exposition 37, 83, 87, 88, 92, 93, 95, 113, 159
Centennial Park 26, 115
Chadwick, Henry 24, 32, 34, 62, 64, 65, 71, 72, 78, 81, 263
Chamberlain, Icebox 155, 157
Champion, Aaron 65
Chapman, Fred 135
Chapman, John 52
Chestnut Street Theater 51, 53, 57, 65, 67, 141, 247
Chicago White Stockings 68, 69, 72–76, 80–86, 89–92, 94–96, 124, 133, 144, 183, 193, 194, 206, 208, 227, 229, 230, 262, 263, 266
Chiles, Pearce 173, 175

Cincinnati Red Stockings 52, 62, 63, 65, 66, 69, 71, 73, 76, 101, 105, 110, 111, 116, 119, 133, 137, 144, 208, 212, 225, 230, 264, 265
City Item Club 60, 61, 67, 141
Civil War 31, 32, 36, 37, 41, 42, 45, 47, 48, 55, 59, 73, 87
Clapp, John 77, 85, 94
Clark, Thomas 20
Clements, Jack 28, 120, 121, 123, 124, 127, 128, 148, 156, 158, 162, 166, 167, 169, 177, 178, 187–189, 201, 231, 232
Cleveland Blues 74, 108, 118, 135, 191, 197, 246
Cleveland Forest Citys 77, 207, 223
Cleveland Spiders 108, 165, 168, 174, 175, 189, 191
Coleman, John 115, 117, 118, 120, 132
College baseball 71, 142, 142, 164, 165, 173, 199, 201, 220
Color Line 2, 4, 55–61, 183, 185, 214
Columbia Park 26, 39, 42, 60, 151
Connor, Roger 162, 163, 256
Conroy, Ben 138, 139
Continental Club 22, 24, 25
Cooley, Duff 171
Cooper, Lewis 20
Coon, William 94
Cope, Elias 45, 46, 53
Corcoran, Tommy 155
Corey, Fred 108, 109, 111
cork-centered baseball 241, 254
Corkhill, Pop 145, 155
Cox, William 5, 244
Coxe, Marcellus 20
Coyne, Andrew 93
Coyne, Matthew 29, 42, 43, 106, 216
Craver, Bill 82–85, 94, 214
"Creeping Commercialism" 62
Creighton, Jim 27, 41, 72, 199, 200, 203, 237, 263
Cricket/Cricket Clubs 18, 21, 32, 41, 46, 59, 81, 82, 141, 224, 225–227, 235–237, 251, 261, 264
Cross, Lave 131, 149, 155, 157, 162, 163, 166, 189–192, 199, 232, 249
Cross, Monte 173, 175, 177
Crowley, Bill 109
Cummings, Candy 82, 223, 225
Cushman, Ed 132
Cuthbert, Maggie 194
Cuthbert, Ned 45, 46, 51, 52,

54, 62, 63, 66, 68, 73, 76, 77, 80, 192–194, 229

Daily, Ed 120, 121, 124
Daily, Hugh 118
Daniels, J.B. 27
Davis, George 194, 195, 256
Davis, James Whyte 55–57
Day, John 114
Defiance Club 145, 146
Delahanty, Ed 125–127, 149, 158, 162, 163, 165–167, 169, 170, 172, 173, 175, 177, 194–197, 211, 219, 245, 257, 258
Desilver, Charles 20
Desilver, Robert 20
Detroit Wolverines 102, 106, 111, 121, 122, 124–126, 167, 188, 198, 204, 258
Dewey, Donald 91, 97, 153, 181, 223, 247, 249
Dick, Billy 53
Diehl, John 20
Dockney, Patsy 49–52
Dolan, Joe 175
Donahue, Red 143, 171, 172, 174, 175
Dorgan, Jerry 101, 102, 109
Douglass, Frederick 55, 185
Douglass, Klondike 175
Doyle, Ed (Dutchy) 144, 145
Dragonslayers 226, 264
Drexel University 47, 142
Dubin, Murray 184–186
Duggleby, Bill 172
Dunlap, Fred 178, 197–199, 235
Dunlap, William 20
Dunn, Charles 20

Easton Club 82, 142, 145
Edwards, James 20
Eggler, Dave 82, 84, 85, 94, 144, 145, 226
1860 All Star Game vs. Excelsior 27
1860 season 21–28
1861 season 31, 32
1862 season 32, 33
1863 season 33, 34
1864 season 34, 36
1879 Pennsylvania championship 145, 146
1890 National Agreement 153–155
1893 pitching changes 163
Ellard, George 65–67
Ellmaker, Frederick 20
Ellmaker, Peter 20
Emlen, George 19, 20
Emot, William 24
English base ball 3, 13, 81
Equity Club: claim as pioneer baseball club 21, 22, 25, 26, 31; 1860 players 27, 203; 1860 season 22, 25–27, 31, 34; first game 22, 26; playing grounds 25, 26; re-formation after Civil War 31, 38, 47, 48, 54, 141
Esper, Duke 138
Esterday, Henry 148
Evans, J.S. 72
Ewing, Buck 149, 187

Faber, Charles/Faber System 175, 192, 197, 200, 208, 210, 217, 256, 258, 260
Farrar, Geraldine 117
Farrar, Sid 116, 117, 120, 123, 127, 148, 159, 201
Fennelly, Frank 146
Ferguson, Bob 107, 116–119, 214
Ferguson, Charlie: background 119; bio 199–202; death 125, 215; 1887 statistics 119; hitting 119–121, 124; pitches first Phillies no-hitter 120; pitching 119–121, 124, 125; playing second base 124; popularity 121, 122, 130
Ferguson, James 81
Fiegal, Virginia 182
Fielding, importance of 32, 66, 74, 193
Fifield, Jack 170, 172
15th Amendment 61, 186
First player transaction 84
Firth, Thomas 20
Fisler, Wes 19, 24, 27, 28, 37, 45, 49, 50, 52, 53, 62–64, 66, 69, 70, 73–77, 80, 82, 84, 85, 94, 95, 144, 145, 178, 202–204, 220, 231
Fitler, Edwin 123
Fitzgerald, Dennis 138
Fitzgerald, Harrington 25
Fitzgerald, Thomas 24, 25, 37, 47, 203, 237–239
Flick, Elmer 172, 173, 175, 246
Fogarty, Jim 119, 123, 127, 137, 149, 158, 204–207, 245
Fogel, Horace 14–21, 25, 244, 250
Force, Davy 85, 86, 90, 91, 94, 95, 119, 214
Forepaugh Park 39, 147, 149, 151, 155, 159
Fort Wayne Kekiongas 72, 223
Fox, Edward John 20
Francis, James 59, 60
Fraser, Chick 77, 174, 175, 246
Frazer, Francis 22
Fulmer, Chick 65, 78–81, 98–101, 142, 144–146, 177, 178, 207–209, 234
Fulmer, Michael 207, 208

Gamesh, Gil 226
Garrigues, James 20
Gaskill, Charles 45, 50
Geary Club 51, 53, 54, 58, 59, 65, 66, 69, 141, 228
Geier, Phil 169
Gilpin, Charles 20
Gleason, Bill 136, 232
Gleason, Kid 125–127, 149
Gosham, Alfred 65–67
Gowen, Franklin 160
Grant, Ulysses S. 93, 95
Green, Ed 138–140
Gross, Emil 116, 117
Guskill, Edward 20

Hagan, Art 115, 117
Halbriter, Ed 103
Hall, George 75, 85, 94, 95
Hall of Fame 45, 86, 124, 125, 127, 134, 135, 158, 162, 163, 169, 171, 172, 175, 178, 181, 192, 194, 201, 209, 211, 221, 224, 231, 246, 252, 254, 255, 257, 259
Hallman, Bill 127, 149, 150, 155, 159
Hamilton, Billy 127, 158, 161–163, 165, 166–170, 172, 177, 197, 209–211, 218, 231, 245, 249, 258, 259
Hamilton Club 18, 25–27, 29, 47
The Handel and Haydn 24
Hanlon, Ned 165, 174, 177, 207
Harbridge, Bill 117
Harper, George 164, 165
Hastings, Scott 74
Hathaway, Edward 20
Hayhurst, Hicks: athletic debut 32; attempted integration of baseball 56; bio 211–215; 1864 season 36; 1865 season 45; 1872 season 76; 1873 season 77, 78, 119; hitting in 1866 50; management role with Athletic 73, 133, 227; member of Winona Club 22; Philadelphia Centennials 83, 84, 220; president of Olympic Club 15; Pythian Pennsylvania application 56; role in 1866–1871 Athletic dynasty 28; role in Force Case 86; role in Pennsylvania State convention 56; role in Philadelphia baseball 237, 246, 247; role with 1877 Athletics 144; town ball star 22, 27

Hecker, Guy 111
Heisler, John 24, 37
Helander, Brock 144–146, 235
Henderson, Rickey 209
Herse, George 20
Heubel, George 73–76
Hicks, Nat 82
Hillborn, Joseph 20
Historical Society of Pennsylvania 56, 60, 144, 185, 213
Holdsworth, Jim 82
Hoover, Buster 147, 148
Hufty, Samuel 20
Hulbert, William: business practices of 89–91, 183; contracts with Adrian Anson 91, 96, 144, 182, 183; death of 113, 114; expulsion of Philadelphia Athletics 95, 95; force case 90, 91; Founding National League 89–92, 266; owner of Chicago White Stockings 86, 91, 96, 144, 182, 183; relations with Philadelphia Athletics 86, 90, 91; Troy/Wise case 102
Hulen, Bill 169
Huntingdon Street Grounds (Philadelphia Base Ball Park, Baker Bowl) 39, 40, 121–124, 126, 127, 161, 162, 164–168, 201, 211, 245
Husted, Bill 149

Idell, Albert 92
Institute for Colored Youth 184–187
Irwin, Art 121, 123, 164, 165, 168, 169, 249

James, Bill 91, 251, 250
James, John 20
Jay Cooke and Company 88
Jefferson Street Grounds (Park) 39, 72, 74, 77, 79, 80, 93, 95, 100, 106, 107, 111, 124, 132, 134, 135, 137, 139, 140, 227
Johnson, Ban 240, 241, 243, 248, 253
Jones, Daniel (Jumping Jack) 106, 198, 111, 112
Jones, Isaac 20
Jones, L.B. 72
Jordan, David 157, 181, 194

Keefe, Tim 112, 124, 150, 163
Kelly, Frank 187
Kelly, King 124, 163, 198, 263
Kerns, James 24, 72
Keystone Club: 1860 season 25, 26; 1861 season 31; 1862 season 32; 1863 season 33, 192; 1864 season 34, 36; 1865 season 38, 44–46, 193; 1866 season 48; 1867 season 51, 53, 54, 63; 1868 season 63, 64, 141; 1869 season 66, 67, 141, 207; 1870 season 67, 142, 207; formation 21, 22, 26, 31; playing grounds 22; style of play 53
Keystone Park 147, 249
Kilroy, Bucko 218
Kilroy, Elmer 218
Kilroy, Matt 149, 150, 215–218
King, Martin Luther, Jr. 184, 186
Kingston, Sam 195
Kleinfelder, Dan 34, 36, 45, 50, 52
Knell, Phil 149
Knickerbocker Club 3, 17, 18, 55, 119, 237, 242, 264
Knight, Frank 27
Knight, Lon 94, 95, 105, 106, 108, 109, 111, 112, 131, 133, 227, 247
Knouff, Ed 132
Krauthoff, Louis 153
Kuklick, Bruce 39, 40, 251, 253

Lajoie, Napoleon 4, 77, 150, 169, 170, 173–176, 194, 197, 198, 246
Landis, Doc 19, 102, 103, 145, 146
Larkin, Henry 131–135, 137, 138, 155, 156, 178, 218–220, 231–233
Latham, Arlie 146. 217. 240
Latham, Juice 101–103, 105, 109
Law, Edward 20
LeCount, Caroline 187
Lewis, Fred 117, 146
Lewis, Joseph 20
Lieb, Fred 21, 135, 191, 192, 253
Lincoln, Abraham 38, 66, 87, 185, 186
Lindsay, Robert 20
Litzenburg, W.H. 27
London Field magazine 81
Lovett, Tom 132
Lowry, Morrow 186
Lucas, Henry 147, 148, 198, 199, 236, 249
Lyons, Denny 135–139, 178

Macht, Norman 247–249
Mack, Connie 5, 25, 76, 149, 151, 191, 192, 197, 215, 216, 221, 237, 238, 241, 248, 251, 253, 254, 266
Mack, Denny 76–79, 81, 142, 143
Malloy, Jerry 56
Malone, Fergy 46, 52, 68, 70, 73, 74, 76–80, 94, 95, 144, 145, 147, 226, 231
Mann, Fred 136, 232
Mann, Lawrence 25
Mann, William 187
Manning, Jack 116, 117, 120, 146
Marylebone Cricket Club 81
Mason, Charlie 97, 100, 101, 104, 107, 112, 129, 132, 133, 143, 145, 146, 220, 221, 247, 248, 256
Mathews, Bobby 103, 108–111, 129, 132, 134, 135, 221–224
McBride, Dick: absence from Athletic roster in 1876 94; athletic debut 32, 193, 235; bio 224–228; Cricketeer 82, 235; 1862 season 32, 235; 1863 season 33, 34; 1864 season 36; 1865 season 44, 45; 1866 season 47, 49, 50, 236; 1867 season 52; 1868 season 63, 64; 1869 season 66, 67; 1870 season 68, 236; 1871 season 73–75; 1874 trip to England 82; 1875 season 83, 85, 94; hitting 44, 45, 50, 52, 64, 82, 85, 213; illness in 1869 67; injury in 1871 74, 75; managing 66, 73, 76, 77, 79, 133; 19th century All-Star Team 178; Philadelphia star 27, 28, 32, 45, 53, 77, 83, 212, 235; pitching 34, 67, 77, 94, 212, 227, 236; playing shortstop 34, 36, 44, 45, 50, 207, 235; professional status 50, 63; role in 1866–1871 dynasty 32, 34, 45, 212; role in 1871 pennant-clincher 75
McBride, Frank 214
McClellan, Bill 116, 117, 120, 146
McCormick, Jerry 148
McCullagh, Robert 20
McFarland, Ed 173, 175
McGarr, Chippy 136
McGeachey, Jack 155
McGill, Willie 168
McGinley, Tim 84
McGuire, Deacon 121, 233
McKnight, Denny 98–100, 102, 113, 114
McMahon, Sadie 138, 139
McMichael, Morton 92
McPhee, Bid 134, 197, 198, 256
McTamanay, Jim 155
McVey, Cal 89
Mencken, August 217
Mercantile Club 21–24, 26, 31, 34, 36, 38, 212
Meyerle, Levi 28, 51, 53, 65–68, 73–77, 80, 94, 95, 144, 145, 148, 177, 178, 220, 228–231

Milligan, Isabella 233
Milligan, Jocko 136, 148, 150, 155, 156, 178, 231–233
Mills, Abraham 113, 114, 240, 242
Minerva Club 17, 18, 21, 22, 26, 27, 31, 36, 38, 45, 46, 48, 54, 141
Morgan, J.P. 160
Morris, Cannonball 146
Mort, Joseph 20
Mountain, Frank 103, 108
Moynahan, Mike 109, 112, 146
Mullane, Tony 102, 111
Mulvey, Joe 123, 127, 148, 150, 155, 159, 162, 163
Murphy, Morgan 177
Mutrie, Jim 105
Myers, Al 127, 148

Nash, Billy 133, 163, 165, 169, 170, 210, 245, 249
National Association (NA) 2–4, 24, 34, 42, 71–86, 89, 90, 94, 95, 98, 100, 101, 105, 108, 116, 117, 121, 141–143, 145, 147, 161, 181, 193, 203, 204, 207, 208, 213, 214, 220, 223–226, 229, 230, 236, 238, 265
National Association of Base Ball Players (NABBP) 2, 3, 16–18, 21, 24–27, 31–34, 36, 38, 41, 42, 44, 45, 47–61, 63–65, 67–73, 76, 83, 108, 132, 141, 142, 185, 186, 193, 203, 204, 212–214, 222, 224, 226, 228, 236–239,265
National League (NL) 2–5, 118, 120–122, 124, 126, 127, 130–132, 135, 139, 141–144, 146, 148–150, 152, 153, 155, 157, 158, 161, 164, 168, 171, 173, 175, 176, 183, 184, 189, 191, 193, 196–198, 200, 202–204, 206, 208, 210, 215, 218, 220, 223–227, 230, 234–236, 240, 243–248, 253, 255–258, 262, 264, 266
Navin, Frank 259
Neagle, Jack 117, 118, 146
Nelson, Candy 143
Nemec, David 1, 97, 98, 103, 107, 112, 114, 116, 130, 139, 153, 155, 181, 217, 219, 235, 256
New York Clipper 15, 62–65, 68, 70–72, 81, 203, 204, 212–215, 220, 224, 229, 238
New York Mutual Club 4, 32, 33, 50–54, 60, 63, 64, 66, 69, 75, 78, 80, 82, 90, 91, 94, 95, 114, 143, 207, 223, 236
New York Metropolitans 98, 109, 110, 112, 114, 132, 146

Newlin, Nicholas 20

Oakdale Grounds 39, 100, 101, 103, 105, 106, 145, 151, 234, 240, 247
O'Brien, Jack 101, 102, 109, 138, 146, 146, 232
O'Day, Hank 223
Olympic Club: adopts NABBP rules 18; clubhouse 14; constitution and bylaws 18–20; 1860 season 17, 18, 21, 22, 24–27; 1861 season 18, 31, 34; 1862 season 32; 1864 season 34, 36; 1865 season 45, 47, 63; 1866 season 48; 1867 season 52, 54; 1868 season 61, 64, 65, 141, 207; 1869 season 61, 67, 141; 1870 season 142; fiftieth anniversary 15; first ball club 3, 17, 18, 21; first baseball game 18, 25, 26; first match 14, 15; Fogel's claims for primacy 14–17, 19; formation 3, 4, 13–15, 212; members 18–20, 25, 63, 65, 215; playing grounds 14, 15, 17–19, 88, 145; style of play 15, 16, 19; union with other clubs 14, 15, 17, 18
O'Neil, Ed 140
O'Neill, Tip 145
Orth, Al 158, 170, 172, 174, 175

Panic of 1873 84, 88
Parvin & Company 166
Pass, John 254
Penn Tiger Club 21, 26
Pennsylvania Club 21, 22, 25–27
Pennsylvania State Convention 55–57, 60, 185, 213, 214
Pennypacker, H.C. 129, 137, 139, 152–154, 177, 221, 248
Pepper, William 201
Peterson, Robert 59, 147
Peverelly, Charles 2, 13–15, 17–19, 21, 22, 24–28, 31–33, 38, 42, 44–47, 51, 212
Phelps, Zack 153, 154
Philadelphia: baseball playing grounds 18, 21, 22, 25–27, 29, 39, 40–44, 47, 49, 60, 64, 72, 74, 77, 79, 80, 93, 95, 100, 101, 103, 105–107, 111, 115, 118, 120–124, 126, 127, 132, 134, 135, 137, 139, 140, 145–147, 149, 151, 155, 159, 161, 162, 164, 165, 201, 211, 227, 234, 240, 245, 247, 249; blue laws 14, 130; Broad Street Station 112, 159, 160; Centennial Exposition 37, 83, 87, 88, 92, 93, 95, 113, 159; center of black baseball 60, 61, 146, 147; changing nature of 28–30, 36–40, 159, 160; Chinese Wall 159, 160; Civil War border city 36; Civil War's effect on 36–38; consolidation 38–40; Fairmount Park 37, 88, 93; first baseball clubs 13, 21, 22, 24, 26, 27; geography of 87, 88; growth of 28, 30, 38–40; industrial center 38, 88, 159; "Iron Age" 159, 160; lower North Philadelphia 29, 30; military quota 36; 19th century All-Star team 177, 178; North Philadelphia 22, 29, 30, 47, 48, 72, 87, 93, 100, 121, 122, 130, 142, 151, 165; Pennsylvania Railroad 40, 47, 159, 160; population growth 28, 38–40, 87; prejudice against ball-playing 14, 17, 18; public transportation 30, 37, 47, 48, 55, 83, 88, 118, 186, 187, 244, 251; racial issues 36, 37, 184–187; railroads 40, 47, 93, 159, 160, 235; Reading Railroad 40, 47, 159, 160; Reading Terminal 160; Republican Party 38, 73, 185–187, 218, 250; role in baseball 3, 4, 13–19, 33, 34, 41, 44, 51, 52, 55–59, 63, 71, 72, 76, 81, 82, 84–86, 90–92, 97–100, 113, 114, 141, 146–150, 152–155; University City 18, 29, 41; West Philadelphia 14, 29, 47, 87, 93, 142
Philadelphia Athletics (3): August 1890 139; Bierbauer/Stovey case 153, 154; disbanding of 139, 140; 1882 season 100–103; 1882 team 101–103; 1883 manager 105; 1883 pennant race 110–112; 1883 post season 112; 1883 season 106–112; 1884 hitting 131; 1884 pitching 131, 132; 1884 turnover 131; 1885 season 132; 1886 season 133–135; 1887 season 135–136; 1888 pennant race 137; 1888 season 136, 137; 1889 season 137, 138; 1890 first half 138, 139; 1890 last road trip 139, 140; 1890 re-construction 138; finishes compared to Phillies 130; fiscal success in 1883 129; formation of 4, 97, 100; lack of support from AA 139; ladies auxiliary 135; manage-

ment of 133, 247, 248; minority owners lawsuit 152; owners 97, 129, 133, 220, 221, 246–248; pitching 131; Players League losses 131; policy on captains 133; reasons for downfall 129–131; return to Philadelphia with 1883 pennant 112; rules on conduct 107; September 1890 139, 140; ticket prices 130; 22 straight losses in 1890 139
Philadelphia Athletics (4) 153, 155–157, 190, 219, 260
Philadelphia Athletics (5) 150, 216
Philadelphia Athletics (6) 1, 2, 4, 5, 76, 151, 191, 192, 197, 215, 216, 238, 241, 248, 251, 253, 254
Philadelphia Base Ball Grounds (Huntingdon Street Grounds) 39, 40, 121–124, 126, 127, 161, 162, 164, 165, 201, 211, 245
Philadelphia Centennials 83, 84, 86, 117, 147, 183, 214, 220
Philadelphia Excelsior Club 58–60, 185, 212
Philadelphia independent/amateur clubs/teams: Ashland of Manayunk 118; Athletics (2) 97–100, 142–146, 204, 208, 215, 220, 230, 234, 239; Defiance Club 145, 146; 1867 season 51–54; 1868 NABBP clubs 62–65; 1869 amateur clubs 67; Excelsior 58–60, 185, 212; Mutual 146, 147; Orion 60, 146, 147; Philadelphias (2) 143–146; Pythian 37, 55–61, 67, 83, 146, 185–187, 213, 214; Shibe Club 144–146, 239, 253
Philadelphia Keystones 147, 148, 187, 188, 231, 236, 249
Philadelphia Phillies: attendance in 1890s 158, 161, 164, 171, 173, 175; building 1884 team 119, 120; buyout of Wagners 157; creation of 107, 112, 114, 115, 239, 243, 255; 1883 City Series 107, 112, 118, 129; 1883 season 112, 115–118; 1884 season 119, 120, 147, 148, 204, 249, 266; 1885 season 120, 200; 1886 season 120, 121, 200; 1887 pennant race 124, 125, 200; 1887 season 121–125, 200, 260; 1888 season 125, 126, 195; 1889 Phillies with other teams 148–150, 155, 159; 1889 season 126, 258; 1890 season 126–128, 148, 210, 266; 1891 season 157–159; 1892 season 161–163, 260; 1893 hitting 163, 164; 1893 pitching 163; 1893 record 163; 1894 adjusted OPS 166; 1894 hitting 164–166; 1894 park fire 164, 164; 1894 pitching 165; 1894 relocation 165; 1894 season 150, 164, 165; 1895 hitting 167; 1895 pitching 168, 260; 1895 season 166–168; 1896 season 168–170; 1897 season 170; 1898 players' revolt 171; 1898 team 171, 172; 1898 turnaround 171, 250; 1899 adjusted OPS 173; 1899 pennant race 174; 1899 pitching staff 173, 174; 1899 team/record 172, 173; electrical sign stealing 177, 250; financial status in 1890 127, 149; Hamilton for Nash trade 169, 210, 245; Huntingdon Street Grounds (Philadelphia Base Ball Park, Baker Bowl) 121–124, 164–168; losses to the Players League 127, 149, 204; makeup of 1883 team 115–117; managers' abuse of pitchers 165, 168, 170; 1900 hitting 175, 177; 1900 lineup 175; 1900 pennant race 177; 1900 pitching 175, 177; owners 115, 127, 130, 149, 153, 157, 169, 240, 241, 244–246; reasons for failures in 1890s 161, 165, 168, 175, 177, 196, 245; Recreation Park 83, 115, 121; re-sign Delahanty and Fogarty 158, 196, 207, 245; rivalry with Athletics 4, 5, 105, 112, 118, 124, 129, 130, 135, 136, 139, 254; Rogers gains majority ownership 169, 241, 245; 20th century 5, 30, 77, 79, 122, 150, 170, 194, 241, 244–246, 250, 254
Philadelphia Quakers 127, 139, 148–150, 153, 155, 162, 190, 206, 219, 232
Philadelphia White Stockings (Philadelphias 1, Pearls): Addy case 78–81; alternative names 77, 81; 1873 collapse 78–80; 1873 playing site 77; 1873 roster 77, 193, 208, 230; 1873 season 77–80, 119; 1874 season 82, 83, 142; 1875 debts 86; 1875 season 86, 230; exclusion from National League in 1876 91, 92; nickname change 81; October 1, 1873 game vs. Nationals 79; October 2, 1873 game vs. Red Stockings 79, 80; players signing with Chicago for 1874 80, 83, 84, 86, 91; possibility of throwing games in 1873 79; raiding Athletics in 1873 77, 149, 193, 230; rebuilding in 1874 81, 82; reputation for hippodroming 79, 82, 91, 95; rivalry vs. Athletics 77, 78, 95; summer 1873 vacation in Cape May 78, 119
Phillips, Horace 97–100, 144–146, 208, 221, 233–235, 240, 247
Piatt, Wiley 171, 172, 174, 175
Piazza, Mike 123, 187, 189
Pickett, John 148
Pike, Lip 47, 49–52
Pittsburgh Pirates 154, 177, 198, 235, 241, 250
Players League 117, 120, 126, 127, 129, 130, 131, 135, 138, 139, 143, 148, 150, 152, 153, 155, 157, 158, 162, 189, 190, 196, 198, 206, 207, 217, 219, 224, 232, 241, 243, 245, 247, 248, 256, 257, 260, 262, 263
Potter, James 241, 244, 245, 250
Pratt, Al 98, 100
Pratt, Tom 22, 26, 31–34, 36, 47–49, 51, 52, 68, 73, 147, 148, 224, 235, 236, 240, 249
Pratt Bros. 147, 236, 249
Purcell, Blondie 116, 117, 120, 138
Pythian Club 37, 55–61, 67, 83, 146, 185–187, 213, 214

Quaker City Club 51–54, 68
Quest, Joe 34

Radbourne, Charles 118
Radcliff, John 51, 52, 62–67, 73–76, 82, 83, 214
Ray, Johnny 140
Reach, Al: bio 237–242; builds Huntingdon Street (Philadelphia) Park 122, 123; on early baseball 21, 33; 1866 season 49, 50; 1867 season 52; 1871 season 73–75; 1872 season 76; 1873 season 82; 1877 season 144; first player paid to change cities 4, 41, 44, 45, 47, 62, 63, 254; on the founding of Athletic (1) 24, 25; hitting in 1868 64; hitting in 1869 67; invitation to new park 166, 167; manages Phillies in 1890 128; member of Brooklyn Eckford

32; offensive records 44, 50, 52, 64, 67, 226; owner of independent Philadelphias 98, 100, 115, 145, 146, 221, 234, 236, 247; ownership of Phillies 107, 114–120, 122, 123, 125–127, 130, 149, 157, 158, 161, 164–167, 169, 171, 188, 196, 199, 207, 210, 244–246, 249, 250, 266; partnership/relationship with Ben Shibe 114, 127, 145, 238–242, 246; rebuilds park in 1895 165, 166; recalling Camac Woods grounds 42–44; sporting goods business 114, 127, 149, 189, 253
Reach, George 241, 242
Reach, Robert 240
Recreation Park 26, 39, 115, 118, 120–123, 132, 145, 146, 240
Reeves, Joseph 20
Reilly, Charlie 164
Reilly, John 137
Revolvers/revolving 41, 50–52, 54, 63, 65, 67, 68, 72–74, 76, 82, 83, 89, 113, 193, 248
Reynolds, Charlie 103
Richardson, Hardie 149, 198
Richmond, John 94
Richter, Francis 1, 15, 16, 18, 21, 22, 25, 41, 44, 47–49, 84, 85, 89, 91, 97, 98, 129, 130, 133, 147, 151, 154, 157, 242–244, 247, 248
Ringo, Frank 117
Robb, Samuel 20
Robb, Thomas 20
Roberts, George 159
Robinson, Jackie 185, 186
Robinson, Wilbert 135, 136, 138, 151, 232, 239
Rockford Forest Citys 52, 74, 76, 181, 182, 207
Rogers, John 5, 114–116, 122, 123, 127, 149, 150, 153, 157–159, 161, 163, 165, 167, 169–171, 177, 189, 195–197, 207, 210, 211, 227, 231, 237, 240, 241, 244–246, 249, 250, 258, 266
Rose, Judge 56, 57
Rowen, Ed 109
Ruth, Babe 73, 124, 162, 166, 167, 178, 202, 210, 226, 229, 241, 258, 261
Ryczek, William 1, 74, 75, 77, 79, 81, 82, 84, 142, 181

St. George Cricket Club 41
St. Louis Browns 95, 100, 110, 111, 112, 133, 136, 137, 142, 144, 156, 171, 188, 189, 217, 232, 258
Sanders, Ben 125–127, 149, 155, 157, 159
Saxton, Joseph 20
Say, Jimmy 101, 109
Say, Lew 101, 109
Schaefer, Harry 66
Schober, George 20
Schofield, J.W. 71, 72
Schriver, Pop 127, 149
Scott, Thomas 159
Sensenderfer, John (Count) 19, 45, 52, 62, 64, 66, 73, 74, 76, 82, 144, 145
Seward, Ed 135–138
Seymour, Harold 1, 5, 18, 21, 38, 51, 90, 91, 98, 100, 131, 133, 143, 152–154
Shaffer, Orator 138, 139
Shaffer, Taylor 138, 139
Shantz family 27, 47
Sharsig, Bill: bio 246–249; 1881 tour 97; 1883 Athletics (3) 103, 106, 109, 112; 1884 Athletics (3) 131, 132; 1885 Athletics (3) 132, 133; 1887 Athletics (3) 135, 232; files 1890 bill of equity 152; formation of Athletics (3) 97, 98, 100, 101, 208, 221, 240; leads last 1890 road trip 139, 140; manager 1888 129, 133, 134, 136; manager 1890 138, 139; manager 1891 155; role in Bierbauer/Stovey case 153, 154; role with Athletic (2) 145, 146, 208, 220, 221, 234; role with Athletics (3) 97, 120, 129, 132–134, 138, 139, 170, 178, 256; sued for use of Athletics name 145; sues Wagner Brothers 155
Shettsline, Bill 5, 133, 147, 170–173, 177, 178, 237, 245, 249–251
Shibe, Ben: bio 251, *252*, 253, 254; manufacturer 24, 114, 239, 240; owner of Athletics (3) 100, 248; owner of Athletics (6) 5, 122, 218, 240, 241, 246, 248; owner of Philadelphias (2) 100; partnership/relationship with Al Reach 114, 127, 145, 238–242, 246; Shibe Baseball Ball Club 114, 145; sponsorship of independent/minor league teams 114, 145, 150, 216
Shibe, Jack 253, 254
Shibe, Tom 253, 254
Shibe Baseball Club 144–146, 239, 253
Shibe Park 39, 42, 166, 215, 216, 218, 251, 254
Shindle, Billy 149, 150
Simmons, Lew 97, 100–102, 104, 105, 107, 112, 129, 132–134, 138, 220, 221, 227, 247, 248, 256
Slagle, Jimmy 175
Smith, Mike 44, 45, 53, 226
Smith, Robert 126, 197
Soden, Arthur 113, 114
Somerville, Ed 84
Spalding, Al 52, 74, 78, 81, 86, 89, 90, 96, 127, 149, 152, 153, 155, 182–184, 206, 223, 225–228, 239, 240–243, 263, 266
Spering, Chris 86, 90
Spink, Al 97, 151, 197, 202, 223, 243
Spitball 222–224
Sporting Life 16, 133, 147, 151, 242, 243
Stallings, George 161, 170–172, 249, 250
Stecher, Charlie 140
Stevens, R.F. 27
"Stonewall Infield" 262
Stovey, Harry: baseball debut 144; Bierbauer/Stovey case 4, 153, 154; bio 254–257; 1877 season 144; 1883 season 107, 109, 111, 112, 132, 222; 1885 hitting 132; 1885 managing 133; 1886 season 133, 134; 1887 season 135; 1888 season 137; 1889 season 138; 1891 season 158; 1892 season 163; family background 107; home run records 112, 132, 162; Mason and Sharsig's support of 133; signing by Athletics (3) 107, 116; signing with Players League 131, 138; skills 107, 177, 178, 228, 231; Worcester Ruby Legs 107, 116
Stow, John 107, 254
Stricker, Cub 101, 109, 110, 131, 145, 146
Sullivan, Dean 1, 19, 21, 57, 59, 71, 154
Sutton, Ezra 77, 85, 94, 95
Sweeney, Bill 102, 103, 108
Swiftfoot Club 21, 26, 27, 38, 48

Taylor, Billy 132
Taylor, Jack 165, 168, 170
Tener, John 202
Thayer, Russell 149
Thomas, Charles 20
Thomas, Joseph 20
Thomas, Roy 142, 173, 175

Thompson, George 95
Thompson, Sam 126, 127, 149, 158, 162, 163, 165–167, 169, 177, 210, 231, 256–259
Thorn, John 1–3, 14–16, 35, 46, 55–57, 68, 85, 99, 115, 123, 143, 156, 162, 181, 200, 212, 217, 223, 260
Thorner, Justus 98, 147
Threston, Christopher 56–58, 146, 185
Thurman, Allan 152, 153, 155
Town ball 13–16, 18, 19, 22, 25, 27, 31, 141, 212
Treacey, Fred 76, 77, 80, 83, 84, 86
Troy, Dasher 102, 105
Troy/Wise case 102, 105
Turner, Tuck 166, 167
Tygiel, Jules 59, 60
Typographical Club 51, 54

Uniforms 19, 22, 25, 35, 42, 77, 81, 185
Union Association 73, 103, 117, 120, 126, 132, 138, 147, 187, 192, 193, 198, 231, 234, 236, 249
Union of Morrisania Club 44, 47, 52
United Club 27, 31
University of Notre Dame 181
University of Pennsylvania 30, 114, 142, 164, 165, 173, 201, 244

Vaccaro, Frank 2, 95, 96, 144–146, 183
Vanderslice, J.M. 148
Vickery, Tom 127
Villanova University 76, 142, 143, 171
Vinton, Bill 120
Voigt, David Quentin 2, 3, 13, 19, 21, 22, 26, 48, 60, 62, 65, 66, 71, 81, 89, 90, 96, 148, 226

Von der Ahe, Chris 100, 133, 136, 137, 193, 232, 243

Wagner, Earl 4, 148, 152–155, 157, 177, 219, 233, 248
Wagner, George 4, 148, 152–155, 157, 177, 219, 233, 248
Wagner Free Institute of Science 43, 44
Ward, John Montgomery 131, 144, 148, 150, 243, 248
Warner, Fred 117
Warner, Sam Bass 28
Warr, William 145
Warrington, Robert 167
Waskie, Andrew 56, 58, 59, 61, 184, 186
Watson, George 20
Weaver, Sam 101–103, 108, 144–146
Welch, Curt 136–138, 232
Wells, Kirk 20
West Philadelphia Club 47, 54, 69, 142, 193
Westcott, Rich 165, 242
Weyhing, Gus 131, 135–138, 150, 155, 157, 162, 163, 165, 168, 178, 260, 261
Wharton, George 20
White, Deacon 89
White, Will 110–112, 117, 223
Whitman, William 20
Whitney, Jim 108, 139
Widener, Peter A.B. 88
Wiedersheim, Theodore 21
Wilkins, Isaac 50, 52, 62, 63, 66
Williamson, Ned 178, 261–263
Wills, Leigh 17, 136, 222
Wilmington clubs 44, 47, 148
Winona Club 21, 22, 25–27, 31, 38, 212, 235
Wise, Sam 102, 105
Wolverton, Harry 175
Wood, Francis 60
Wood, George 121, 124, 125, 127, 148, 149, 155, 157, 159, 206

Wood, Jimmy 78–80, 263
Worcester Ruby Legs 101, 103, 106–108, 113, 114, 116, 120, 255
Wright, Al 94, 144, 145
Wright, Carrie 264, 266
Wright, George 66, 67, 69, 82, 239
Wright, Harry: antipathy towards Philadelphia teams 50, 75, 78, 86, 90, 91, 119, 224; Bio 263–267; blindness 128; Boston Red Stockings 73, 86, 214; Cincinnati Red Stockings 66, 67, 119, 212, 214; Cricketeer 81, 82, 226, 227; 1873 season 78, 119, 214; fired in 1893 161, 163–165, 245; formation of National League 90; "Harry Wright's League" (National Association) 71, 72, 214; history with Philadelphia 50, 75, 78, 86, 96, 119, 214; lack of knowledge of baseball's origins 81; Phillies manager 115, 119–128, 130, 133, 135, 148, 149, 161, 163, 168, 169, 178, 188, 200–202, 204, 205, 210, 245; reaction to Force case 90, 91; support of 1876 Athletics 96; trip to England 81, 82
Wright, Isabelle 169, 241, 245, 266
Wright, Marshall 1, 7, 31, 42, 44, 49, 58, 67, 69–71, 181, 212
Wright, Samuel, Jr. 264
Wright, Samuel, Sr. 264

York, Tom 82
Young, Cy 168, 261
Young, George 80
Young, Nick 71, 72

Zettlein, George 75, 78–80, 86, 94, 95, 143, 225, 236

www.ingramcontent.com/pod-product-compliance
Lightning Source LLC
Chambersburg PA
CBHW081542300426
44116CB00015B/2723